Shojo Beat

Rasetsu

Vol. 2

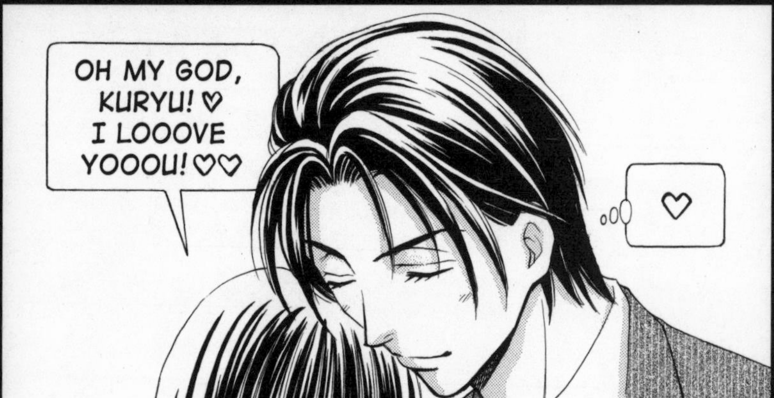
OH MY GOD, KURYU! ♡ I LOOOVE YOOOU! ♡♡
♡

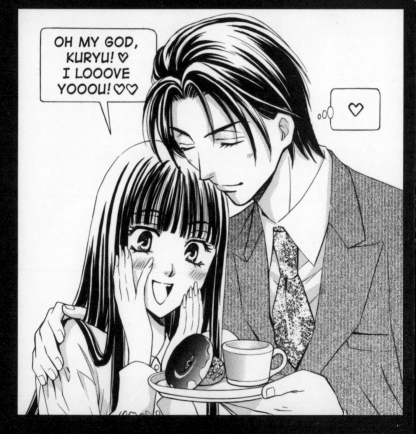

Story & Art by

Chika Shiomi

Characters

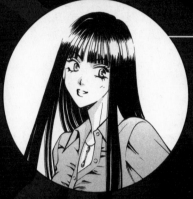

Rasetsu Hyuga

A powerful 18-year-old exorcist, Rasetsu has a flower-like mark on her chest—a memento left by a demon. Rasetsu eats lots of sweets to recharge her psychic powers. She's currently looking for a boyfriend.

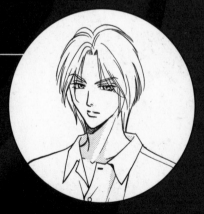

Yako Hoshino

An ace psychic who controls water, Yako was headhunted by Rasetsu. He still has feelings for the spirit he was in love with in high school…

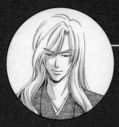

Hiichiro Amakawa

The chief of the agency where Rasetsu and Yako work. A very powerful psychic.

Kuryu Iwatsuki

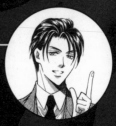

A psychic who uses *kotodama* (spiritual power manifested through words). His power works on humans and animals alike.

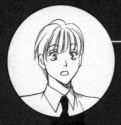

Aoi

Does administrative work for the agency. Ever since Yako came to the office, however, he's been left with nothing to do.

Story

The Hiichiro Amakawa Agency deals with exorcisms, and Rasetsu and Kuryu are psychics who work there. One day, Yako Hoshino visits their office because he needs help with a possessed book. Rasetsu recognizes Yako's supernatural powers and tries to recruit him. He eventually joins the agency and learns that Rasetsu is actually cursed by a malevolent spirit. However, Yako doesn't know that the only way for Rasetsu to break her curse is to find true love!

Rasetsu

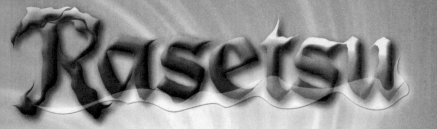

Volume 2
Contents

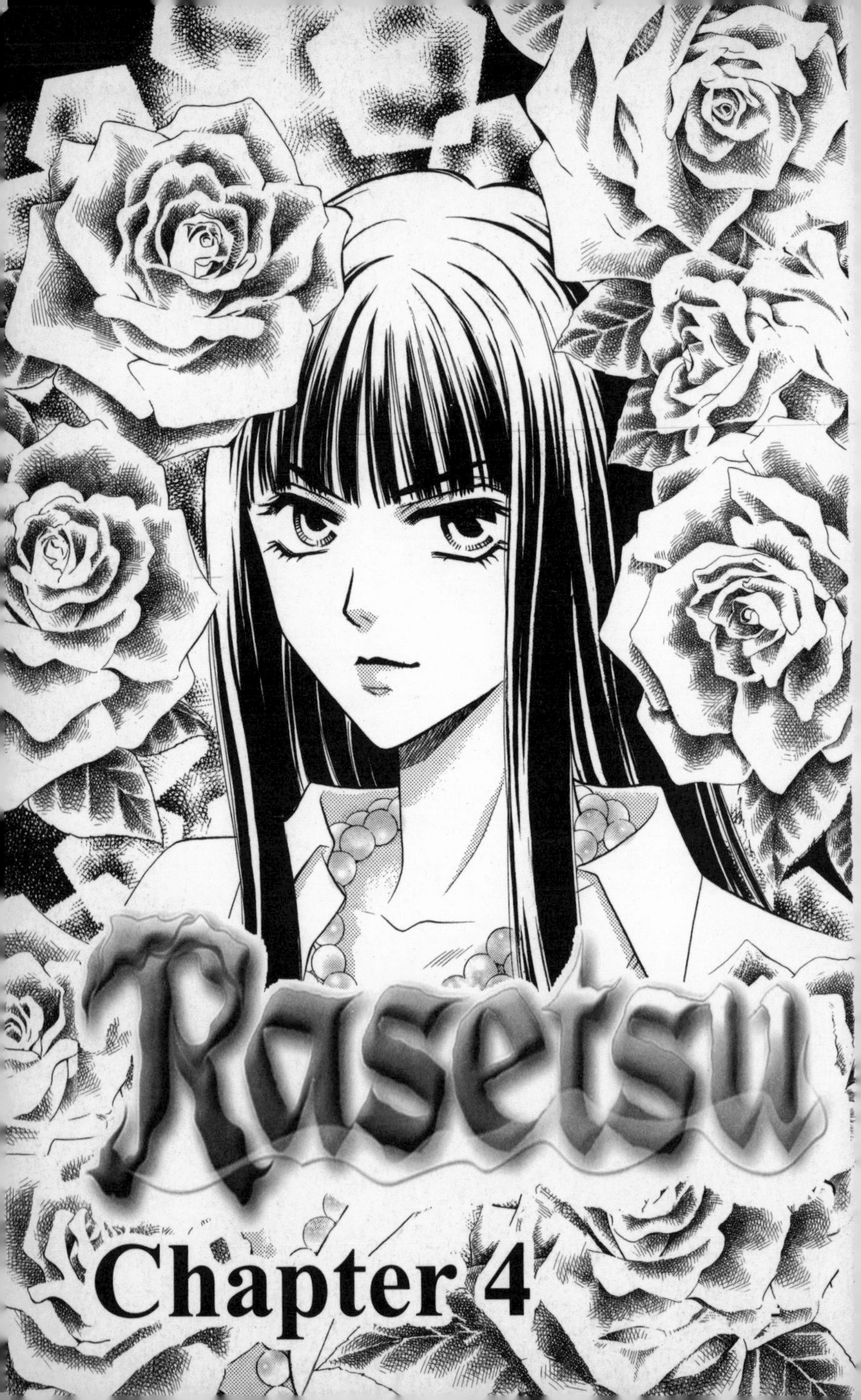
Rasetsu
Chapter 4

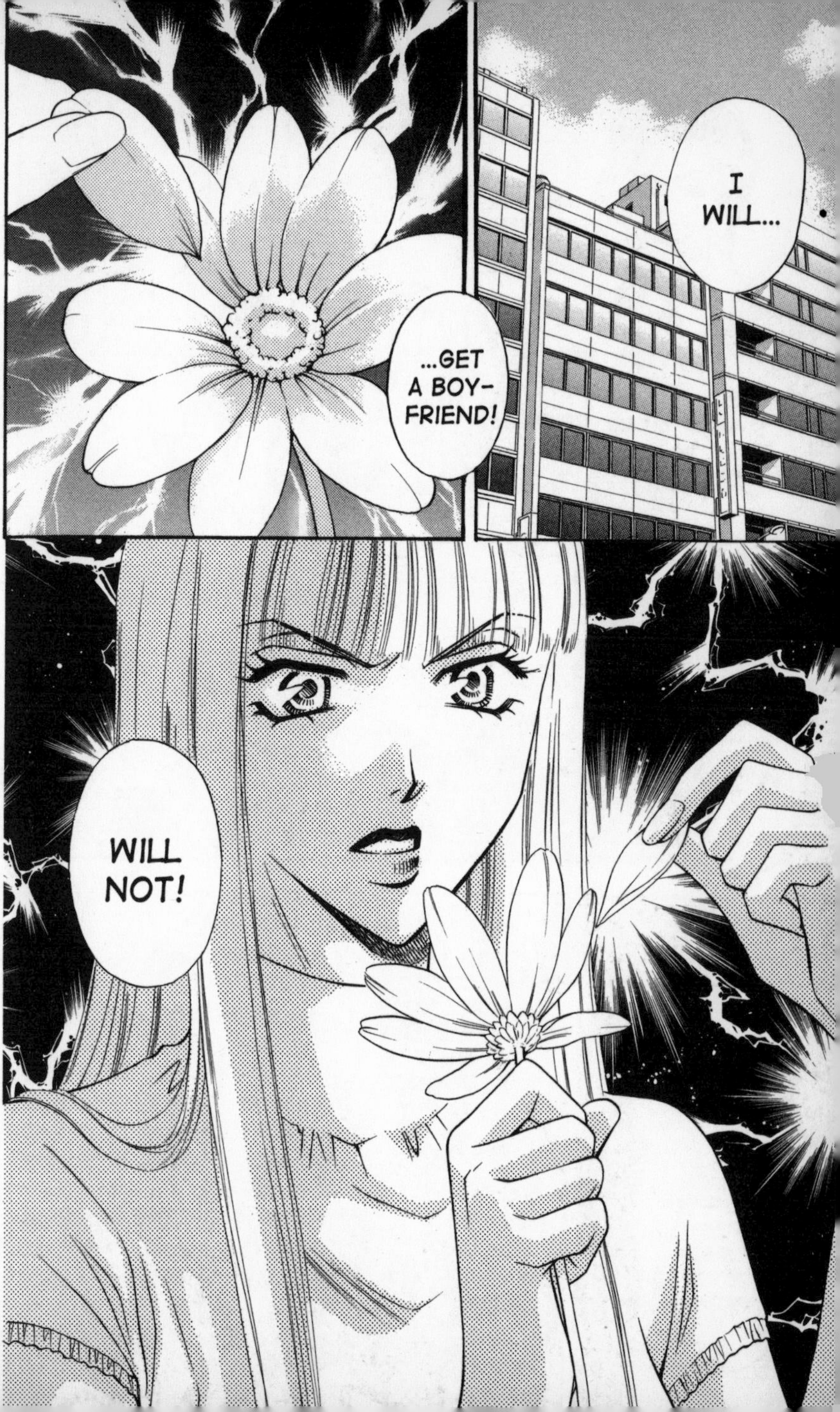
I WILL...
...GET A BOY-FRIEND!
WILL NOT!

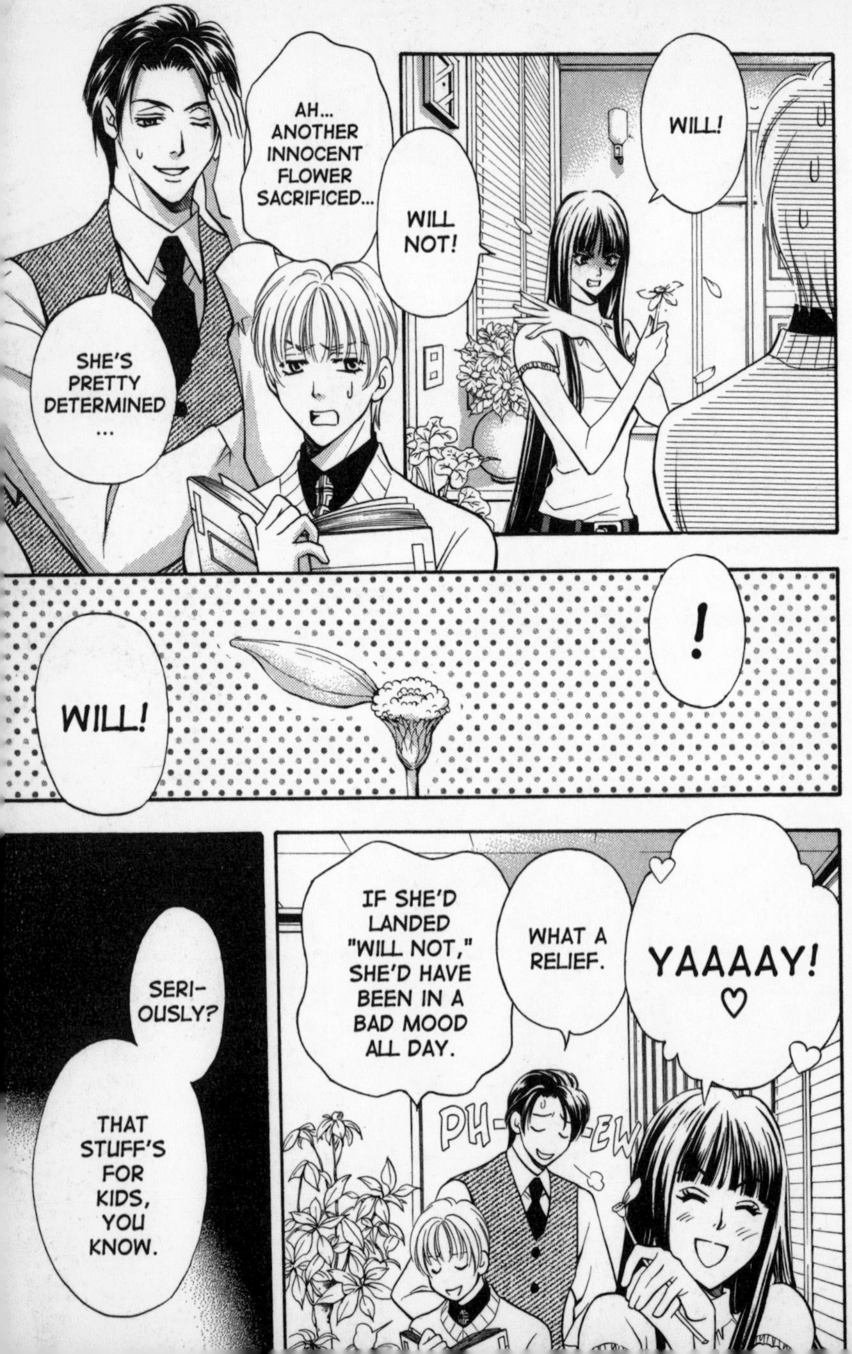

WILL!
AH... ANOTHER INNOCENT FLOWER SACRIFICED...
WILL NOT!
SHE'S PRETTY DETERMINED ...
!
WILL!
YAAAAY! ♡
WHAT A RELIEF.
IF SHE'D LANDED "WILL NOT," SHE'D HAVE BEEN IN A BAD MOOD ALL DAY.
PH--EW
SERI-OUSLY?
THAT STUFF'S FOR KIDS, YOU KNOW.

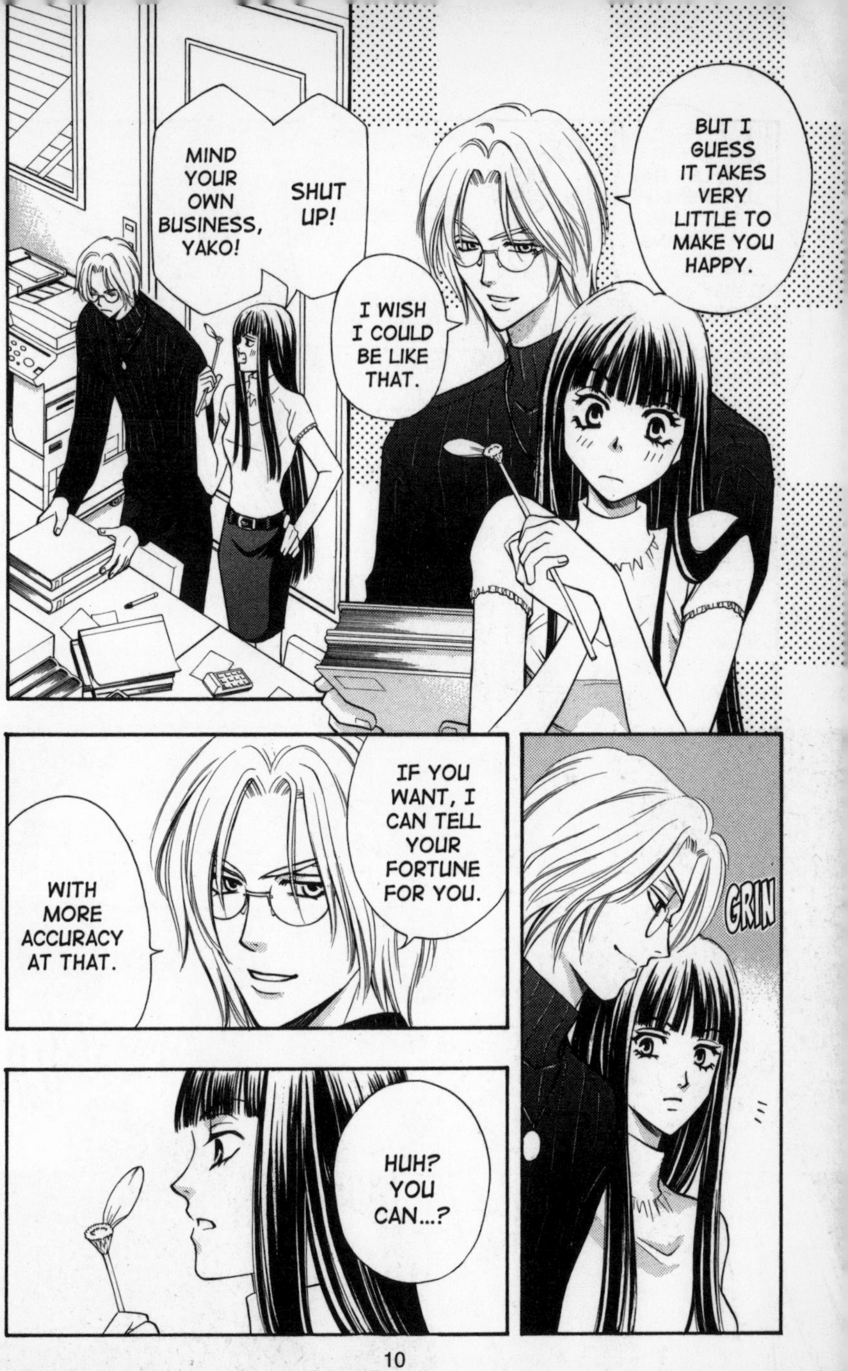

BUT I GUESS IT TAKES VERY LITTLE TO MAKE YOU HAPPY.
I WISH I COULD BE LIKE THAT.
SHUT UP!
MIND YOUR OWN BUSINESS, YAKO!
GRIN
IF YOU WANT, I CAN TELL YOUR FORTUNE FOR YOU.
WITH MORE ACCURACY AT THAT.
HUH? YOU CAN...?

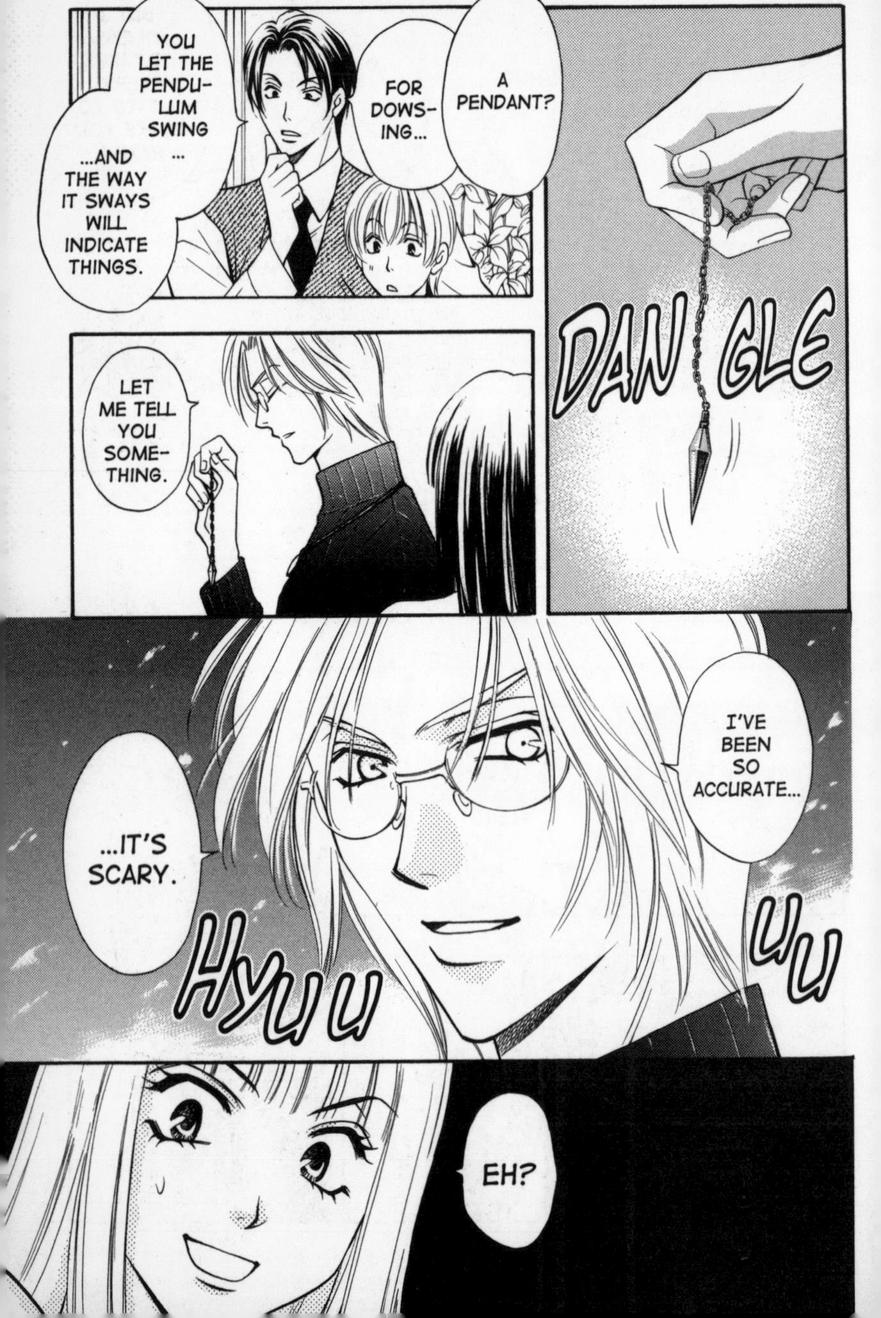
DAN GLE
A PENDANT?
FOR DOWSING...
YOU LET THE PENDULUM SWING ...
...AND THE WAY IT SWAYS WILL INDICATE THINGS.
LET ME TELL YOU SOMETHING.
I'VE BEEN SO ACCURATE...
...IT'S SCARY.
HYUU UU
EH?

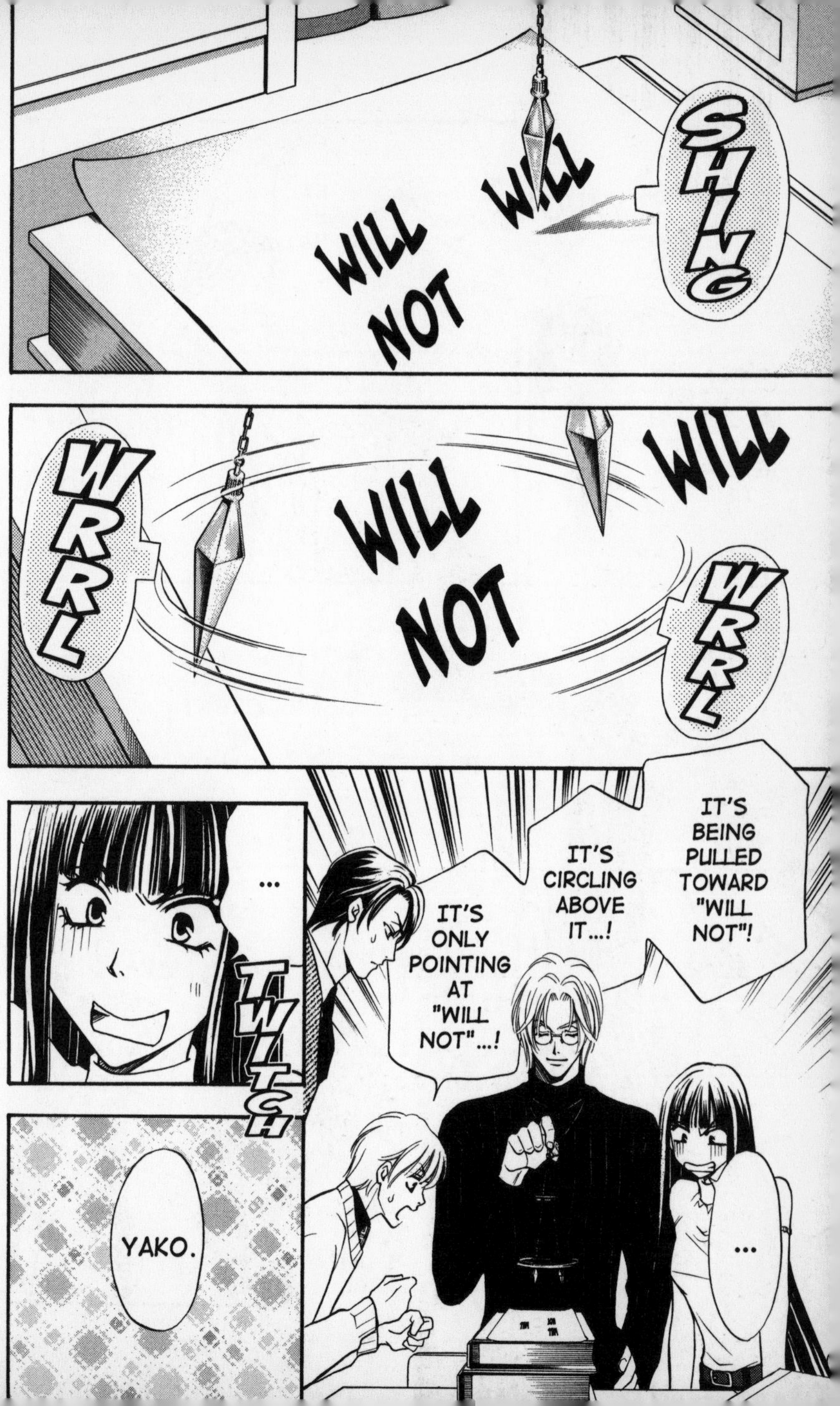
SHING
WILL
WILL NOT
WILL
WRRL
WILL NOT
WRRL
IT'S BEING PULLED TOWARD "WILL NOT"!
IT'S CIRCLING ABOVE IT...!
IT'S ONLY POINTING AT "WILL NOT"...!
...
...
TWITCH
YAKO.

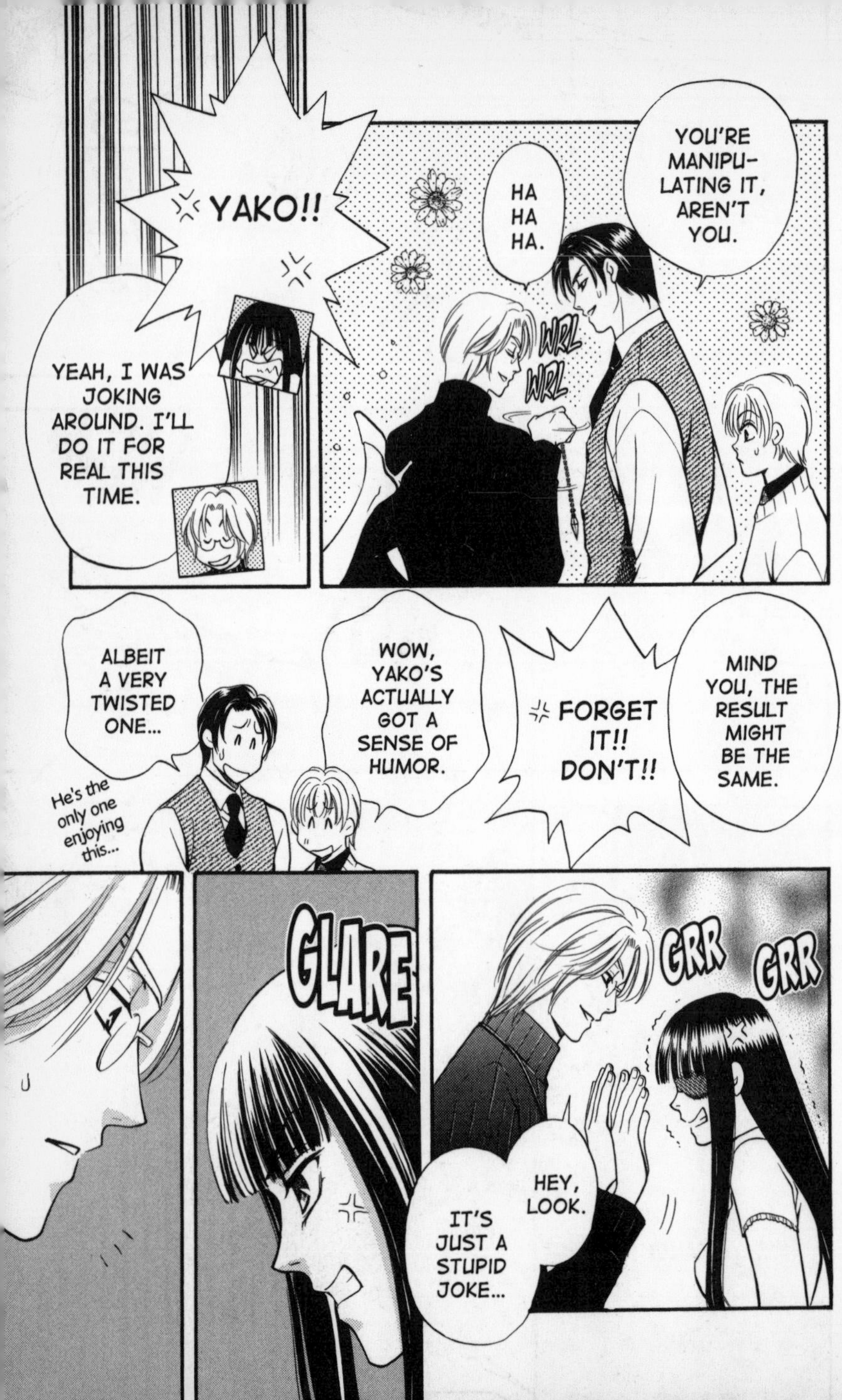
YOU'RE MANIPU-LATING IT, AREN'T YOU.
HA HA HA.
WRL WRL
YAKO!!
YEAH, I WAS JOKING AROUND. I'LL DO IT FOR REAL THIS TIME.
MIND YOU, THE RESULT MIGHT BE THE SAME.
FORGET IT!! DON'T!!
WOW, YAKO'S ACTUALLY GOT A SENSE OF HUMOR.
ALBEIT A VERY TWISTED ONE...
He's the only one enjoying this...
GRR GRR
HEY, LOOK.
IT'S JUST A STUPID JOKE...
GLARE

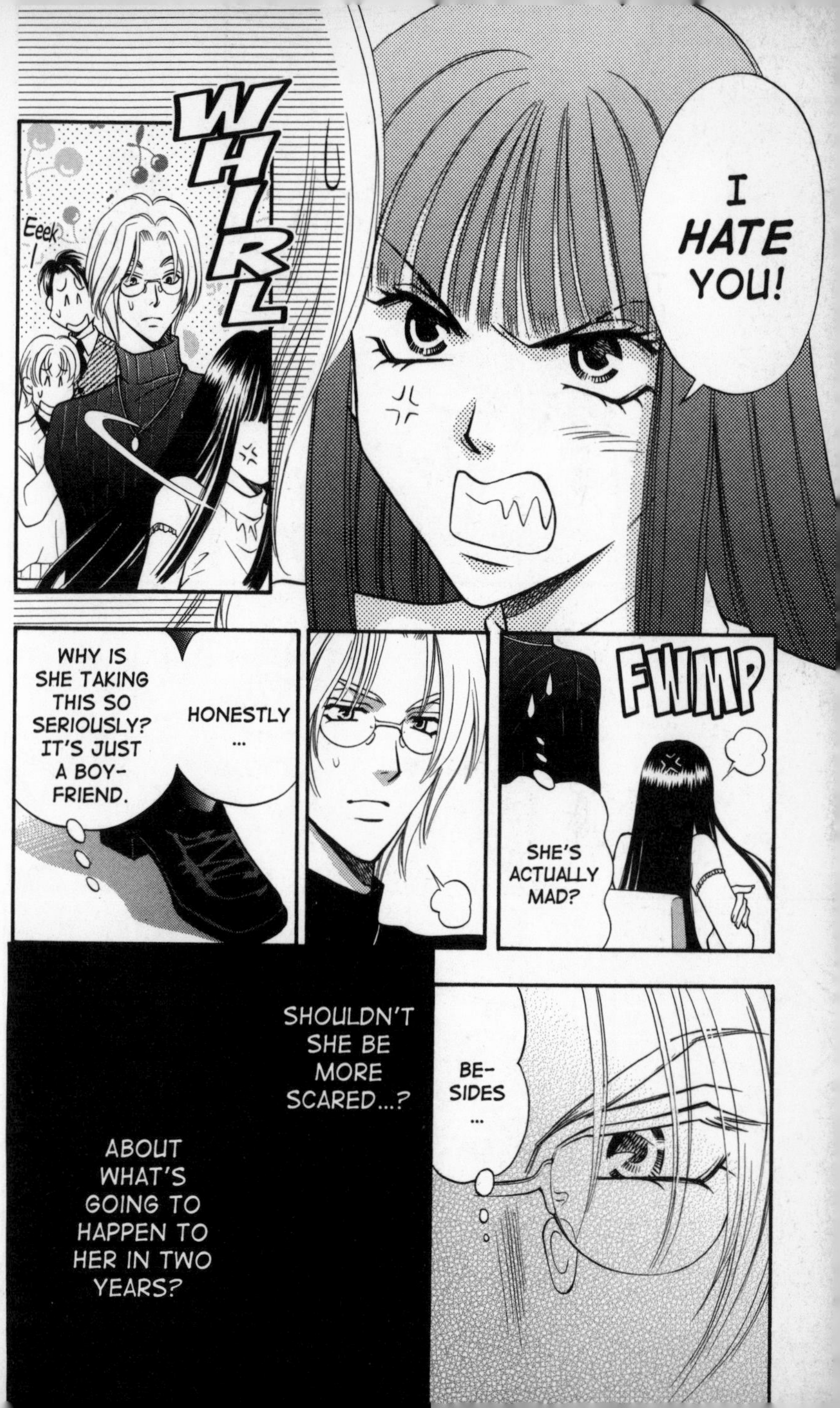
I HATE YOU!
WHIRL
Eeek!
FWMP
SHE'S ACTUALLY MAD?
HONESTLY ...
WHY IS SHE TAKING THIS SO SERIOUSLY? IT'S JUST A BOY-FRIEND.
BE-SIDES ...
SHOULDN'T SHE BE MORE SCARED...?
ABOUT WHAT'S GOING TO HAPPEN TO HER IN TWO YEARS?

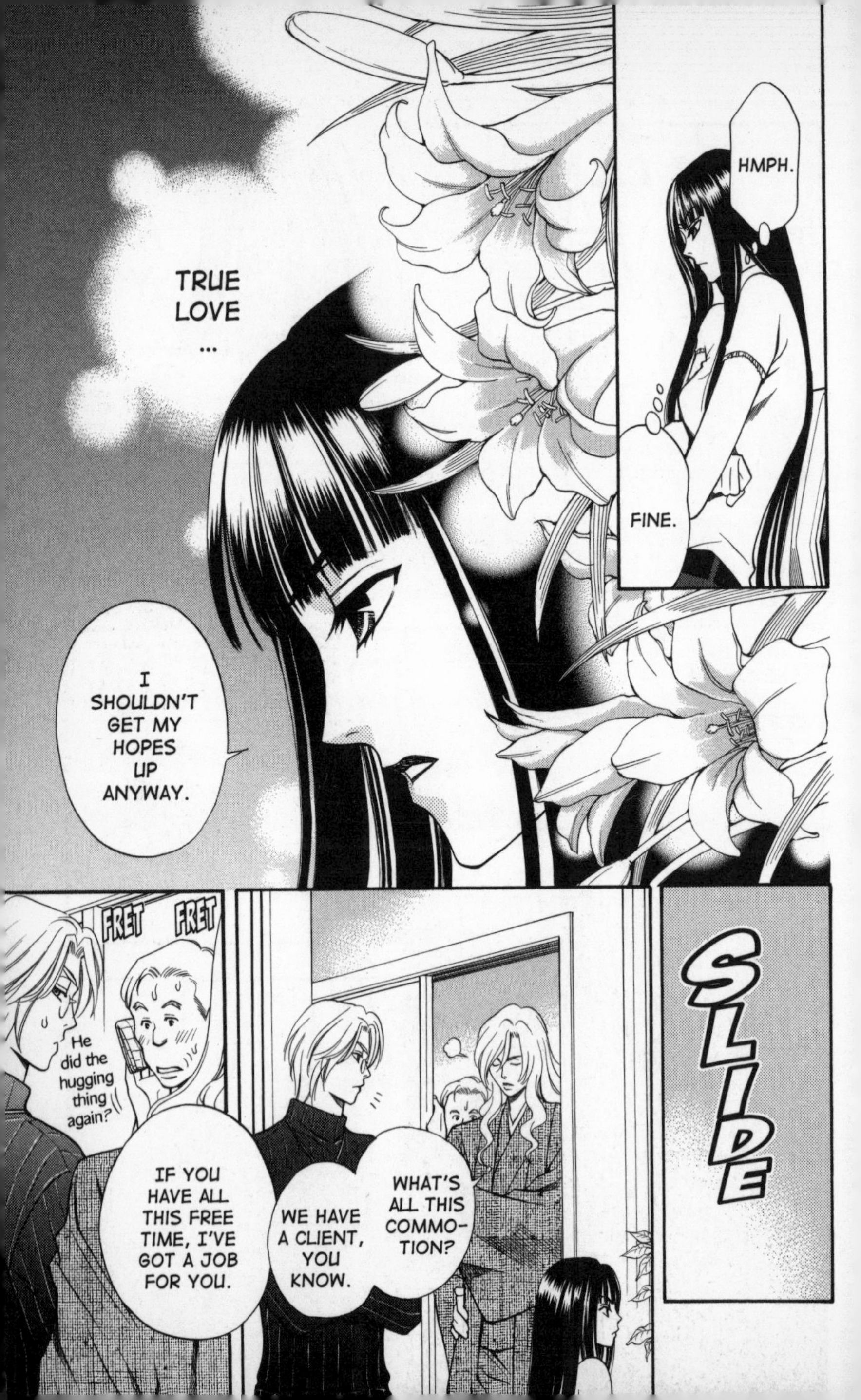
HMPH.
FINE.
TRUE LOVE ...
I SHOULDN'T GET MY HOPES UP ANYWAY.
SLIDE
WHAT'S ALL THIS COMMO-TION?
WE HAVE A CLIENT, YOU KNOW.
IF YOU HAVE ALL THIS FREE TIME, I'VE GOT A JOB FOR YOU.
FRET FRET
He did the hugging thing again?

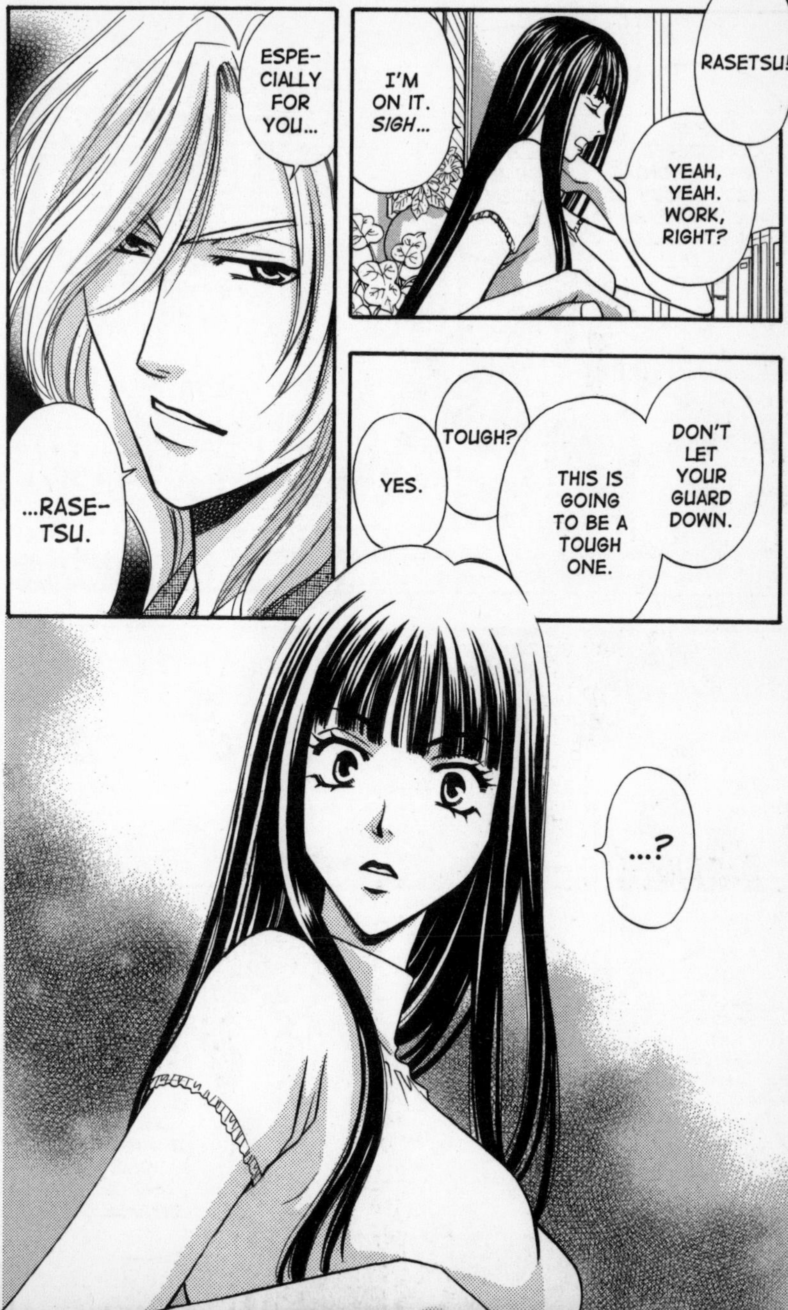
RASETSU!
YEAH, YEAH. WORK, RIGHT?
I'M ON IT. *SIGH*...
DON'T LET YOUR GUARD DOWN.
THIS IS GOING TO BE A TOUGH ONE.
TOUGH?
YES.
ESPE-CIALLY FOR YOU...
...RASE-TSU.
...?

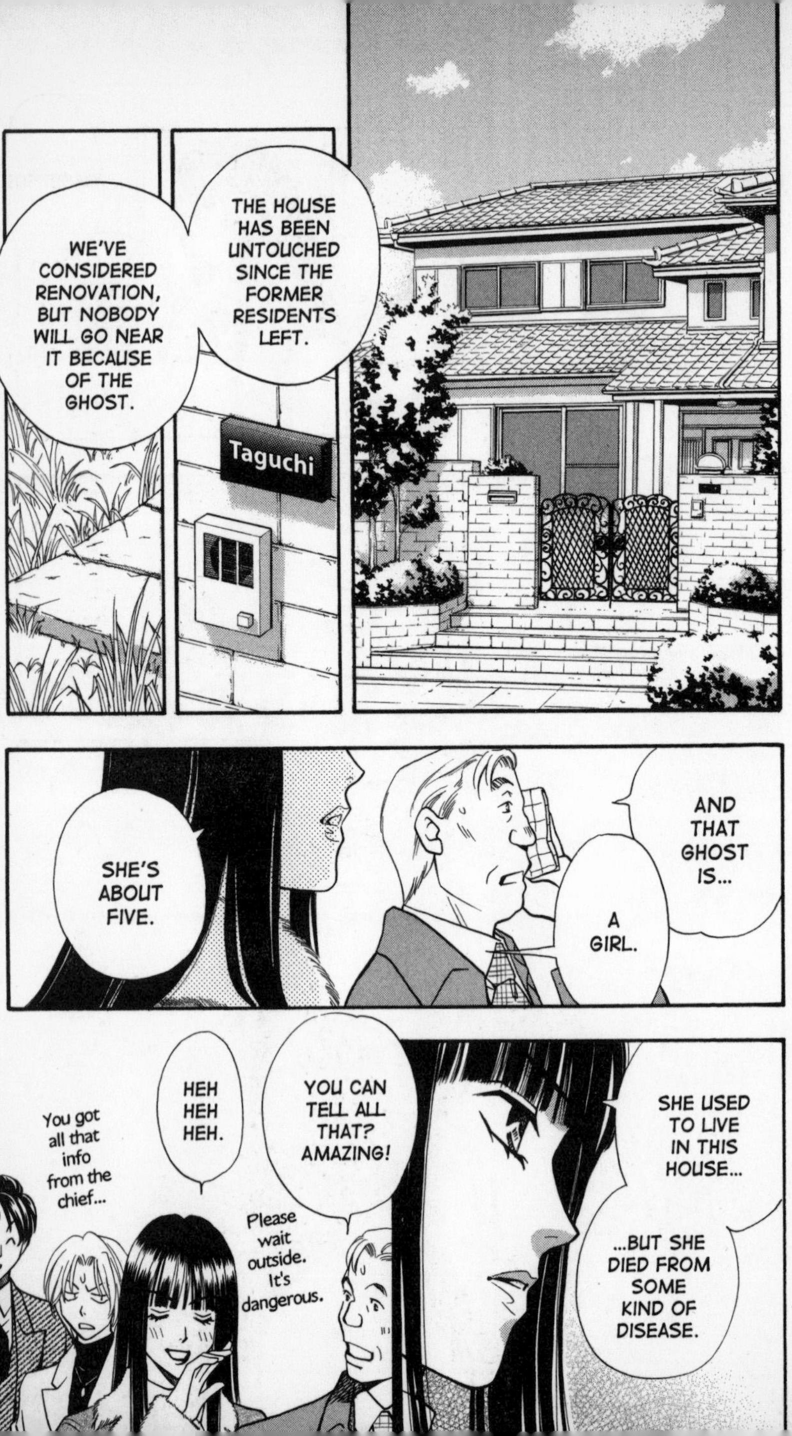
THE HOUSE HAS BEEN UNTOUCHED SINCE THE FORMER RESIDENTS LEFT.
WE'VE CONSIDERED RENOVATION, BUT NOBODY WILL GO NEAR IT BECAUSE OF THE GHOST.
Taguchi
AND THAT GHOST IS...
A GIRL.
SHE'S ABOUT FIVE.
SHE USED TO LIVE IN THIS HOUSE...
...BUT SHE DIED FROM SOME KIND OF DISEASE.
YOU CAN TELL ALL THAT? AMAZING!
HEH HEH HEH.
Please wait outside. It's dangerous.
You got all that info from the chief...

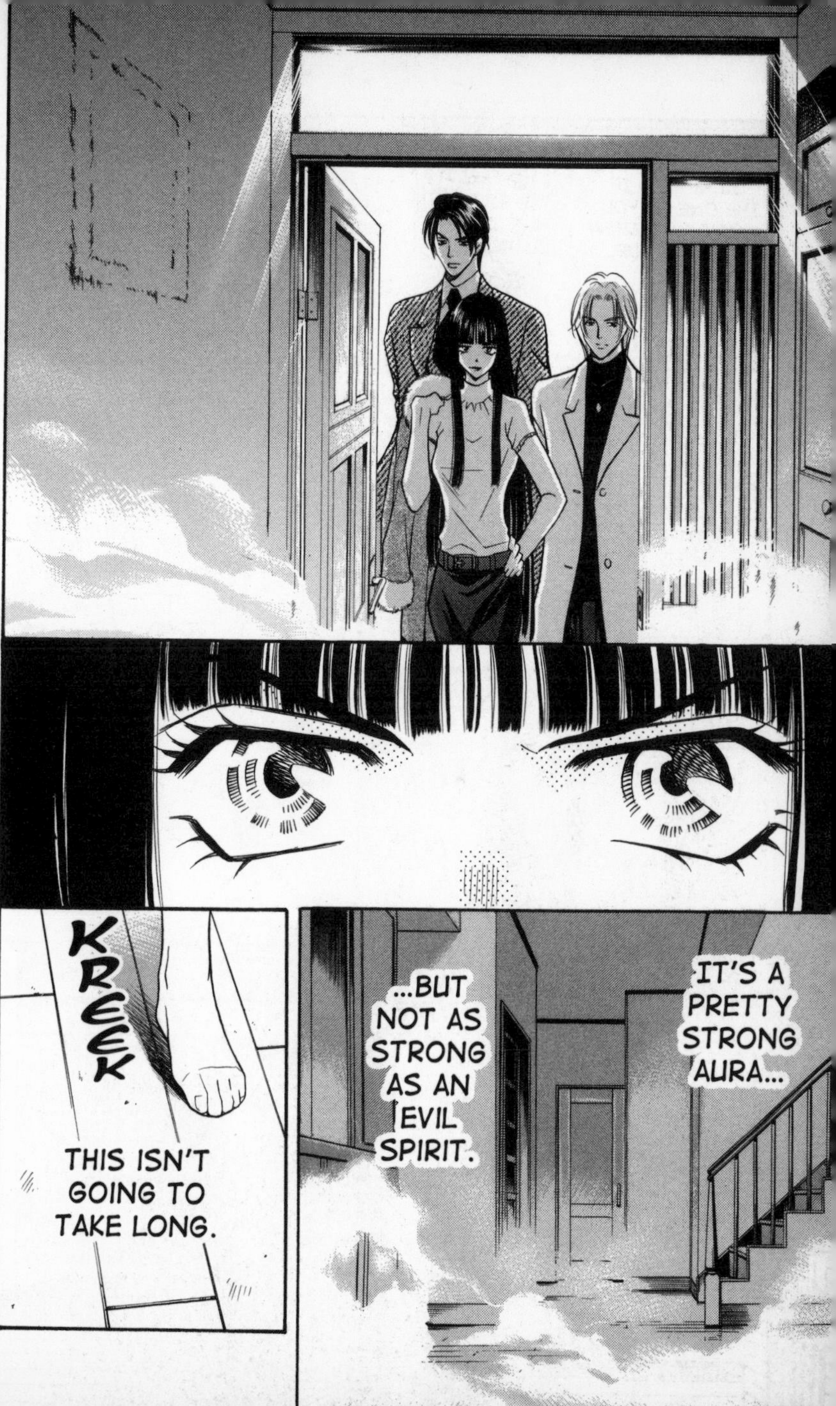
IT'S A PRETTY STRONG AURA...
...BUT NOT AS STRONG AS AN EVIL SPIRIT.
KREEK
THIS ISN'T GOING TO TAKE LONG.

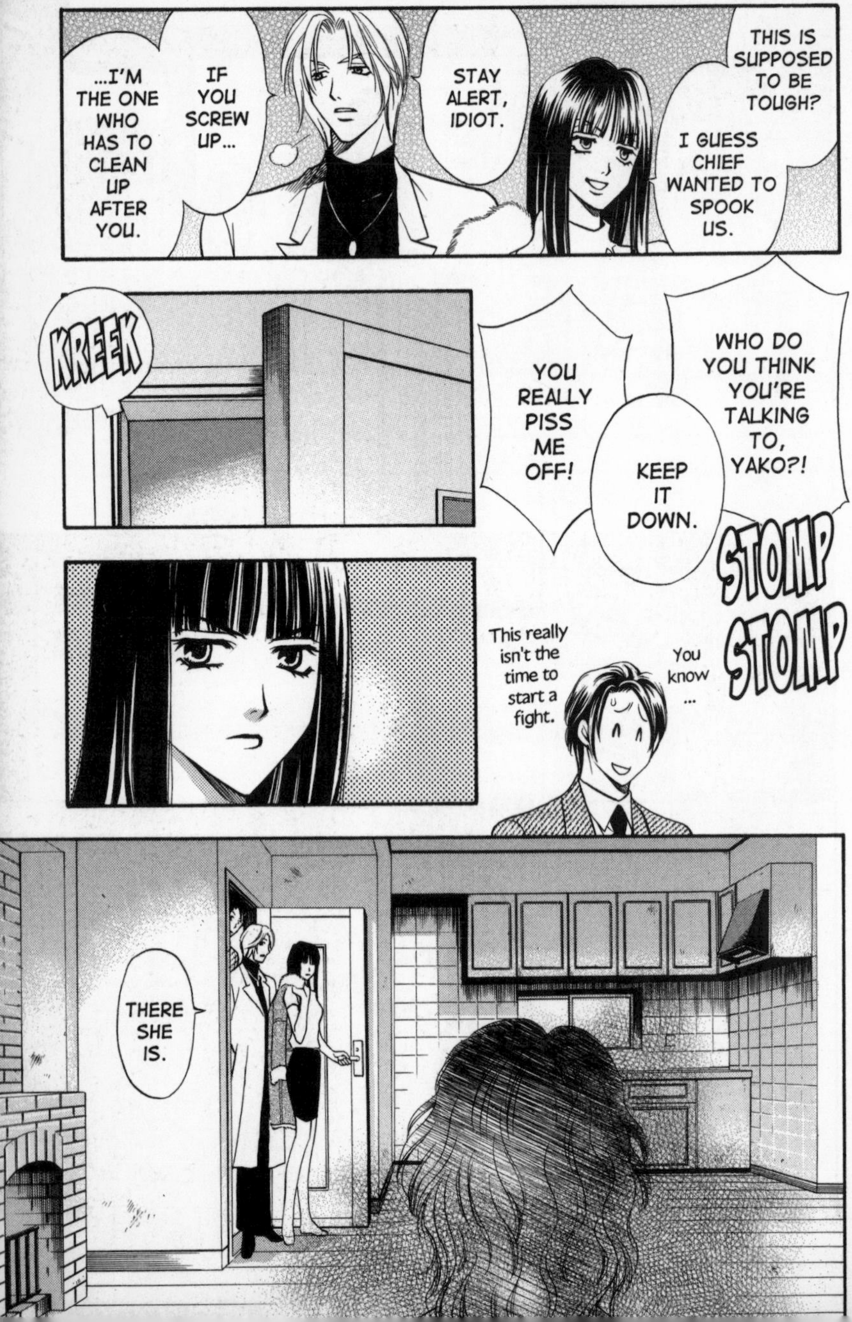
THIS IS SUPPOSED TO BE TOUGH?
I GUESS CHIEF WANTED TO SPOOK US.
STAY ALERT, IDIOT.
IF YOU SCREW UP...
...I'M THE ONE WHO HAS TO CLEAN UP AFTER YOU.
WHO DO YOU THINK YOU'RE TALKING TO, YAKO?!
YOU REALLY PISS ME OFF!
KEEP IT DOWN.
STOMP STOMP
You know ...
This really isn't the time to start a fight.
KREEK
THERE SHE IS.

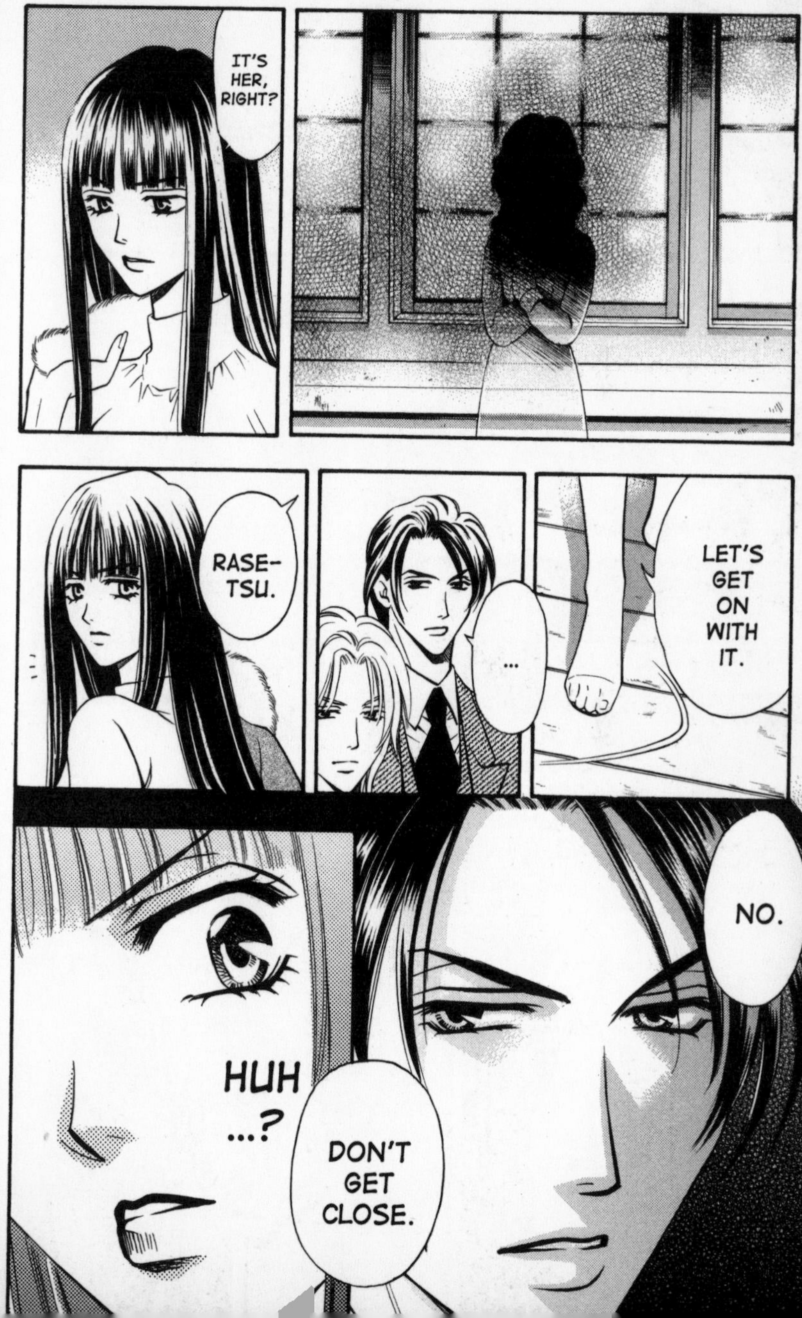
IT'S HER, RIGHT?
LET'S GET ON WITH IT.
...
RASE-TSU.
NO.
DON'T GET CLOSE.
HUH ...?

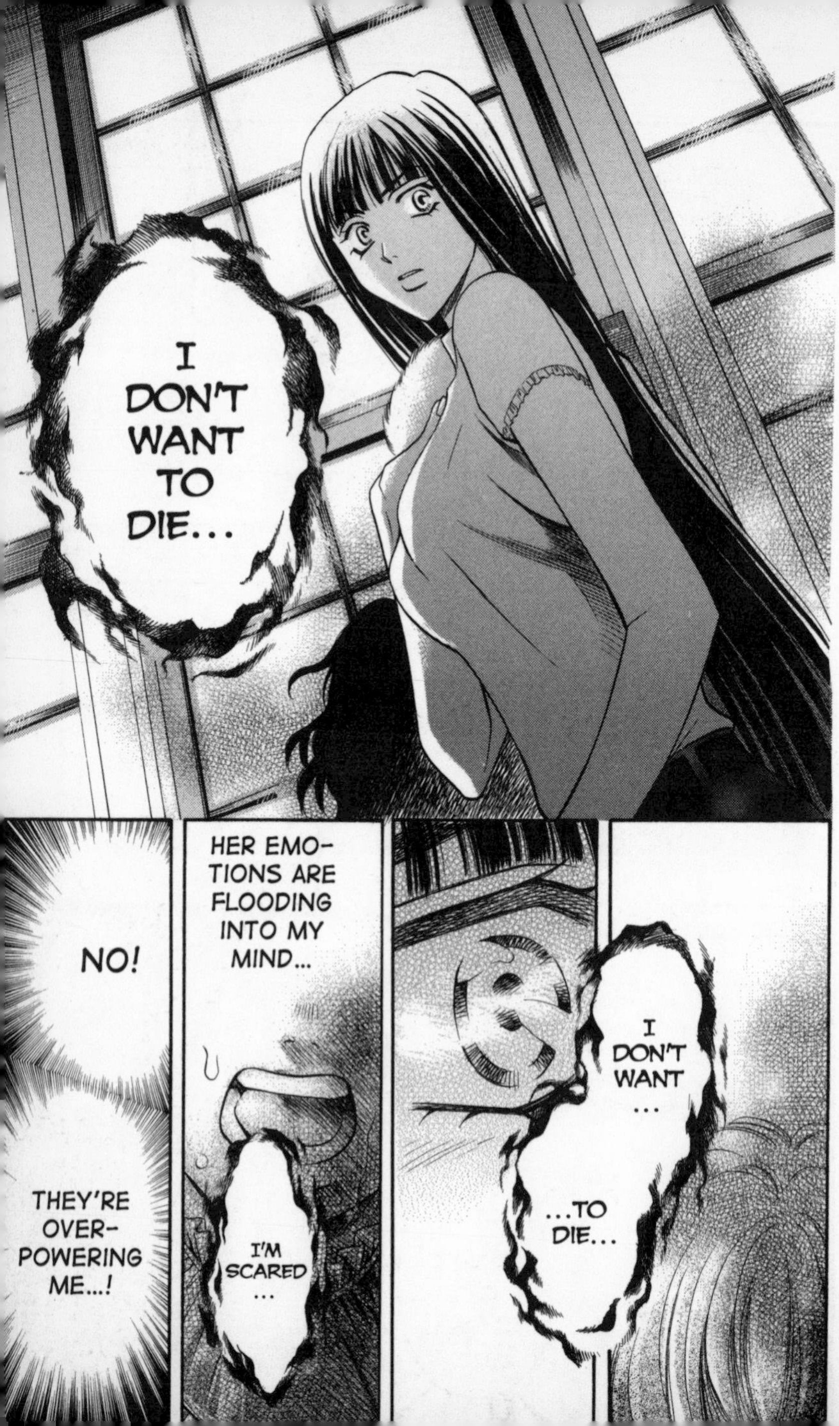
I DON'T WANT TO DIE...
I DON'T WANT...
...TO DIE...
HER EMO-TIONS ARE FLOODING INTO MY MIND...
I'M SCARED...
NO!
THEY'RE OVER-POWERING ME...!

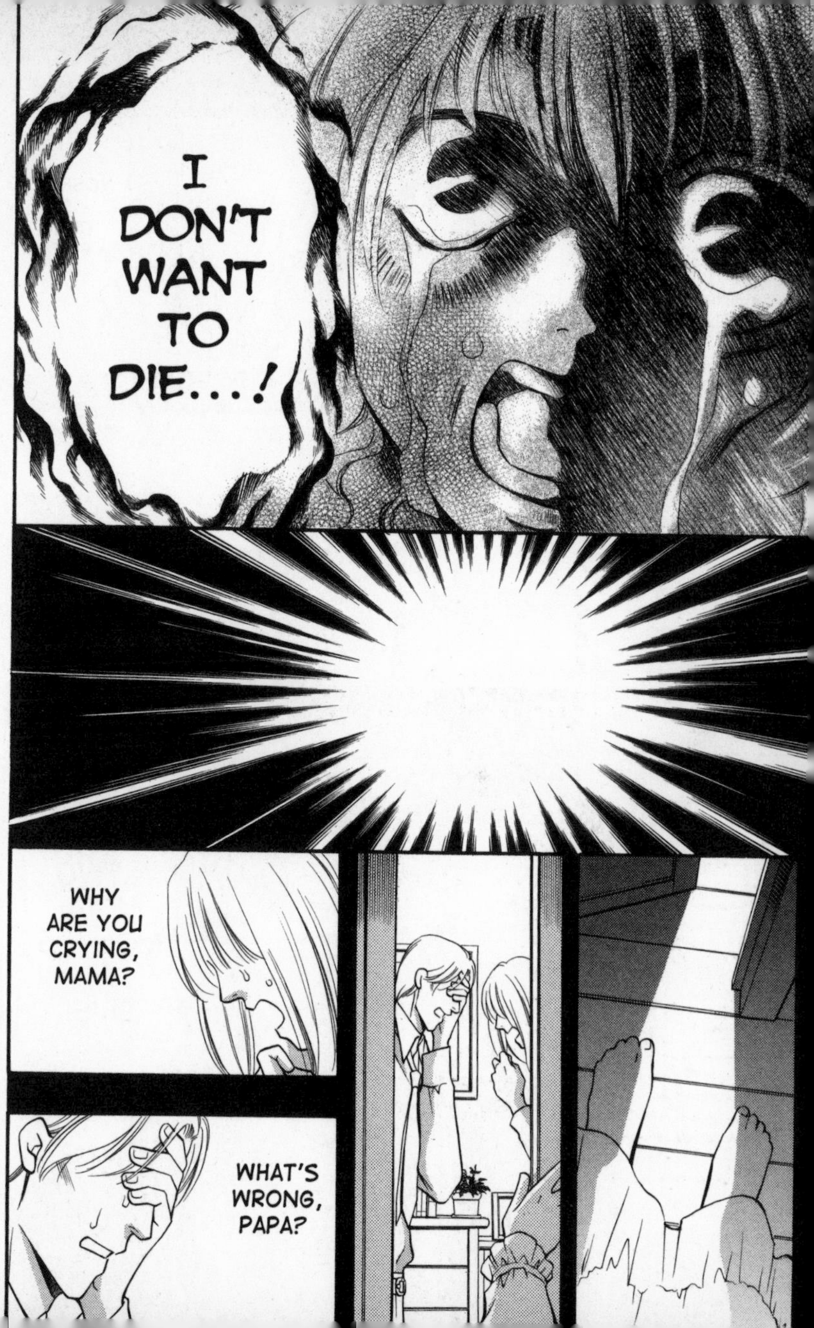
I DON'T WANT TO DIE...!
WHY ARE YOU CRYING, MAMA?
WHAT'S WRONG, PAPA?

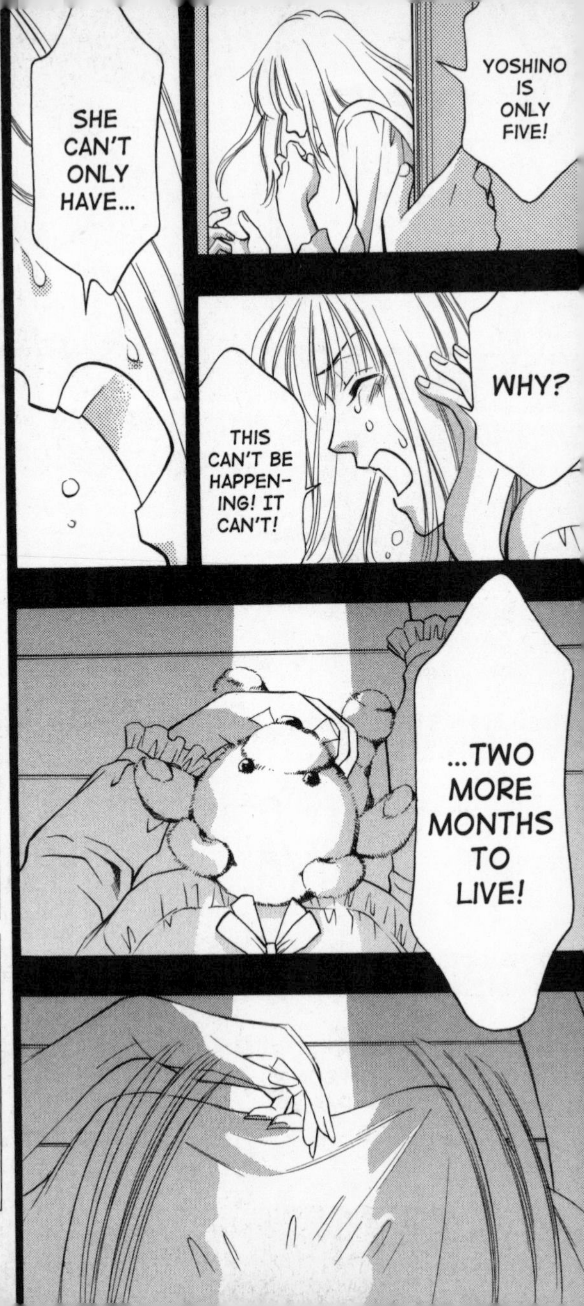
YOSHINO IS ONLY FIVE!
WHY?
THIS CAN'T BE HAPPEN-ING! IT CAN'T!
SHE CAN'T ONLY HAVE...
...TWO MORE MONTHS TO LIVE!

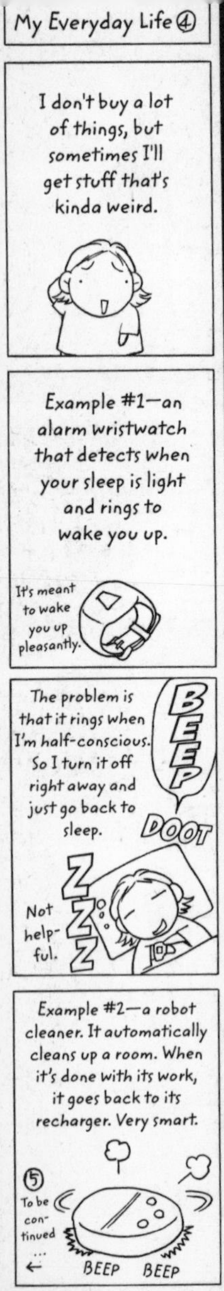
My Everyday Life ④
I don't buy a lot of things, but sometimes I'll get stuff that's kinda weird.
Example #1—an alarm wristwatch that detects when your sleep is light and rings to wake you up.
It's meant to wake you up pleasantly.
The problem is that it rings when I'm half-conscious. So I turn it off right away and just go back to sleep.
BEEP
DOOT
Z Z Z
Not help-ful.
Example #2—a robot cleaner. It automatically cleans up a room. When it's done with its work, it goes back to its recharger. Very smart.
⑤ To be con-tinued ... ←
BEEP BEEP

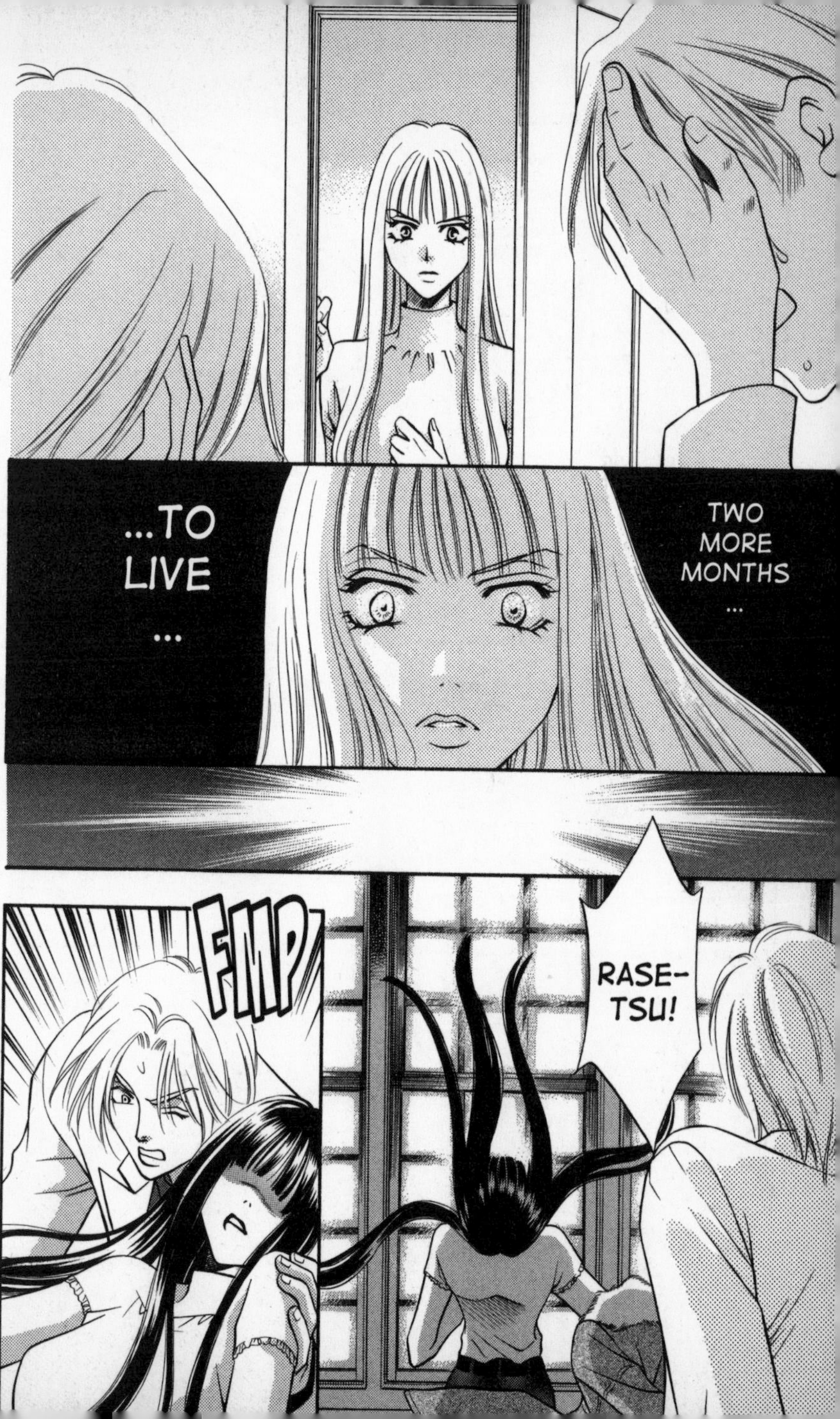
TWO MORE MONTHS ...
...TO LIVE ...
RASE-TSU!
FMP

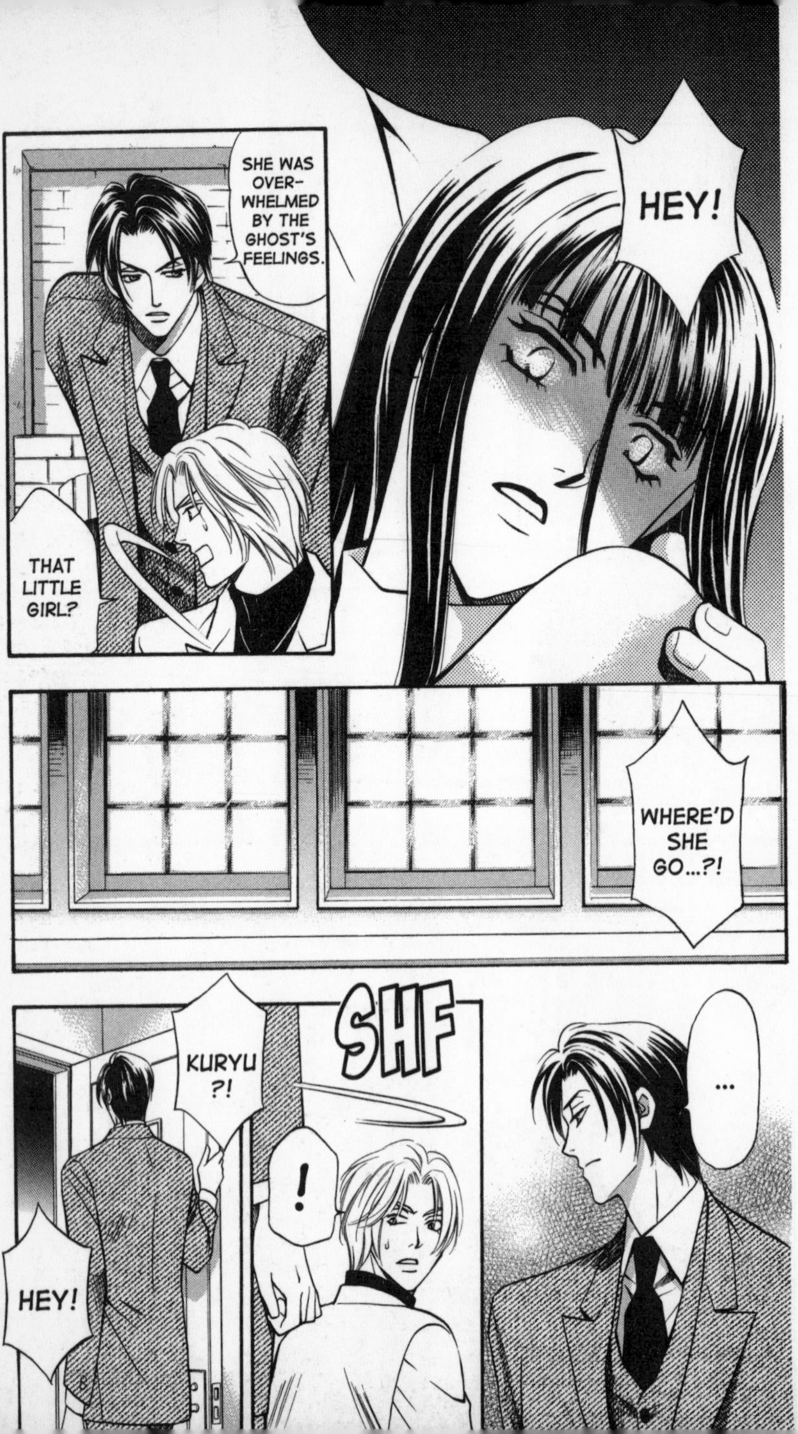
HEY!
SHE WAS OVER-WHELMED BY THE GHOST'S FEELINGS.
THAT LITTLE GIRL?
WHERE'D SHE GO...?!
...
SHF
KURYU ?!
!
HEY!

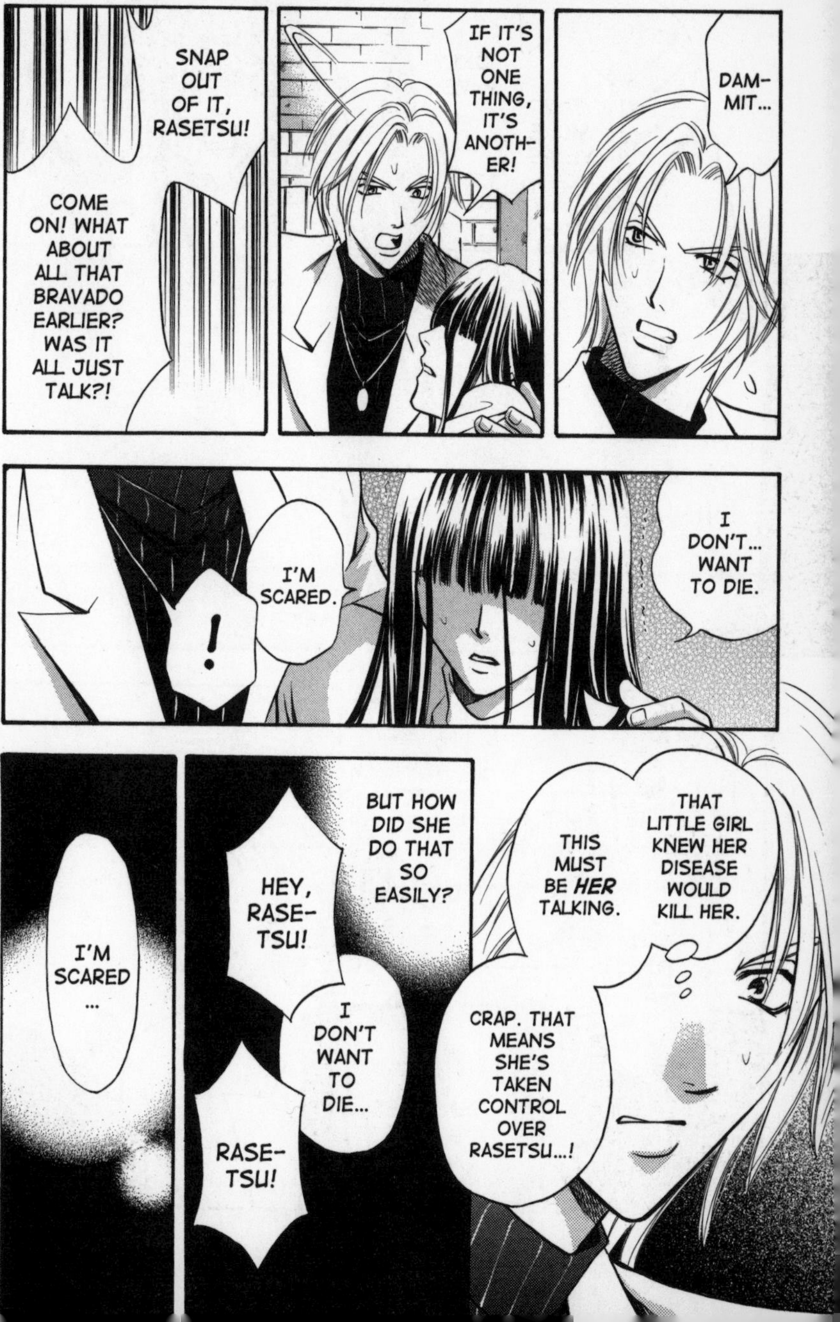
DAMMIT...
IF IT'S NOT ONE THING, IT'S ANOTHER!
SNAP OUT OF IT, RASETSU!
COME ON! WHAT ABOUT ALL THAT BRAVADO EARLIER? WAS IT ALL JUST TALK?!
I DON'T... WANT TO DIE.
I'M SCARED.
!
THAT LITTLE GIRL KNEW HER DISEASE WOULD KILL HER.
THIS MUST BE *HER* TALKING.
CRAP. THAT MEANS SHE'S TAKEN CONTROL OVER RASETSU...!
BUT HOW DID SHE DO THAT SO EASILY?
HEY, RASETSU!
I DON'T WANT TO DIE...
RASETSU!
I'M SCARED...

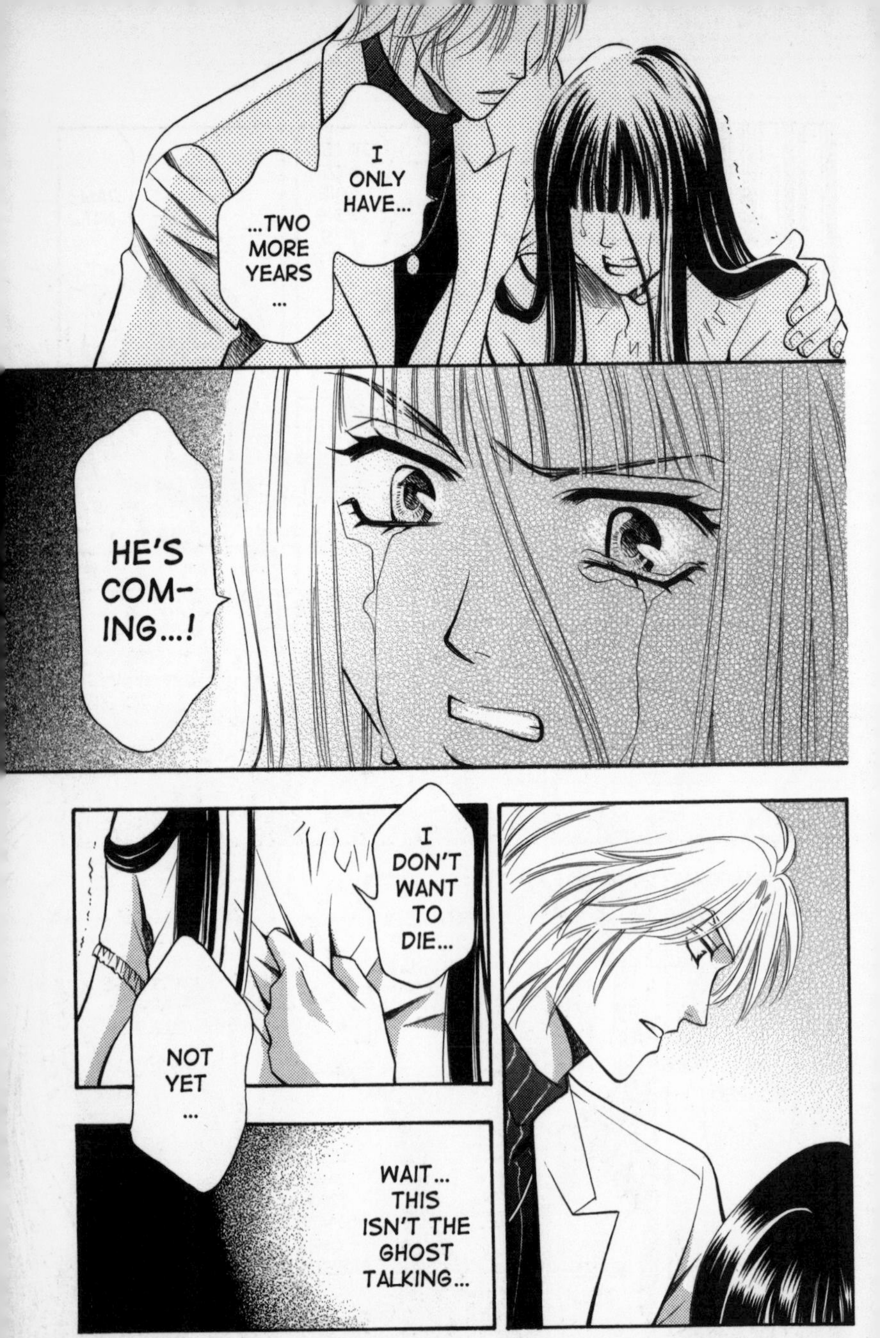
I ONLY HAVE...
...TWO MORE YEARS ...
HE'S COMING...!
I DON'T WANT TO DIE...
NOT YET ...
WAIT... THIS ISN'T THE GHOST TALKING...

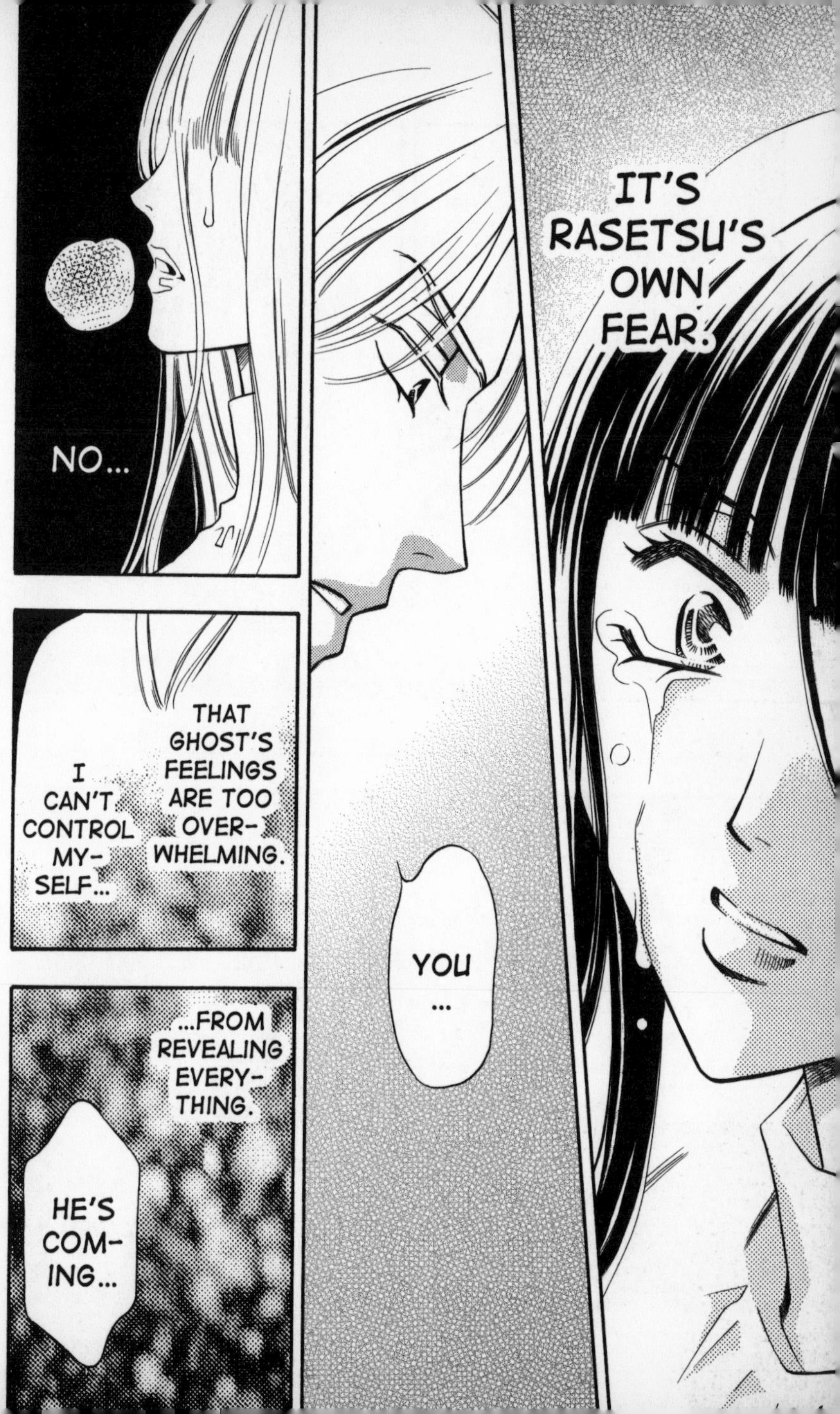
IT'S RASETSU'S OWN FEAR.
YOU ...
NO...
THAT GHOST'S FEELINGS ARE TOO OVER-WHELMING.
I CAN'T CONTROL MY-SELF...
...FROM REVEALING EVERY-THING.
HE'S COM-ING...

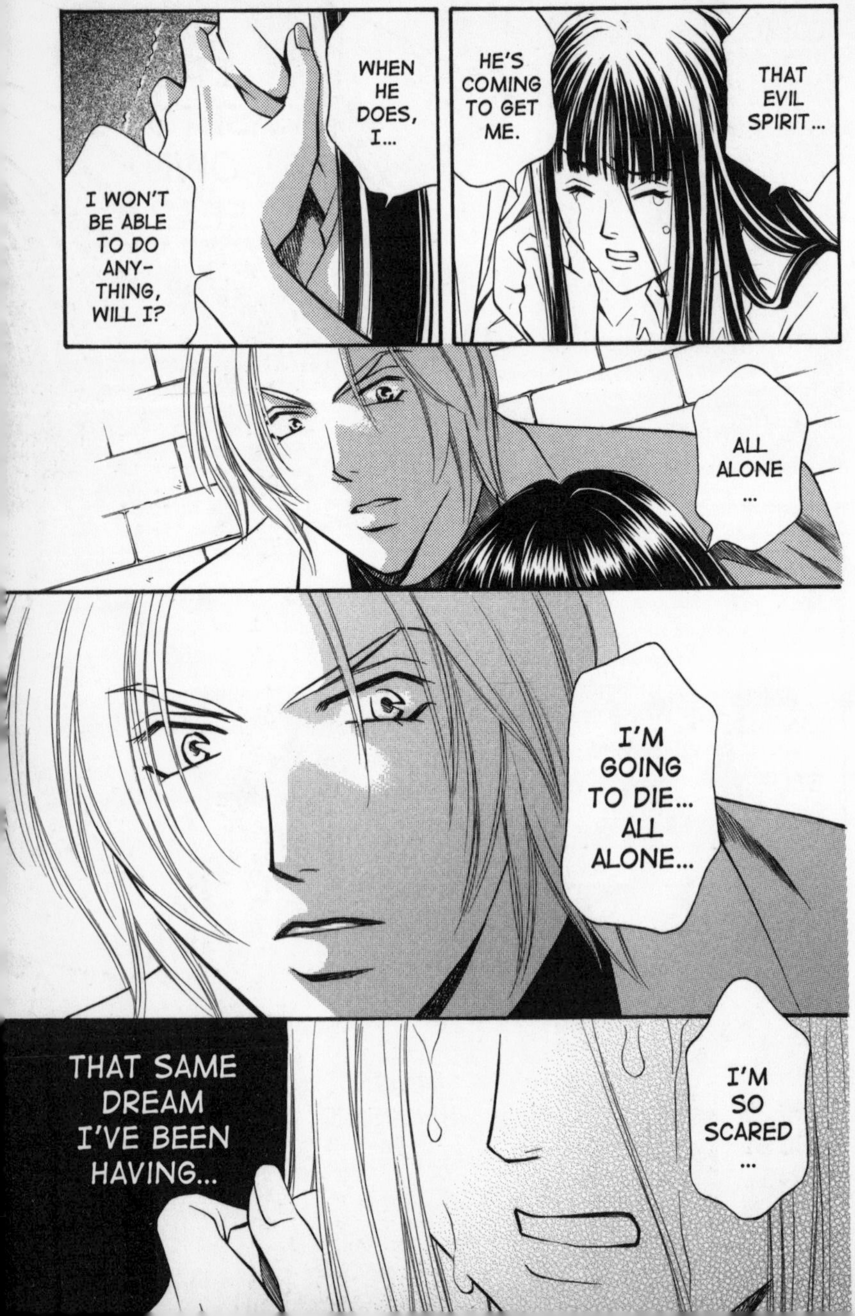
THAT EVIL SPIRIT...
HE'S COMING TO GET ME.
WHEN HE DOES, I...
I WON'T BE ABLE TO DO ANYTHING, WILL I?
ALL ALONE...
I'M GOING TO DIE... ALL ALONE...
I'M SO SCARED...
THAT SAME DREAM I'VE BEEN HAVING...

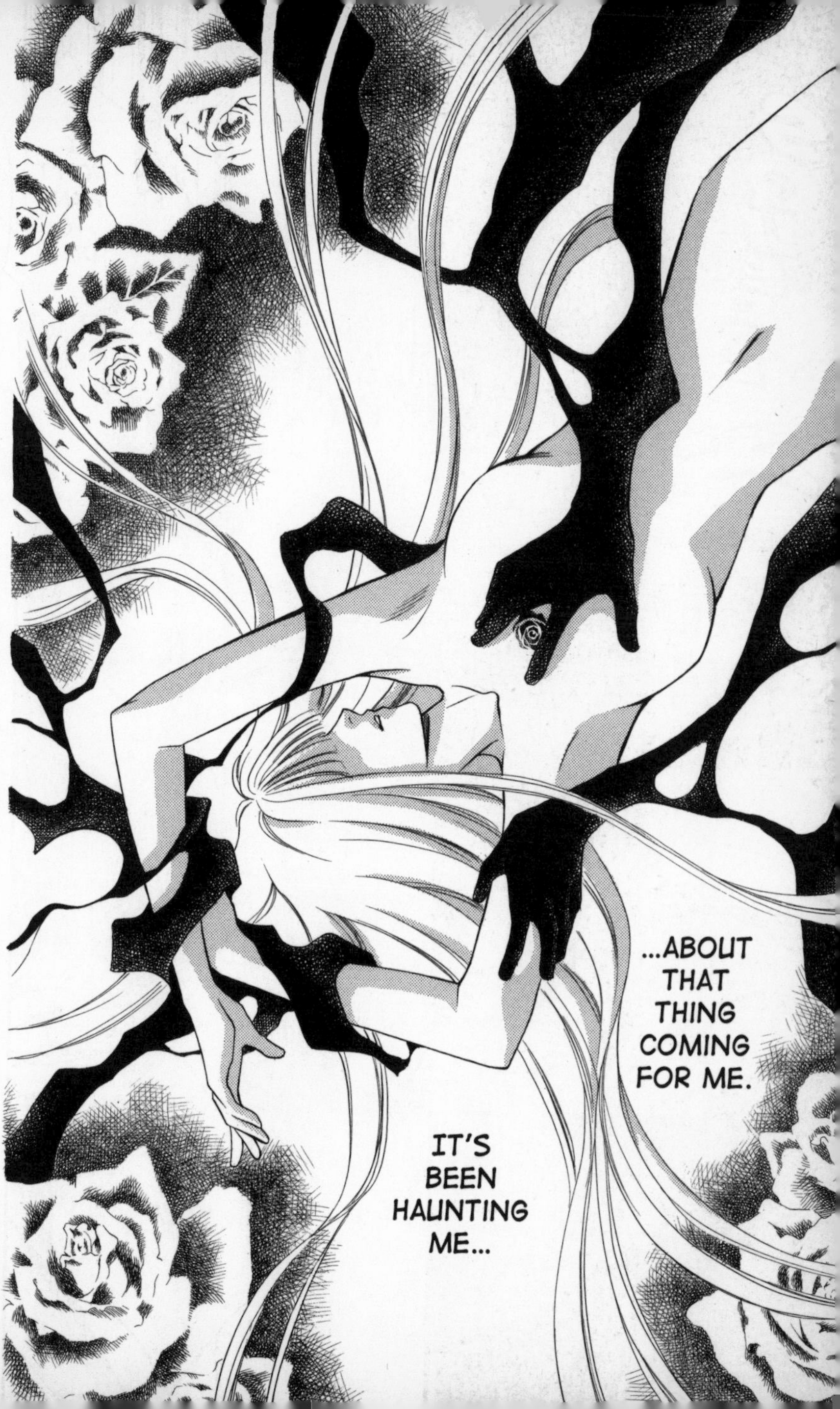
IT'S BEEN HAUNTING ME...
...ABOUT THAT THING COMING FOR ME.

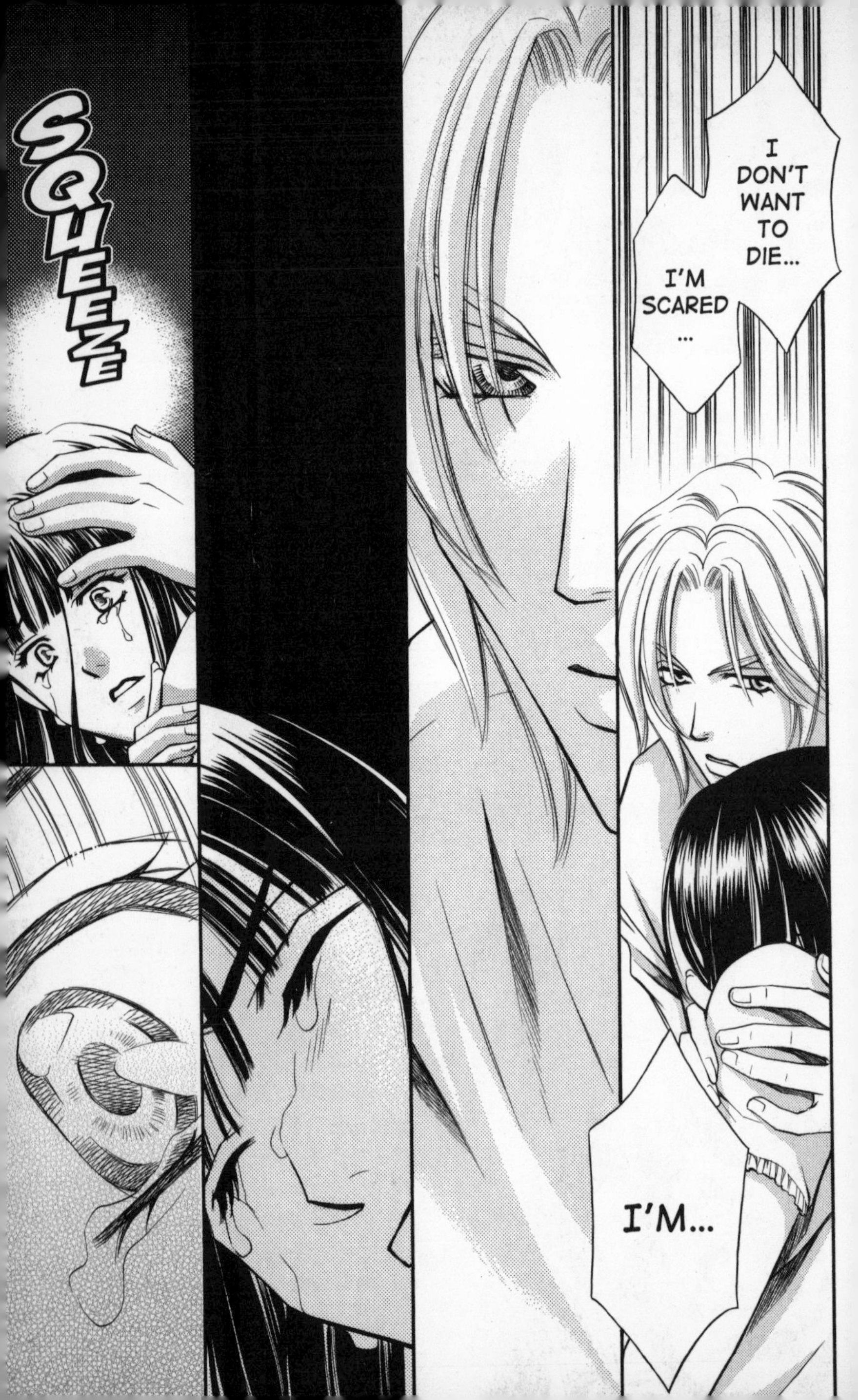
I DON'T WANT TO DIE...
I'M SCARED...
I'M...
SQUEEZE

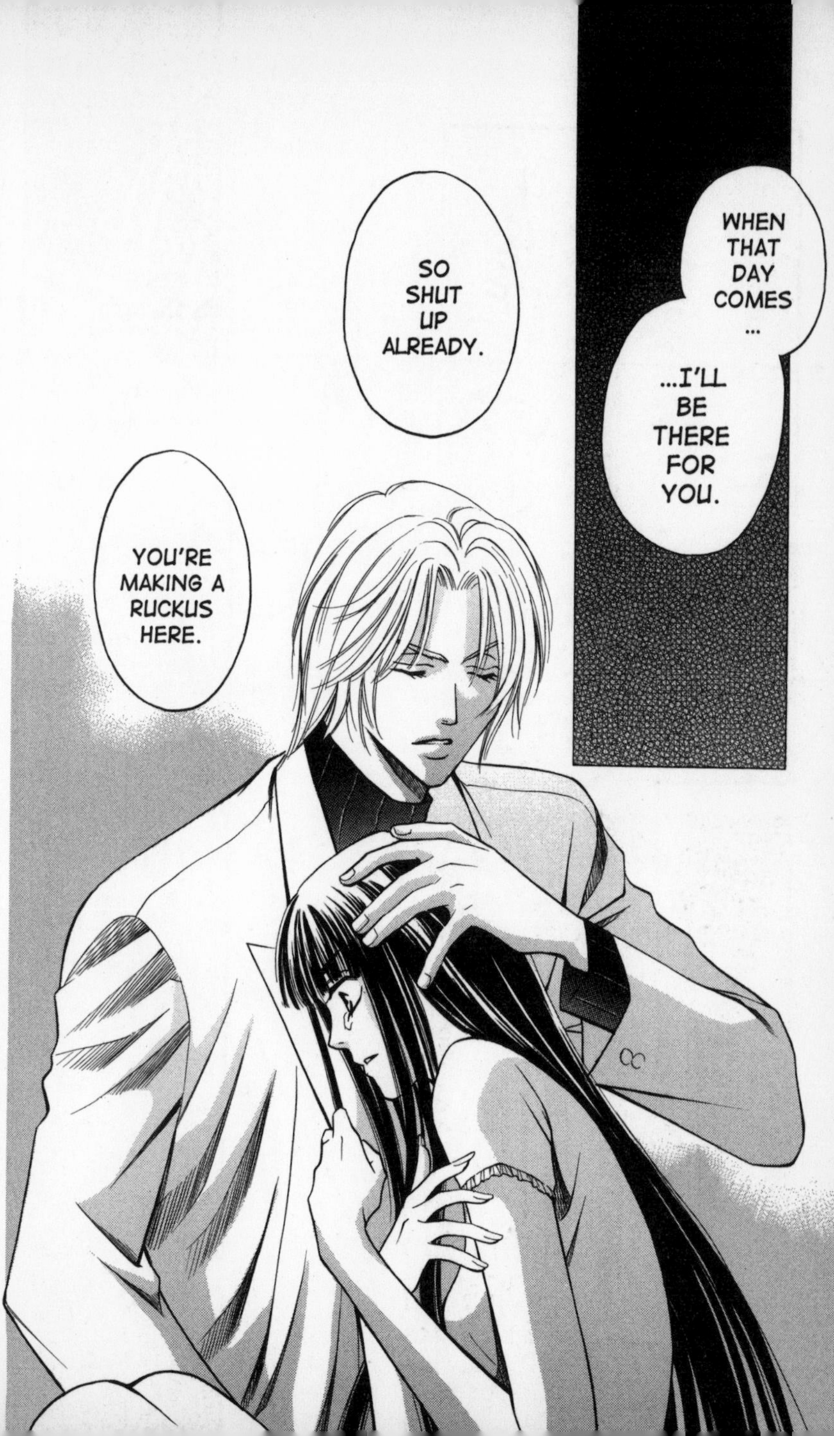
WHEN THAT DAY COMES ...
...I'LL BE THERE FOR YOU.
SO SHUT UP ALREADY.
YOU'RE MAKING A RUCKUS HERE.

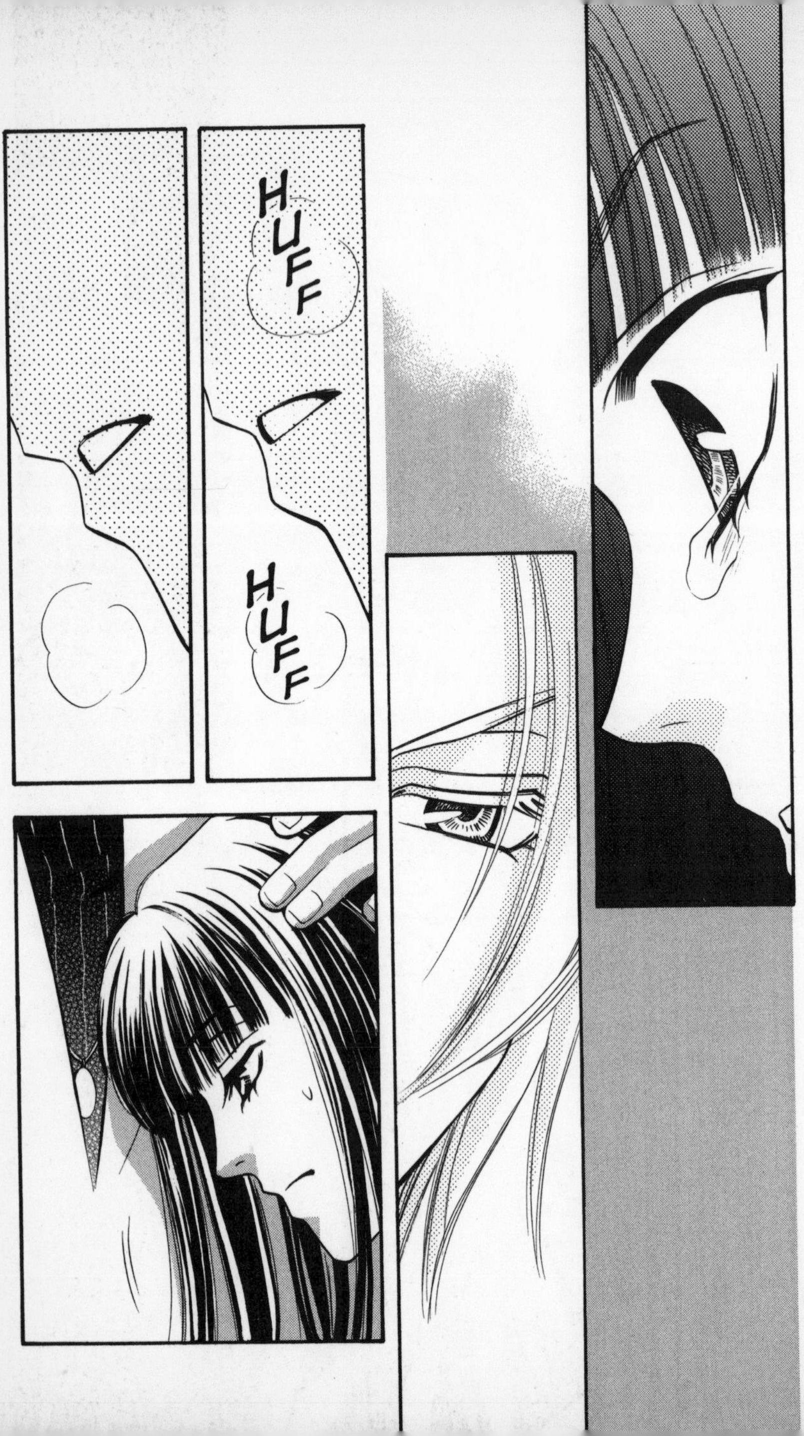
HUFF
HUFF

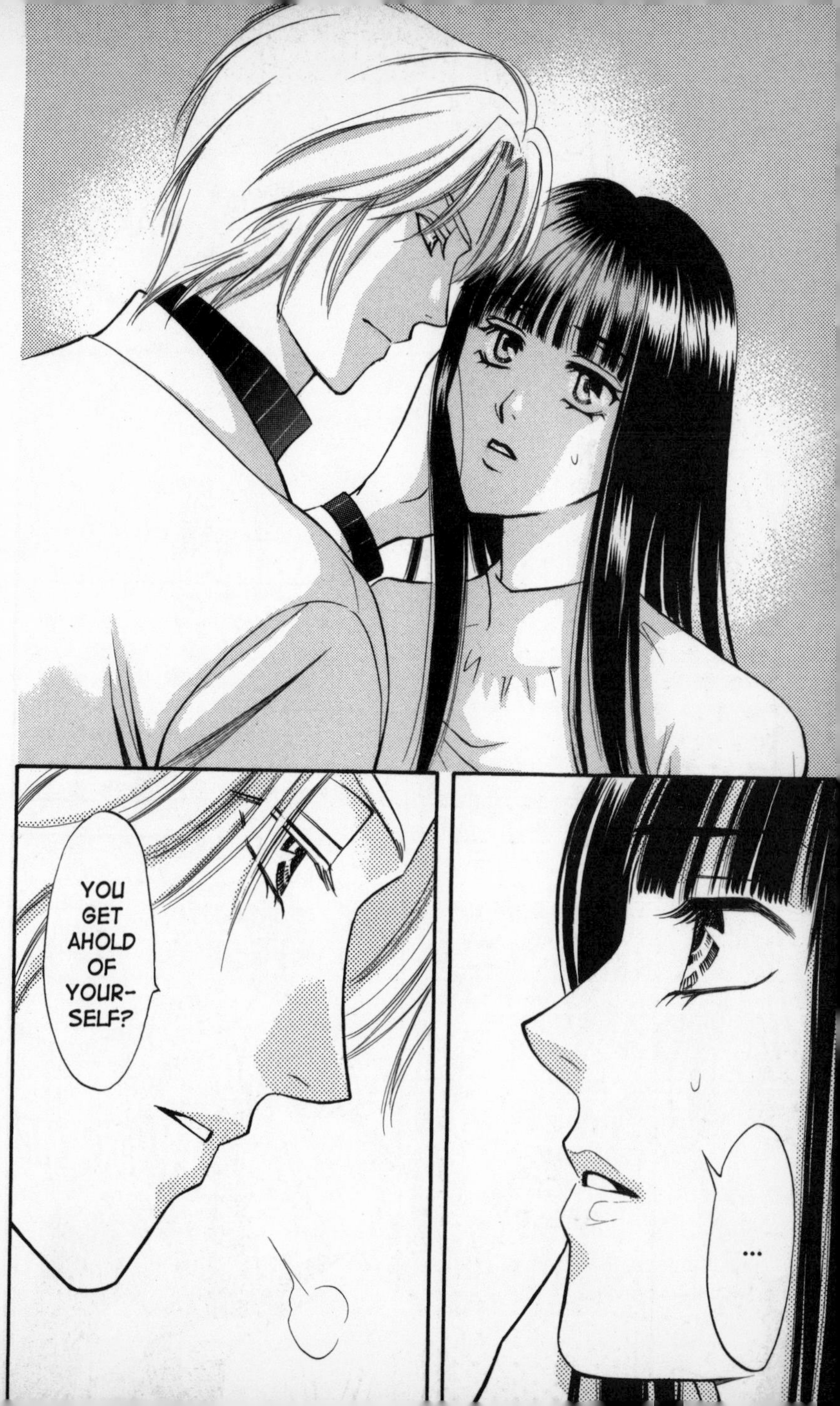
...
YOU GET AHOLD OF YOURSELF?

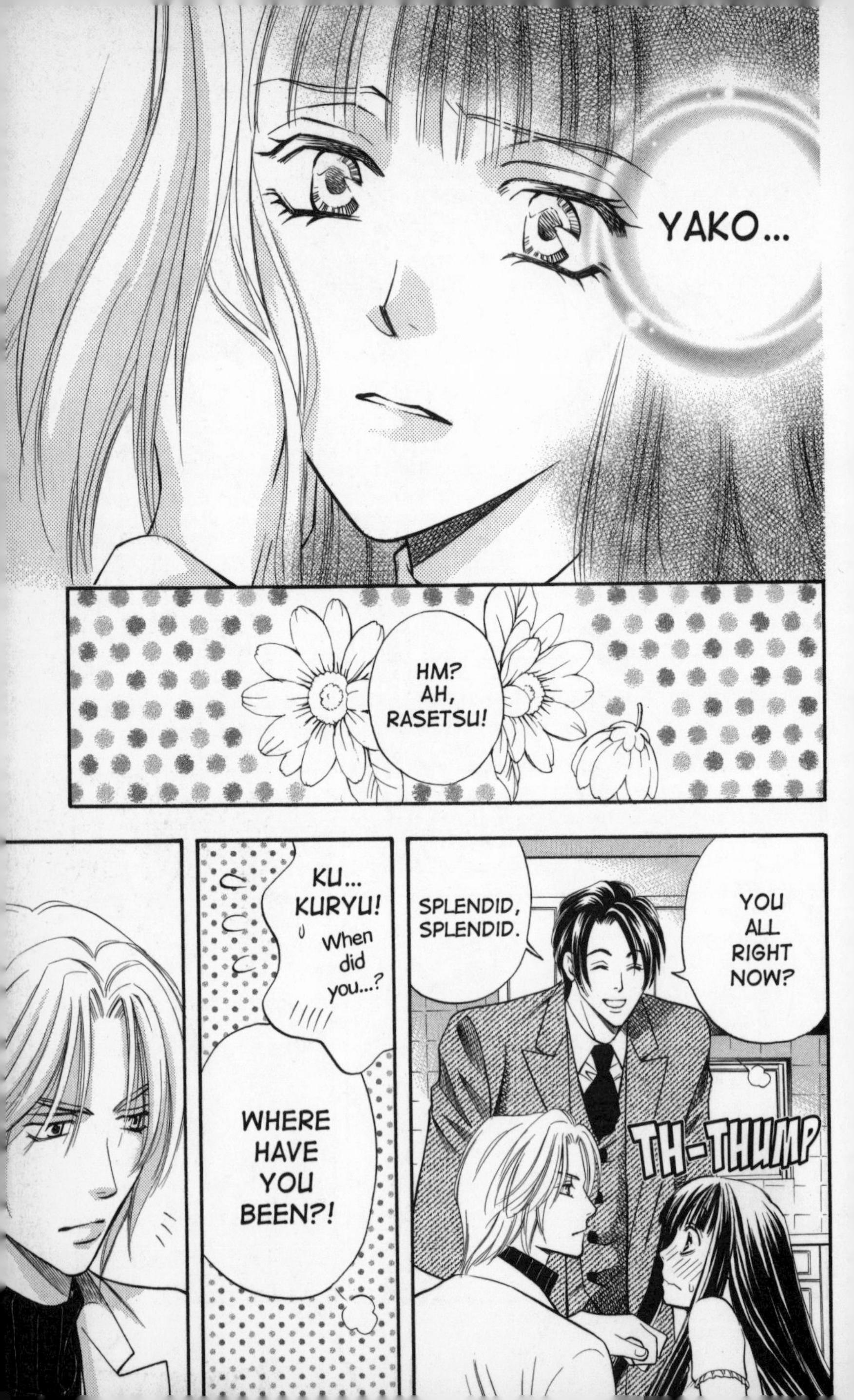
YAKO...
HM? AH, RASETSU!
YOU ALL RIGHT NOW?
SPLENDID, SPLENDID.
TH-THUMP
KU... KURYU!
When did you...?
WHERE HAVE YOU BEEN?!

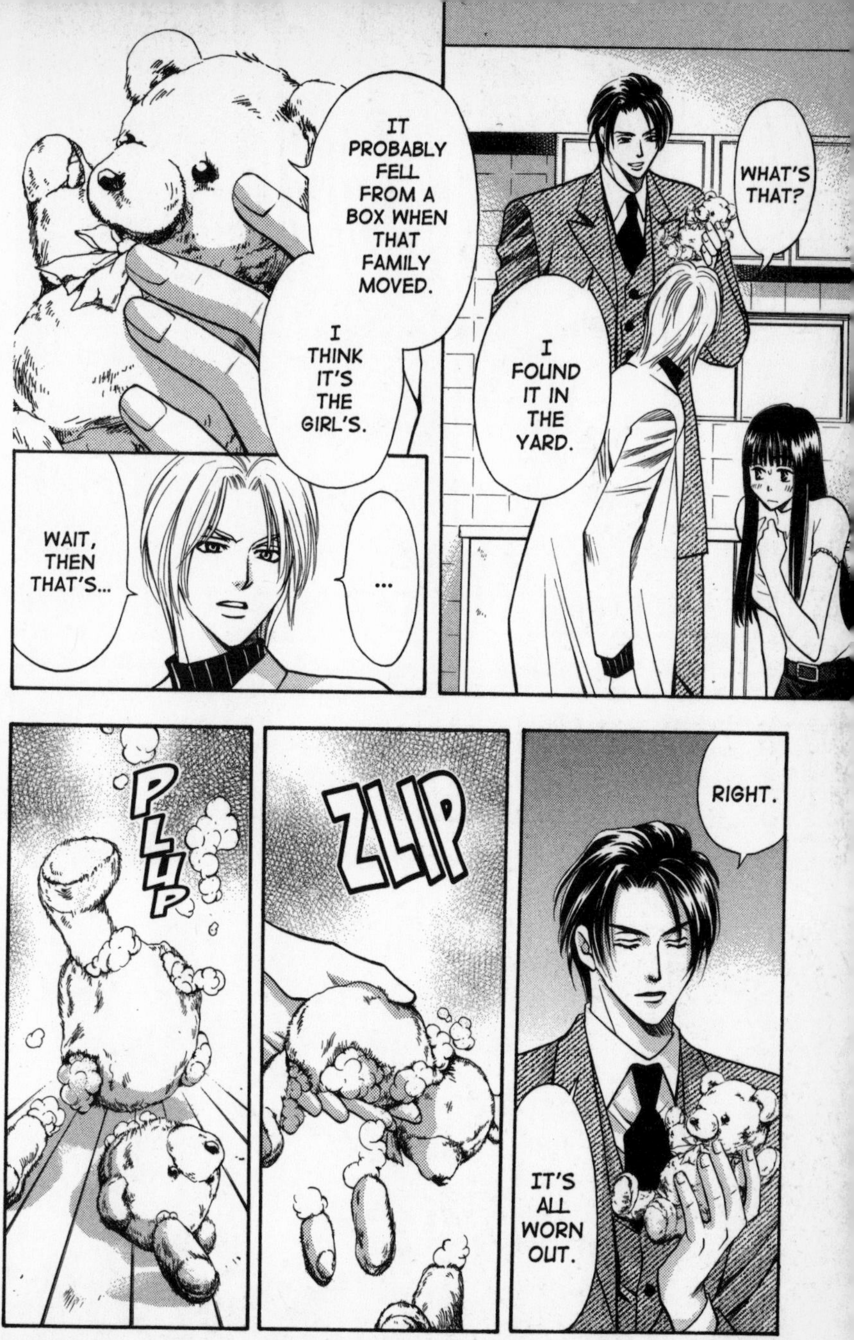
WHAT'S THAT?
I FOUND IT IN THE YARD.
IT PROBABLY FELL FROM A BOX WHEN THAT FAMILY MOVED.
I THINK IT'S THE GIRL'S.
...
WAIT, THEN THAT'S...
RIGHT.
IT'S ALL WORN OUT.
ZLIP
PLUP

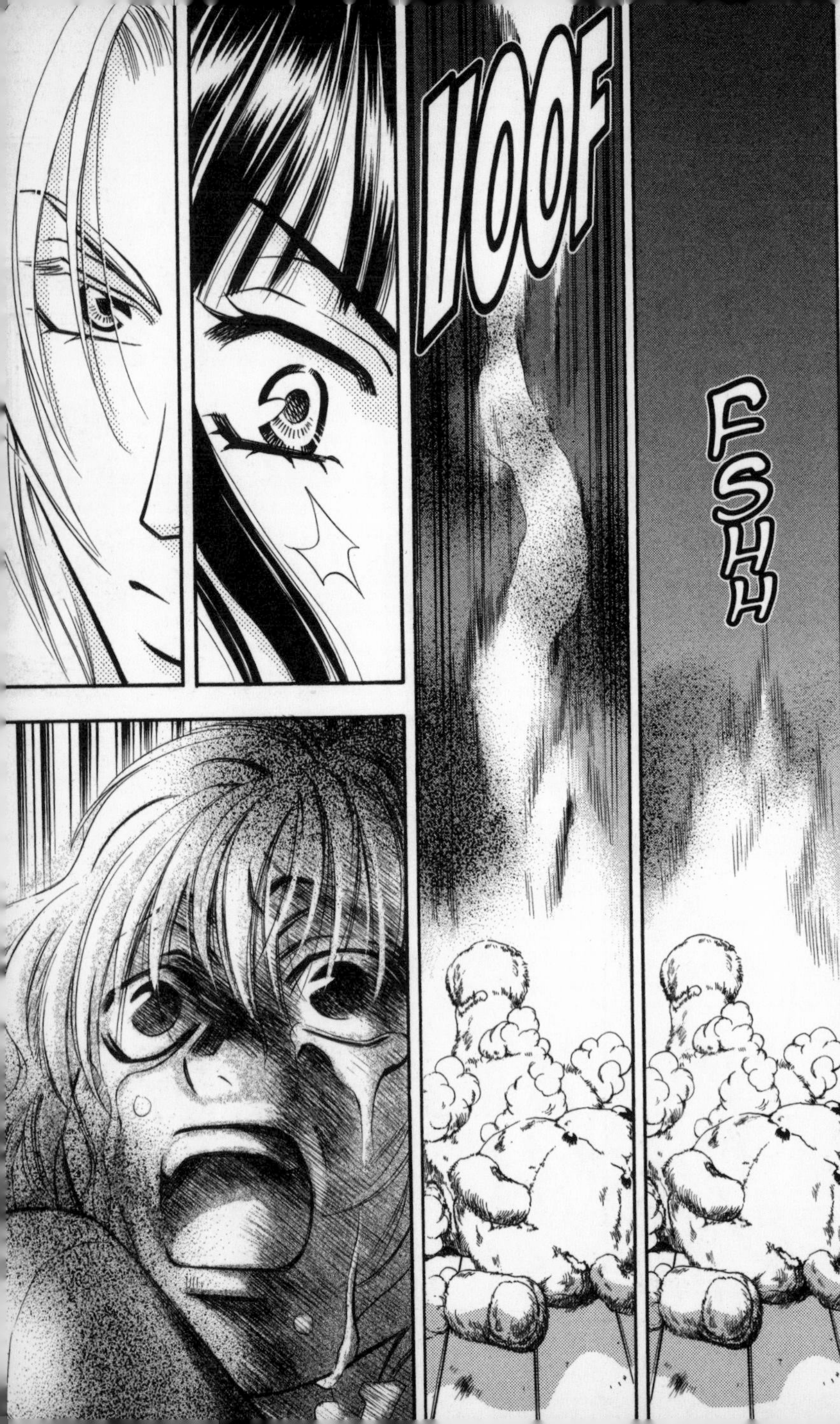
FSHH
VOOF

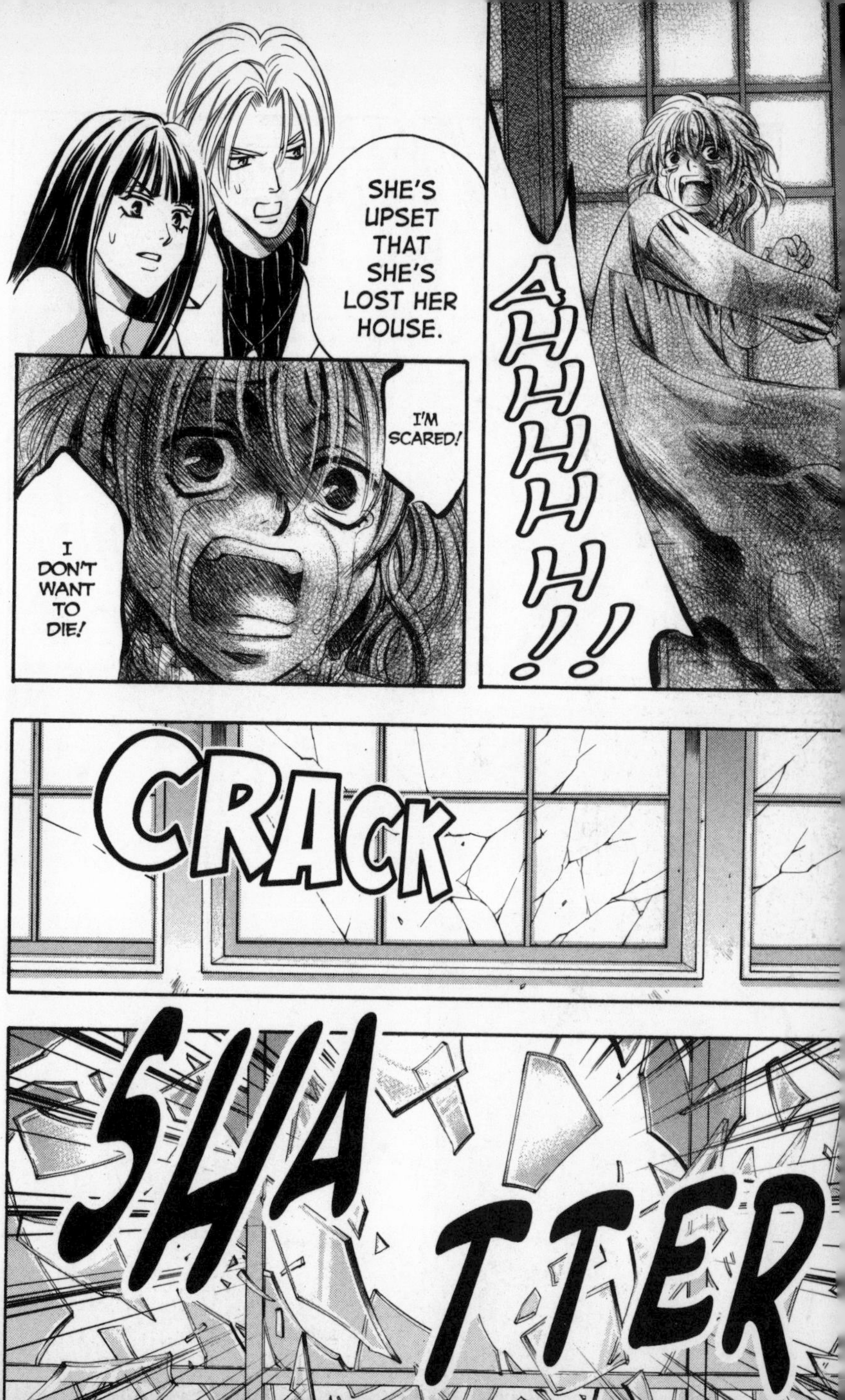
AHHHHH!!
SHE'S UPSET THAT SHE'S LOST HER HOUSE.
I'M SCARED!
I DON'T WANT TO DIE!
CRACK
SHATTER

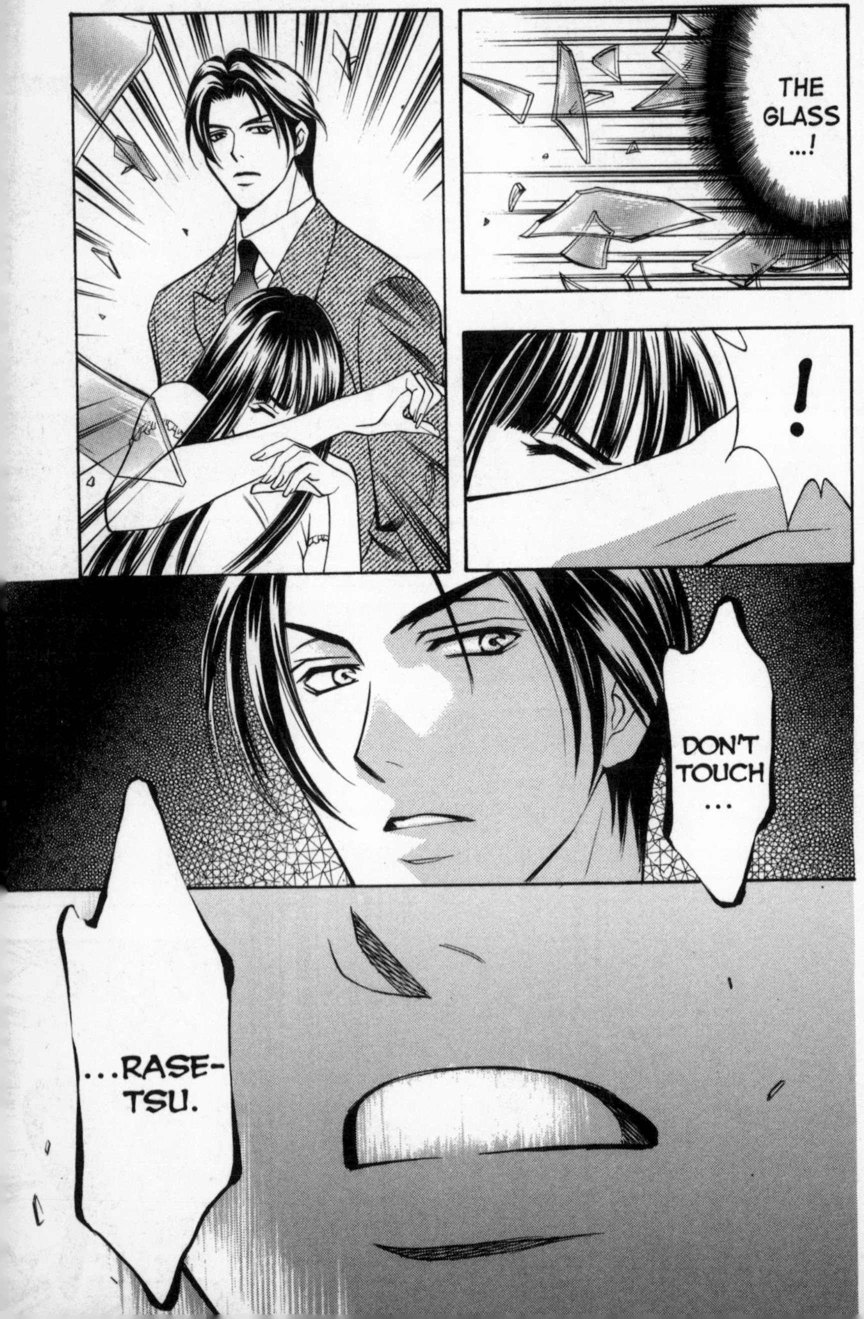
THE GLASS ...!
!
DON'T TOUCH ...
...RASE-TSU.

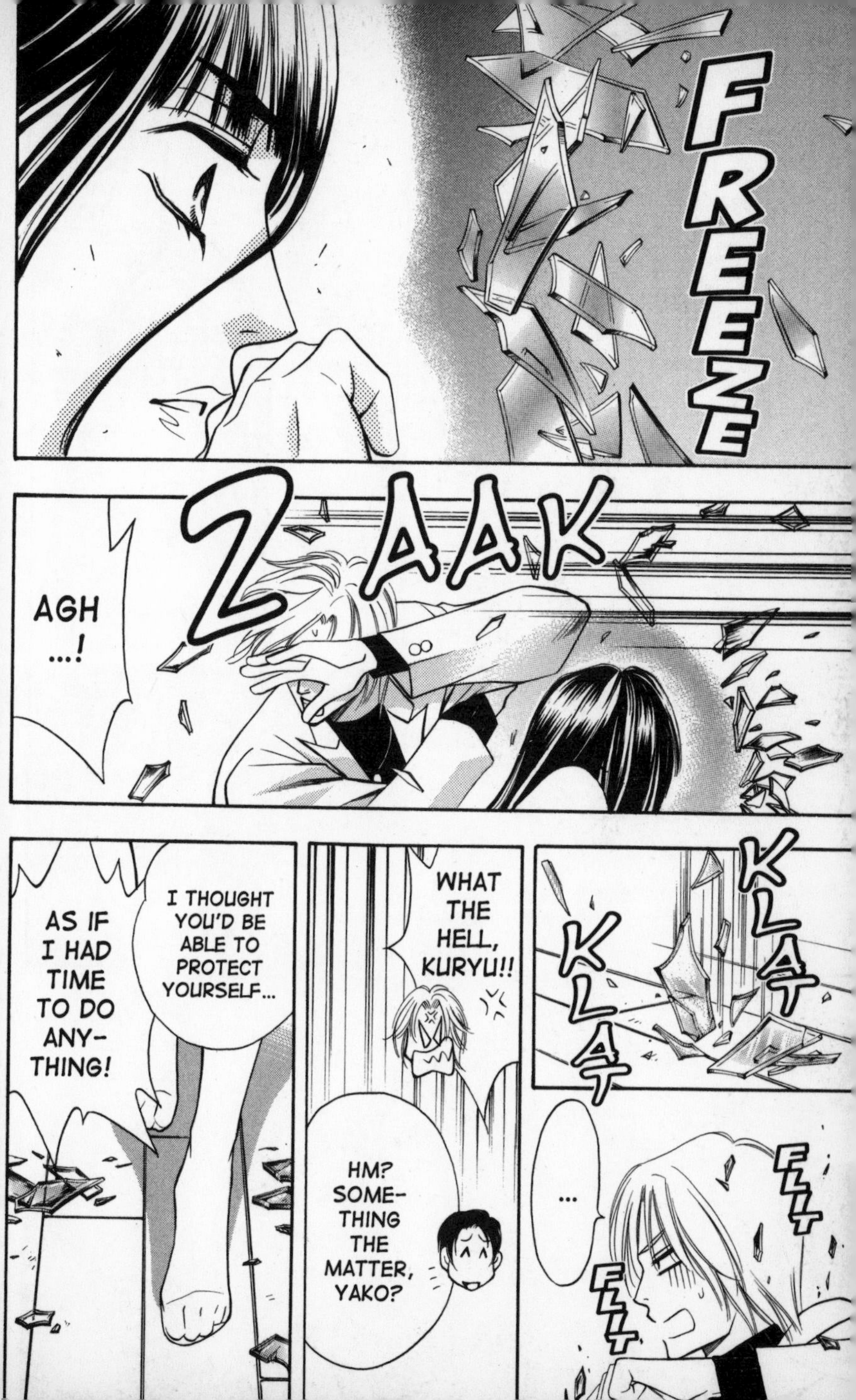
FREEZE
ZAAK
AGH ...!
KLAT
KLAT
...
FLIT
FLIT
WHAT THE HELL, KURYU!!
HM? SOMETHING THE MATTER, YAKO?
I THOUGHT YOU'D BE ABLE TO PROTECT YOURSELF...
AS IF I HAD TIME TO DO ANYTHING!

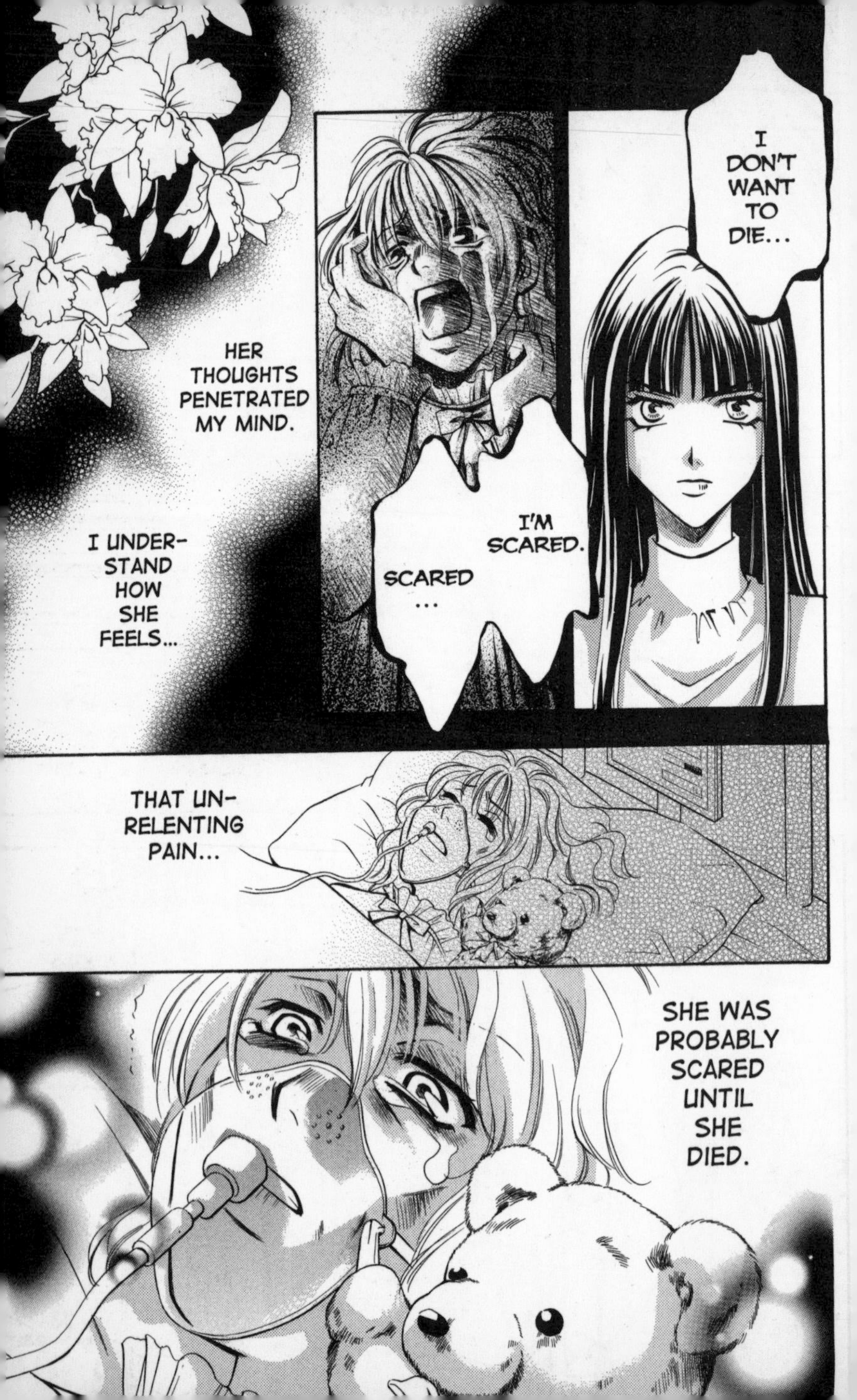
I DON'T WANT TO DIE...
I'M SCARED.
SCARED...
HER THOUGHTS PENETRATED MY MIND.
I UNDERSTAND HOW SHE FEELS...
THAT UNRELENTING PAIN...
SHE WAS PROBABLY SCARED UNTIL SHE DIED.

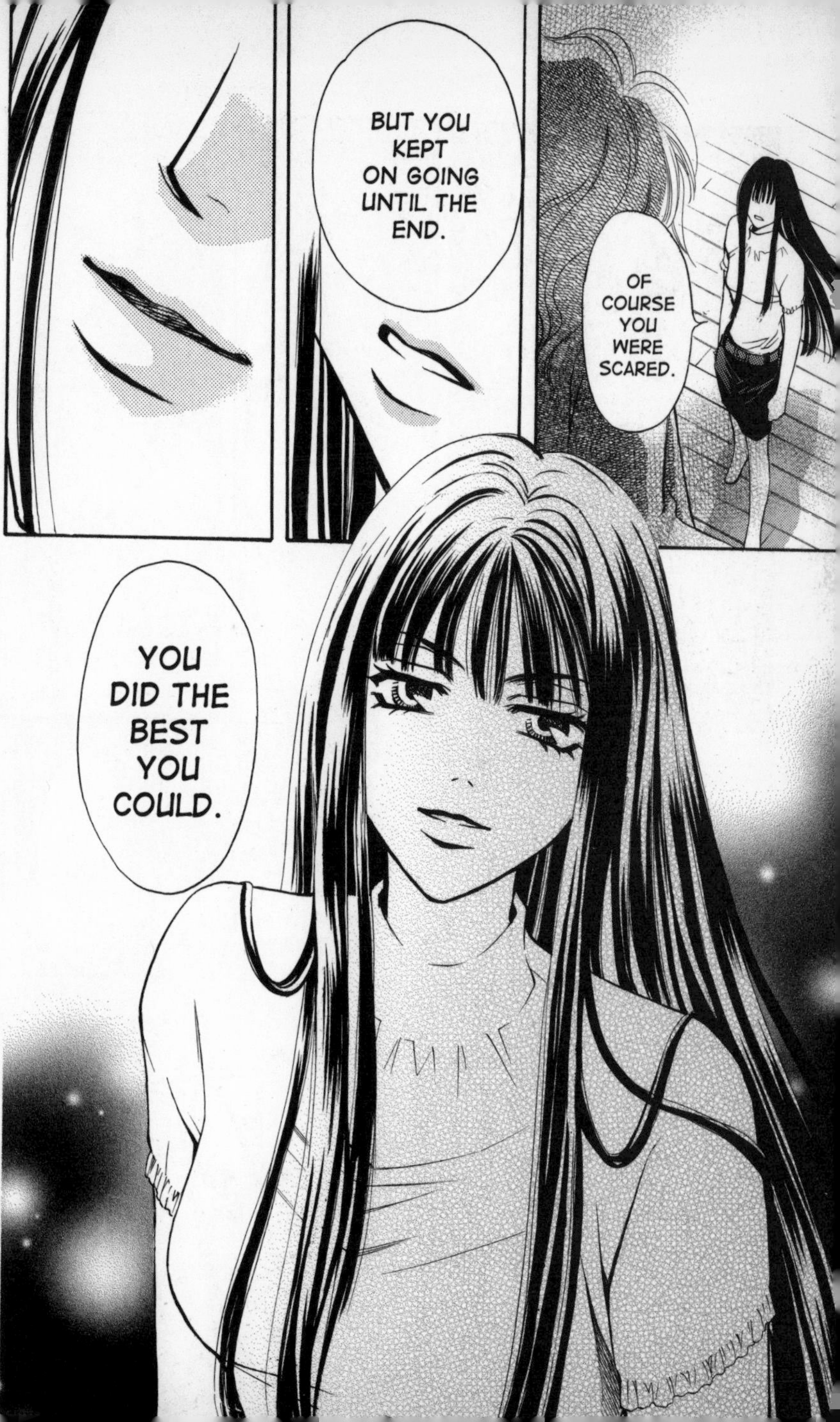
OF COURSE YOU WERE SCARED.
BUT YOU KEPT ON GOING UNTIL THE END.
YOU DID THE BEST YOU COULD.

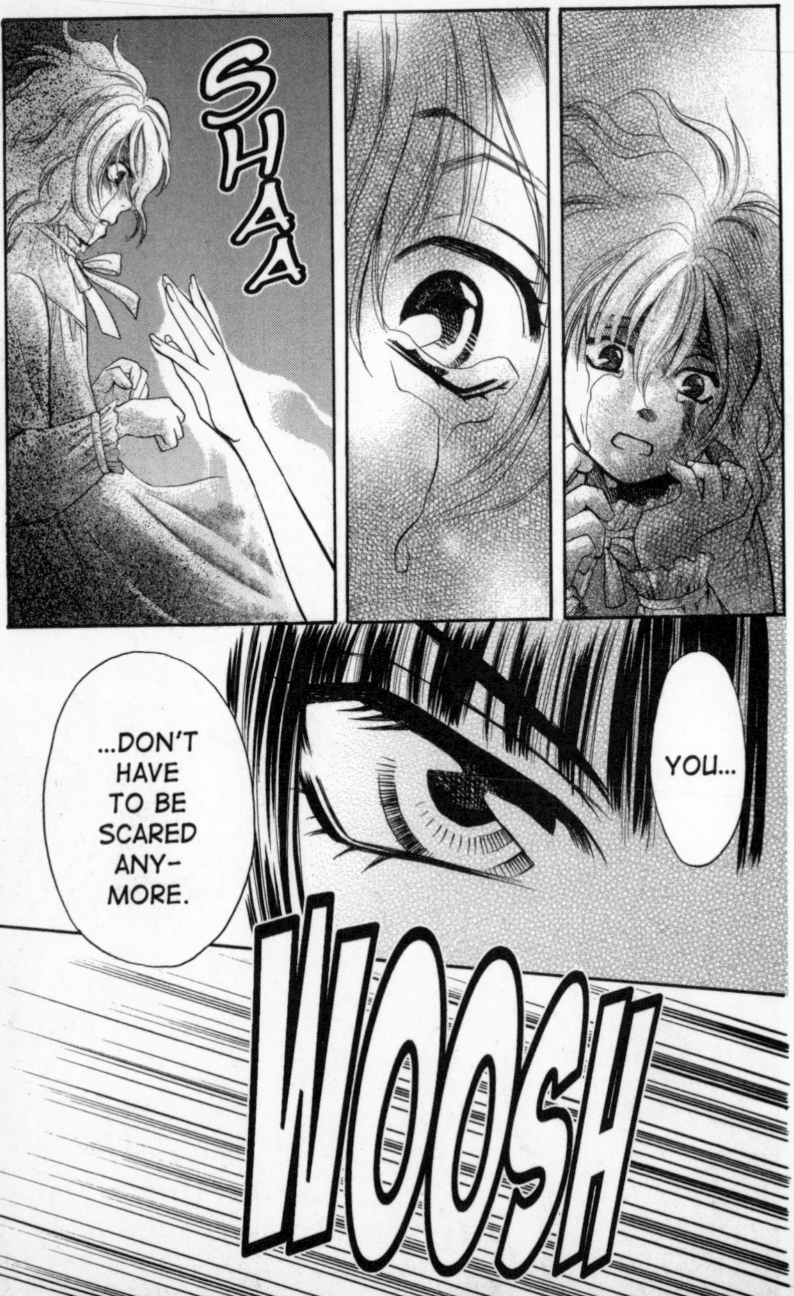
SHAA
YOU...
...DON'T HAVE TO BE SCARED ANY-MORE.
WOOSH

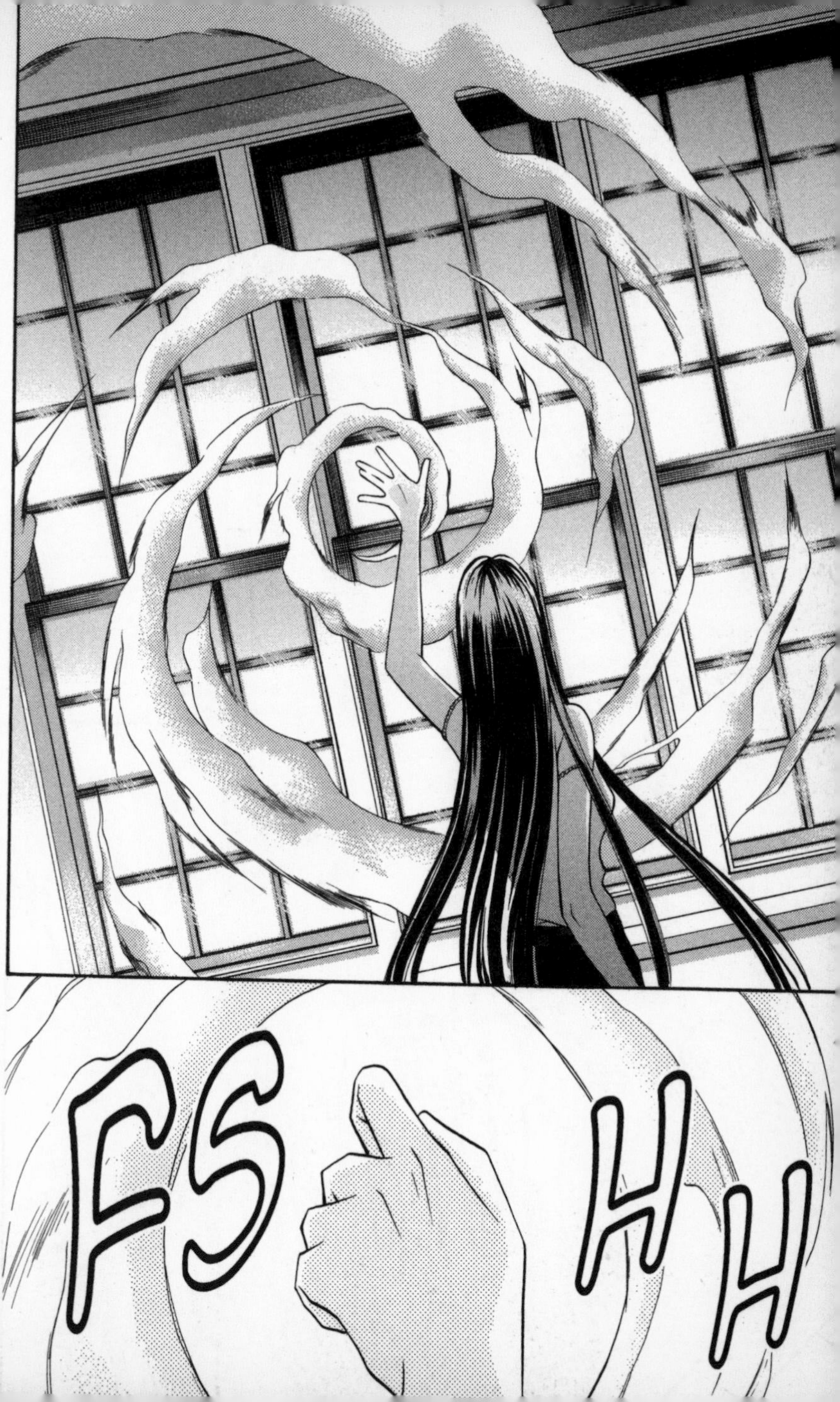
FSHH

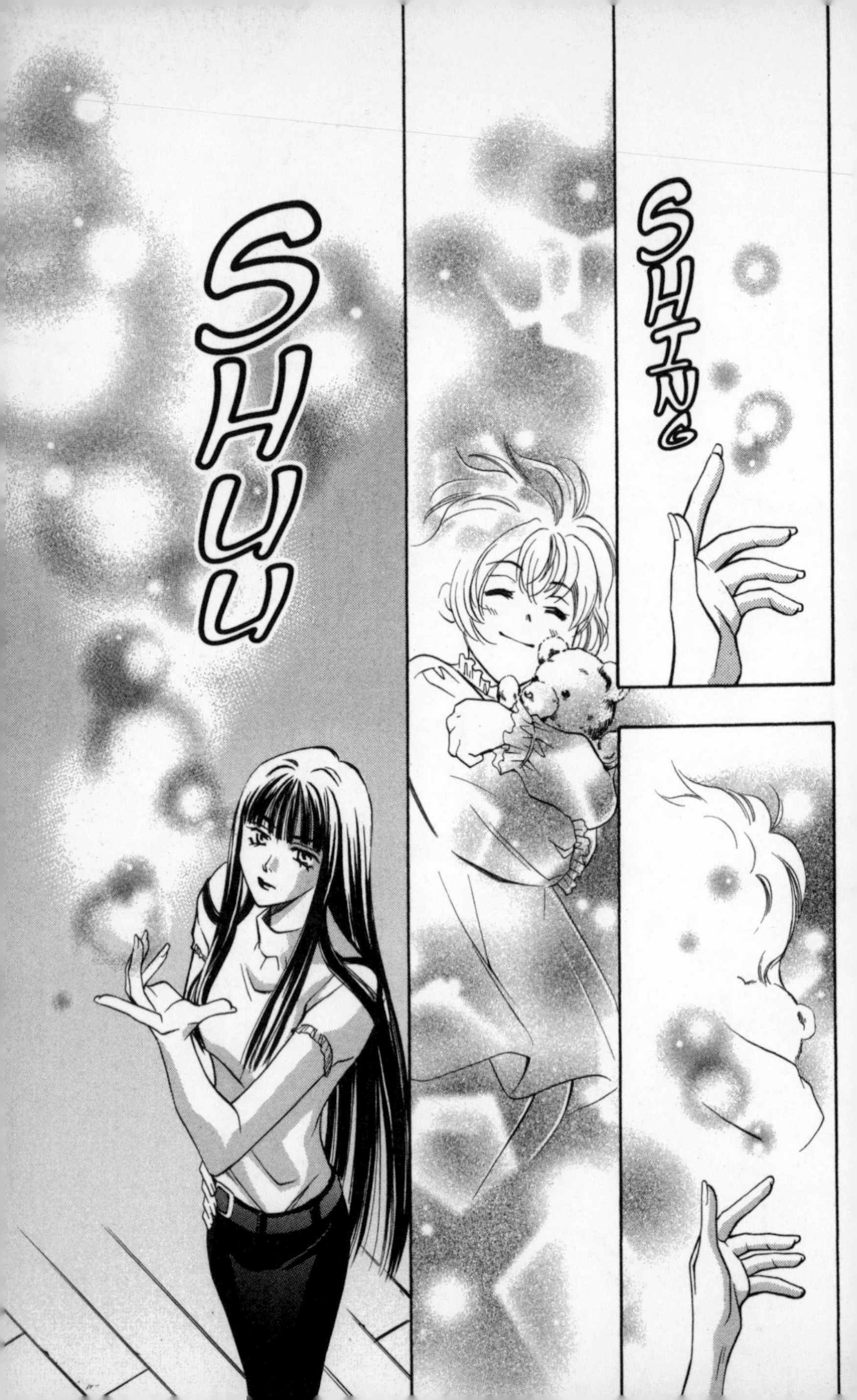
SHING
SHUU

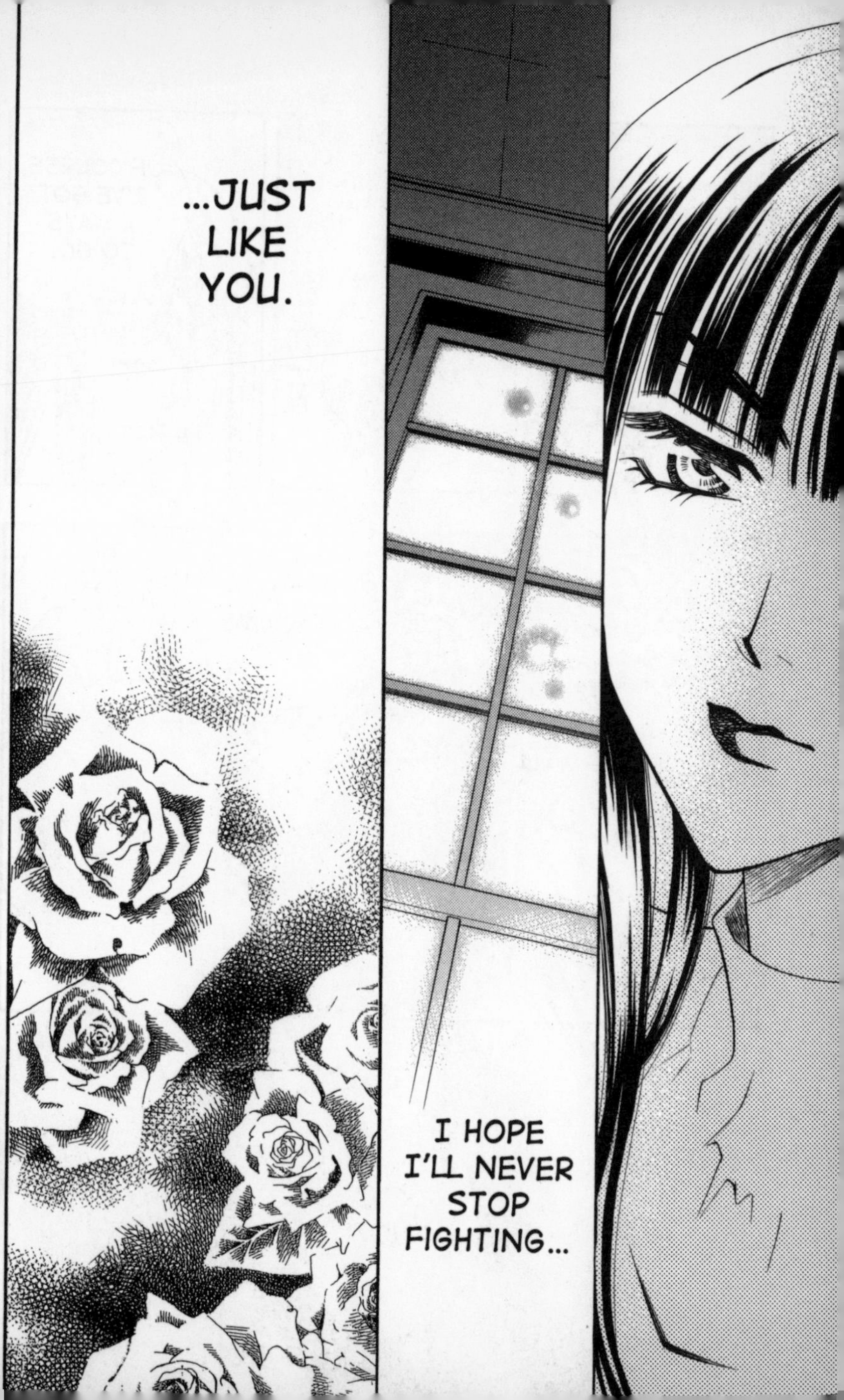
I HOPE I'LL NEVER STOP FIGHTING...
...JUST LIKE YOU.

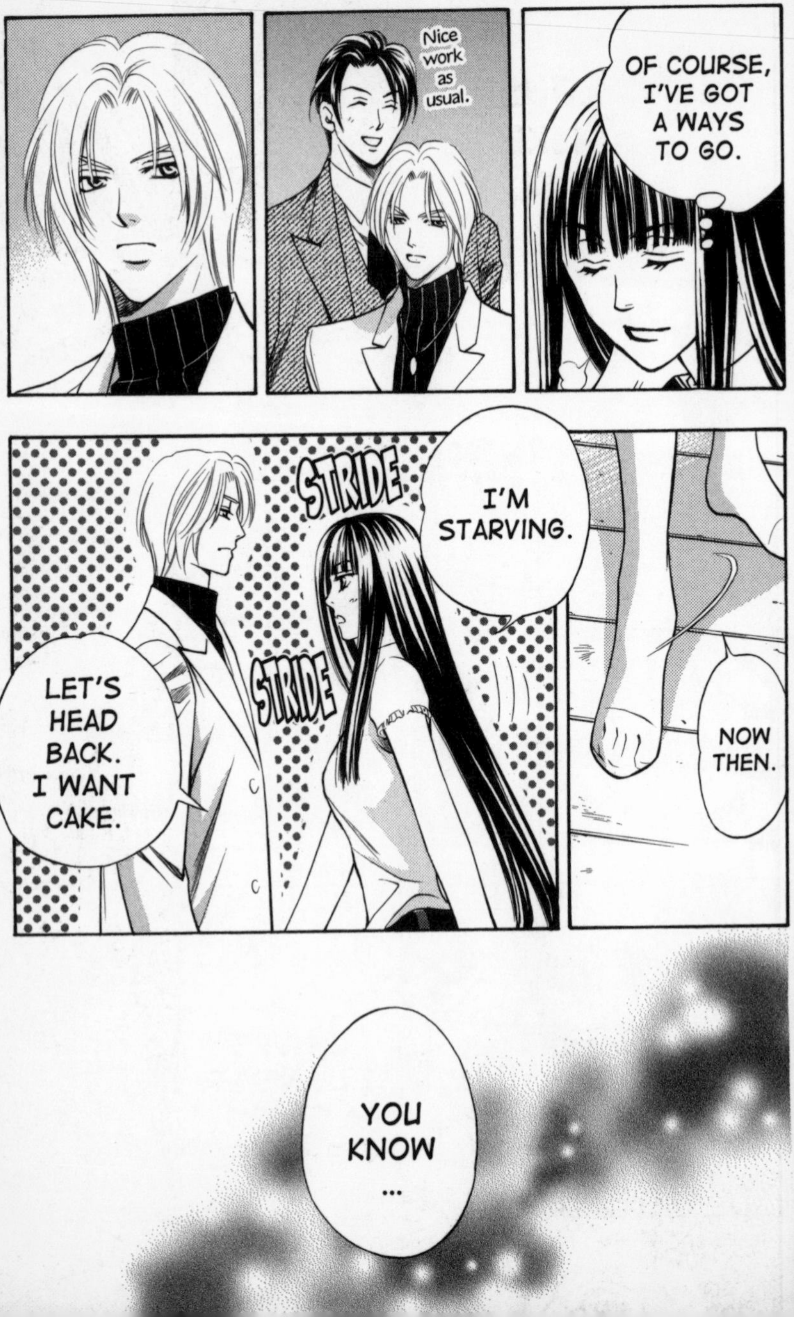
OF COURSE, I'VE GOT A WAYS TO GO.
Nice work as usual.
NOW THEN.
I'M STARVING.
STRIDE
STRIDE
LET'S HEAD BACK. I WANT CAKE.
YOU KNOW ...

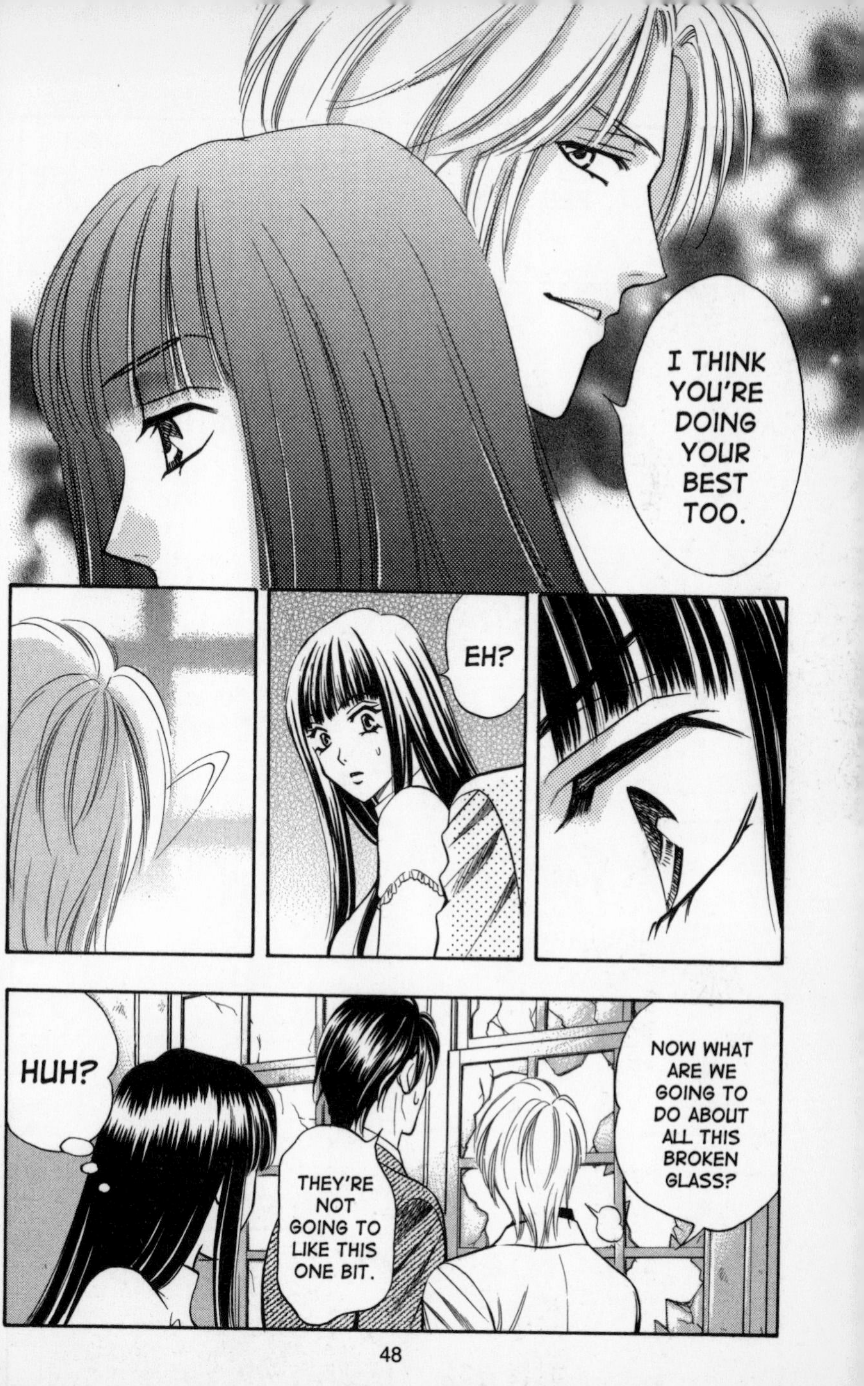
I THINK YOU'RE DOING YOUR BEST TOO.
EH?
NOW WHAT ARE WE GOING TO DO ABOUT ALL THIS BROKEN GLASS?
THEY'RE NOT GOING TO LIKE THIS ONE BIT.
HUH?

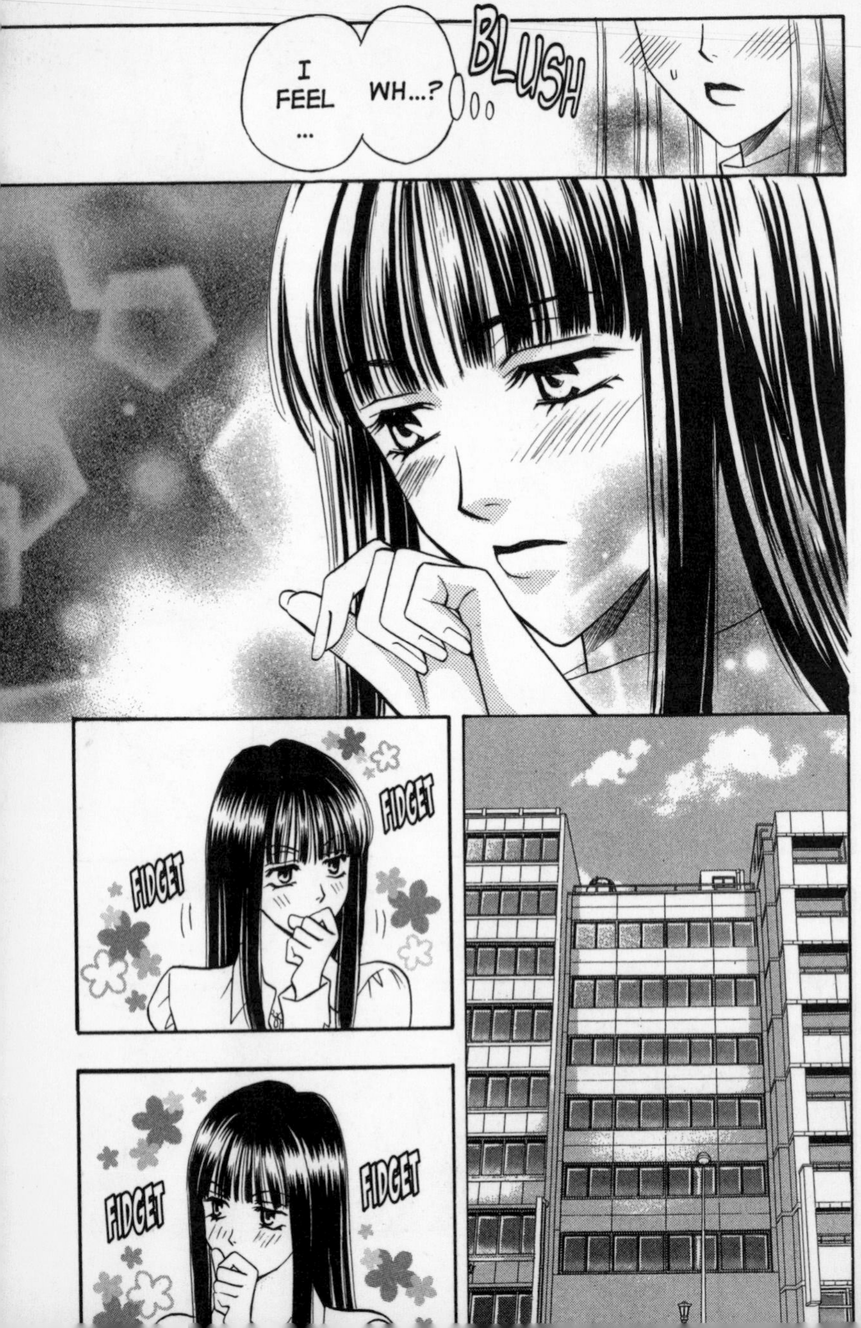
BLUSH
WH...?
I FEEL ...
FIDGET
FIDGET
FIDGET
FIDGET

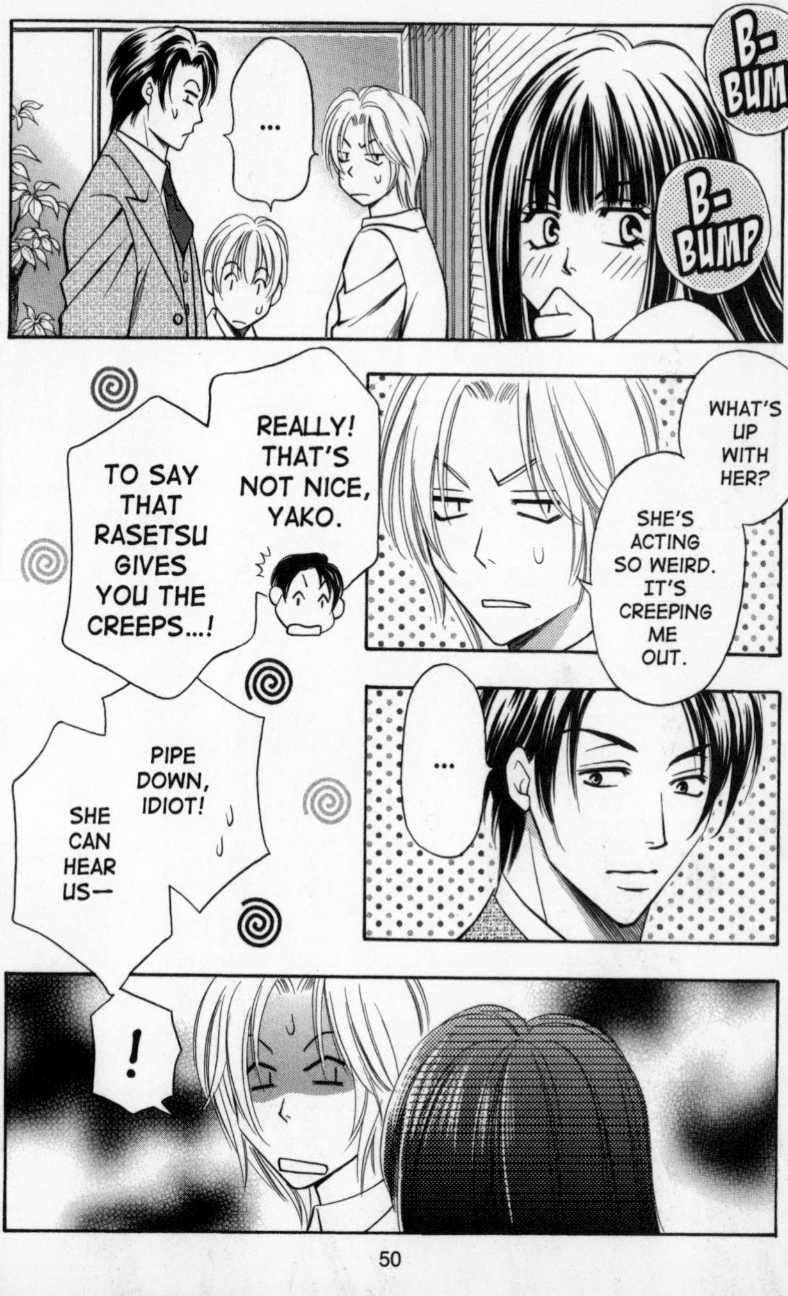
B-BUMP
B-BUMP
...
WHAT'S UP WITH HER?
SHE'S ACTING SO WEIRD. IT'S CREEPING ME OUT.
REALLY! THAT'S NOT NICE, YAKO.
TO SAY THAT RASETSU GIVES YOU THE CREEPS...!
...
PIPE DOWN, IDIOT!
SHE CAN HEAR US—
!

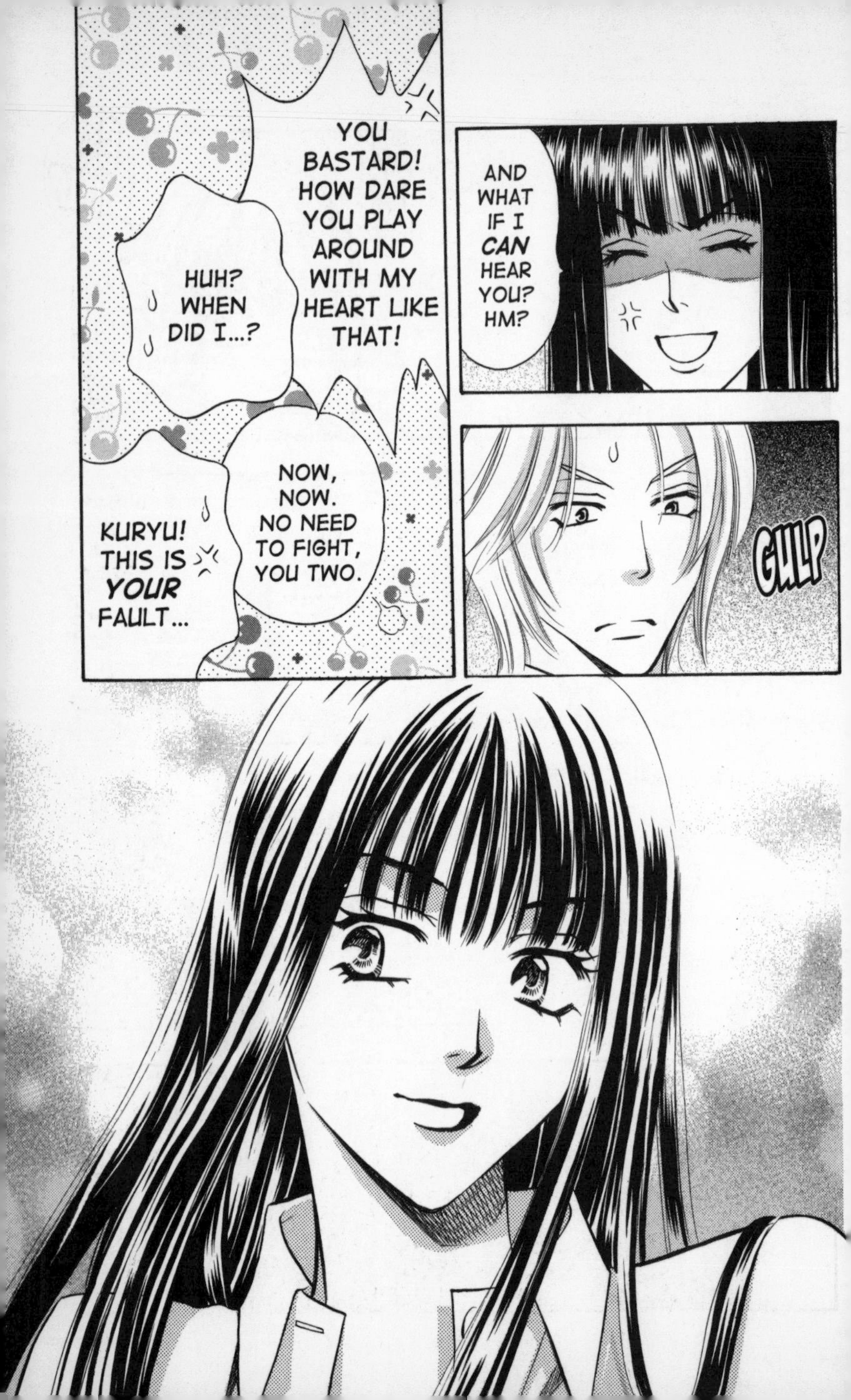
AND WHAT IF I CAN HEAR YOU? HM?
GULP
YOU BASTARD! HOW DARE YOU PLAY AROUND WITH MY HEART LIKE THAT!
HUH? WHEN DID I...?
NOW, NOW. NO NEED TO FIGHT, YOU TWO.
KURYU! THIS IS YOUR FAULT...

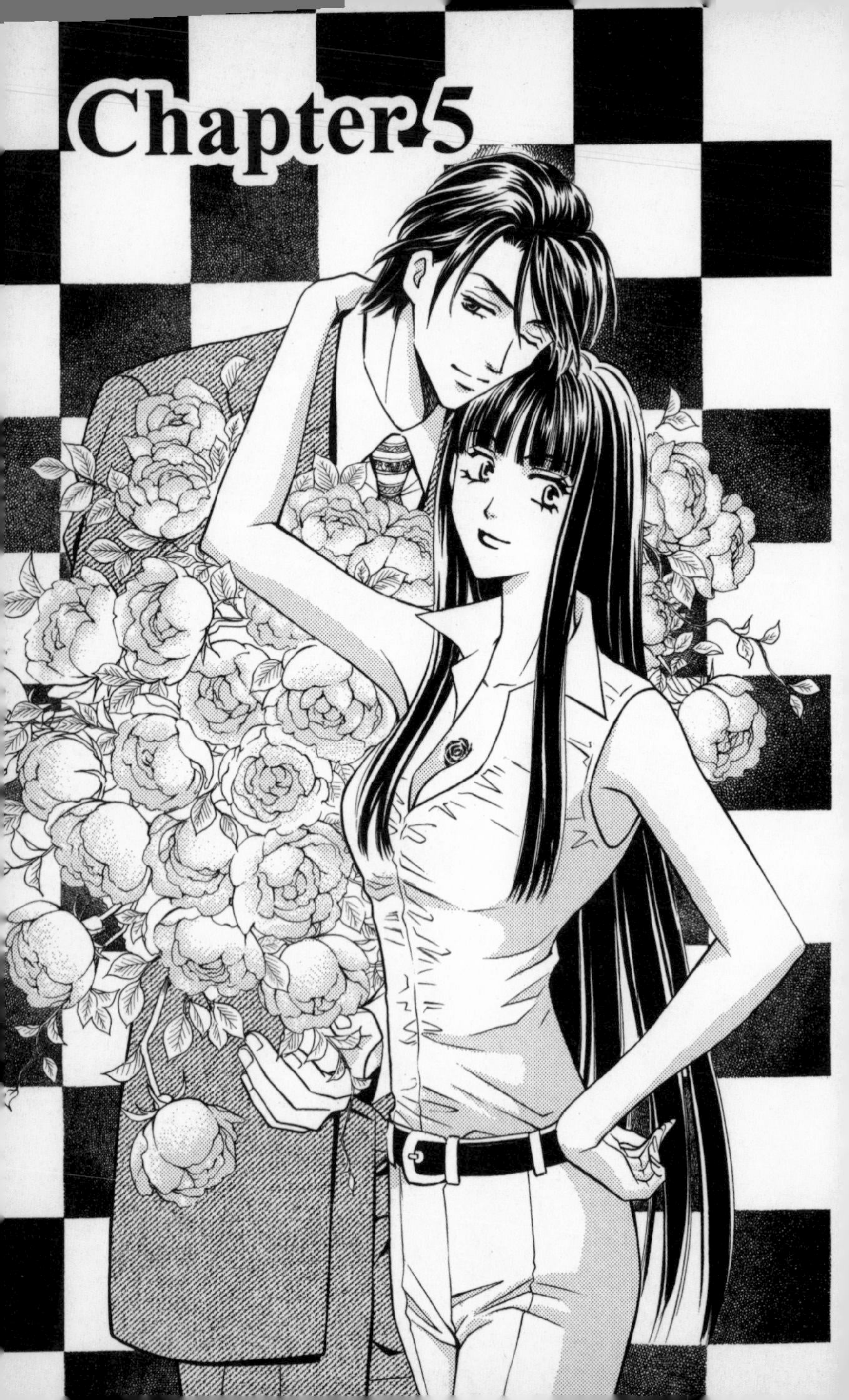
Chapter 5

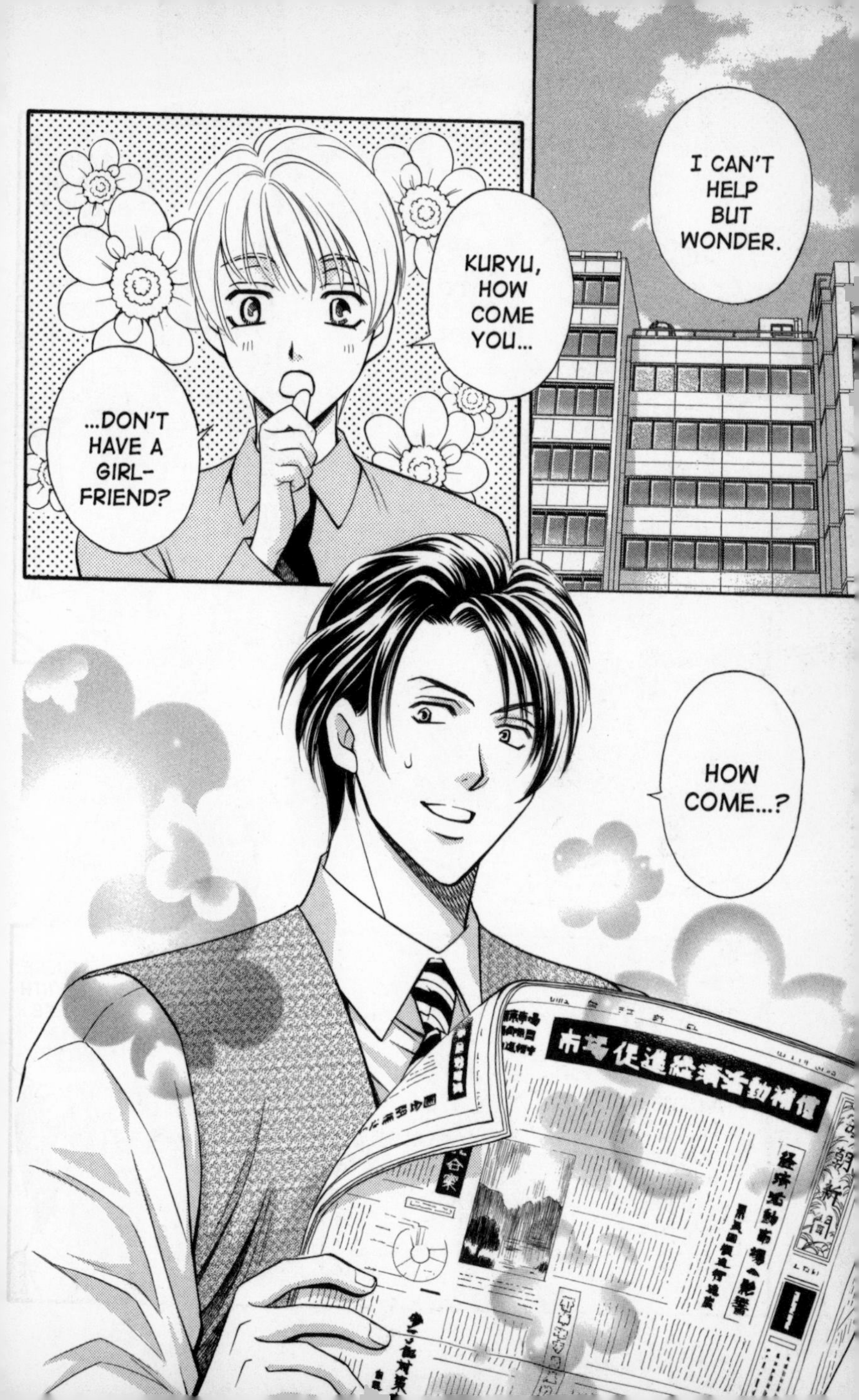
I CAN'T HELP BUT WONDER.
KURYU, HOW COME YOU...
...DON'T HAVE A GIRL-FRIEND?
HOW COME...?

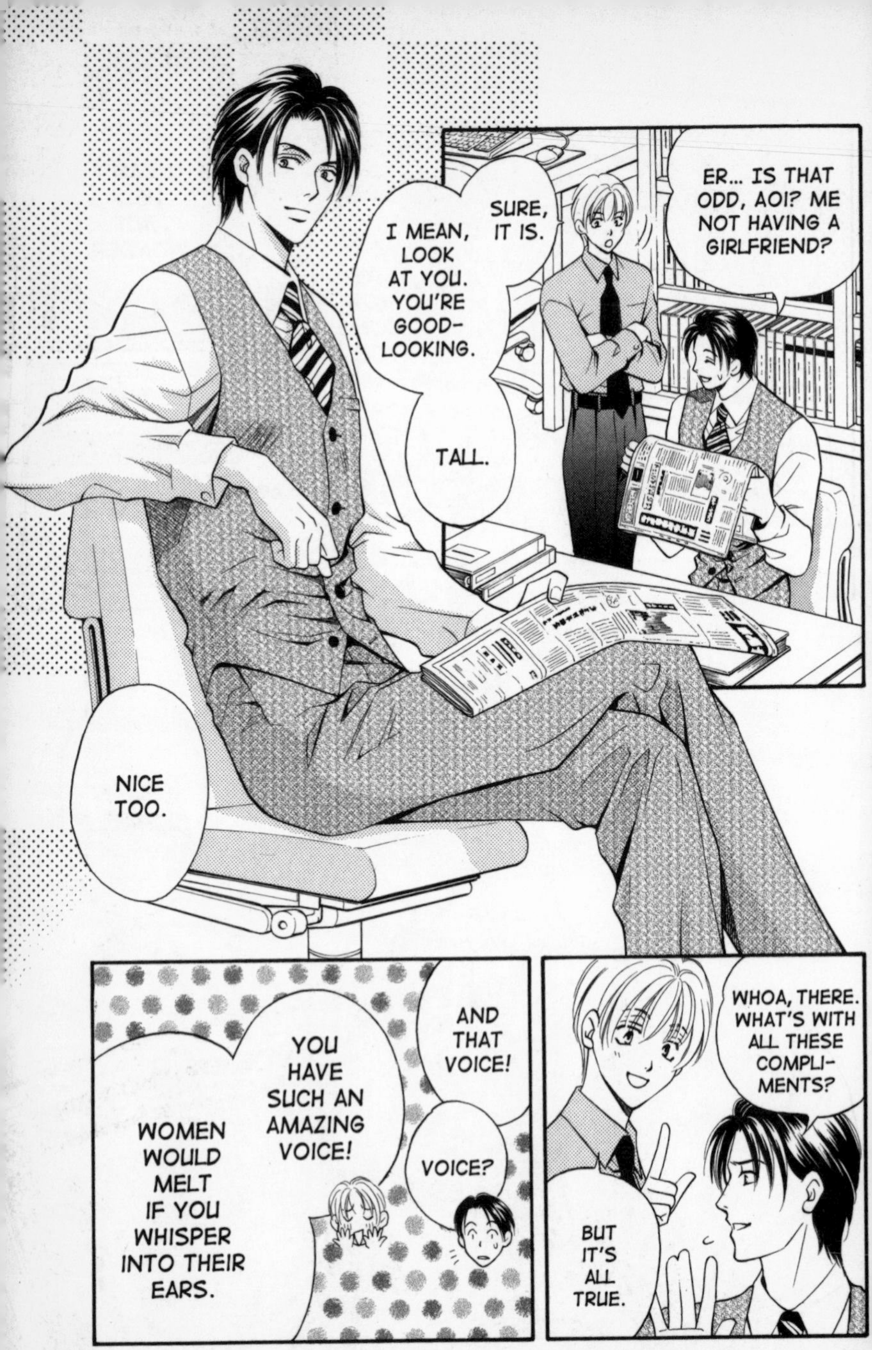
ER... IS THAT ODD, AOI? ME NOT HAVING A GIRLFRIEND?
SURE, IT IS.
I MEAN, LOOK AT YOU. YOU'RE GOOD-LOOKING.
TALL.
NICE TOO.
WHOA, THERE. WHAT'S WITH ALL THESE COMPLI-MENTS?
BUT IT'S ALL TRUE.
AND THAT VOICE!
YOU HAVE SUCH AN AMAZING VOICE!
VOICE?
WOMEN WOULD MELT IF YOU WHISPER INTO THEIR EARS.

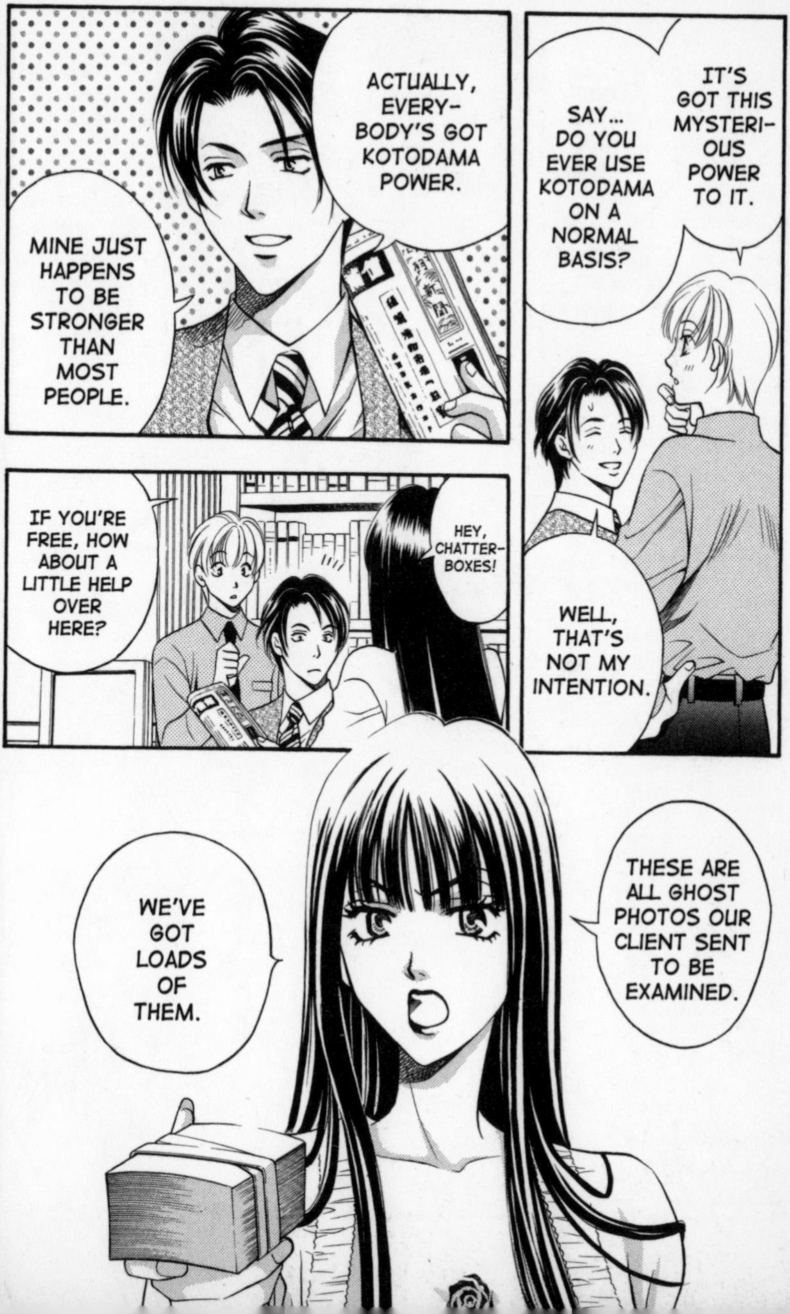
IT'S GOT THIS MYSTERIOUS POWER TO IT.
SAY... DO YOU EVER USE KOTODAMA ON A NORMAL BASIS?
WELL, THAT'S NOT MY INTENTION.
ACTUALLY, EVERYBODY'S GOT KOTODAMA POWER.
MINE JUST HAPPENS TO BE STRONGER THAN MOST PEOPLE.
HEY, CHATTERBOXES!
IF YOU'RE FREE, HOW ABOUT A LITTLE HELP OVER HERE?
THESE ARE ALL GHOST PHOTOS OUR CLIENT SENT TO BE EXAMINED.
WE'VE GOT LOADS OF THEM.

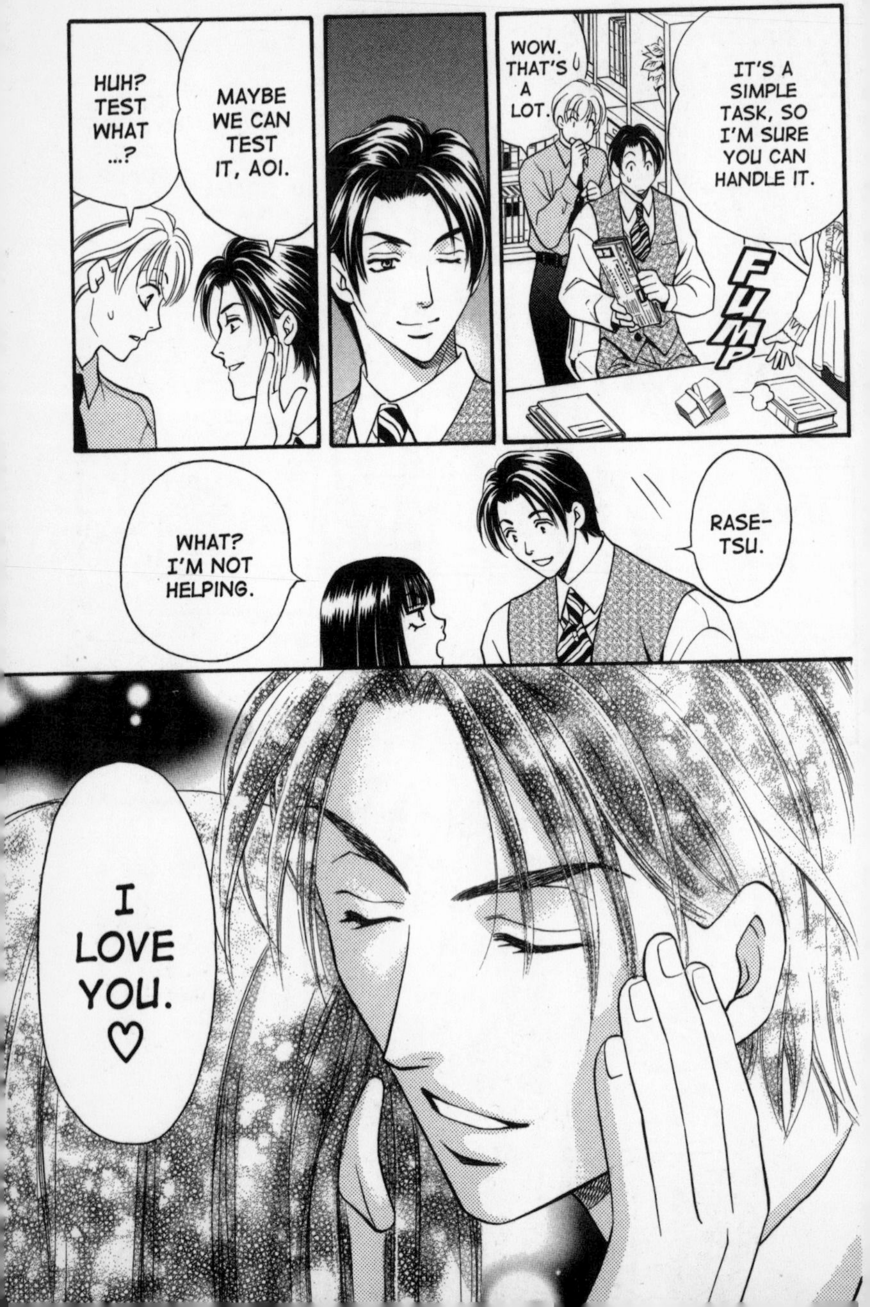
IT'S A SIMPLE TASK, SO I'M SURE YOU CAN HANDLE IT.
WOW. THAT'S A LOT.
FUMP
MAYBE WE CAN TEST IT, AOI.
HUH? TEST WHAT ...?
RASE-TSU.
WHAT? I'M NOT HELPING.
I LOVE YOU. ♡

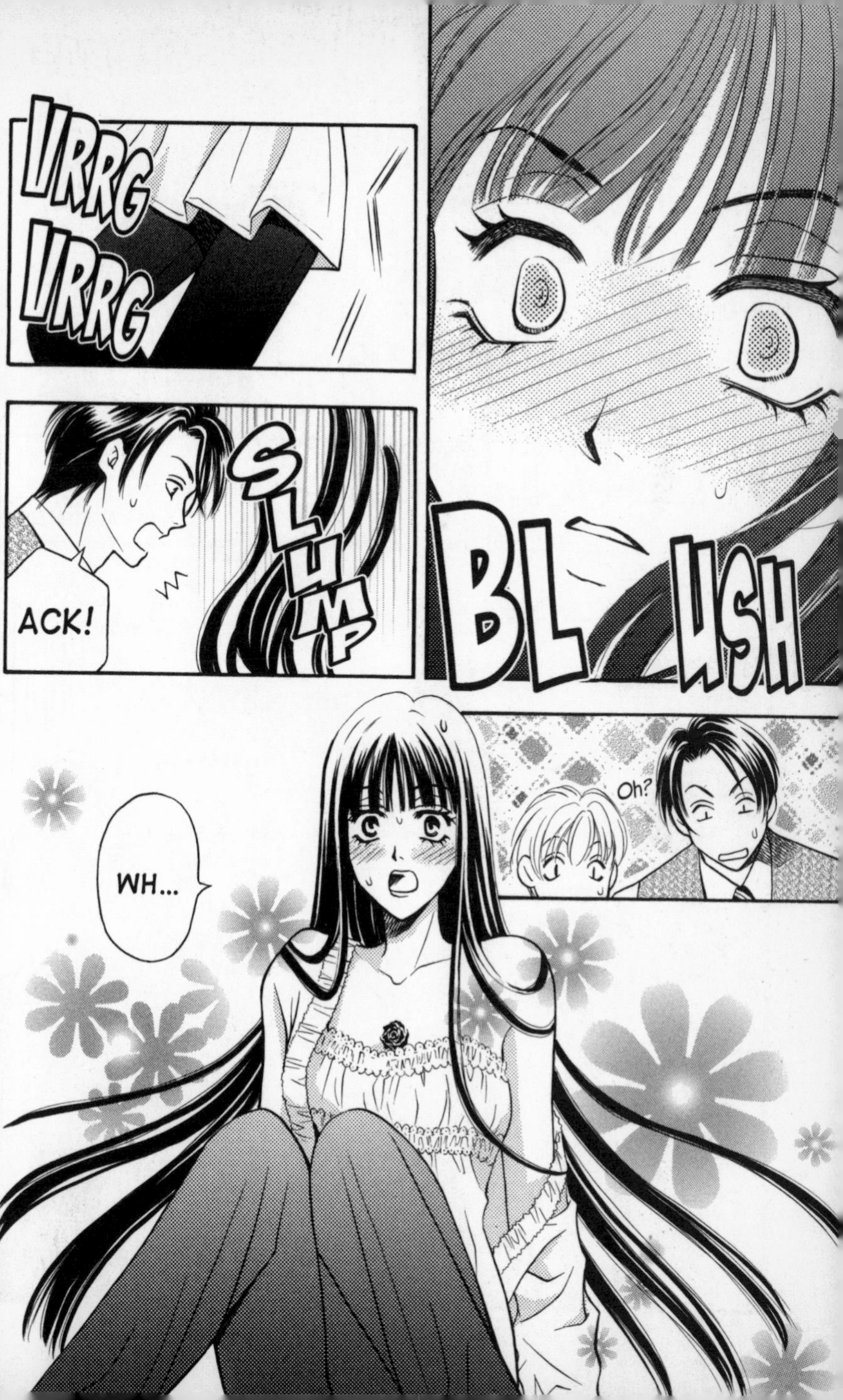
BLUSH
URRG URRG
SLUMP
ACK!
Oh?
WH...

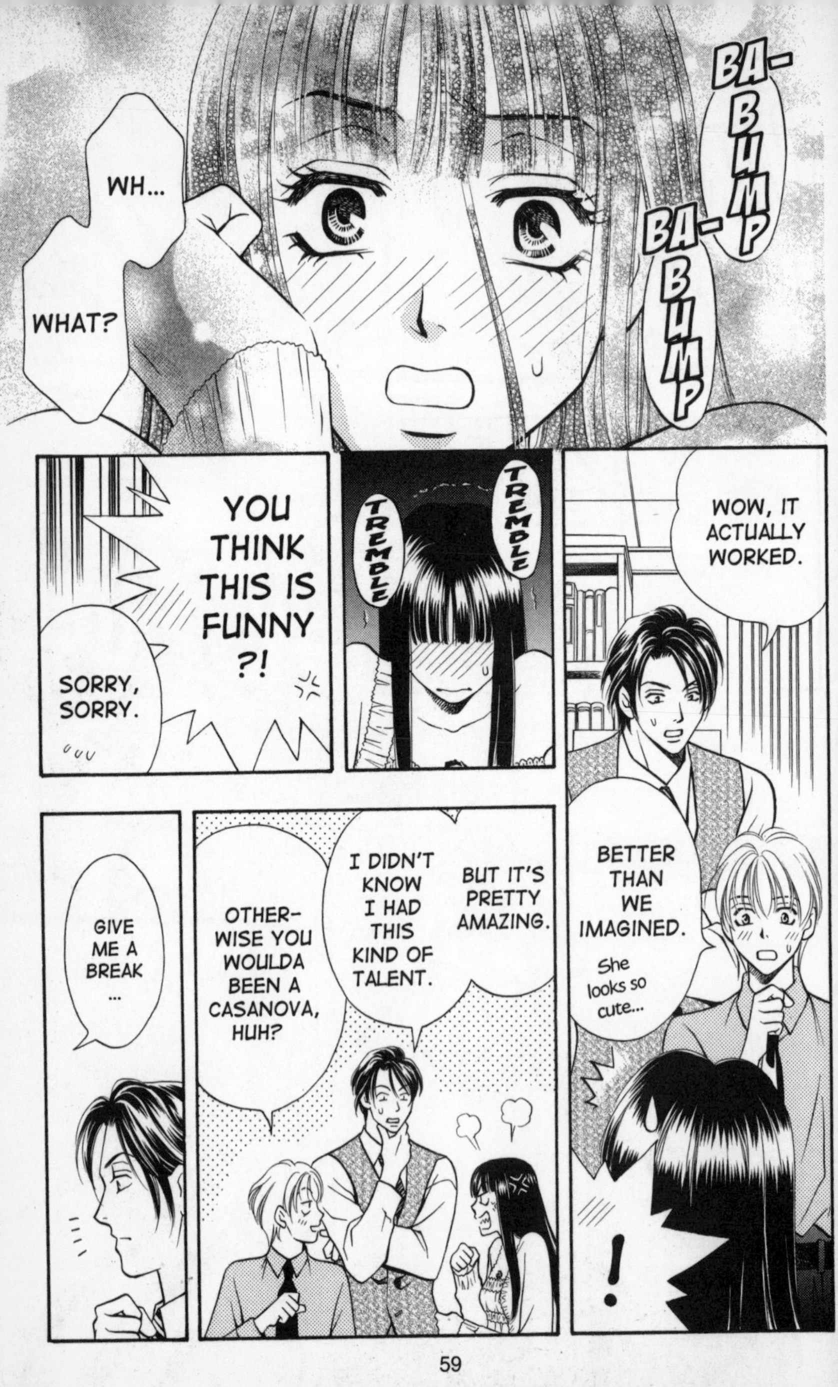
BA-BUMP
BA-BUMP
WH...
WHAT?
WOW, IT ACTUALLY WORKED.
BETTER THAN WE IMAGINED.
She looks so cute...
!
TREMBLE
TREMBLE
YOU THINK THIS IS FUNNY?!
SORRY, SORRY.
BUT IT'S PRETTY AMAZING.
I DIDN'T KNOW I HAD THIS KIND OF TALENT.
OTHER-WISE YOU WOULDA BEEN A CASANOVA, HUH?
GIVE ME A BREAK...

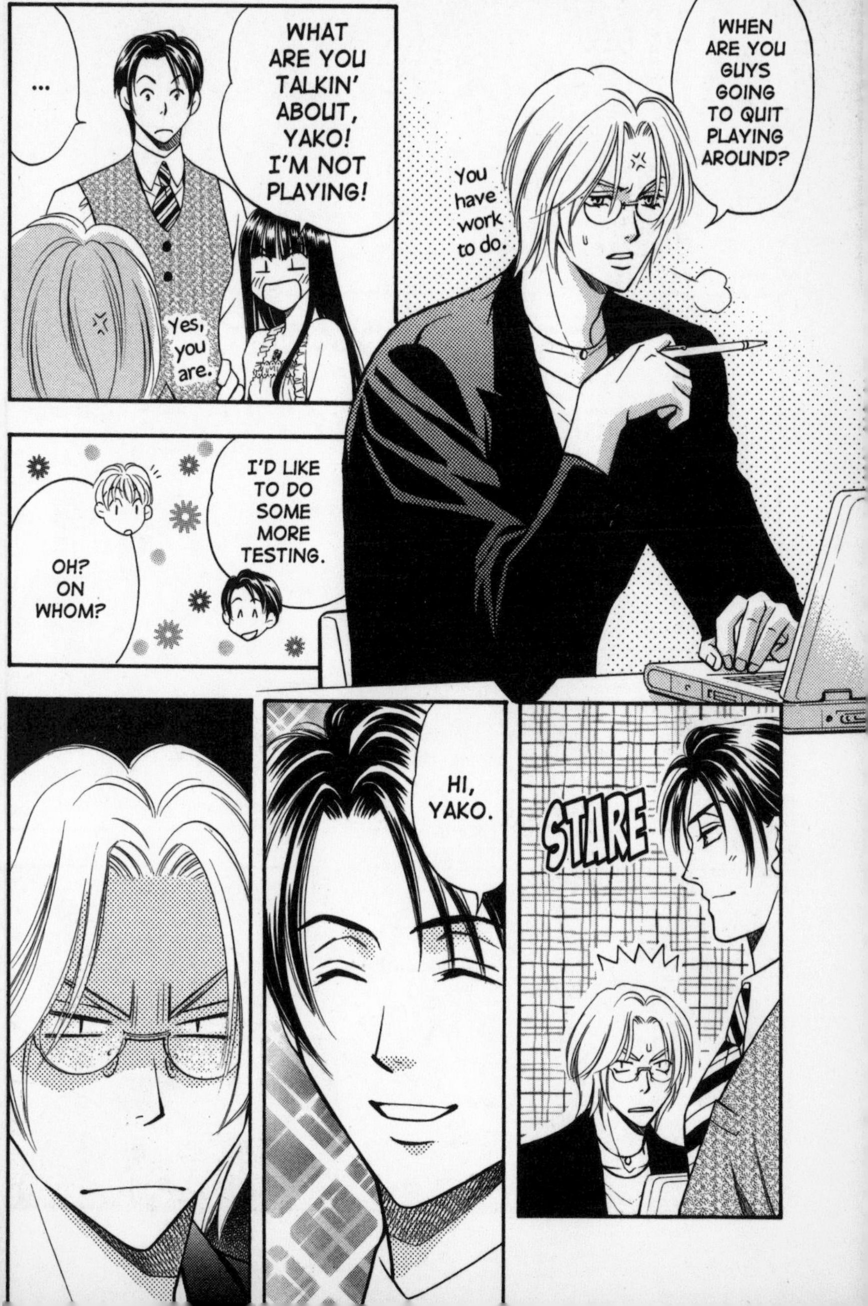
WHEN ARE YOU GUYS GOING TO QUIT PLAYING AROUND?
You have work to do.
WHAT ARE YOU TALKIN' ABOUT, YAKO! I'M NOT PLAYING!
...
Yes, you are.
I'D LIKE TO DO SOME MORE TESTING.
OH? ON WHOM?
STARE
HI, YAKO.

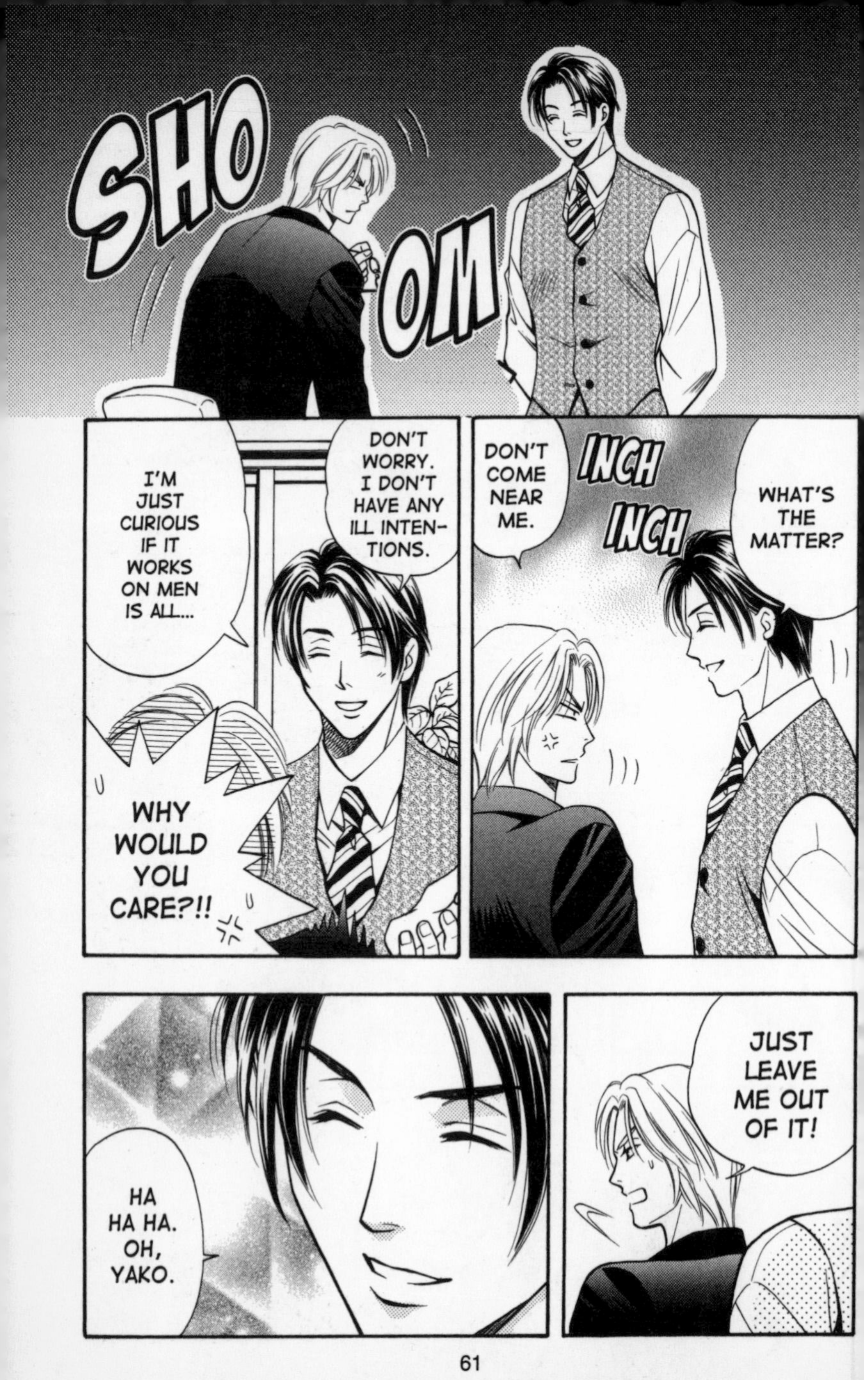
SHOOM
WHAT'S THE MATTER?
INCH INCH
DON'T COME NEAR ME.
DON'T WORRY. I DON'T HAVE ANY ILL INTENTIONS.
I'M JUST CURIOUS IF IT WORKS ON MEN IS ALL...
WHY WOULD YOU CARE?!!
JUST LEAVE ME OUT OF IT!
HA HA HA. OH, YAKO.

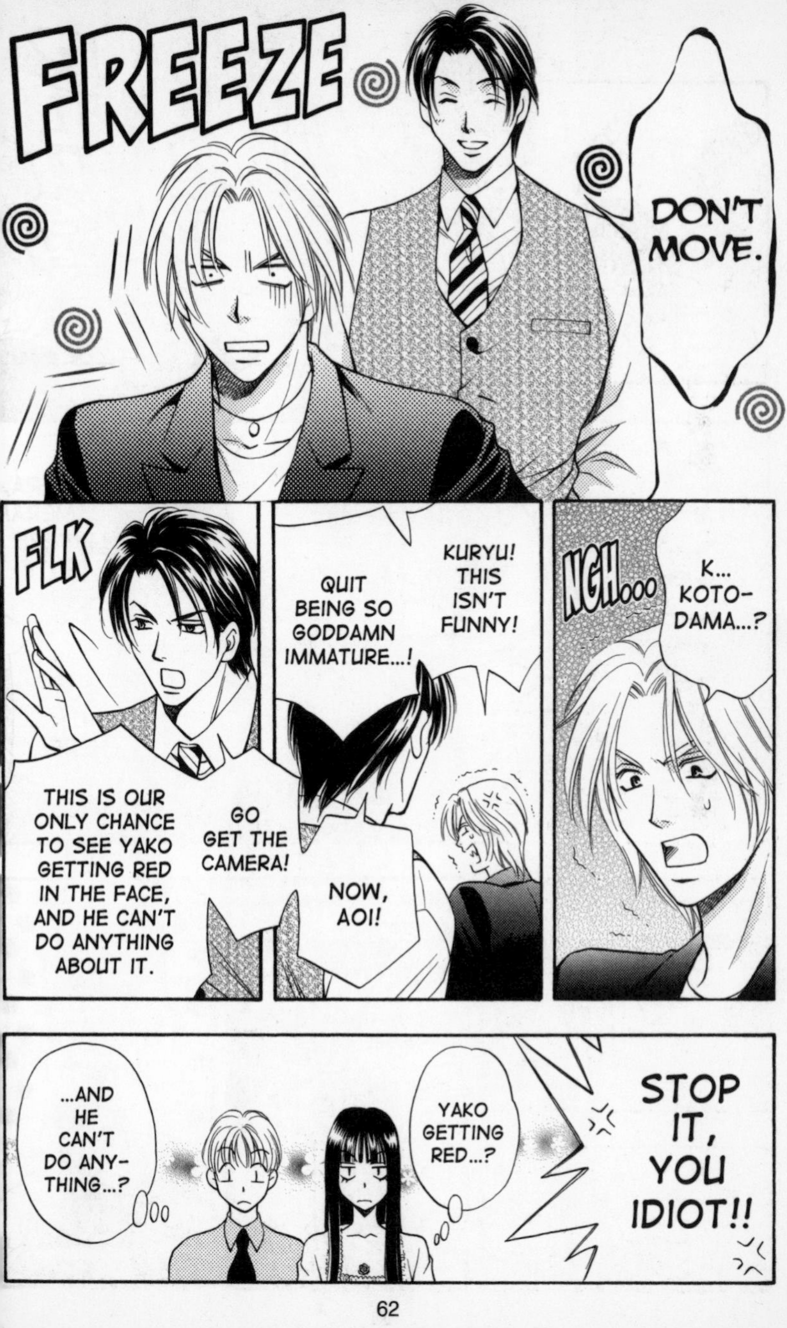
DON'T MOVE.
FREEZE
K... KOTO-DAMA...?
NGHooo
KURYU! THIS ISN'T FUNNY!
QUIT BEING SO GODDAMN IMMATURE...!
NOW, AOI!
FLK
GO GET THE CAMERA!
THIS IS OUR ONLY CHANCE TO SEE YAKO GETTING RED IN THE FACE, AND HE CAN'T DO ANYTHING ABOUT IT.
STOP IT, YOU IDIOT!!
YAKO GETTING RED...?
...AND HE CAN'T DO ANY-THING...?

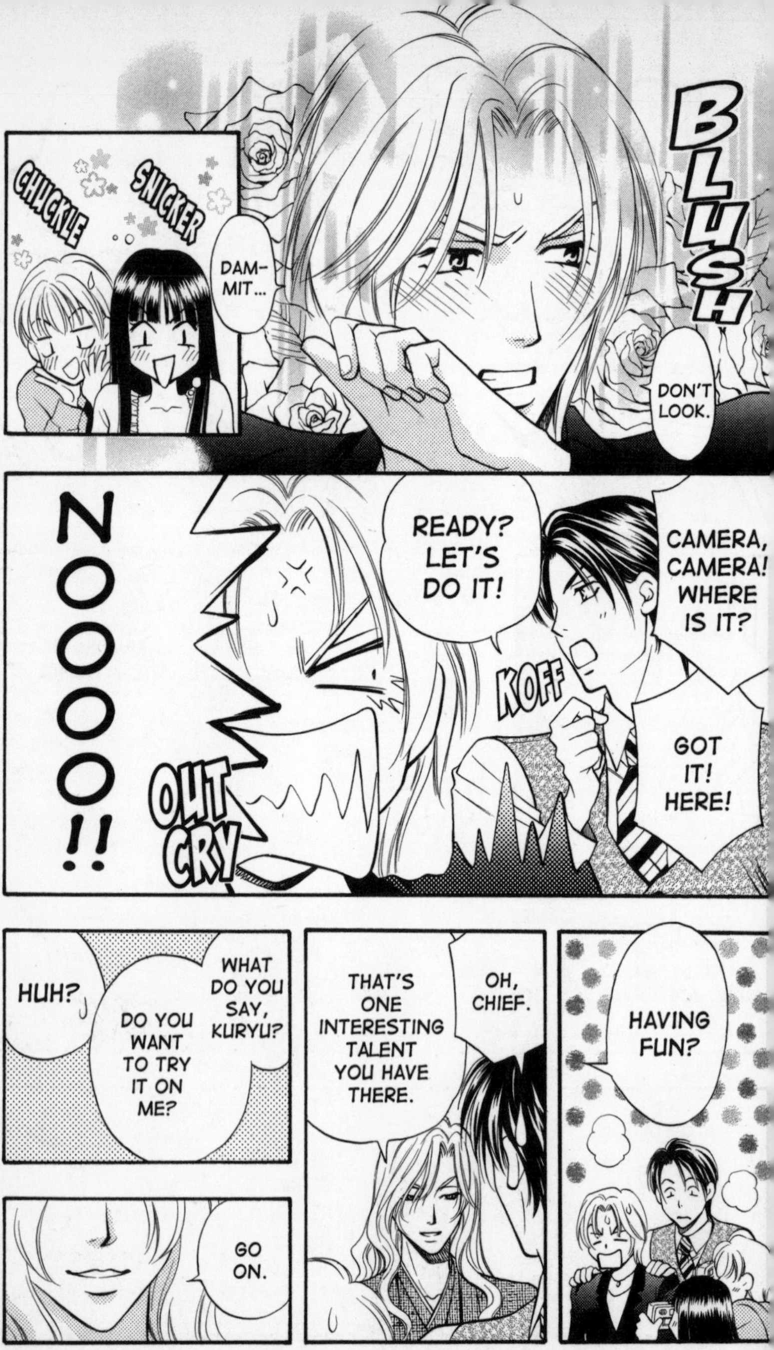
BLUSH
DON'T LOOK.
DAM-MIT...
SNICKER
CHUCKLE
CAMERA, CAMERA! WHERE IS IT?
READY? LET'S DO IT!
GOT IT! HERE!
KOFF
OUT CRY
NOOOOO!!
HAVING FUN?
OH, CHIEF.
THAT'S ONE INTERESTING TALENT YOU HAVE THERE.
WHAT DO YOU SAY, KURYU?
DO YOU WANT TO TRY IT ON ME?
HUH?
GO ON.

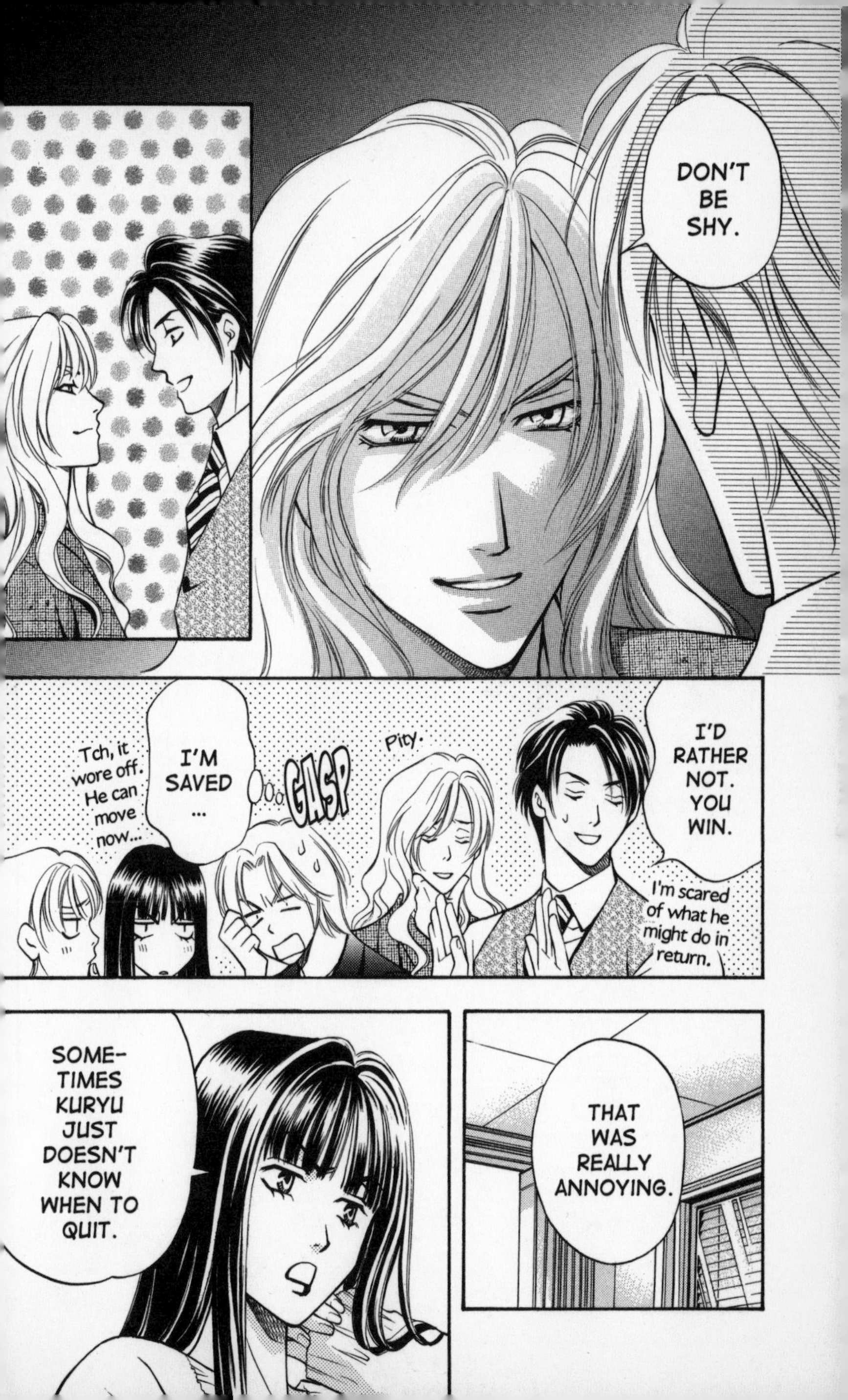
DON'T BE SHY.
I'D RATHER NOT. YOU WIN.
I'm scared of what he might do in return.
Pity.
GASP
I'M SAVED ...
Tch, it wore off. He can move now...
THAT WAS REALLY ANNOYING.
SOME-TIMES KURYU JUST DOESN'T KNOW WHEN TO QUIT.

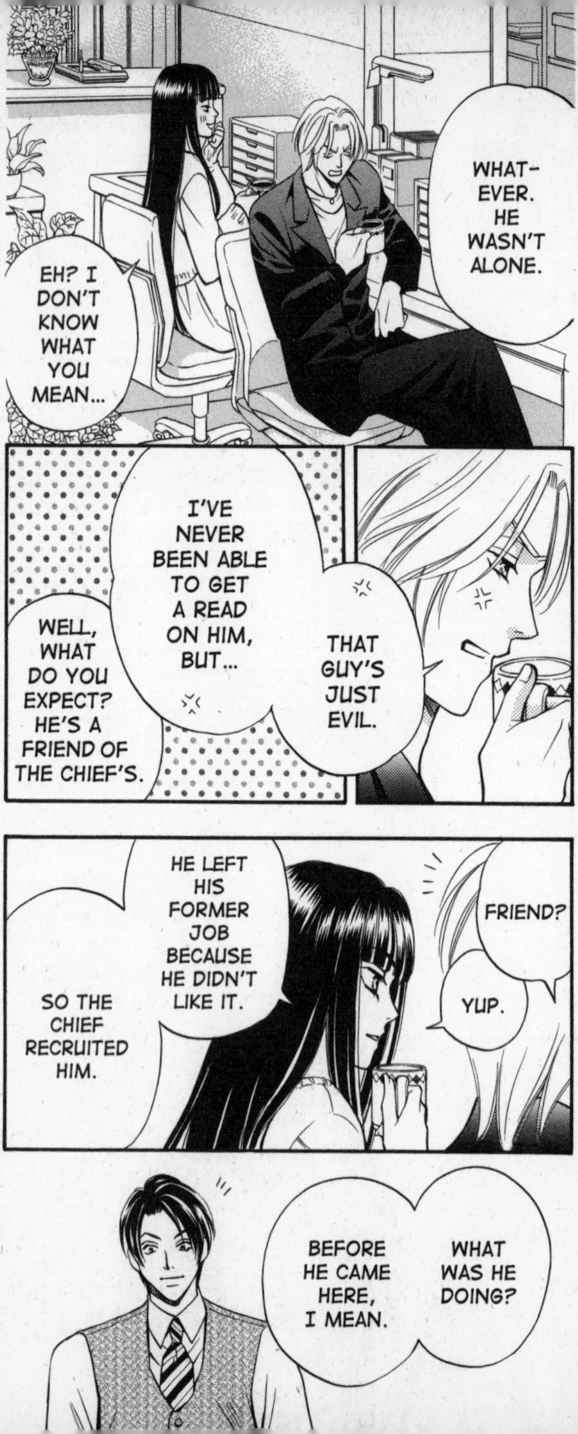
WHAT-EVER. HE WASN'T ALONE.
EH? I DON'T KNOW WHAT YOU MEAN...
THAT GUY'S JUST EVIL.
I'VE NEVER BEEN ABLE TO GET A READ ON HIM, BUT...
WELL, WHAT DO YOU EXPECT? HE'S A FRIEND OF THE CHIEF'S.
FRIEND?
YUP.
HE LEFT HIS FORMER JOB BECAUSE HE DIDN'T LIKE IT.
SO THE CHIEF RECRUITED HIM.
WHAT WAS HE DOING?
BEFORE HE CAME HERE, I MEAN.

My Everyday Life ⑤

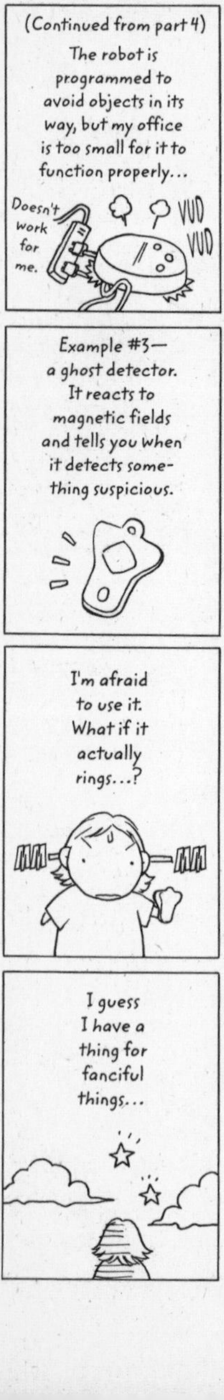
(Continued from part 4)
The robot is programmed to avoid objects in its way, but my office is too small for it to function properly...
Doesn't work for me.
VUD VUD
Example #3— a ghost detector. It reacts to magnetic fields and tells you when it detects something suspicious.
I'm afraid to use it. What if it actually rings...?
I guess I have a thing for fanciful things...

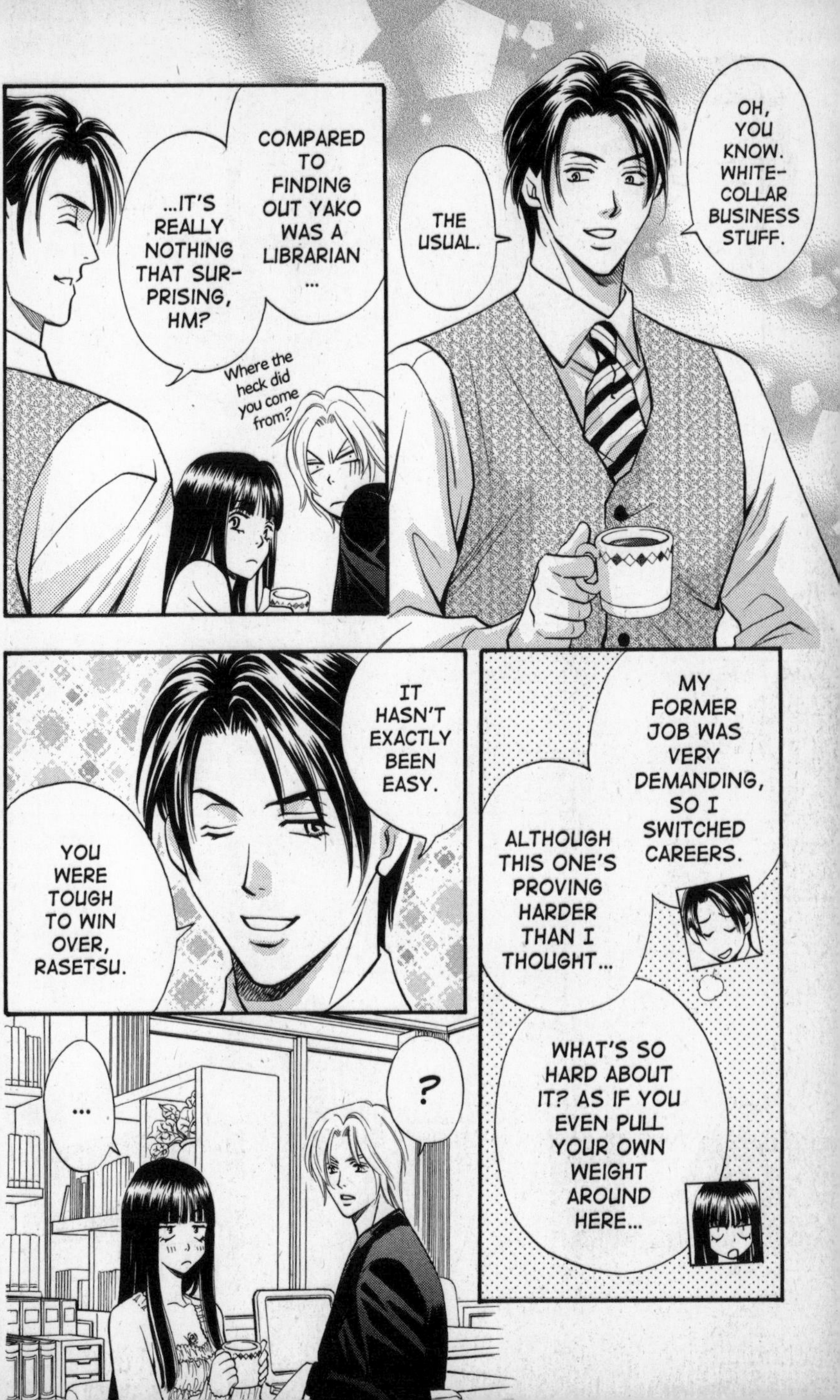
OH, YOU KNOW. WHITE-COLLAR BUSINESS STUFF.
THE USUAL.
COMPARED TO FINDING OUT YAKO WAS A LIBRARIAN...
...IT'S REALLY NOTHING THAT SUR-PRISING, HM?
Where the heck did you come from?
MY FORMER JOB WAS VERY DEMANDING, SO I SWITCHED CAREERS.
ALTHOUGH THIS ONE'S PROVING HARDER THAN I THOUGHT...
WHAT'S SO HARD ABOUT IT? AS IF YOU EVEN PULL YOUR OWN WEIGHT AROUND HERE...
IT HASN'T EXACTLY BEEN EASY.
YOU WERE TOUGH TO WIN OVER, RASETSU.
?
...

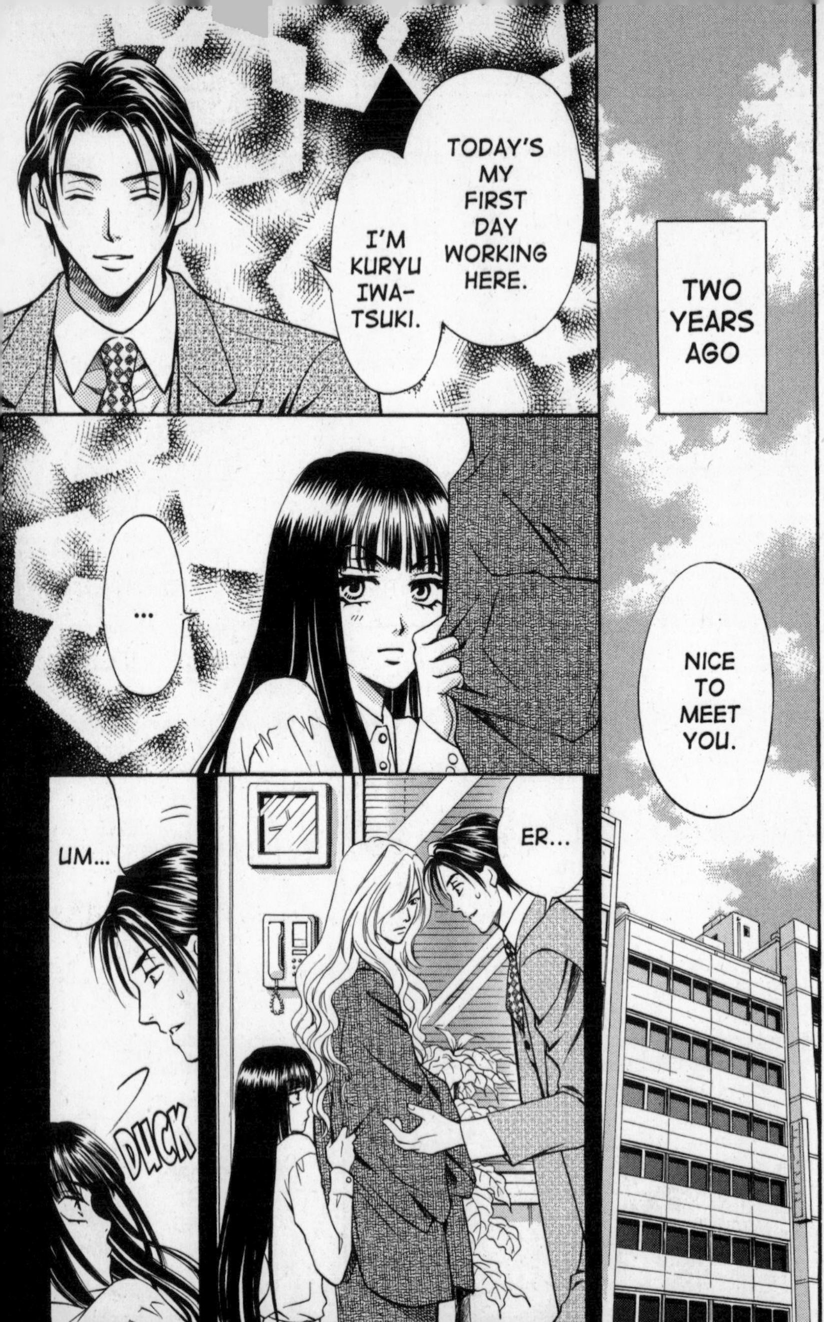
TWO YEARS AGO
NICE TO MEET YOU.
TODAY'S MY FIRST DAY WORKING HERE.
I'M KURYU IWA-TSUKI.
...
ER...
UM...
DUCK

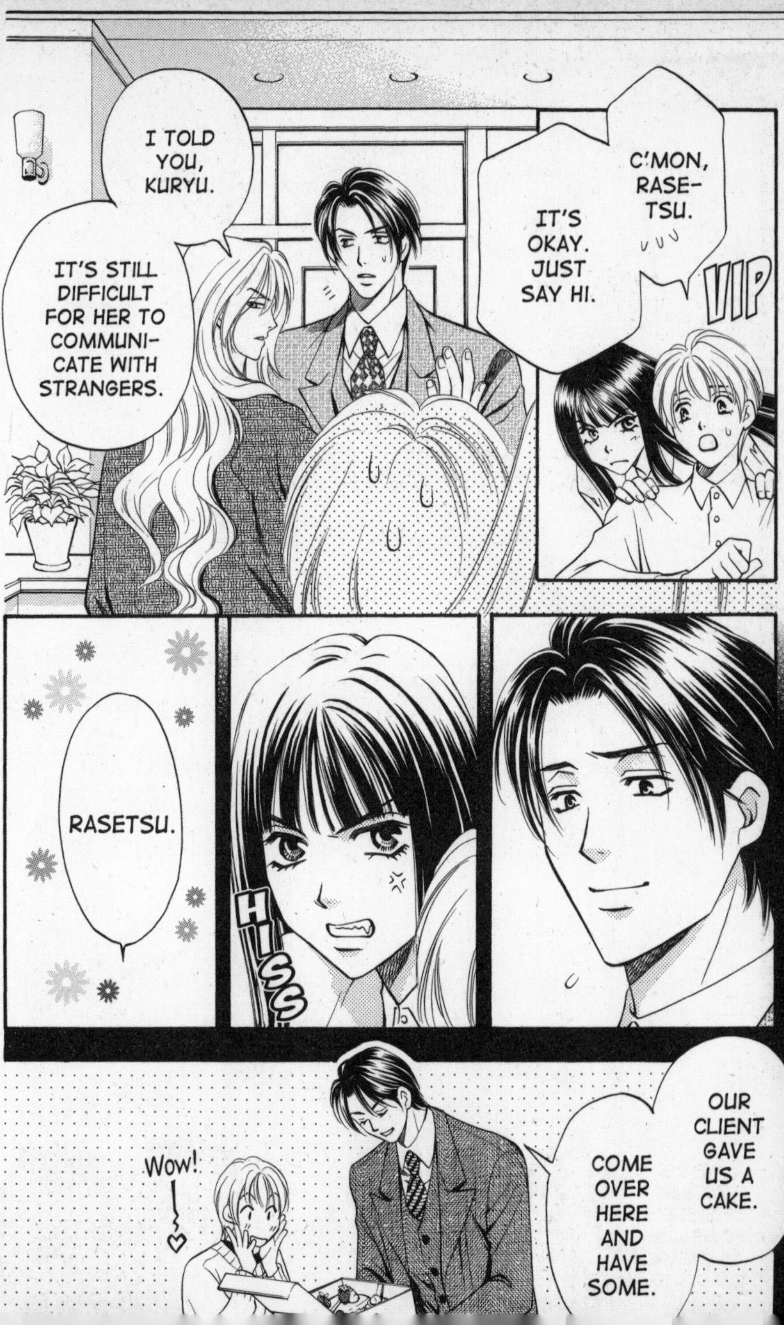
C'MON, RASE-TSU.
IT'S OKAY. JUST SAY HI.
VIP
I TOLD YOU, KURYU.
IT'S STILL DIFFICULT FOR HER TO COMMUNI-CATE WITH STRANGERS.
HISS
RASETSU.
OUR CLIENT GAVE US A CAKE.
COME OVER HERE AND HAVE SOME.
Wow!

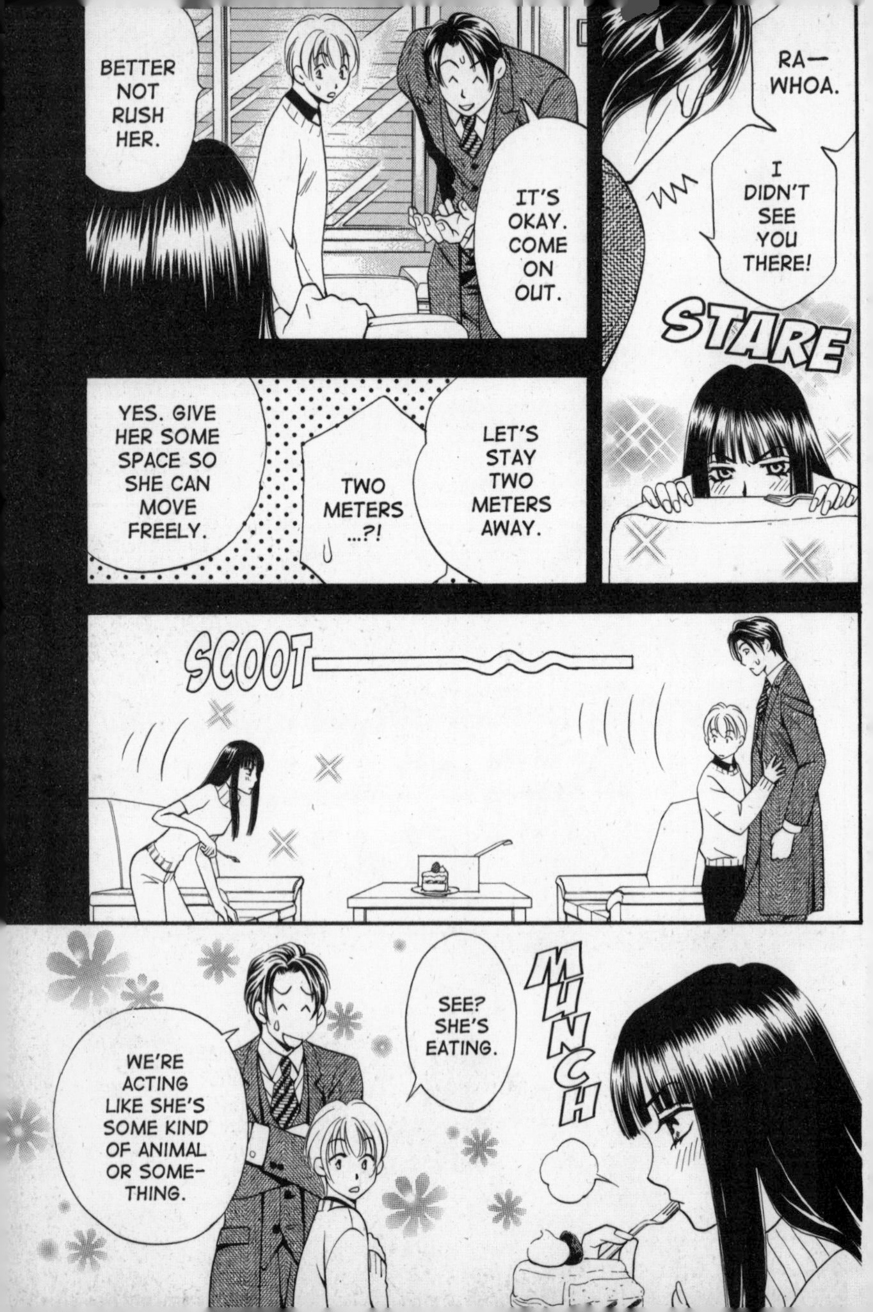
RA— WHOA.
I DIDN'T SEE YOU THERE!
STARE
IT'S OKAY. COME ON OUT.
BETTER NOT RUSH HER.
LET'S STAY TWO METERS AWAY.
TWO METERS ...?!
YES. GIVE HER SOME SPACE SO SHE CAN MOVE FREELY.
SCOOT
MUNCH
SEE? SHE'S EATING.
WE'RE ACTING LIKE SHE'S SOME KIND OF ANIMAL OR SOME-THING.

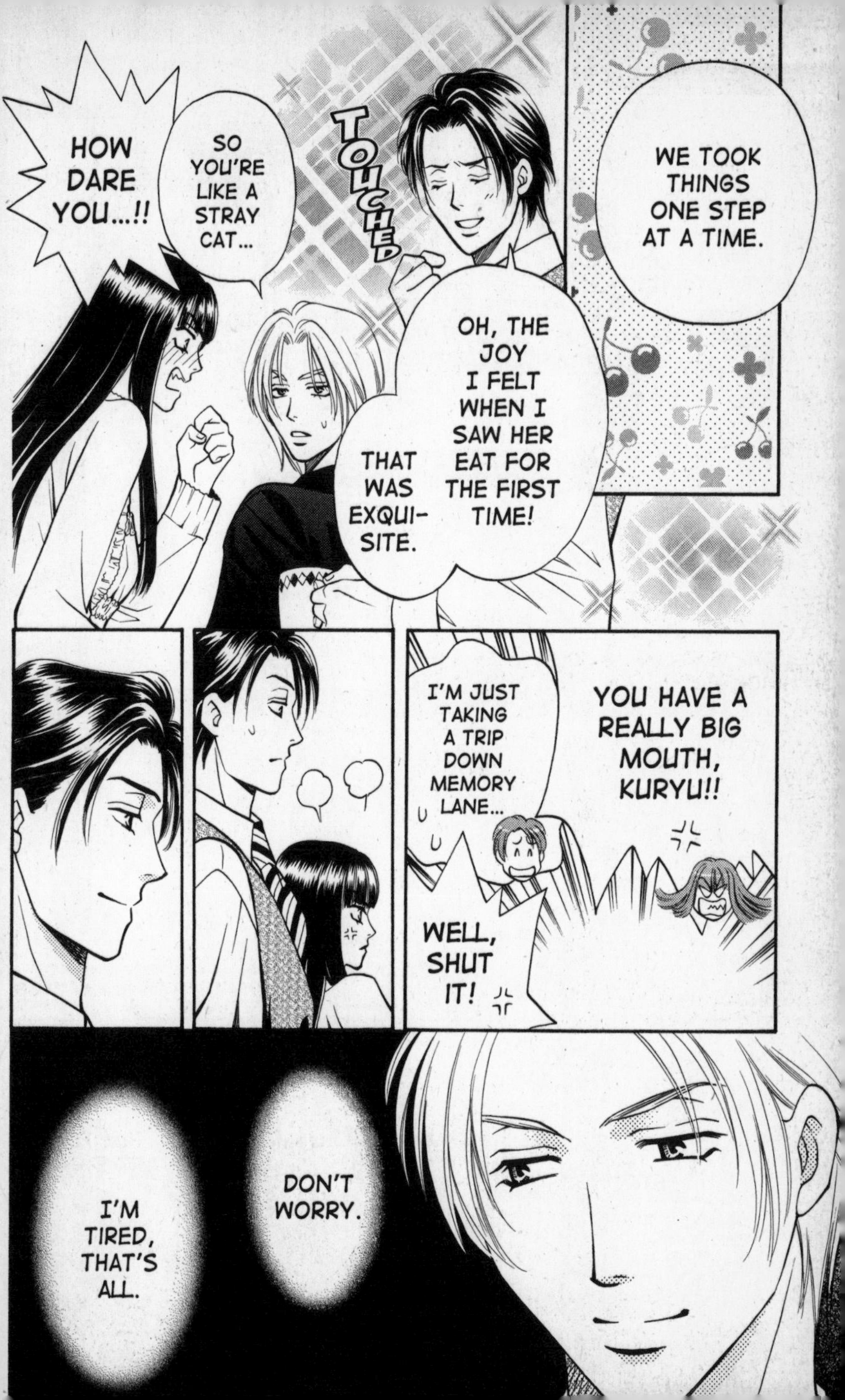
WE TOOK THINGS ONE STEP AT A TIME.
TOUCHED
OH, THE JOY I FELT WHEN I SAW HER EAT FOR THE FIRST TIME!
THAT WAS EXQUISITE.
SO YOU'RE LIKE A STRAY CAT...
HOW DARE YOU...!!
YOU HAVE A REALLY BIG MOUTH, KURYU!!
I'M JUST TAKING A TRIP DOWN MEMORY LANE...
WELL, SHUT IT!
DON'T WORRY.
I'M TIRED, THAT'S ALL.

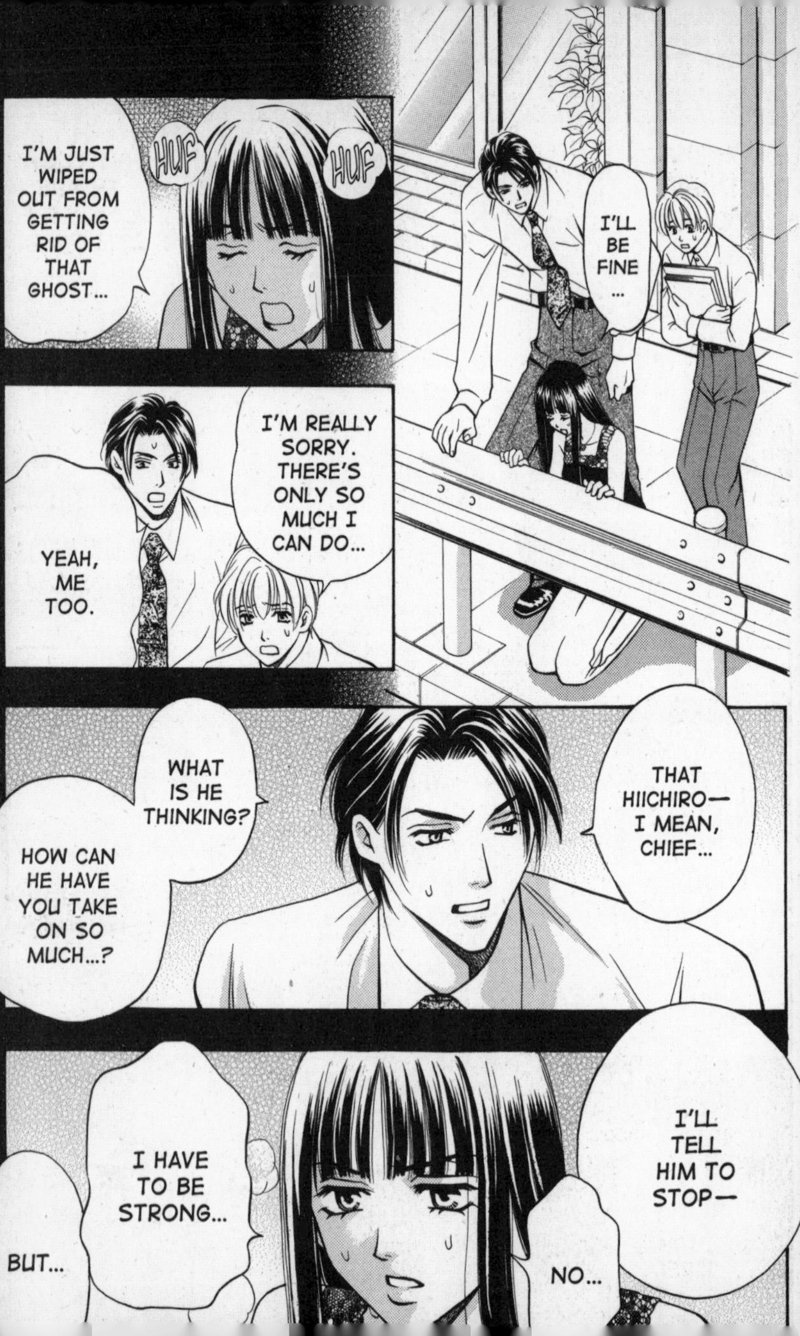
I'LL BE FINE...
HUF HUF
I'M JUST WIPED OUT FROM GETTING RID OF THAT GHOST...
I'M REALLY SORRY. THERE'S ONLY SO MUCH I CAN DO...
YEAH, ME TOO.
THAT HIICHIRO— I MEAN, CHIEF...
WHAT IS HE THINKING?
HOW CAN HE HAVE YOU TAKE ON SO MUCH...?
I'LL TELL HIM TO STOP—
NO...
I HAVE TO BE STRONG...
BUT...

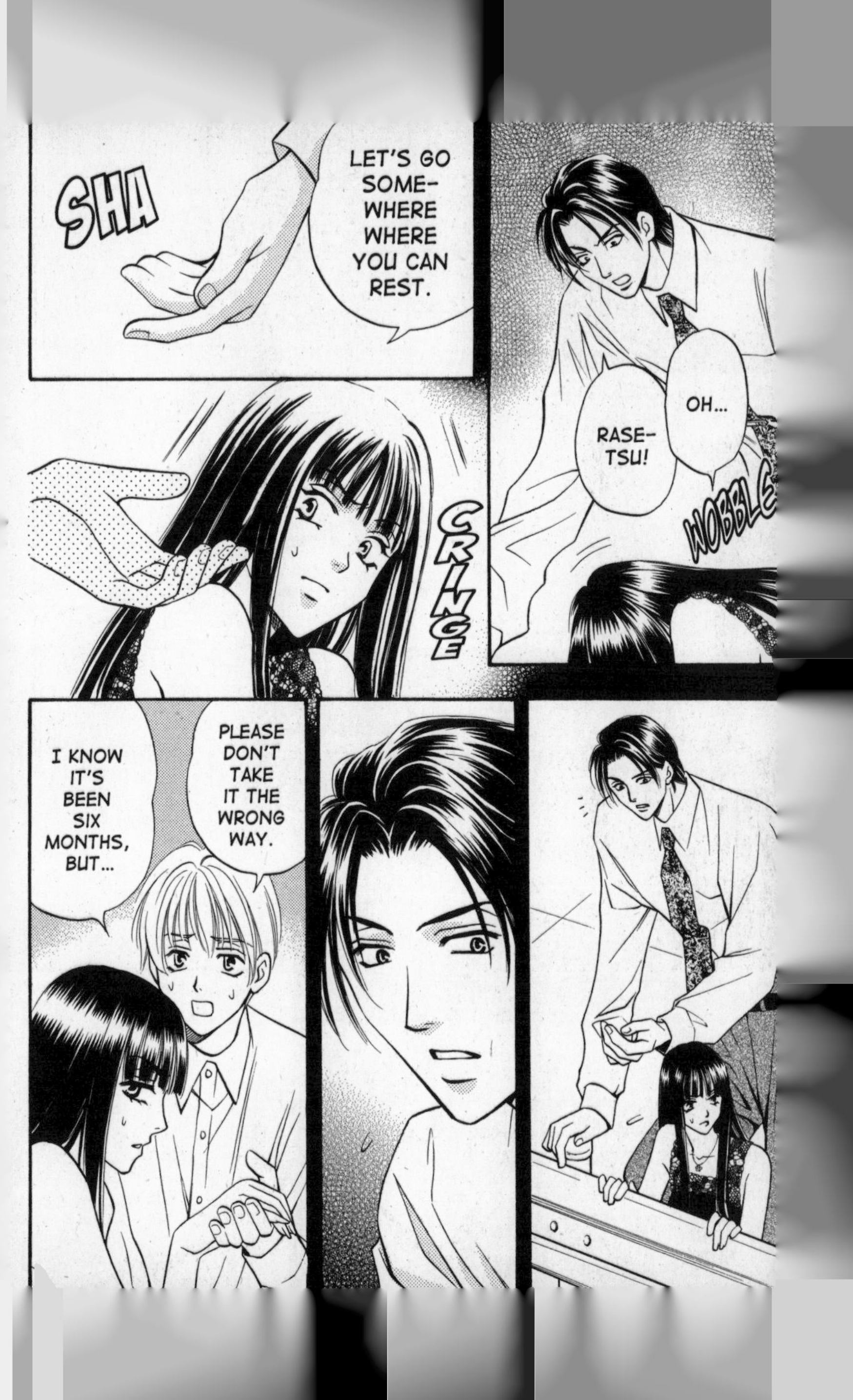
OH...
RASE-TSU!
WOBBLE
LET'S GO SOME-WHERE WHERE YOU CAN REST.
SHA
CRINGE
PLEASE DON'T TAKE IT THE WRONG WAY.
I KNOW IT'S BEEN SIX MONTHS, BUT...

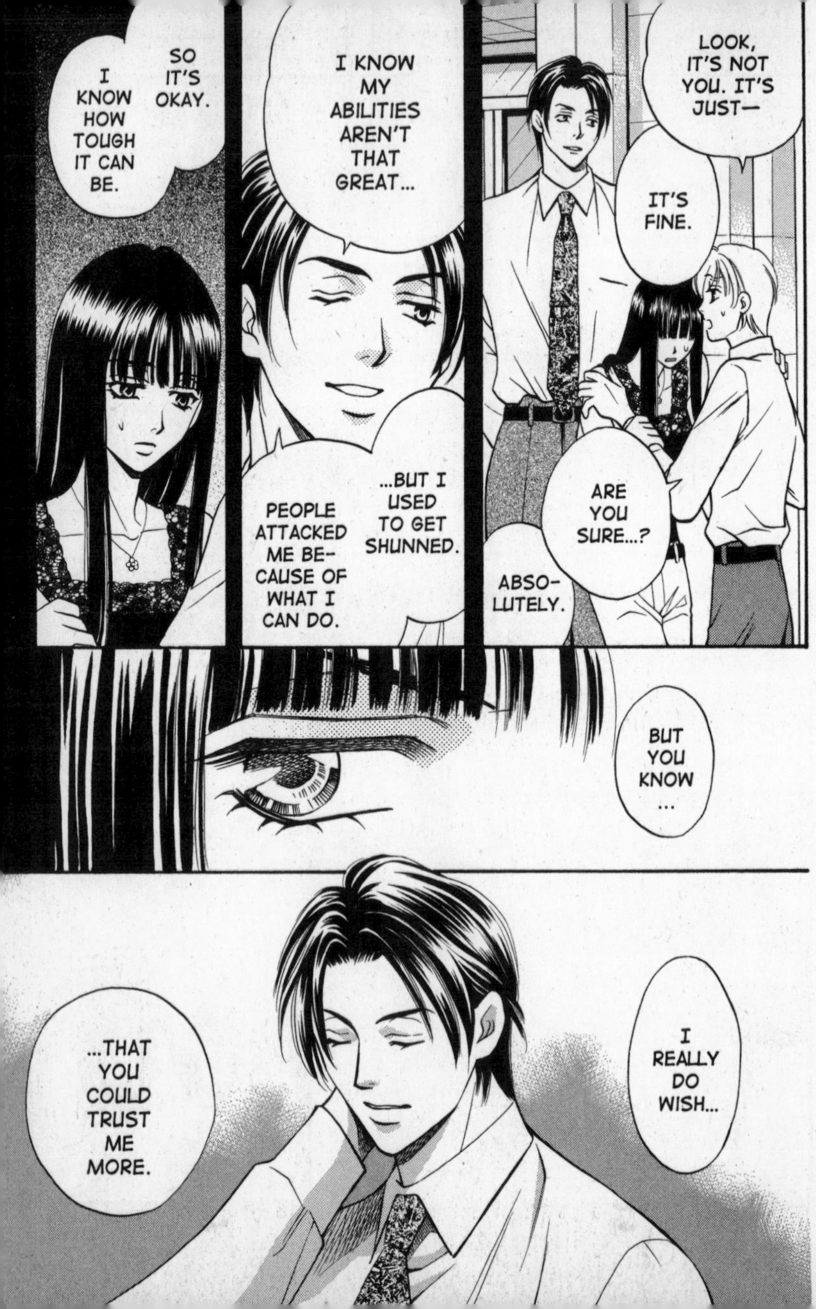
LOOK, IT'S NOT YOU. IT'S JUST—
IT'S FINE.
ARE YOU SURE...?
ABSO-LUTELY.
I KNOW MY ABILITIES AREN'T THAT GREAT...
...BUT I USED TO GET SHUNNED.
PEOPLE ATTACKED ME BE-CAUSE OF WHAT I CAN DO.
SO IT'S OKAY.
I KNOW HOW TOUGH IT CAN BE.
BUT YOU KNOW ...
I REALLY DO WISH...
...THAT YOU COULD TRUST ME MORE.

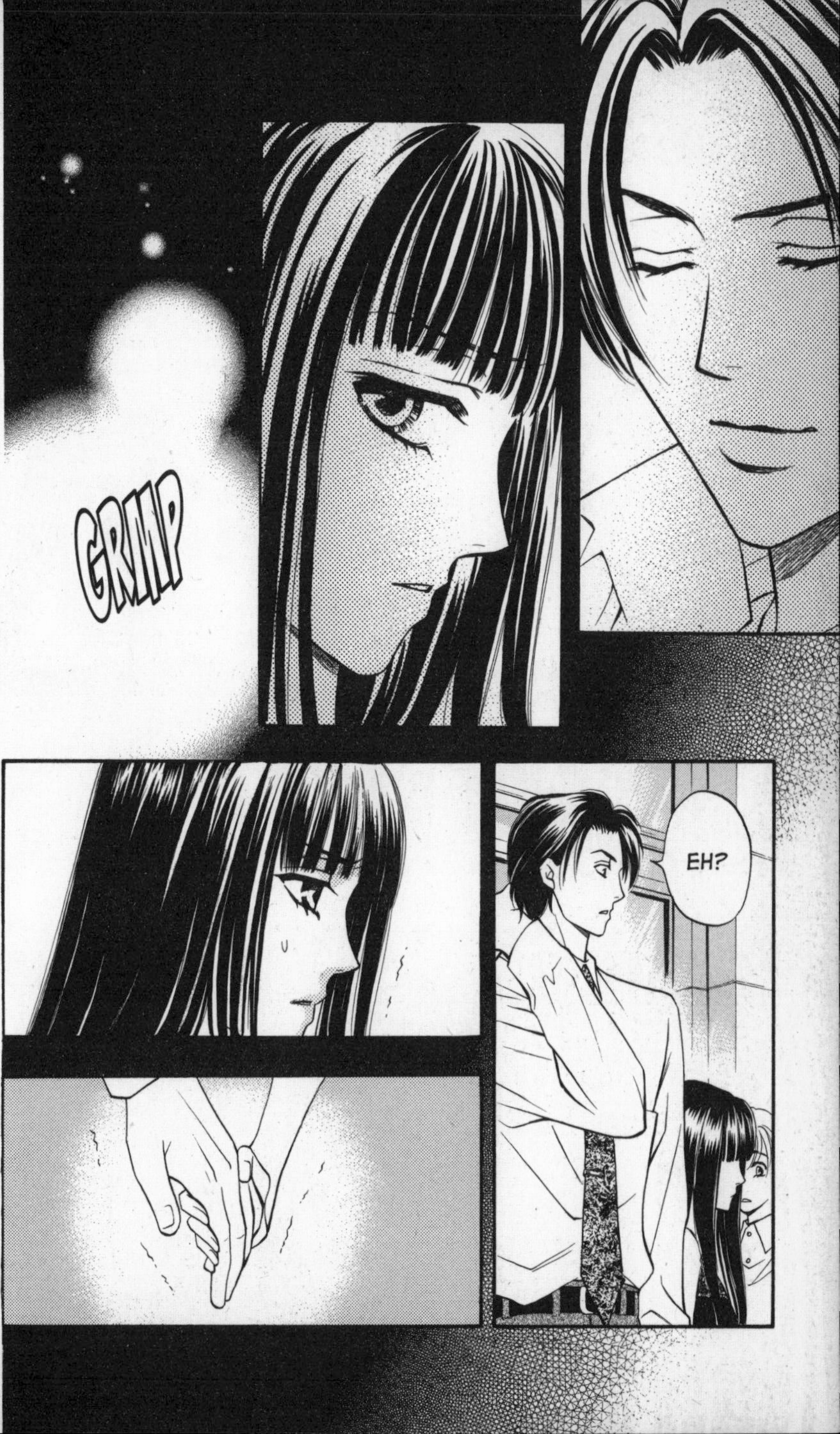
GRMP
EH?

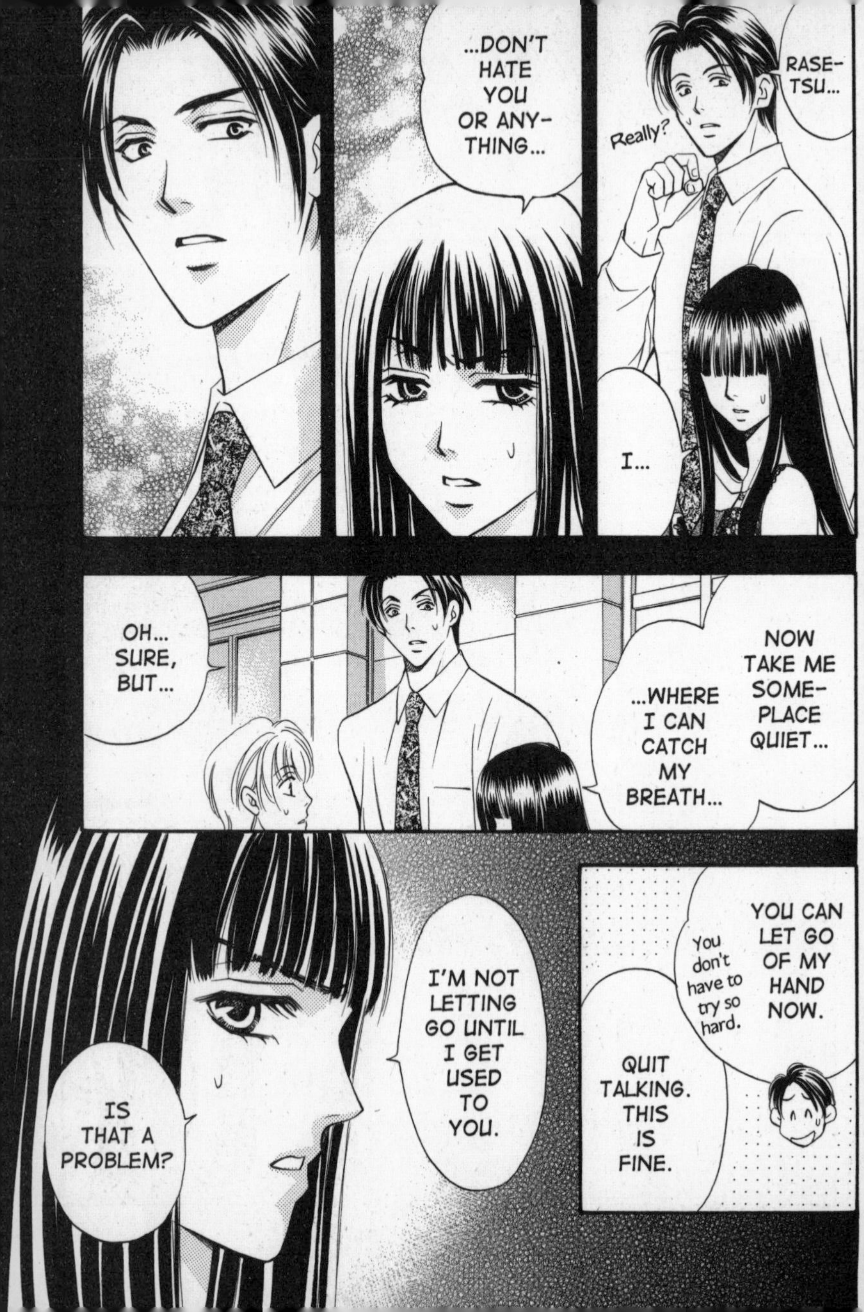
RASE-TSU...
Really?
I...
...DON'T HATE YOU OR ANY-THING...
NOW TAKE ME SOME-PLACE QUIET...
...WHERE I CAN CATCH MY BREATH...
OH... SURE, BUT...
YOU CAN LET GO OF MY HAND NOW.
You don't have to try so hard.
QUIT TALKING. THIS IS FINE.
I'M NOT LETTING GO UNTIL I GET USED TO YOU.
IS THAT A PROBLEM?

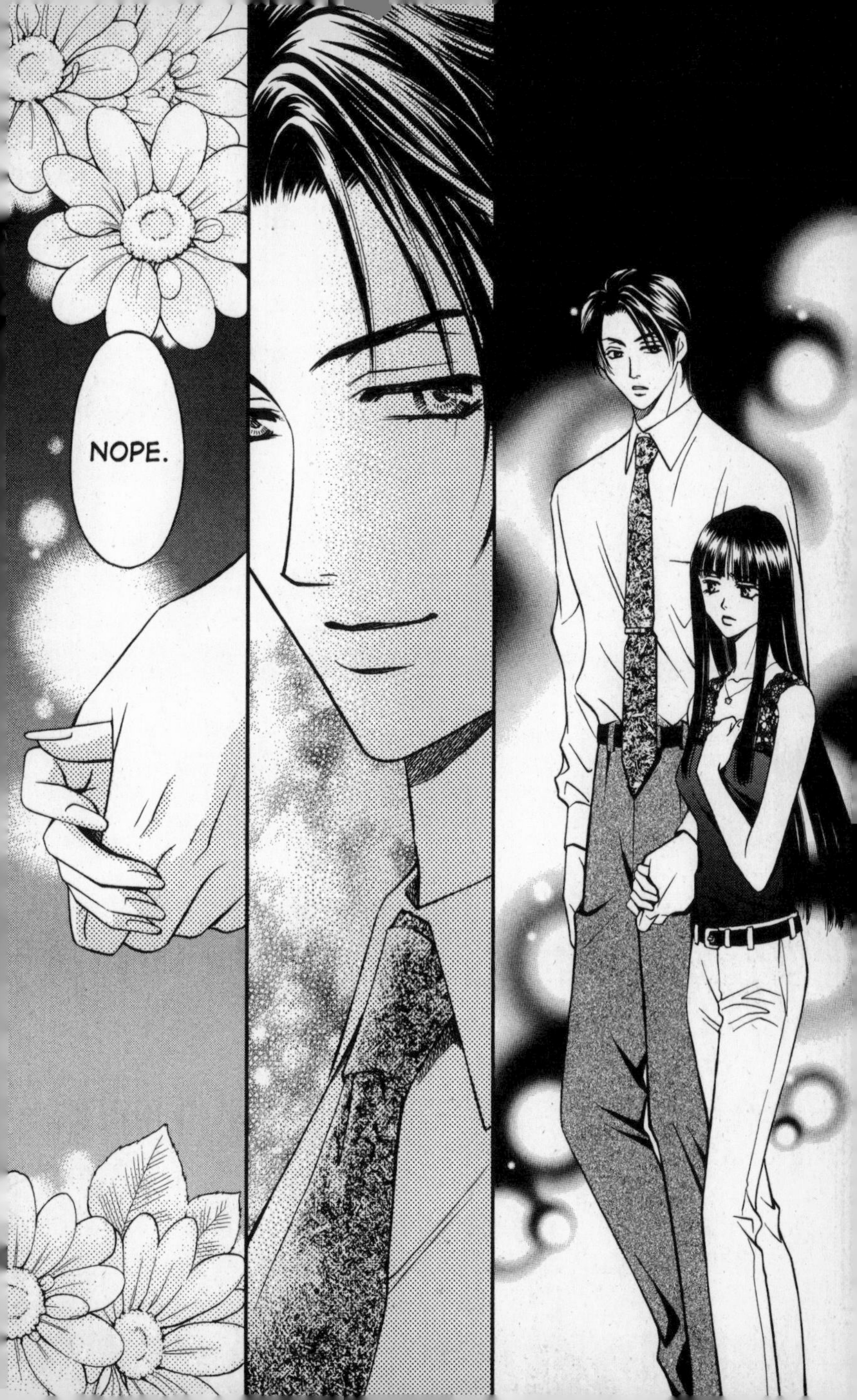
NOPE.

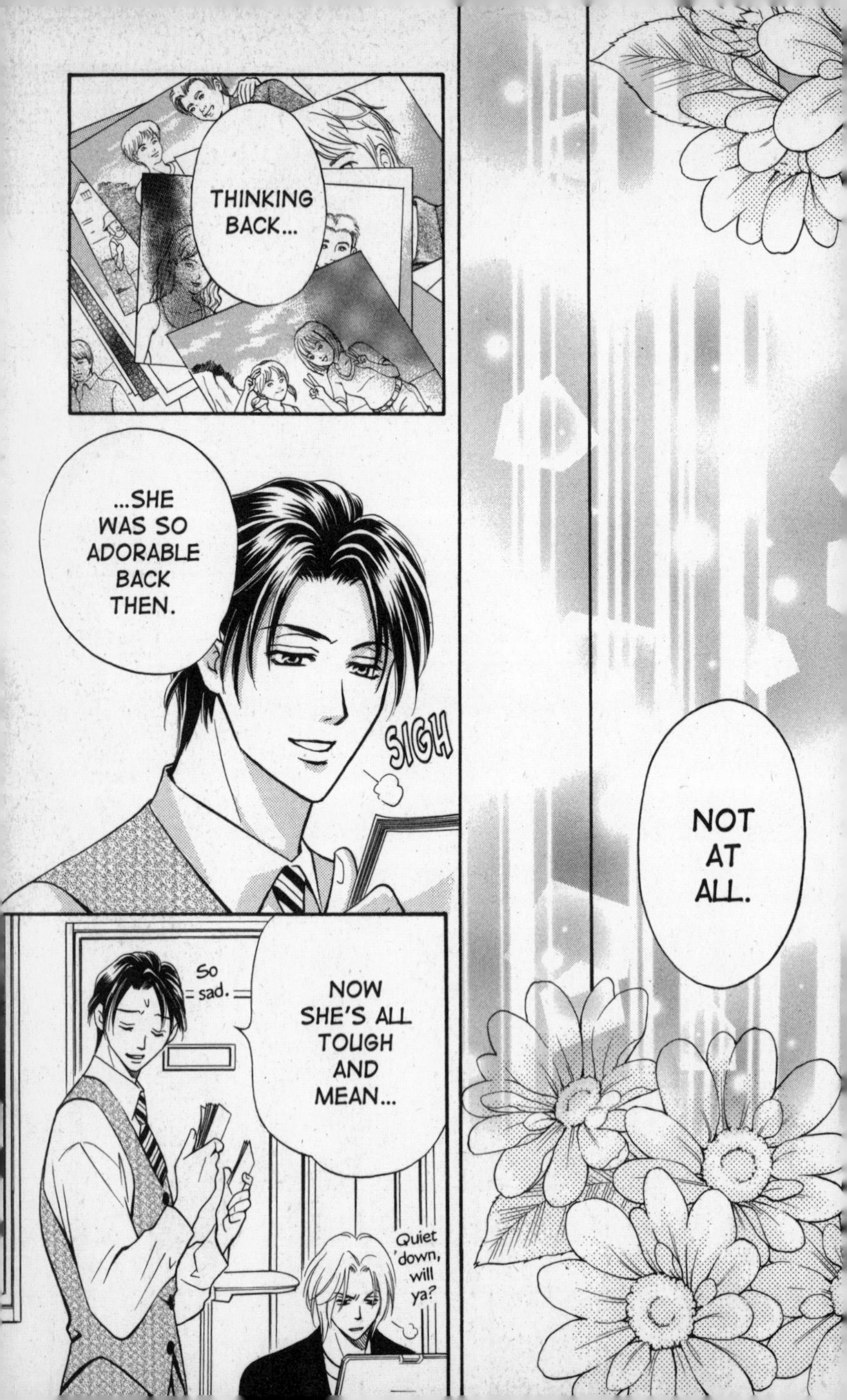
NOT AT ALL.
THINKING BACK...
...SHE WAS SO ADORABLE BACK THEN.
SIGH
NOW SHE'S ALL TOUGH AND MEAN...
So sad.
Quiet down, will ya?

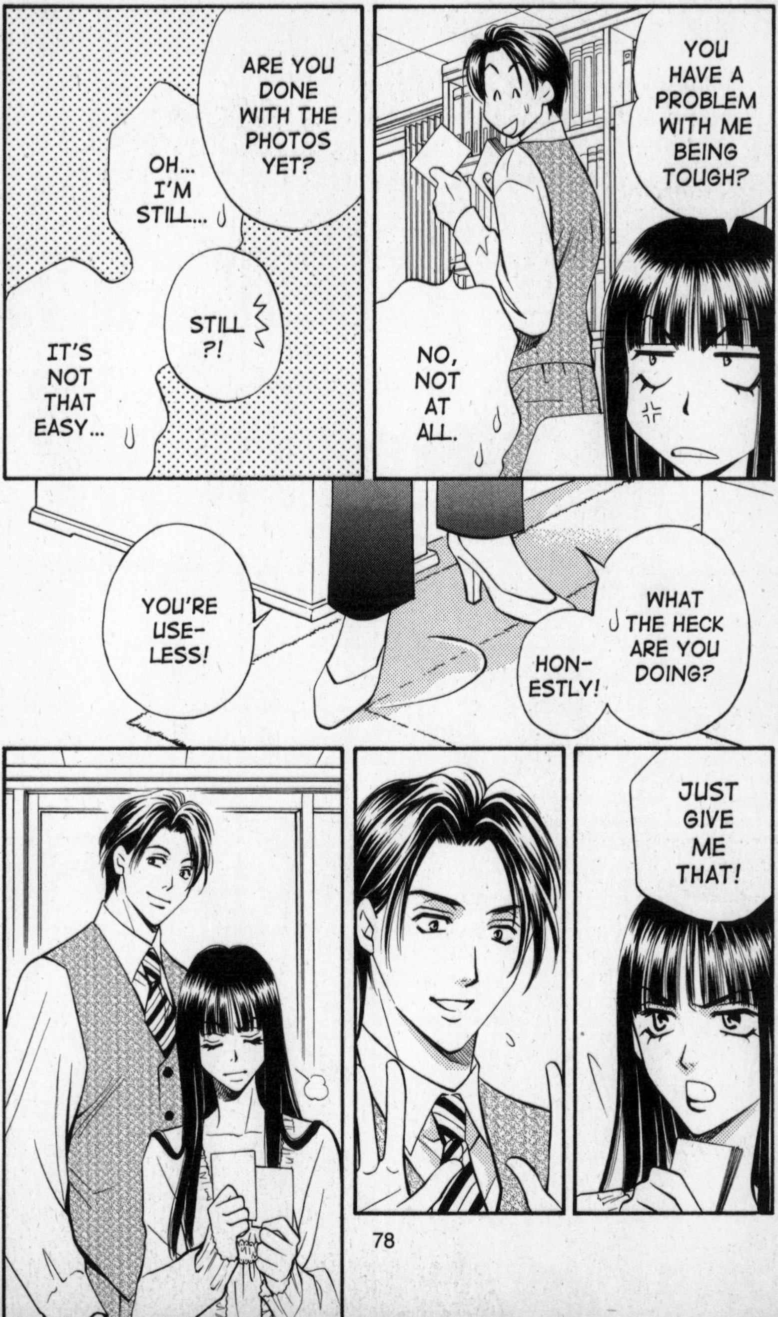
YOU HAVE A PROBLEM WITH ME BEING TOUGH?
NO, NOT AT ALL.
ARE YOU DONE WITH THE PHOTOS YET?
OH... I'M STILL...
STILL?!
IT'S NOT THAT EASY...
WHAT THE HECK ARE YOU DOING?
HON-ESTLY!
YOU'RE USE-LESS!
JUST GIVE ME THAT!

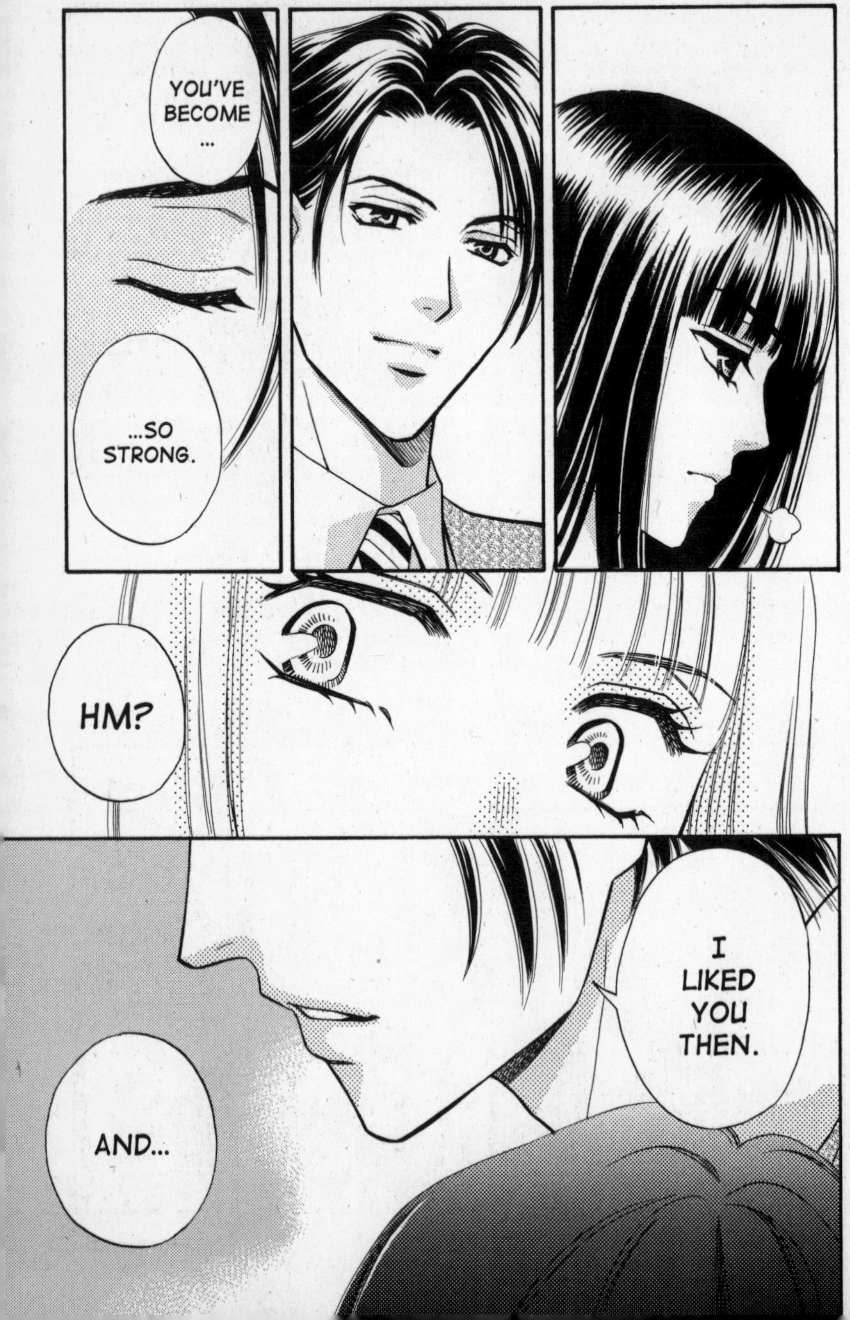
YOU'VE BECOME ...
...SO STRONG.
HM?
I LIKED YOU THEN.
AND...

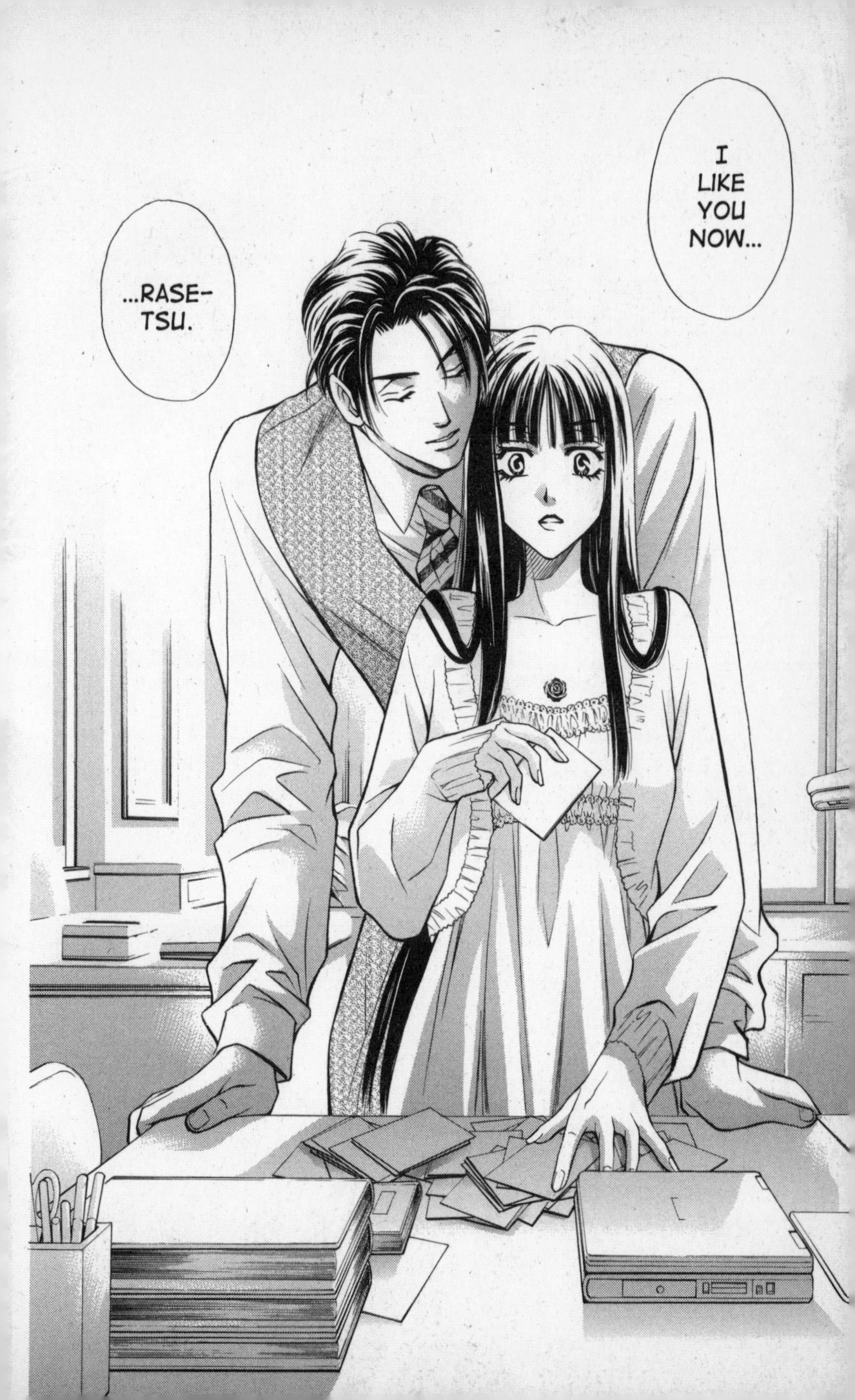
I LIKE YOU NOW...
...RASE-TSU.

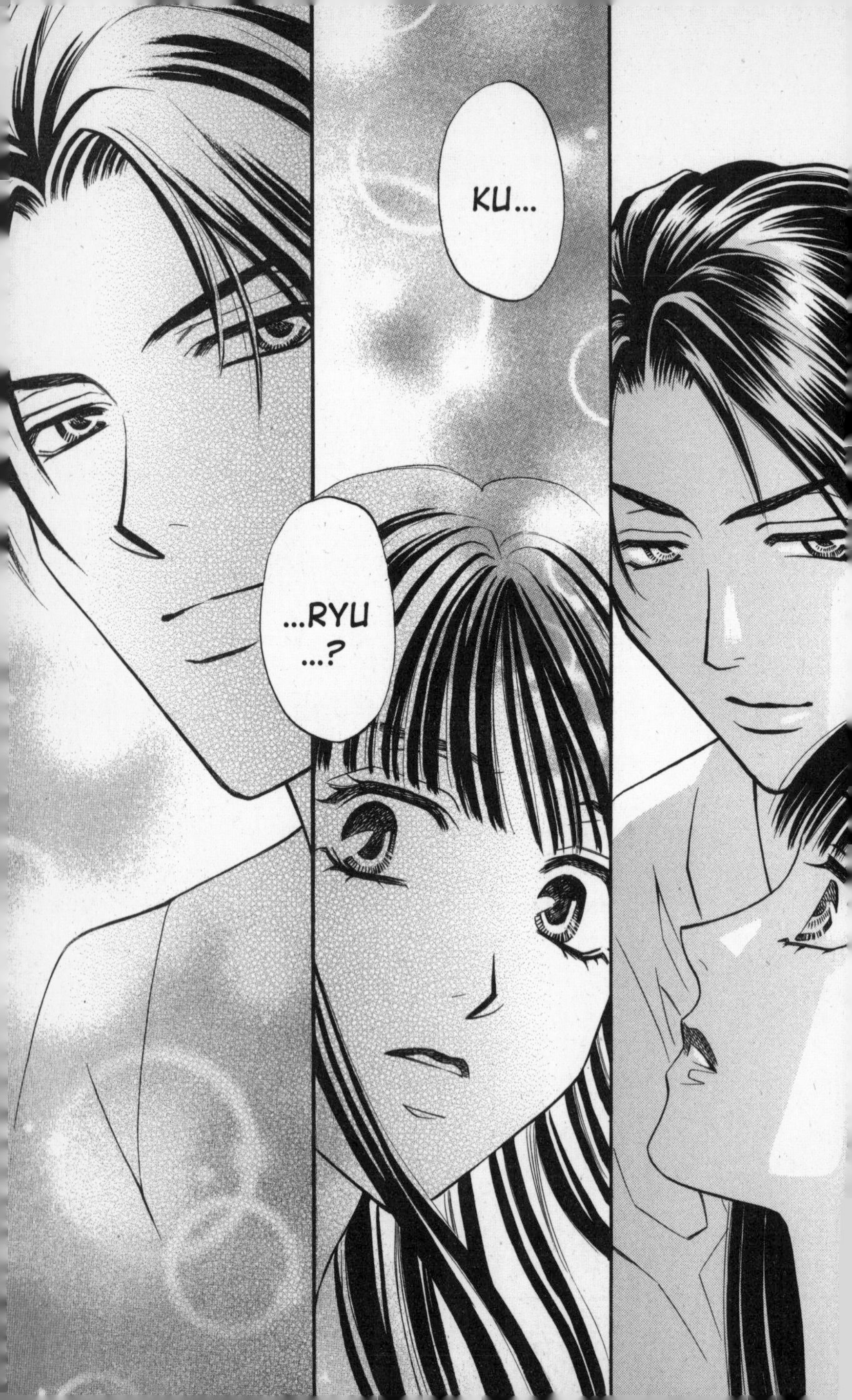
KU...
...RYU ...?

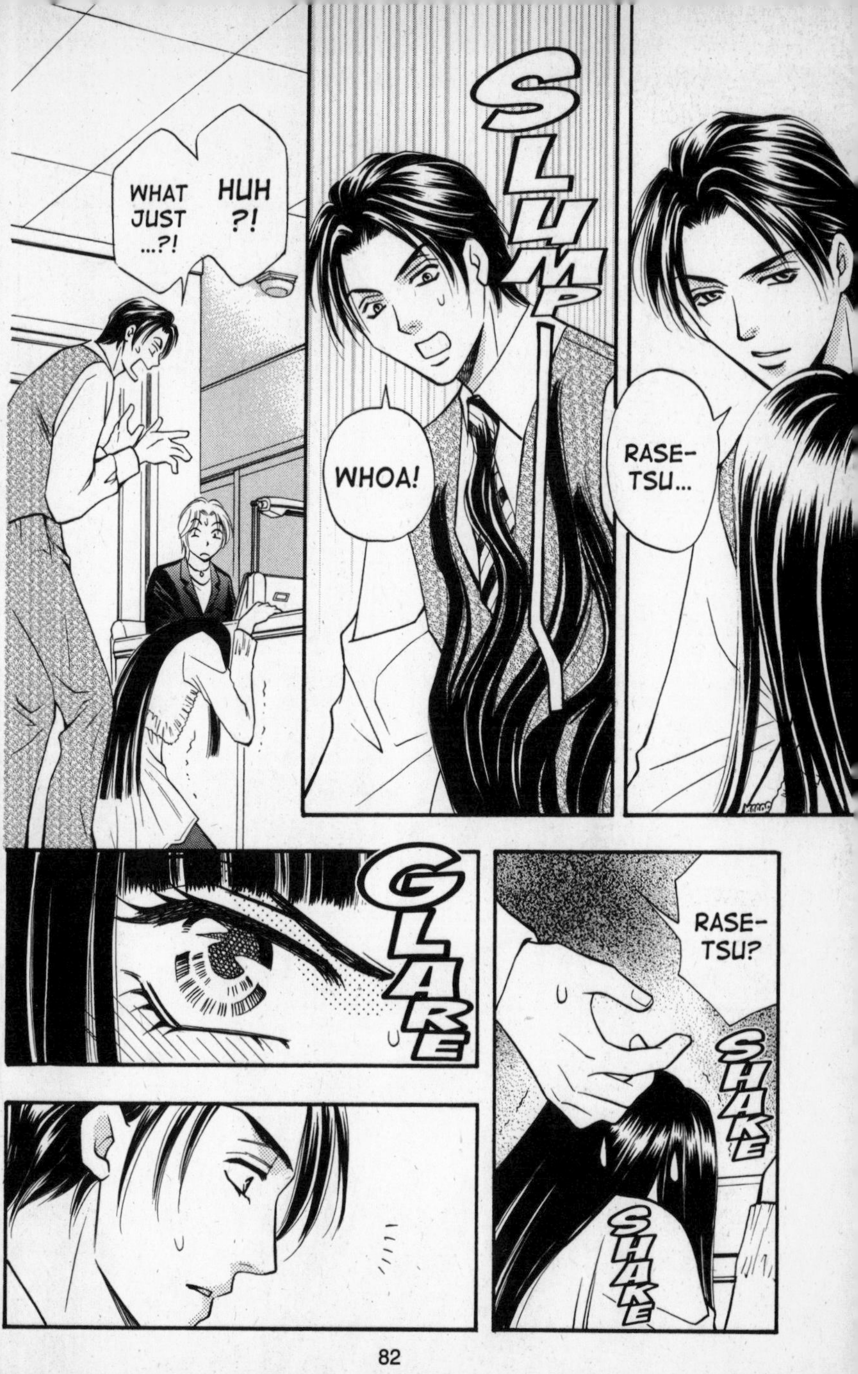
RASE-TSU...
SLUMP
WHOA!
HUH ?!
WHAT JUST ...?!
RASE-TSU?
SHAKE
SHAKE
GLARE

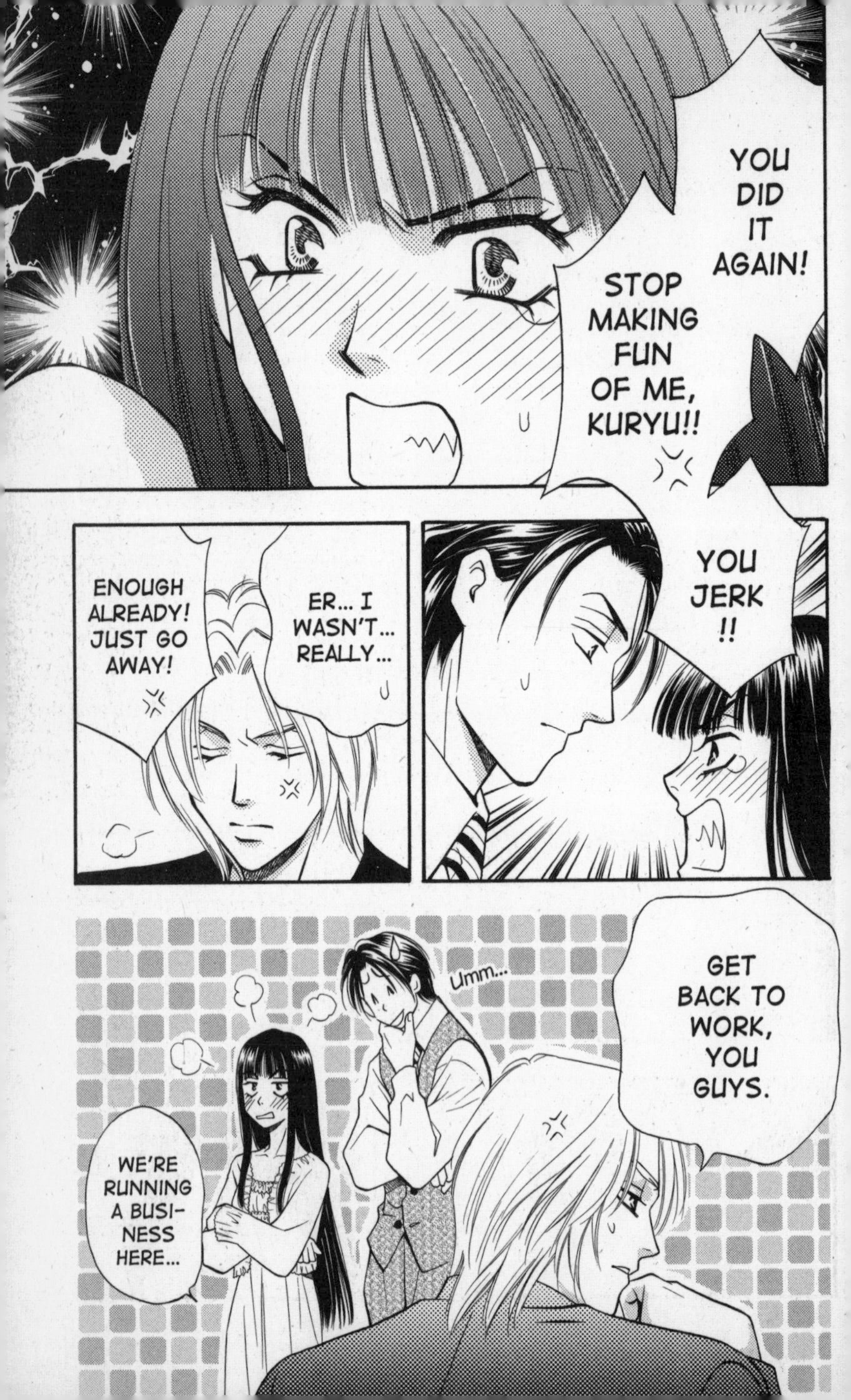
YOU DID IT AGAIN!
STOP MAKING FUN OF ME, KURYU!!
YOU JERK !!
ER... I WASN'T... REALLY...
ENOUGH ALREADY! JUST GO AWAY!
GET BACK TO WORK, YOU GUYS.
Umm...
WE'RE RUNNING A BUSI-NESS HERE...

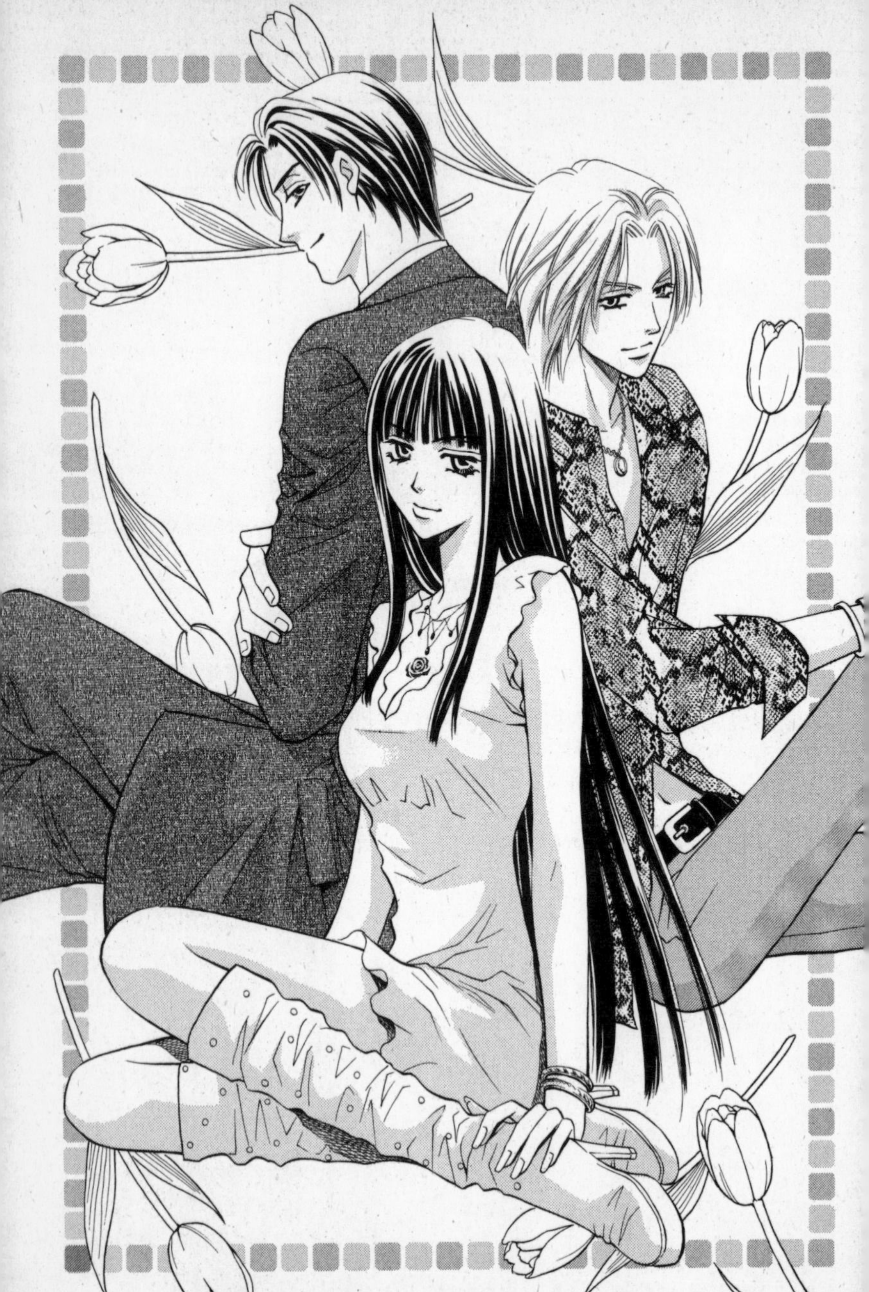

Chapter 6

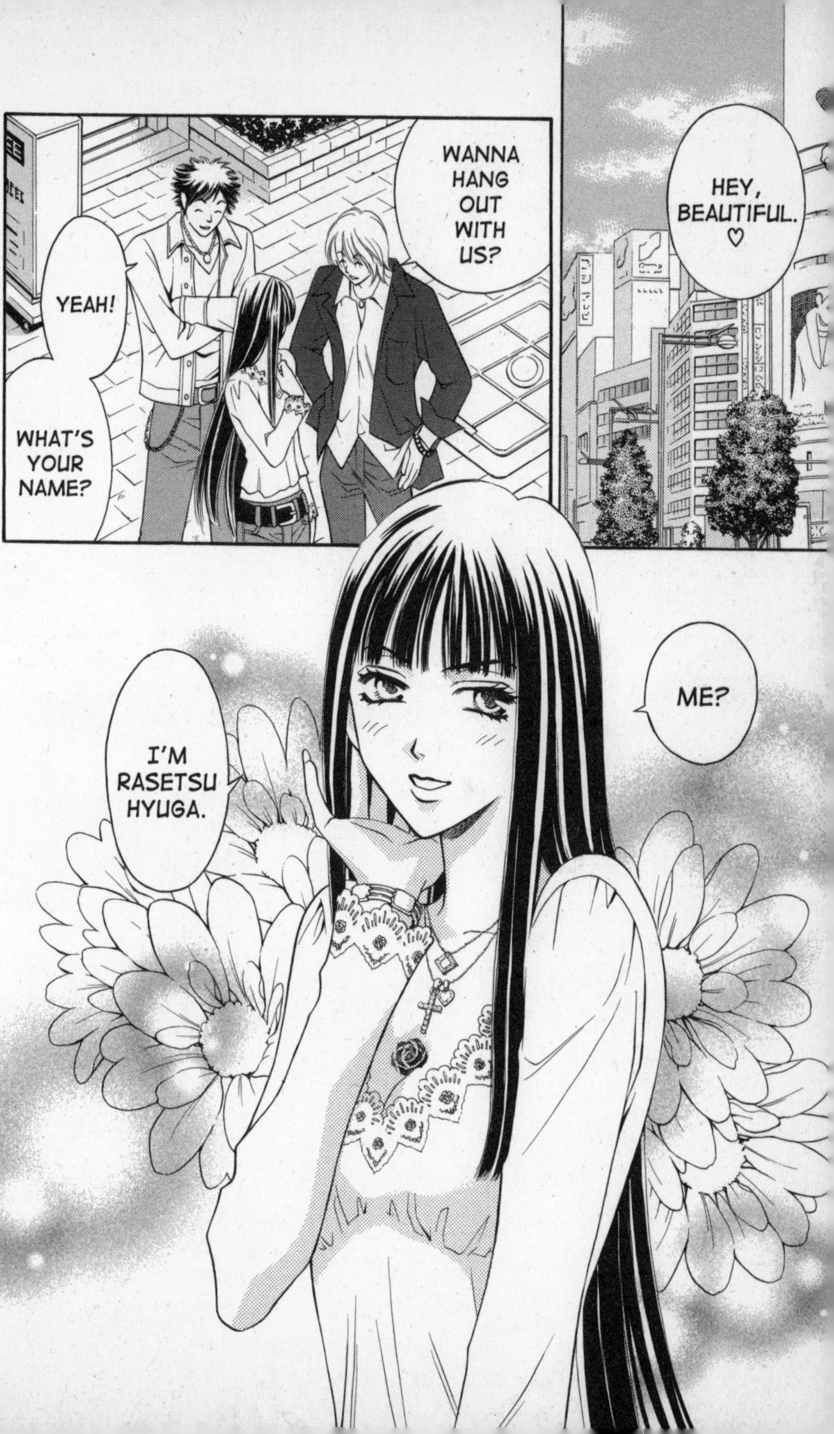
HEY, BEAUTIFUL. ♡
WANNA HANG OUT WITH US?
YEAH!
WHAT'S YOUR NAME?
ME?
I'M RASETSU HYUGA.

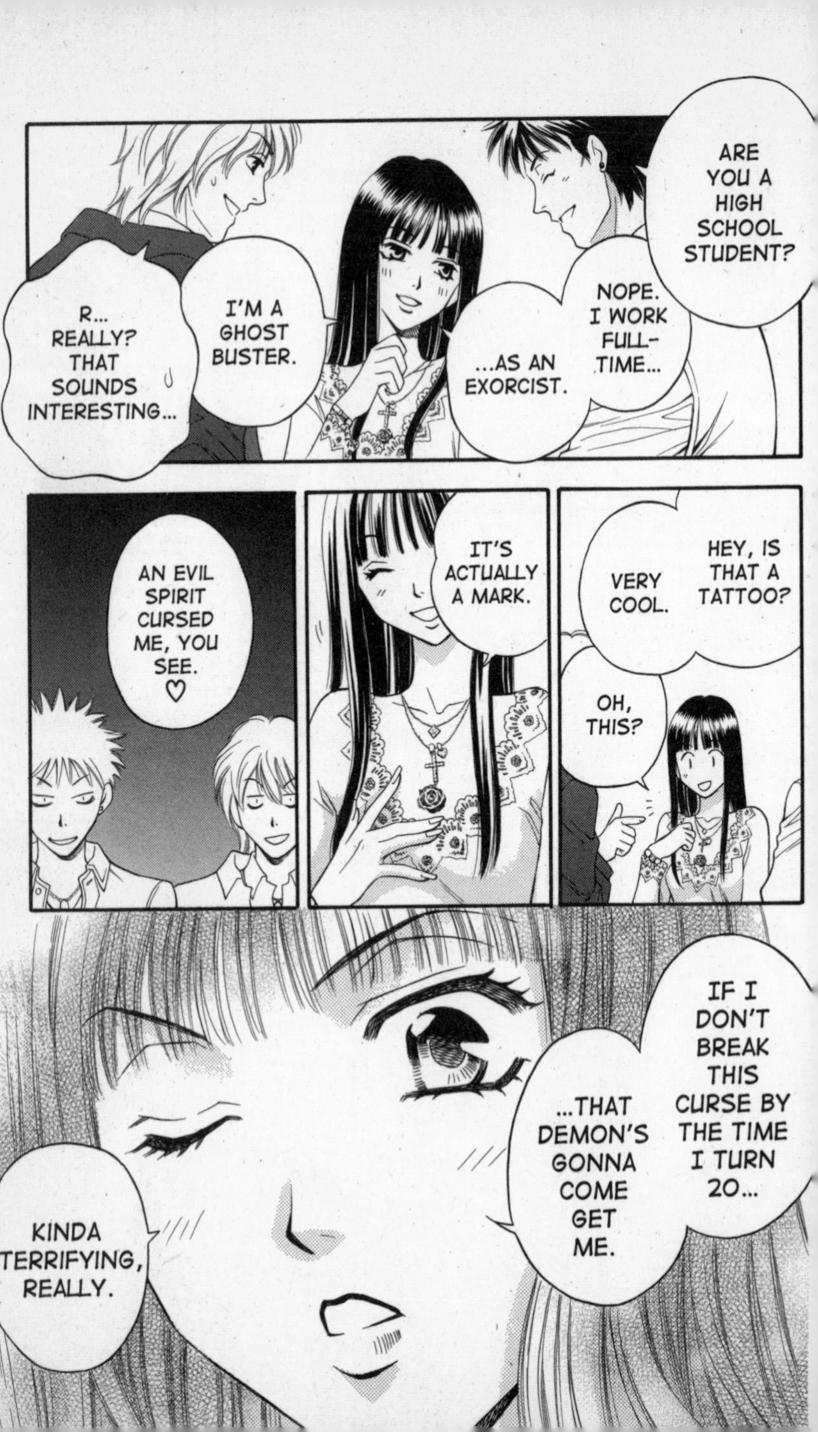
ARE YOU A HIGH SCHOOL STUDENT?
NOPE. I WORK FULL-TIME...
...AS AN EXORCIST.
I'M A GHOST BUSTER.
R... REALLY? THAT SOUNDS INTERESTING...
HEY, IS THAT A TATTOO?
VERY COOL.
OH, THIS?
IT'S ACTUALLY A MARK.
AN EVIL SPIRIT CURSED ME, YOU SEE. ♡
IF I DON'T BREAK THIS CURSE BY THE TIME I TURN 20...
...THAT DEMON'S GONNA COME GET ME.
KINDA TERRIFYING, REALLY.

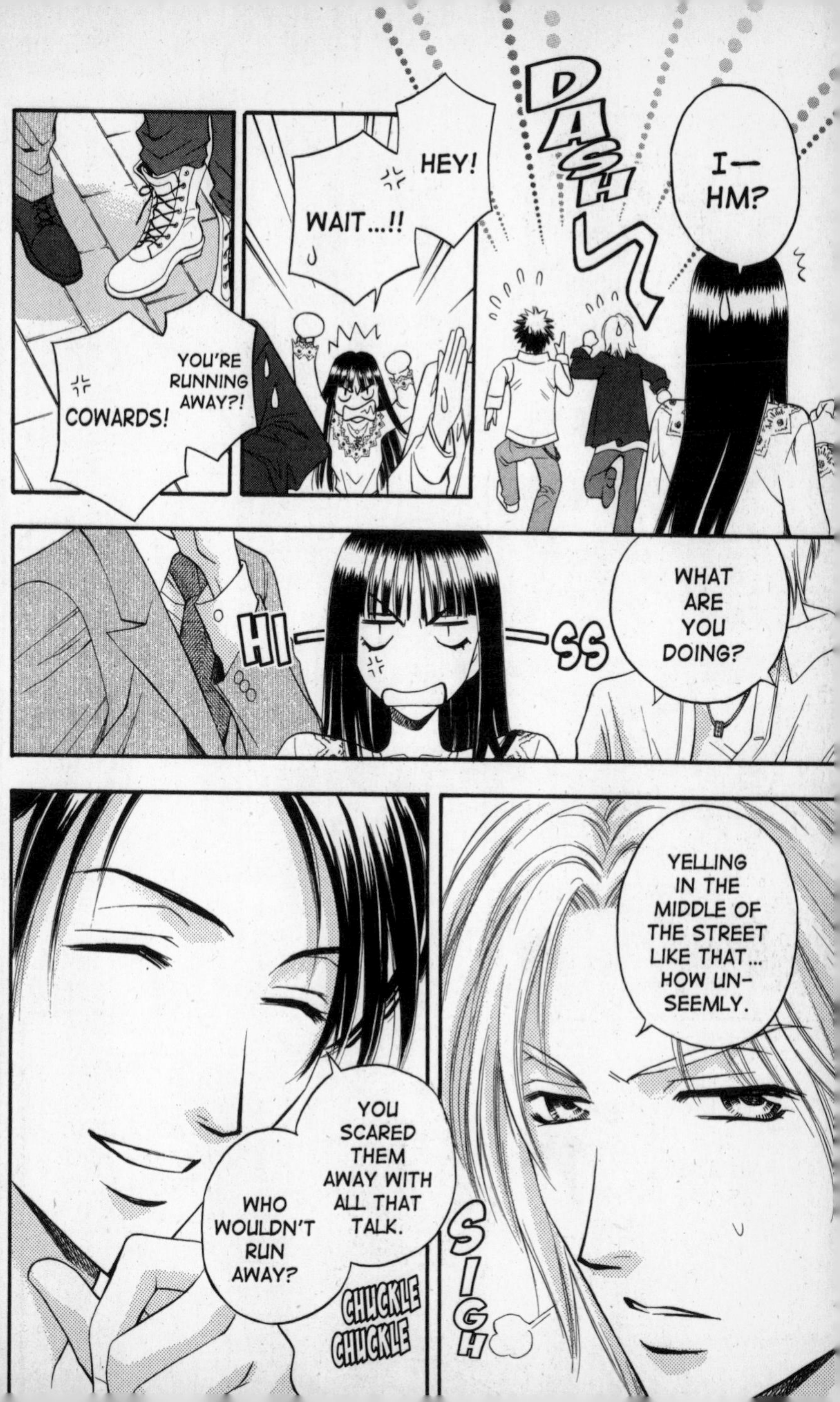
DASH
I— HM?
HEY!
WAIT...!!
YOU'RE RUNNING AWAY?!
COWARDS!
WHAT ARE YOU DOING?
HI—SS
YELLING IN THE MIDDLE OF THE STREET LIKE THAT... HOW UN-SEEMLY.
SIGH
YOU SCARED THEM AWAY WITH ALL THAT TALK.
WHO WOULDN'T RUN AWAY?
CHUCKLE CHUCKLE

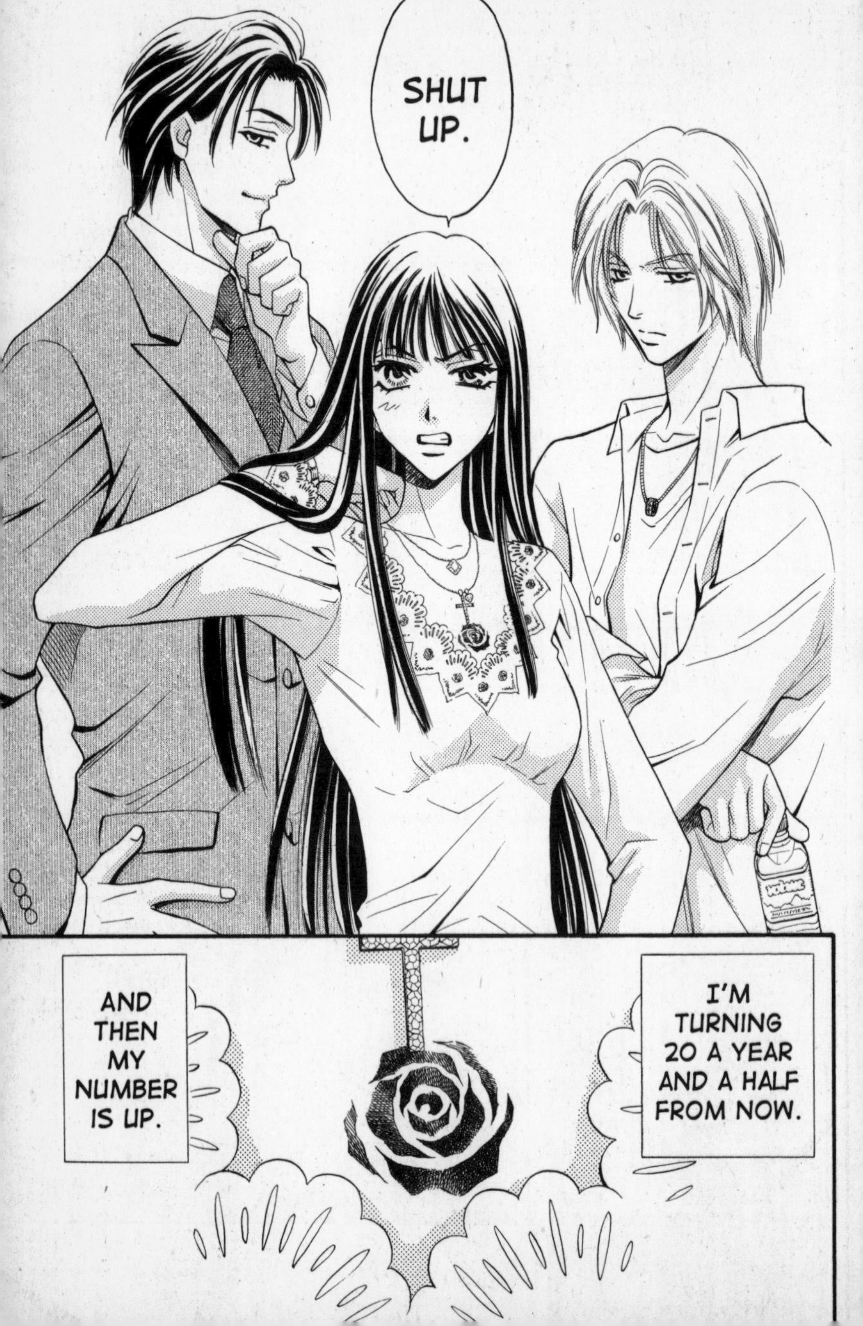
SHUT UP.
I'M TURNING 20 A YEAR AND A HALF FROM NOW.
AND THEN MY NUMBER IS UP.

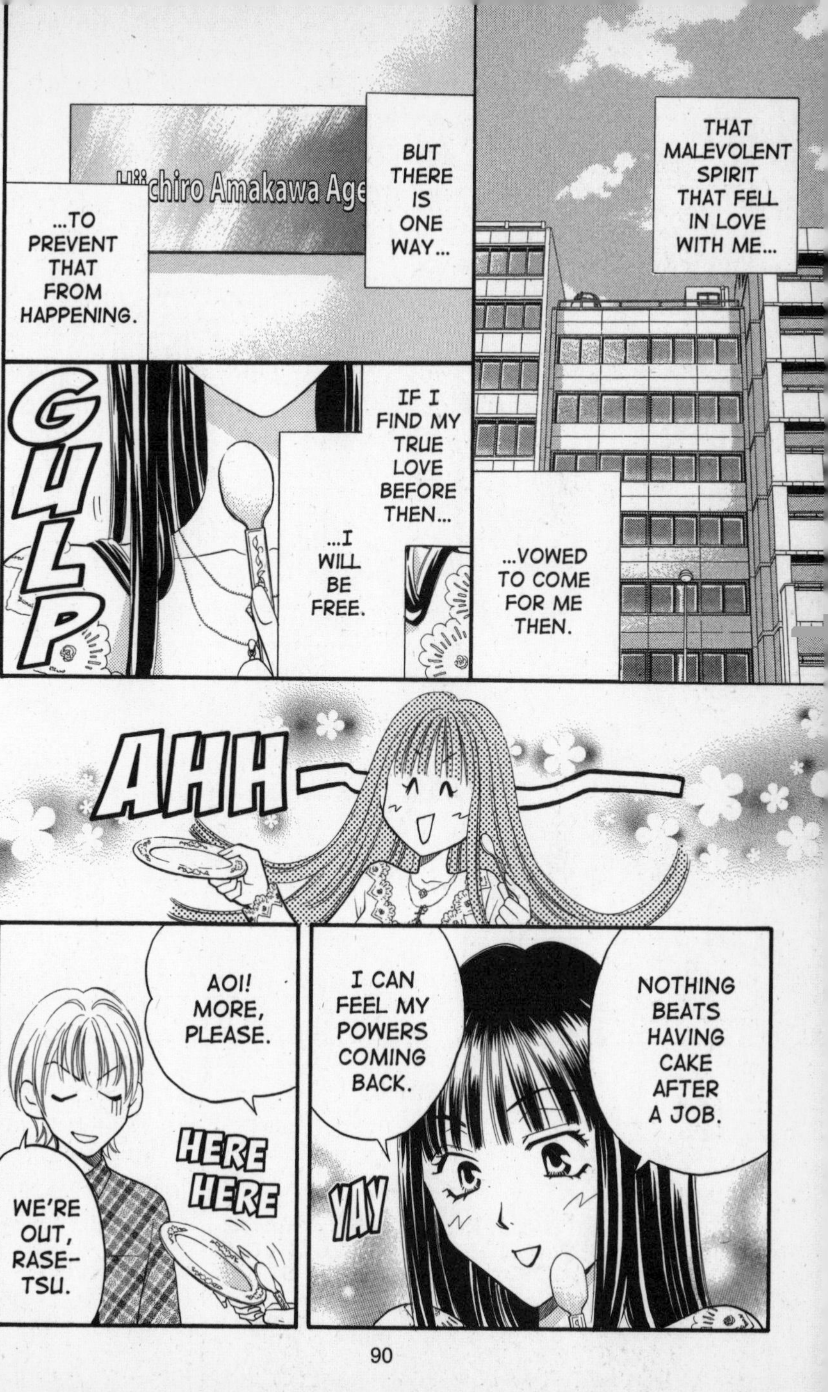
THAT MALEVOLENT SPIRIT THAT FELL IN LOVE WITH ME...
...VOWED TO COME FOR ME THEN.
BUT THERE IS ONE WAY...
chiro Amakawa Age
...TO PREVENT THAT FROM HAPPENING.
IF I FIND MY TRUE LOVE BEFORE THEN...
...I WILL BE FREE.
GULP
AHH—
NOTHING BEATS HAVING CAKE AFTER A JOB.
I CAN FEEL MY POWERS COMING BACK.
YAY
AOI! MORE, PLEASE.
HERE HERE
WE'RE OUT, RASETSU.

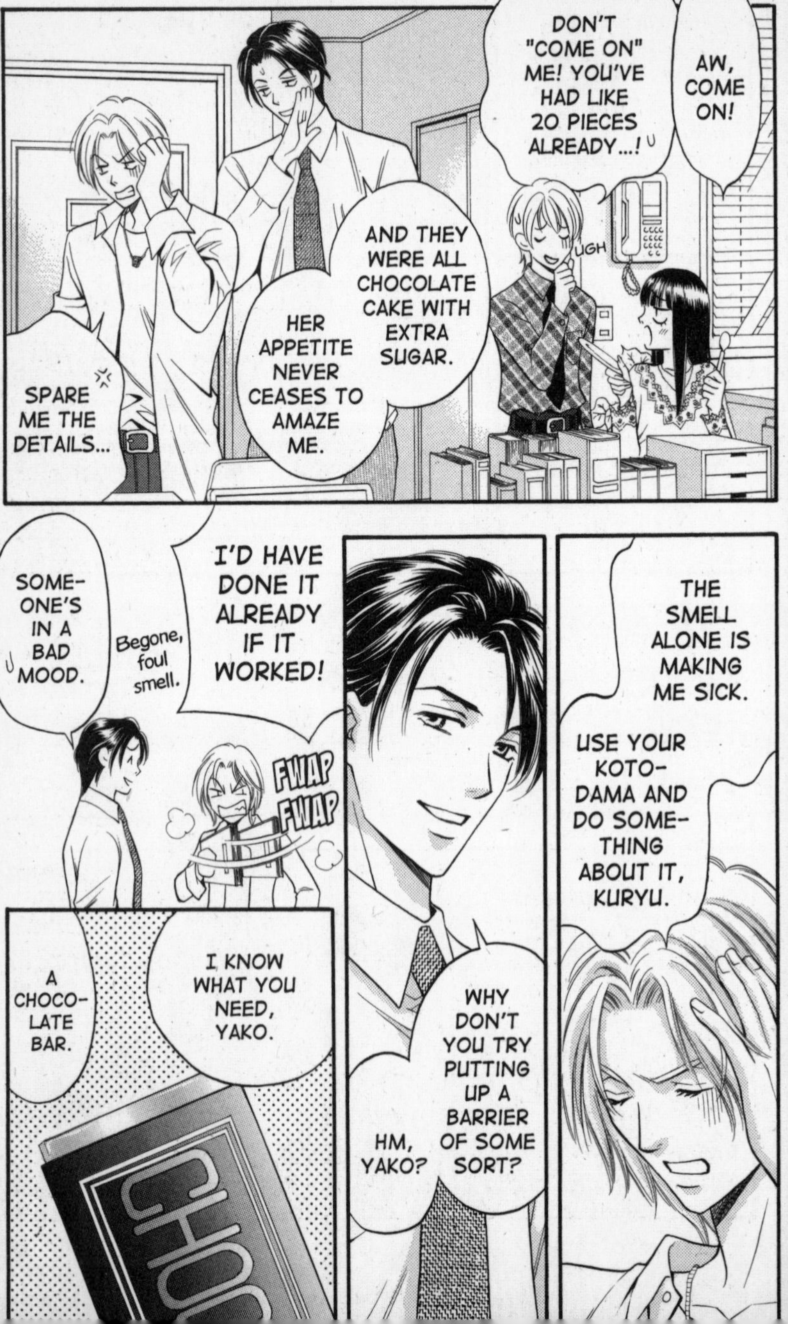
AW, COME ON!
DON'T "COME ON" ME! YOU'VE HAD LIKE 20 PIECES ALREADY...!
UGH
AND THEY WERE ALL CHOCOLATE CAKE WITH EXTRA SUGAR.
HER APPETITE NEVER CEASES TO AMAZE ME.
SPARE ME THE DETAILS...
THE SMELL ALONE IS MAKING ME SICK.
USE YOUR KOTO-DAMA AND DO SOME-THING ABOUT IT, KURYU.
WHY DON'T YOU TRY PUTTING UP A BARRIER OF SOME SORT?
HM, YAKO?
I'D HAVE DONE IT ALREADY IF IT WORKED!
FWAP FWAP
Begone, foul smell.
SOME-ONE'S IN A BAD MOOD.
I KNOW WHAT YOU NEED, YAKO.
A CHOCO-LATE BAR.
CHO

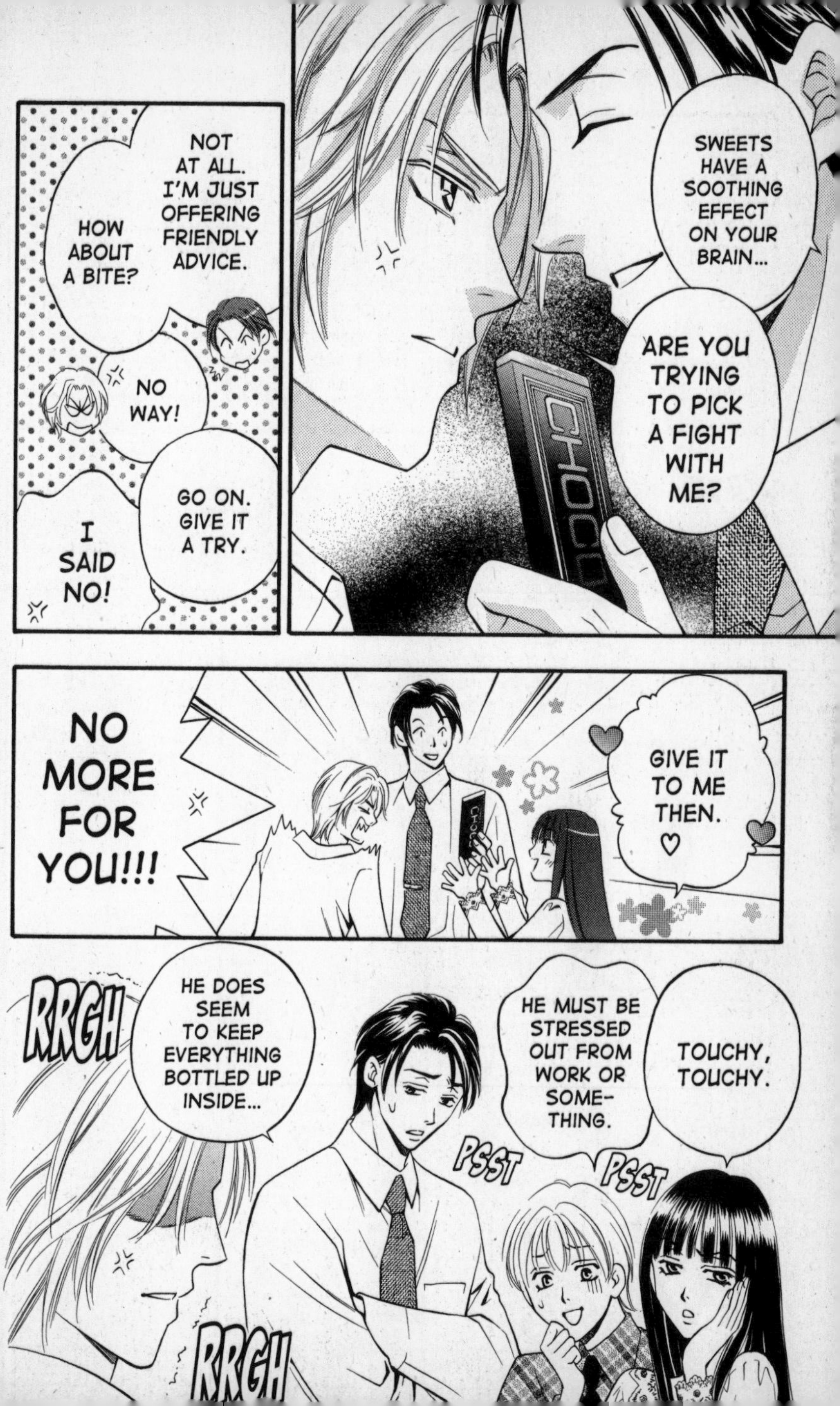
SWEETS HAVE A SOOTHING EFFECT ON YOUR BRAIN...
ARE YOU TRYING TO PICK A FIGHT WITH ME?
NOT AT ALL. I'M JUST OFFERING FRIENDLY ADVICE.
HOW ABOUT A BITE?
NO WAY!
GO ON. GIVE IT A TRY.
I SAID NO!
GIVE IT TO ME THEN. ♡
NO MORE FOR YOU!!!
TOUCHY, TOUCHY.
HE MUST BE STRESSED OUT FROM WORK OR SOME-THING.
PSST
PSST
HE DOES SEEM TO KEEP EVERYTHING BOTTLED UP INSIDE...
RRGH
RRGH

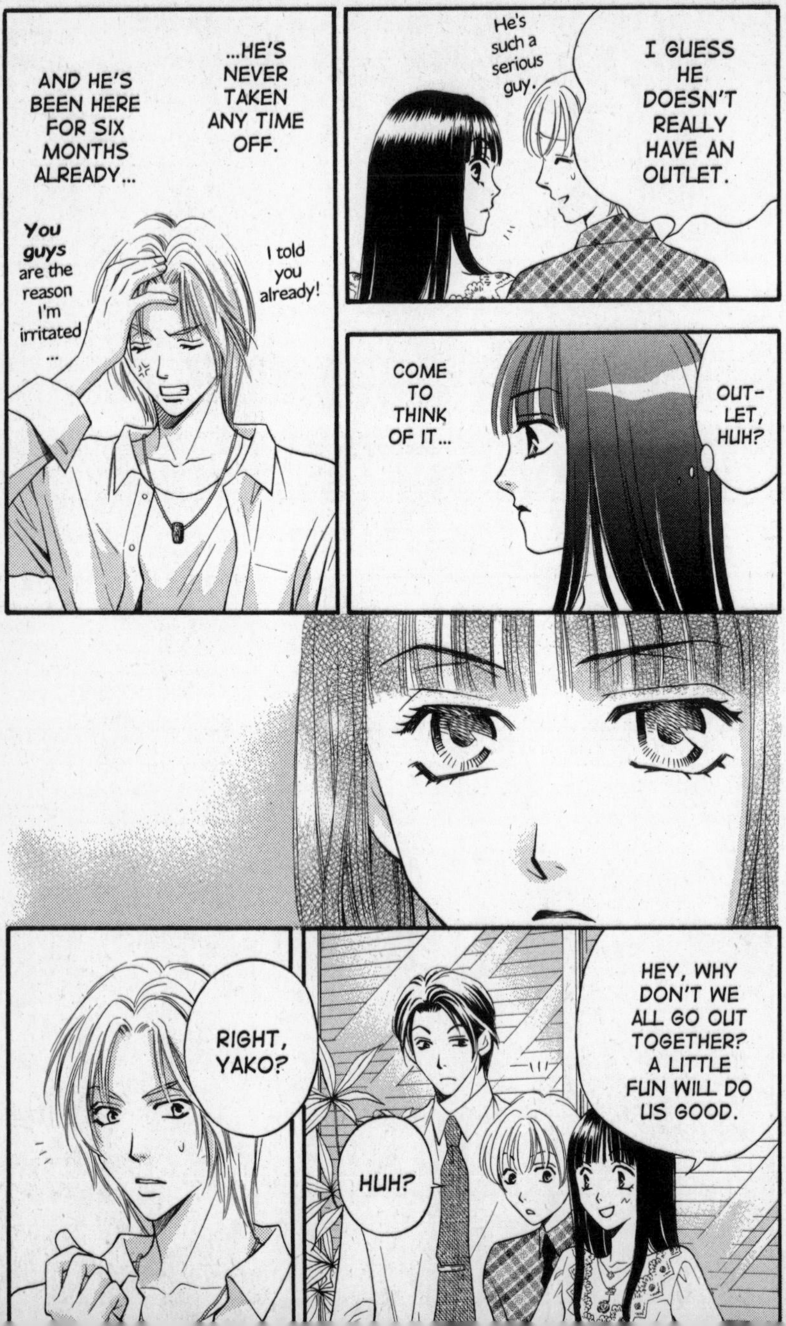
I GUESS HE DOESN'T REALLY HAVE AN OUTLET.
He's such a serious guy.
OUT-LET, HUH?
COME TO THINK OF IT...
AND HE'S BEEN HERE FOR SIX MONTHS ALREADY...
...HE'S NEVER TAKEN ANY TIME OFF.
I told you already!
You guys are the reason I'm irritated...
HEY, WHY DON'T WE ALL GO OUT TOGETHER? A LITTLE FUN WILL DO US GOOD.
HUH?
RIGHT, YAKO?

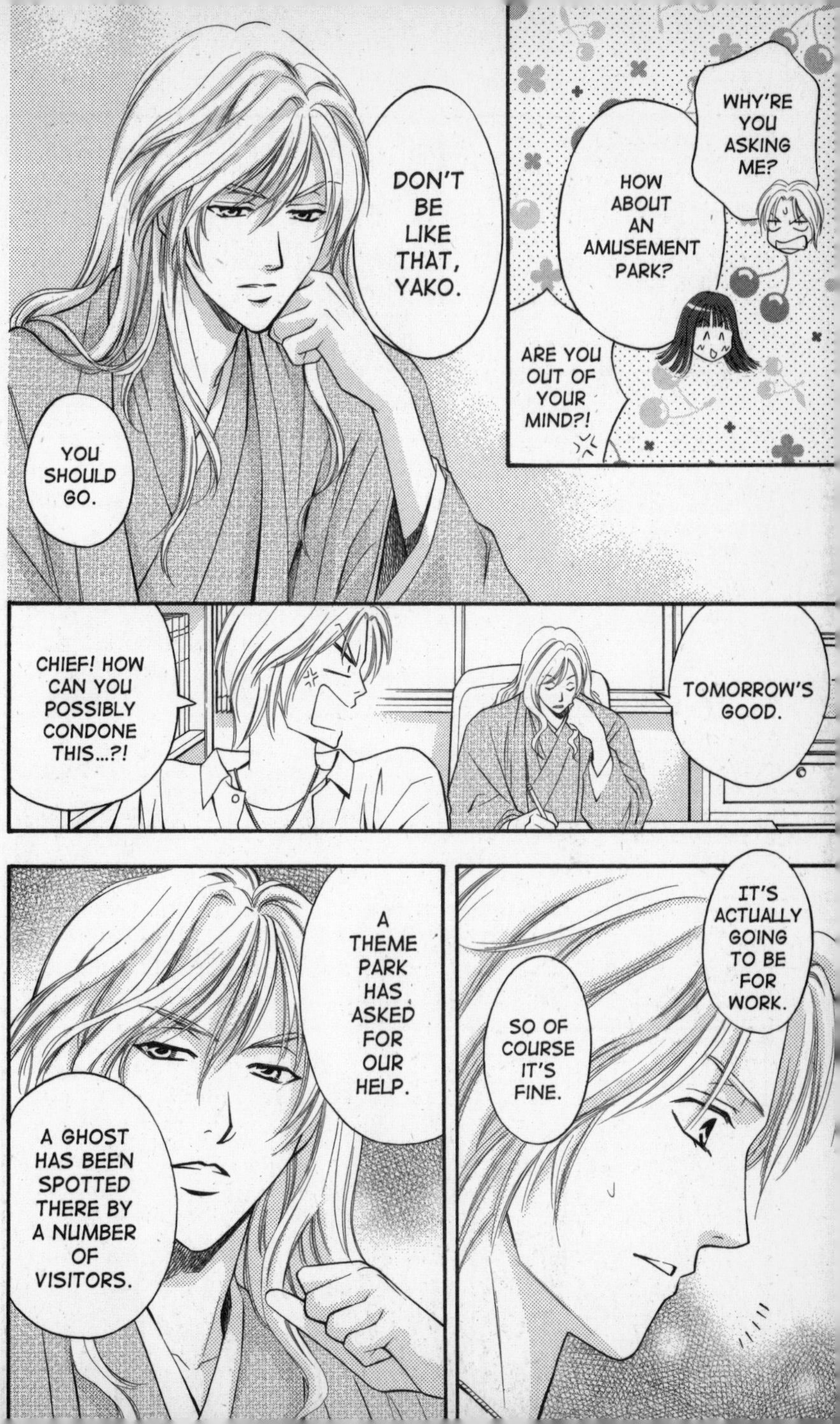
WHY'RE YOU ASKING ME?
HOW ABOUT AN AMUSEMENT PARK?
ARE YOU OUT OF YOUR MIND?!
DON'T BE LIKE THAT, YAKO.
YOU SHOULD GO.
TOMORROW'S GOOD.
CHIEF! HOW CAN YOU POSSIBLY CONDONE THIS...?!
IT'S ACTUALLY GOING TO BE FOR WORK.
SO OF COURSE IT'S FINE.
A THEME PARK HAS ASKED FOR OUR HELP.
A GHOST HAS BEEN SPOTTED THERE BY A NUMBER OF VISITORS.

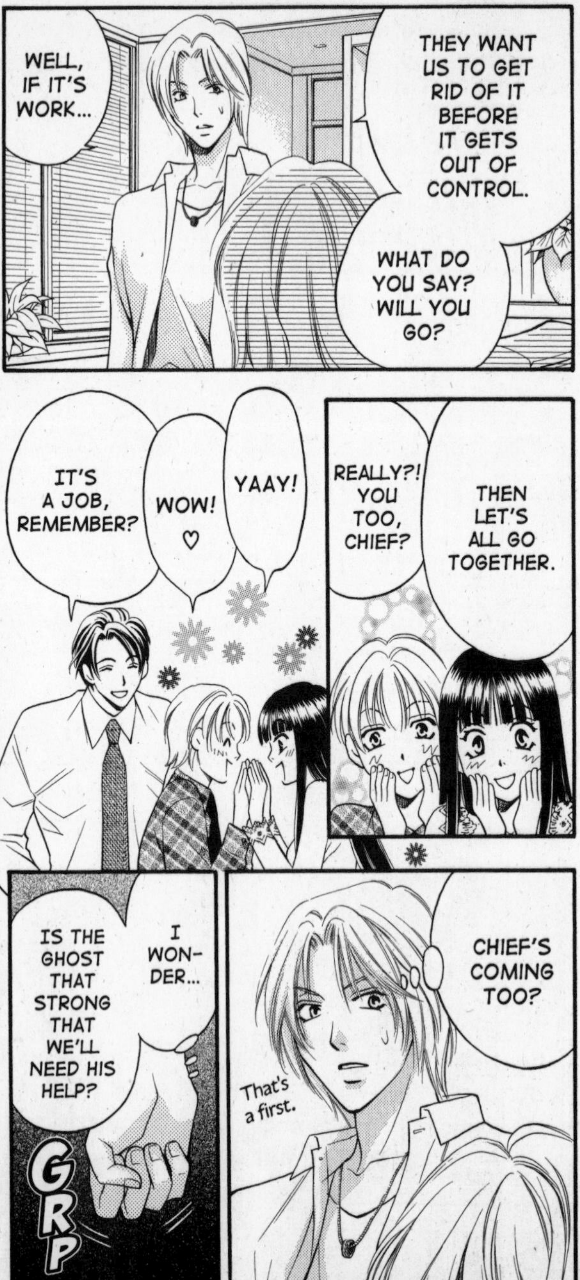
THEY WANT US TO GET RID OF IT BEFORE IT GETS OUT OF CONTROL.
WHAT DO YOU SAY? WILL YOU GO?
WELL, IF IT'S WORK...
THEN LET'S ALL GO TOGETHER.
REALLY?! YOU TOO, CHIEF?
YAAY!
WOW! ♡
IT'S A JOB, REMEMBER?
CHIEF'S COMING TOO?
That's a first.
I WON-DER...
IS THE GHOST THAT STRONG THAT WE'LL NEED HIS HELP?
GRP

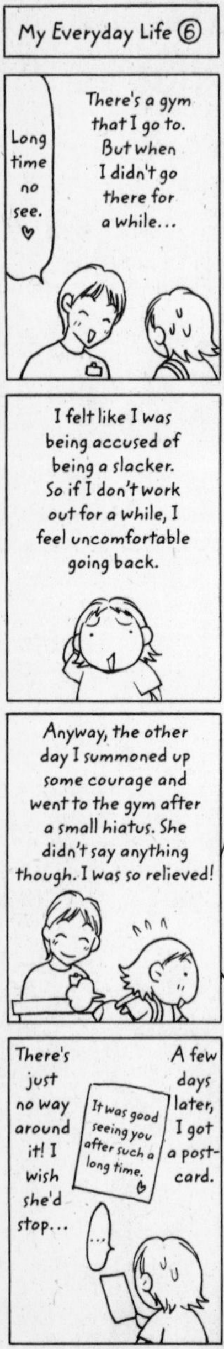
My Everyday Life ⑥
There's a gym that I go to. But when I didn't go there for a while...
Long time no see. ♡
I felt like I was being accused of being a slacker. So if I don't work out for a while, I feel uncomfortable going back.
Anyway, the other day I summoned up some courage and went to the gym after a small hiatus. She didn't say anything though. I was so relieved!
A few days later, I got a post-card.
It was good seeing you after such a long time. ♡
There's just no way around it! I wish she'd stop...
...

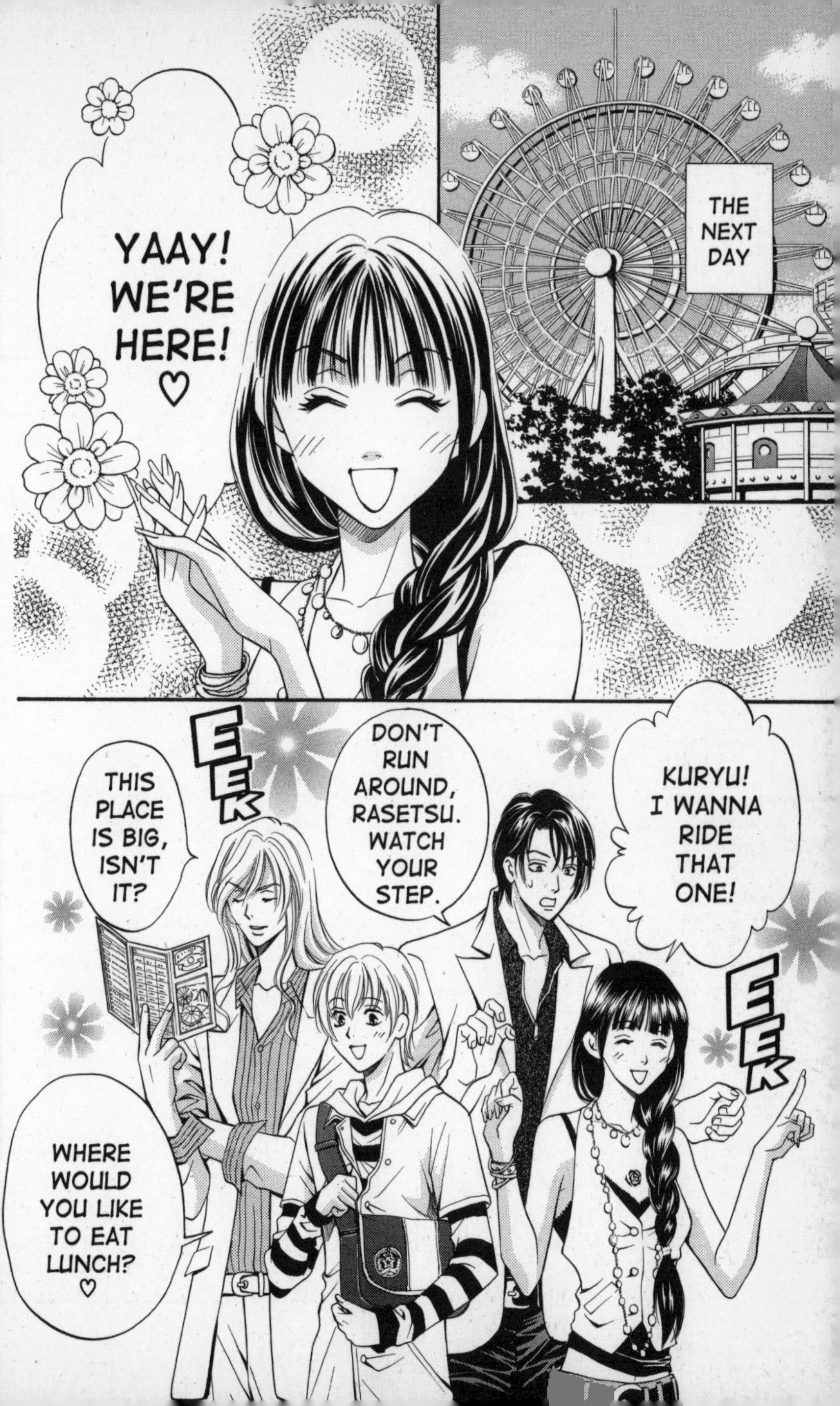
THE NEXT DAY
YAAY! WE'RE HERE! ♡
KURYU! I WANNA RIDE THAT ONE!
EEK
DON'T RUN AROUND, RASETSU. WATCH YOUR STEP.
EEK
THIS PLACE IS BIG, ISN'T IT?
WHERE WOULD YOU LIKE TO EAT LUNCH? ♡

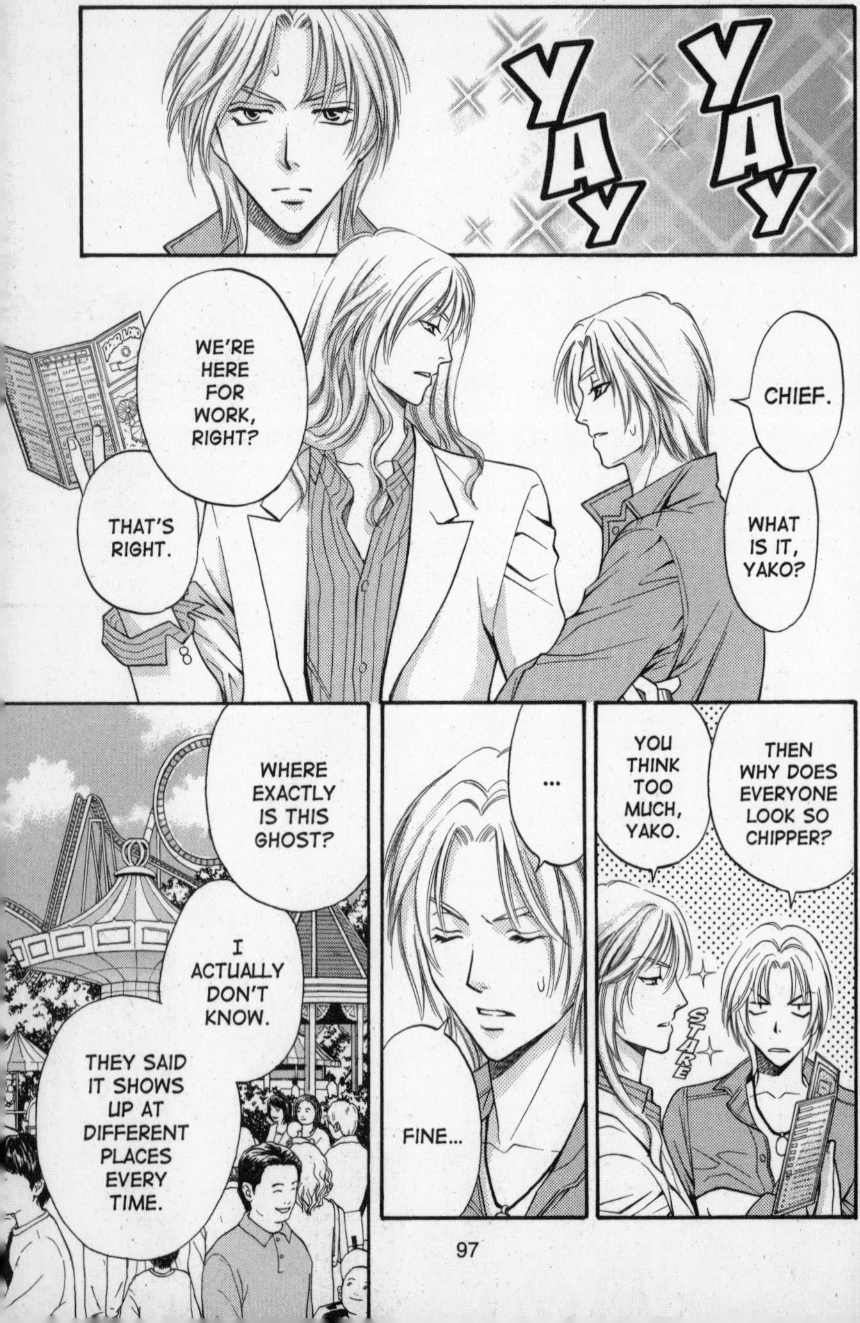
YAY YAY
CHIEF.
WHAT IS IT, YAKO?
WE'RE HERE FOR WORK, RIGHT?
THAT'S RIGHT.
THEN WHY DOES EVERYONE LOOK SO CHIPPER?
YOU THINK TOO MUCH, YAKO.
STARE
...
FINE...
WHERE EXACTLY IS THIS GHOST?
I ACTUALLY DON'T KNOW.
THEY SAID IT SHOWS UP AT DIFFERENT PLACES EVERY TIME.

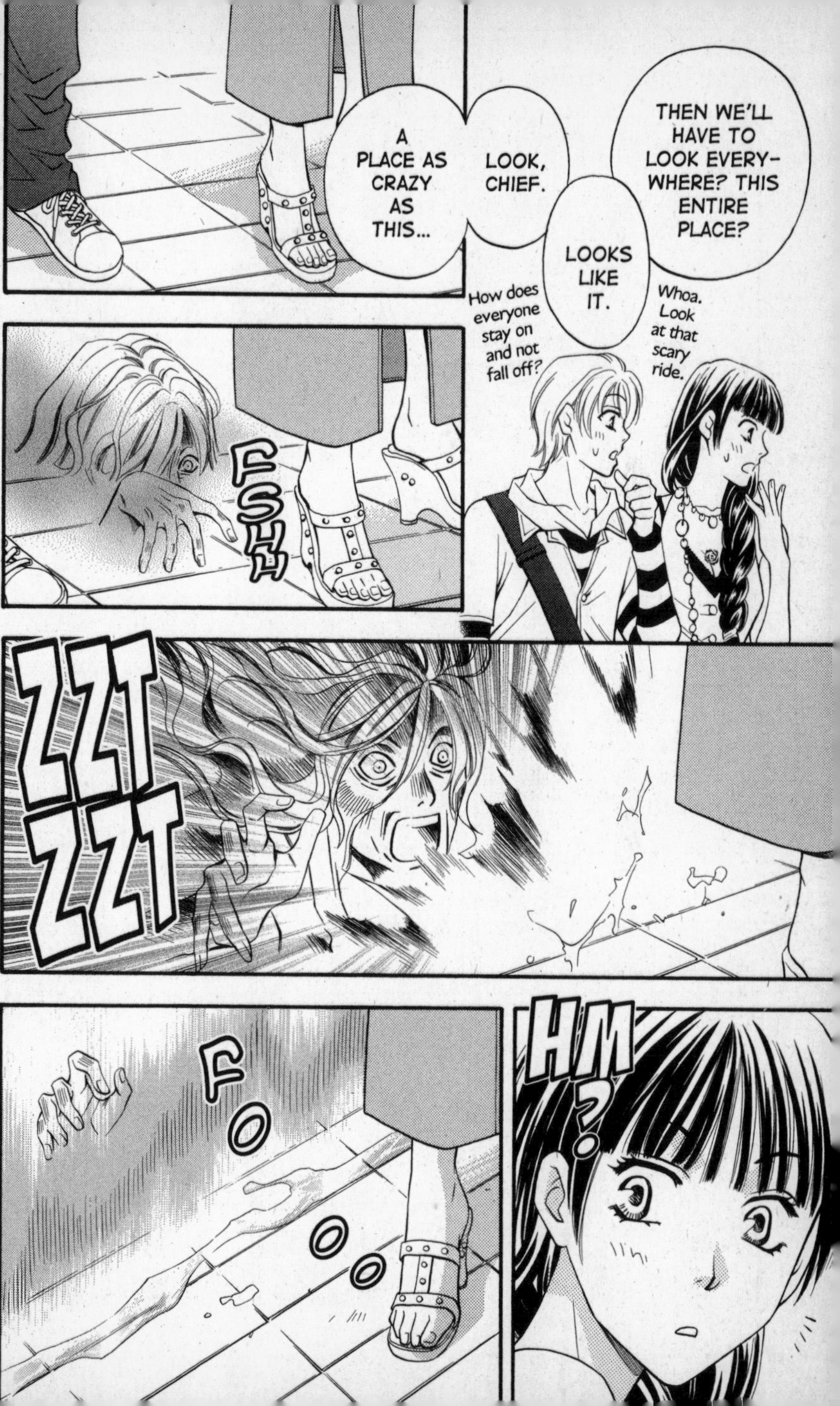
THEN WE'LL HAVE TO LOOK EVERY-WHERE? THIS ENTIRE PLACE?
LOOKS LIKE IT.
LOOK, CHIEF.
A PLACE AS CRAZY AS THIS...
Whoa. Look at that scary ride.
How does everyone stay on and not fall off?
FSHH
ZZT ZZT
HM?
FOOOO

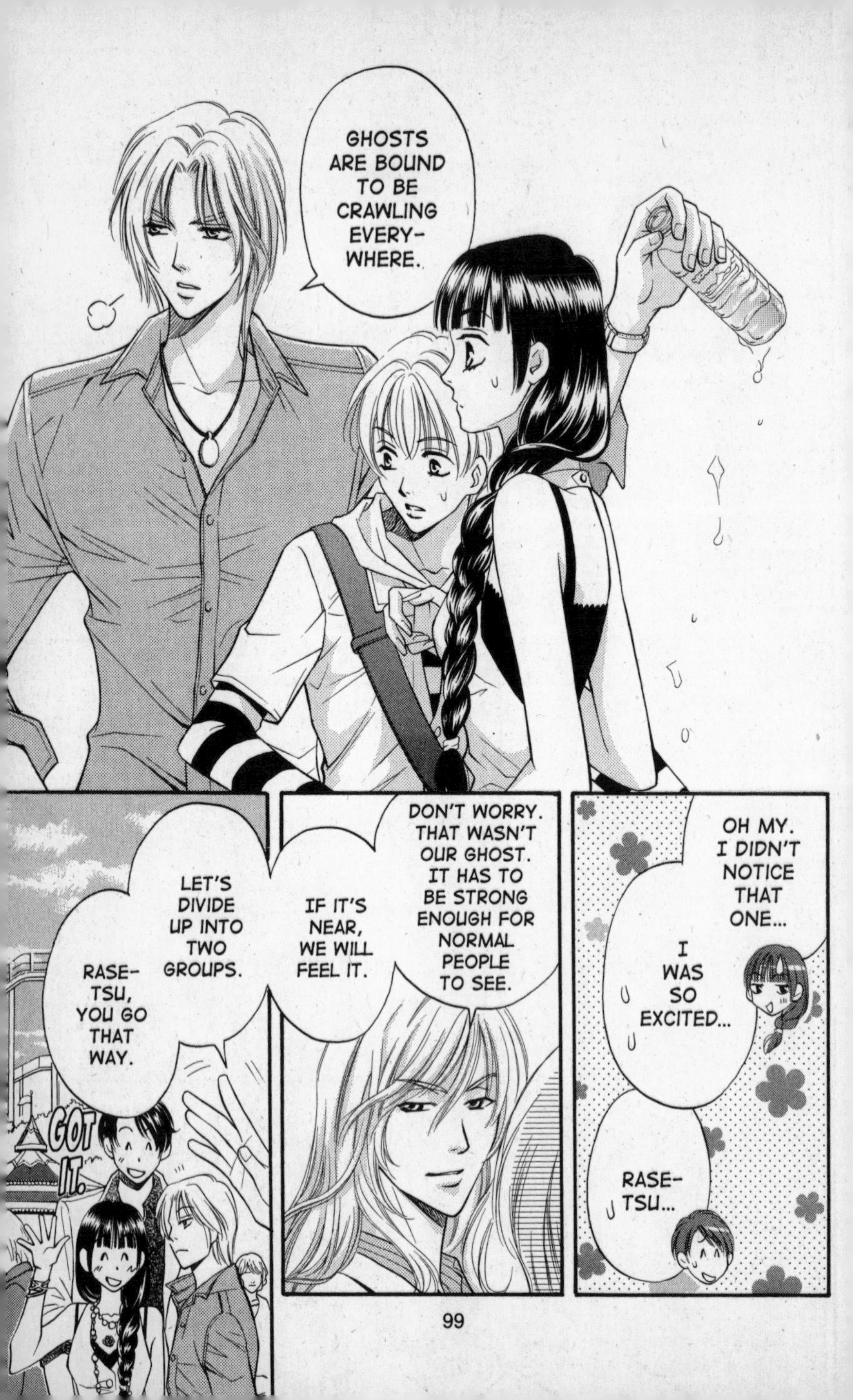
GHOSTS ARE BOUND TO BE CRAWLING EVERY-WHERE.
OH MY. I DIDN'T NOTICE THAT ONE...
I WAS SO EXCITED...
RASE-TSU...
DON'T WORRY. THAT WASN'T OUR GHOST. IT HAS TO BE STRONG ENOUGH FOR NORMAL PEOPLE TO SEE.
IF IT'S NEAR, WE WILL FEEL IT.
LET'S DIVIDE UP INTO TWO GROUPS.
RASE-TSU, YOU GO THAT WAY.
GOT IT.

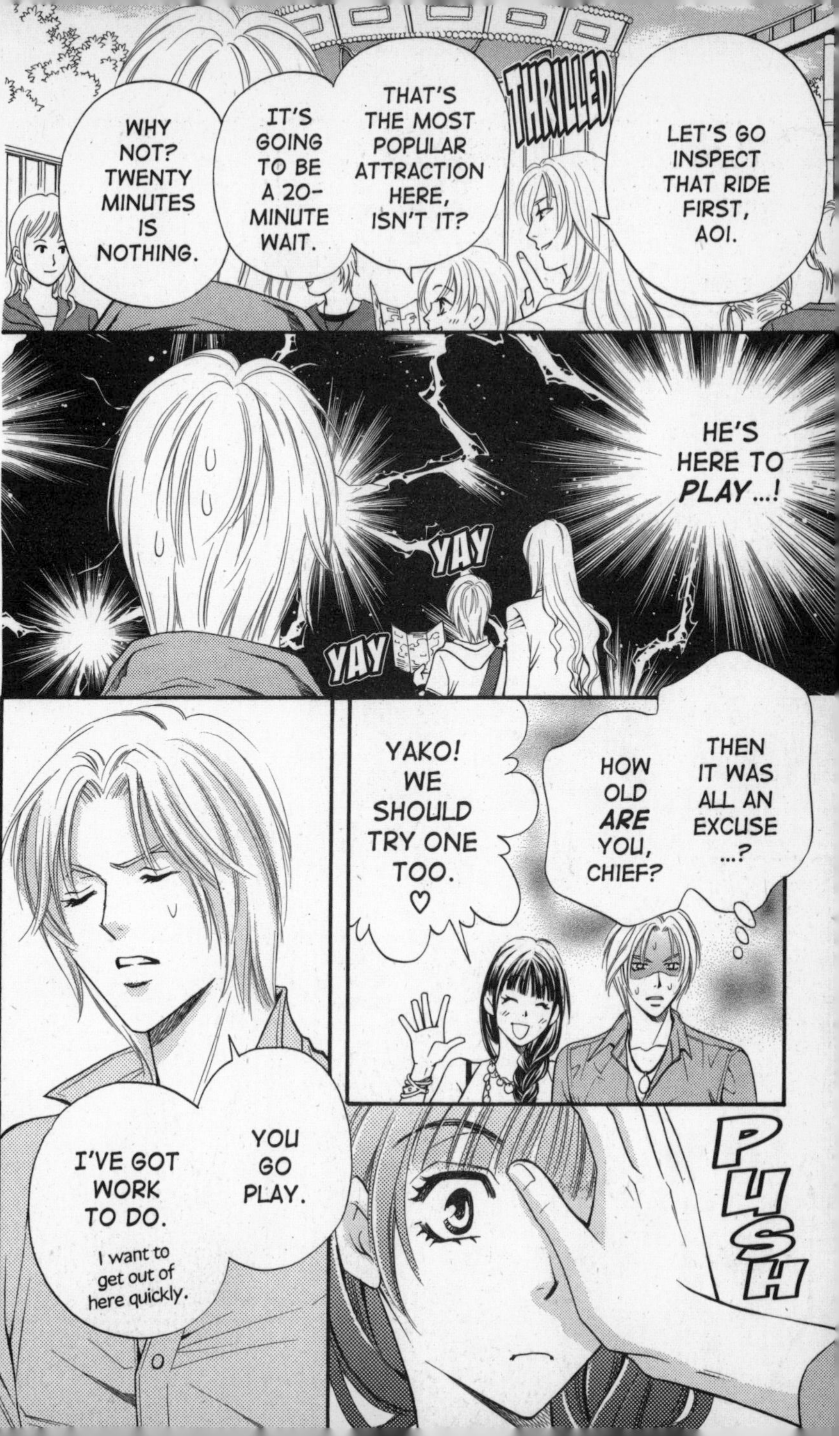
THRILLED
LET'S GO INSPECT THAT RIDE FIRST, AOI.
THAT'S THE MOST POPULAR ATTRACTION HERE, ISN'T IT?
IT'S GOING TO BE A 20-MINUTE WAIT.
WHY NOT? TWENTY MINUTES IS NOTHING.
HE'S HERE TO PLAY...!
YAY
YAY
THEN IT WAS ALL AN EXCUSE ...?
HOW OLD ARE YOU, CHIEF?
YAKO! WE SHOULD TRY ONE TOO. ♡
PUSH
YOU GO PLAY.
I'VE GOT WORK TO DO.
I want to get out of here quickly.

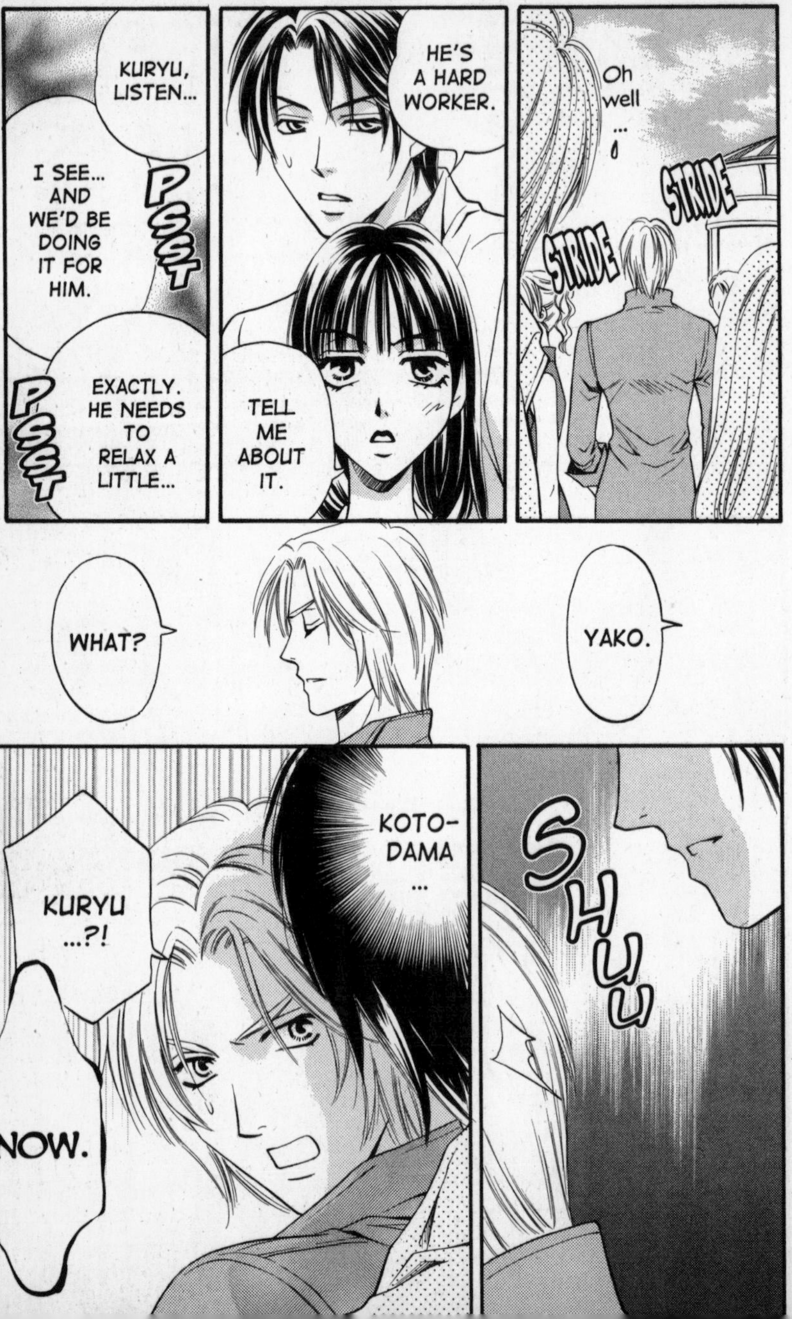
STRIDE
Oh well...
STRIDE
HE'S A HARD WORKER.
TELL ME ABOUT IT.
KURYU, LISTEN...
I SEE... AND WE'D BE DOING IT FOR HIM.
PSST
EXACTLY. HE NEEDS TO RELAX A LITTLE...
PSST
YAKO.
WHAT?
SHUU
KOTO-DAMA...
KURYU...?!
NOW.

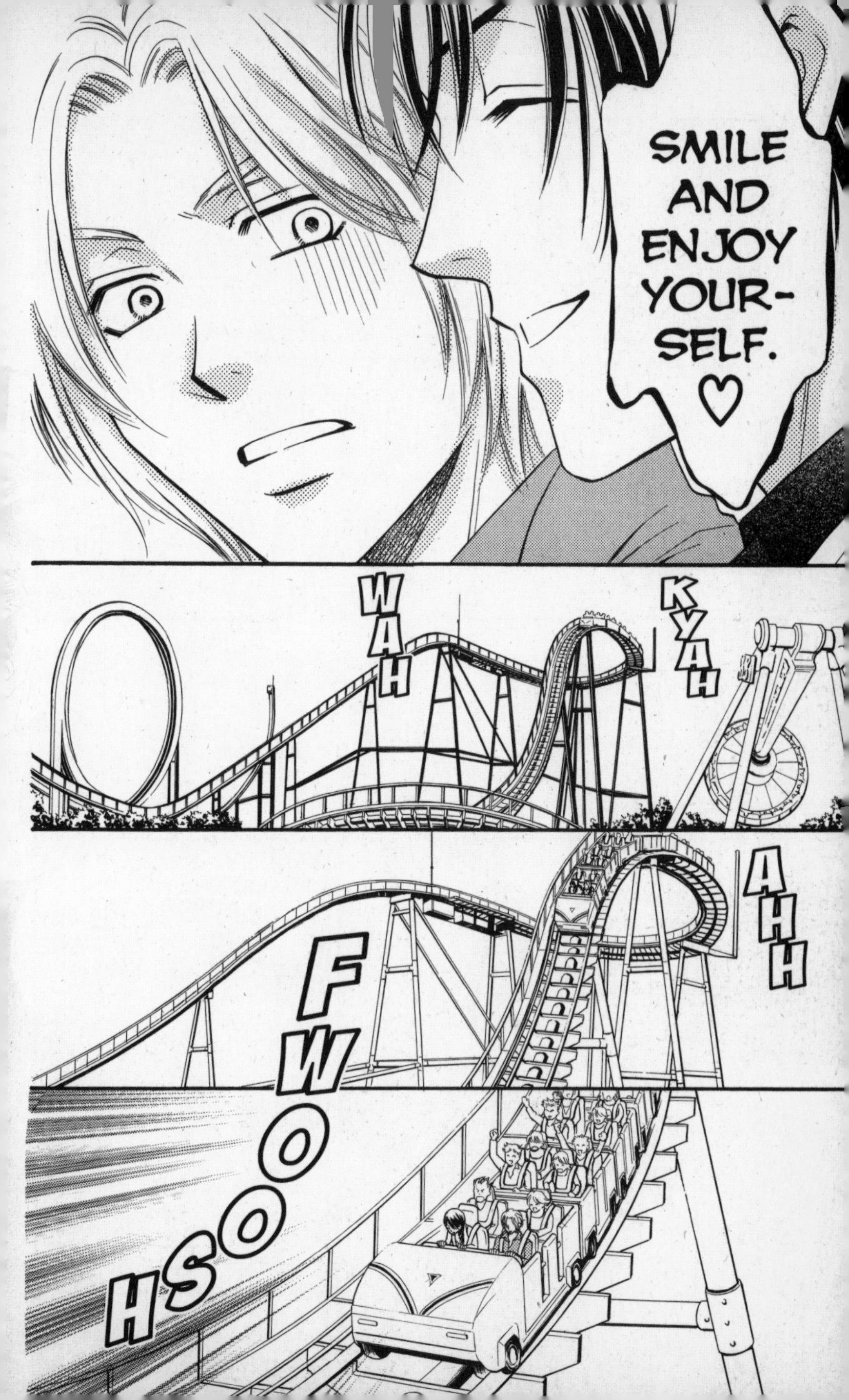
SMILE AND ENJOY YOURSELF. ♥
KYAH
WAH
AHH
FWOOSH

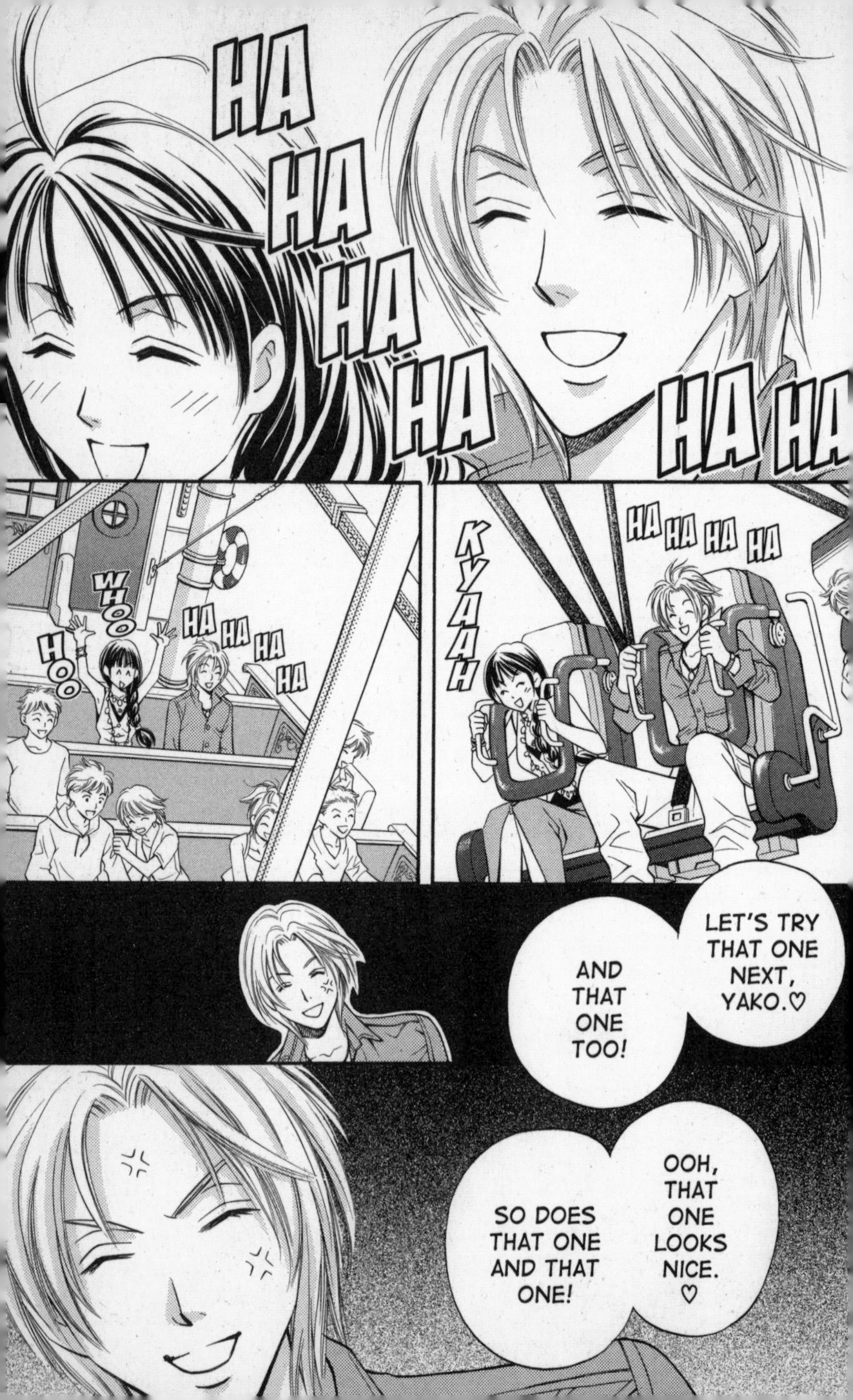
HA HA HA HA
HA HA
HA HA HA HA
KYAAAH
WHOO
HOO
HA HA HA HA
LET'S TRY THAT ONE NEXT, YAKO.♡
AND THAT ONE TOO!
OOH, THAT ONE LOOKS NICE. ♡
SO DOES THAT ONE AND THAT ONE!

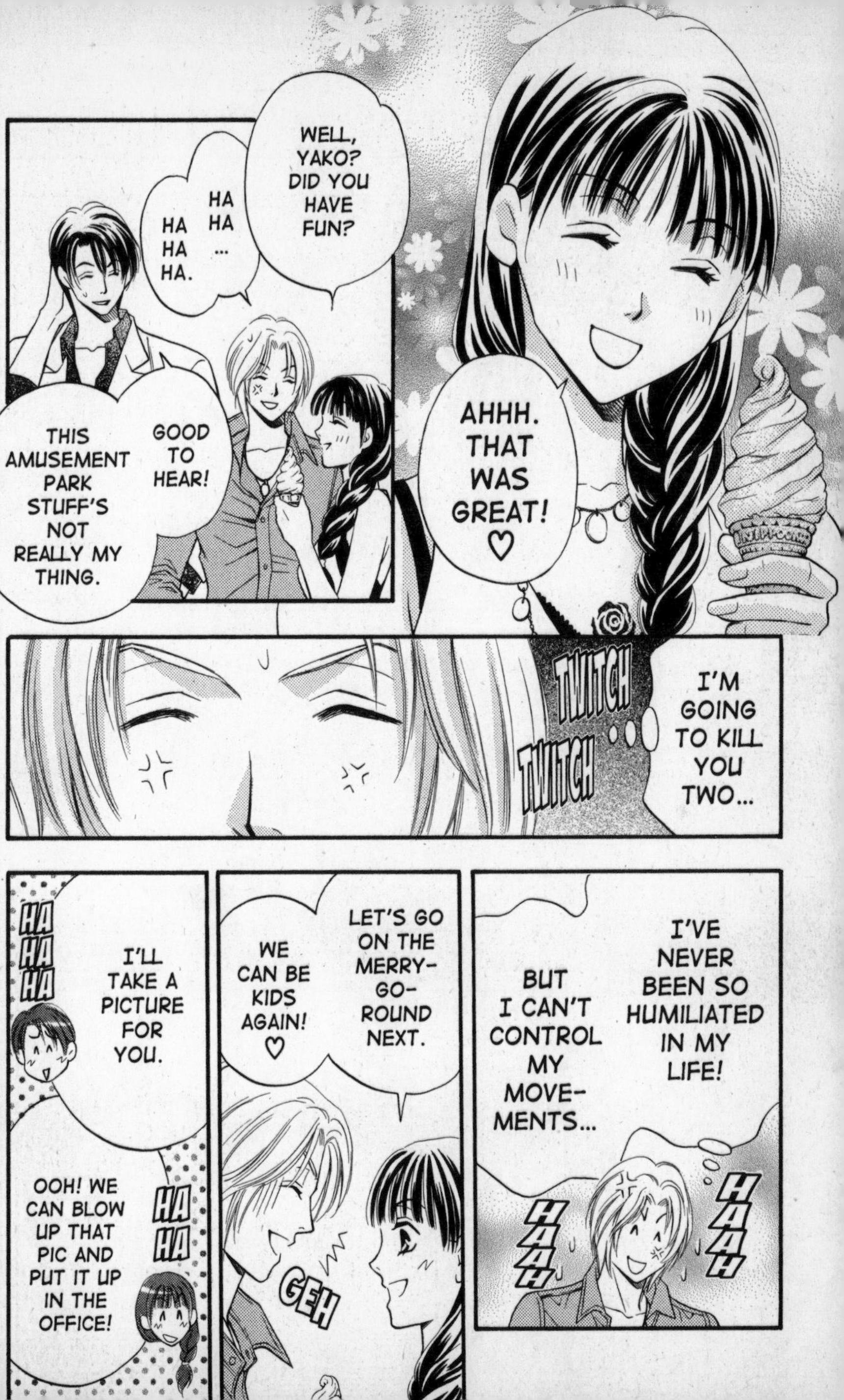
AHHH. THAT WAS GREAT! ♡
WELL, YAKO? DID YOU HAVE FUN?
HA HA ...
HA HA HA.
GOOD TO HEAR!
THIS AMUSEMENT PARK STUFF'S NOT REALLY MY THING.
TWITCH
TWITCH
I'M GOING TO KILL YOU TWO...
I'VE NEVER BEEN SO HUMILIATED IN MY LIFE!
BUT I CAN'T CONTROL MY MOVEMENTS...
HAAH
HAAH
LET'S GO ON THE MERRY-GO-ROUND NEXT.
WE CAN BE KIDS AGAIN! ♡
GEH
HA HA HA
I'LL TAKE A PICTURE FOR YOU.
HA HA
OOH! WE CAN BLOW UP THAT PIC AND PUT IT UP IN THE OFFICE!

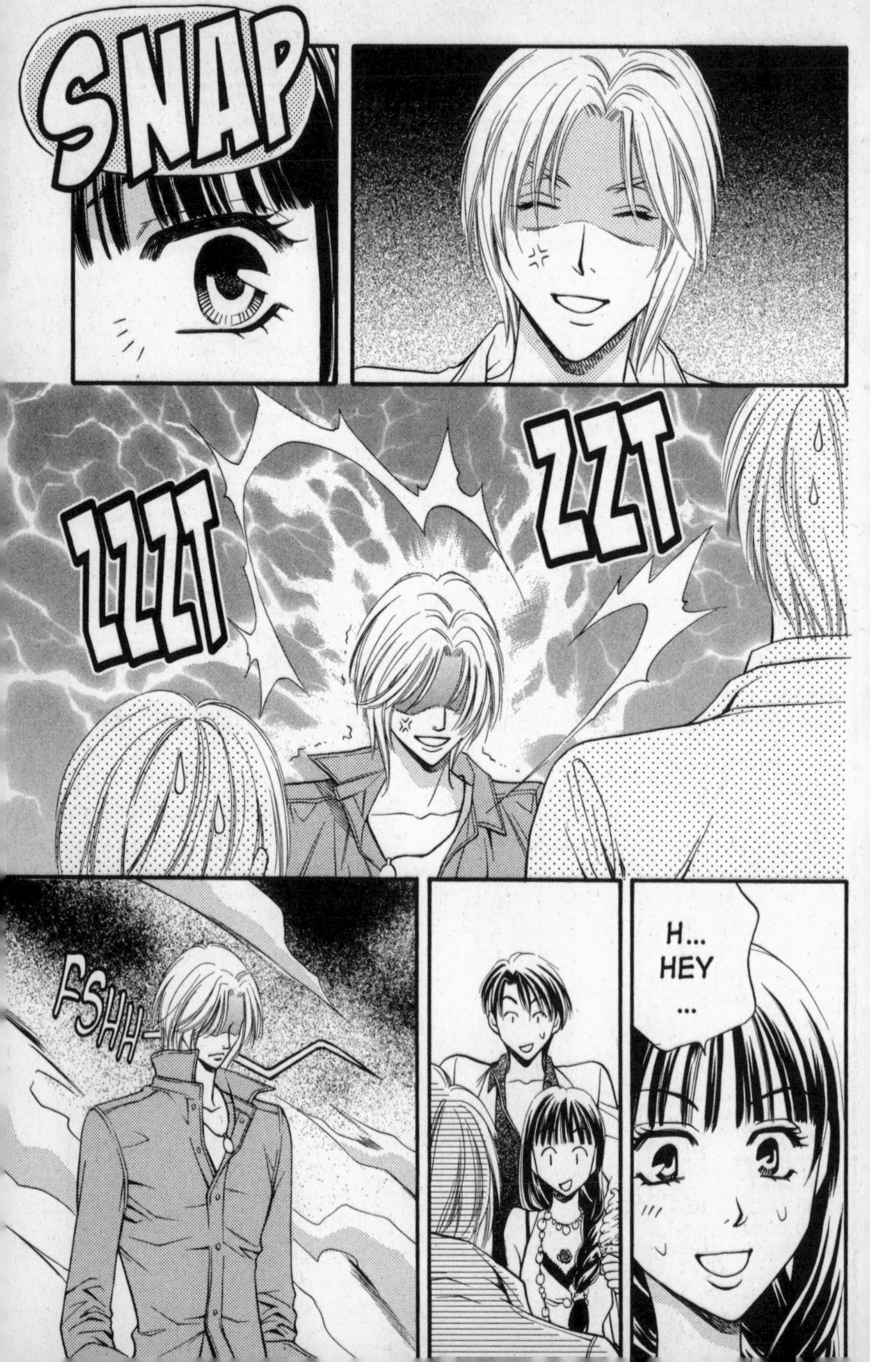
SNAP
ZZT
ZZZT
H... HEY ...
FSHH-

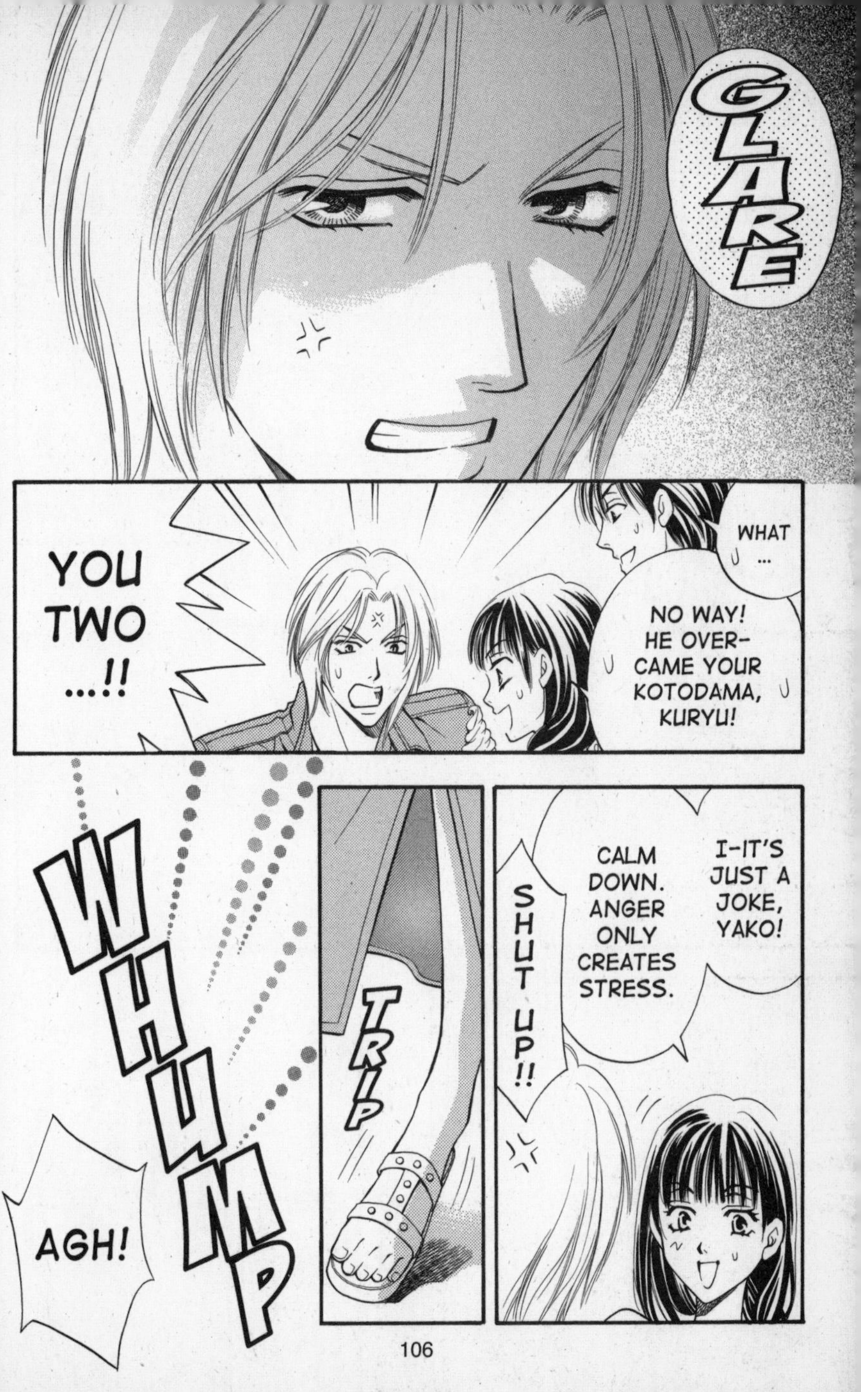
GLARE
WHAT ...
NO WAY! HE OVER-CAME YOUR KOTODAMA, KURYU!
YOU TWO ...!!
I-IT'S JUST A JOKE, YAKO!
CALM DOWN. ANGER ONLY CREATES STRESS.
SHUT UP!!
TRIP
WHUMP
AGH!

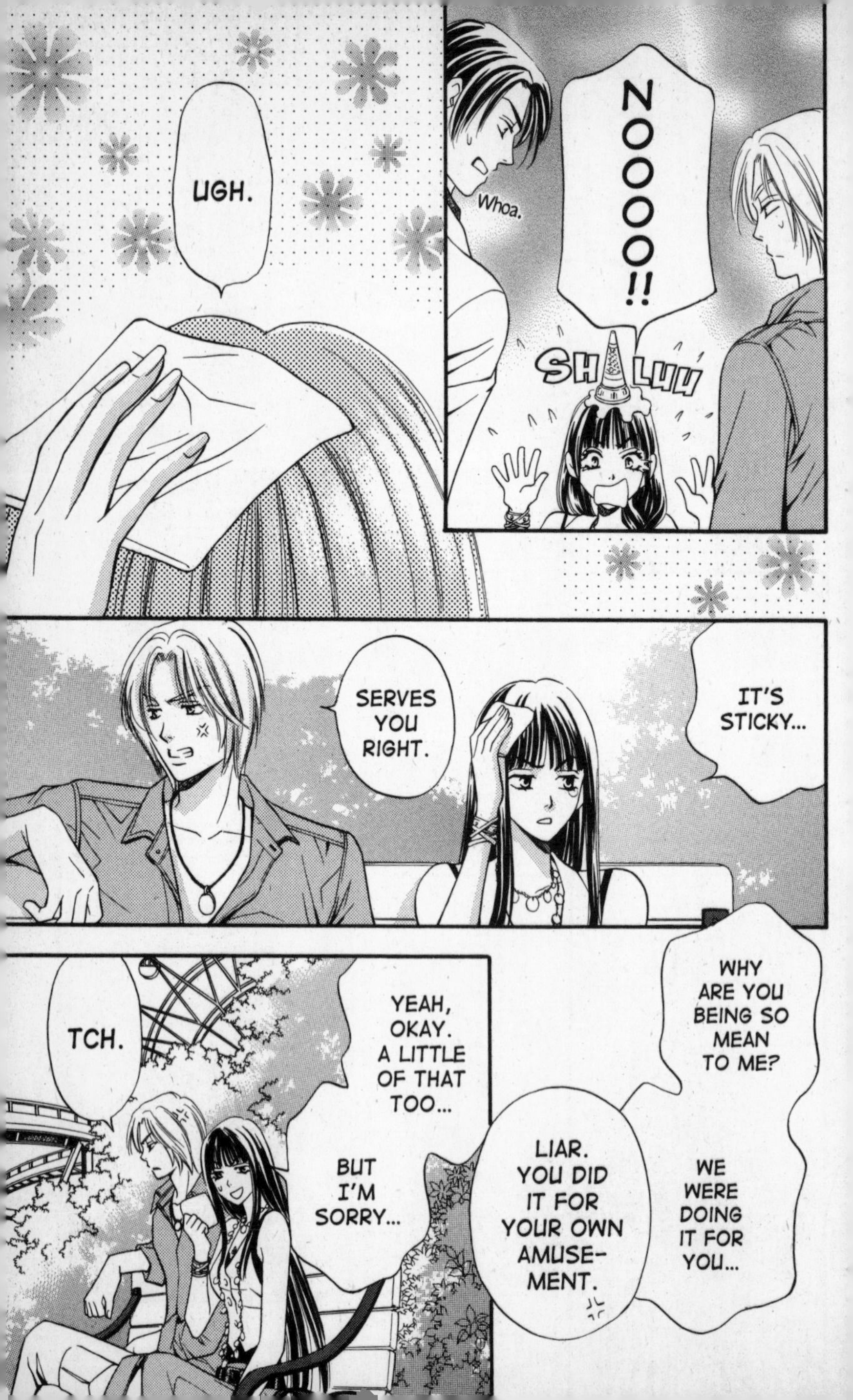
NOOOO!!
Whoa.
SH LUH
UGH.
IT'S STICKY...
SERVES YOU RIGHT.
WHY ARE YOU BEING SO MEAN TO ME?
WE WERE DOING IT FOR YOU...
LIAR. YOU DID IT FOR YOUR OWN AMUSE-MENT.
YEAH, OKAY. A LITTLE OF THAT TOO...
BUT I'M SORRY...
TCH.

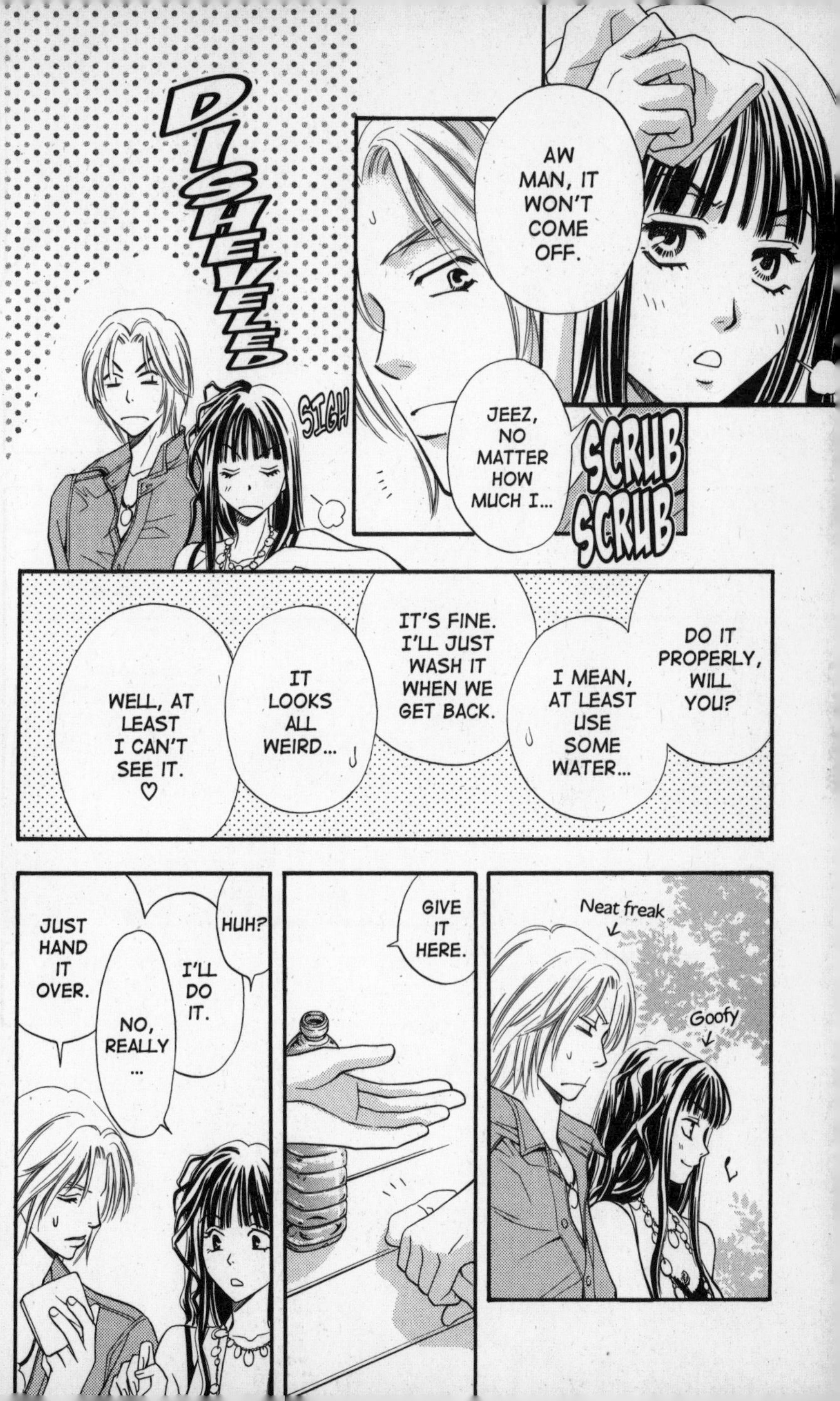
AW MAN, IT WON'T COME OFF.
JEEZ, NO MATTER HOW MUCH I...
SCRUB SCRUB
DISHEVELED
SIGH
DO IT PROPERLY, WILL YOU?
I MEAN, AT LEAST USE SOME WATER...
IT'S FINE. I'LL JUST WASH IT WHEN WE GET BACK.
IT LOOKS ALL WEIRD...
WELL, AT LEAST I CAN'T SEE IT. ♡
Neat freak
Goofy
GIVE IT HERE.
HUH?
I'LL DO IT.
NO, REALLY...
JUST HAND IT OVER.

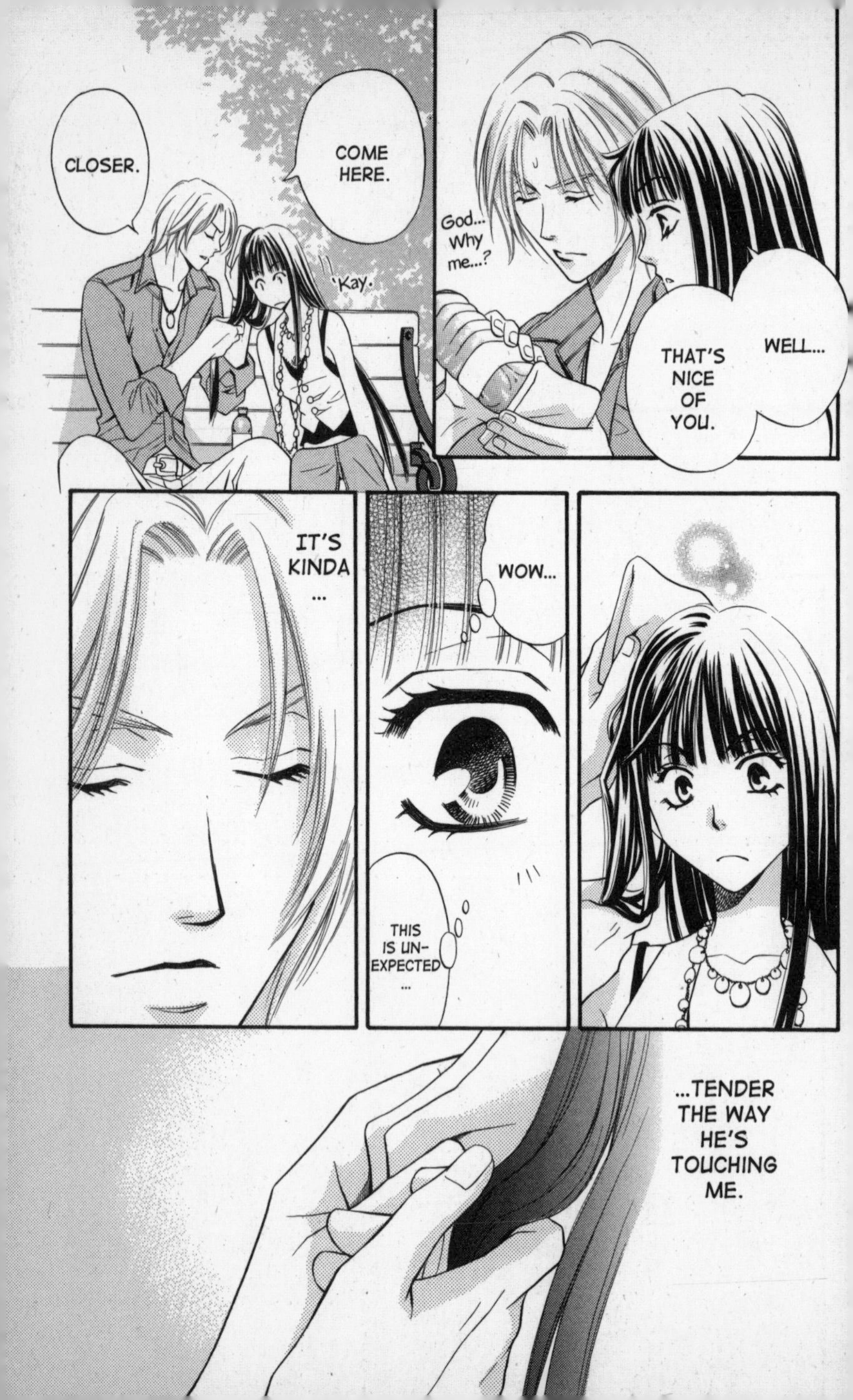
WELL...
THAT'S NICE OF YOU.
God... Why me...?
COME HERE.
CLOSER.
'Kay.
WOW...
THIS IS UN-EXPECTED...
IT'S KINDA ...
...TENDER THE WAY HE'S TOUCHING ME.

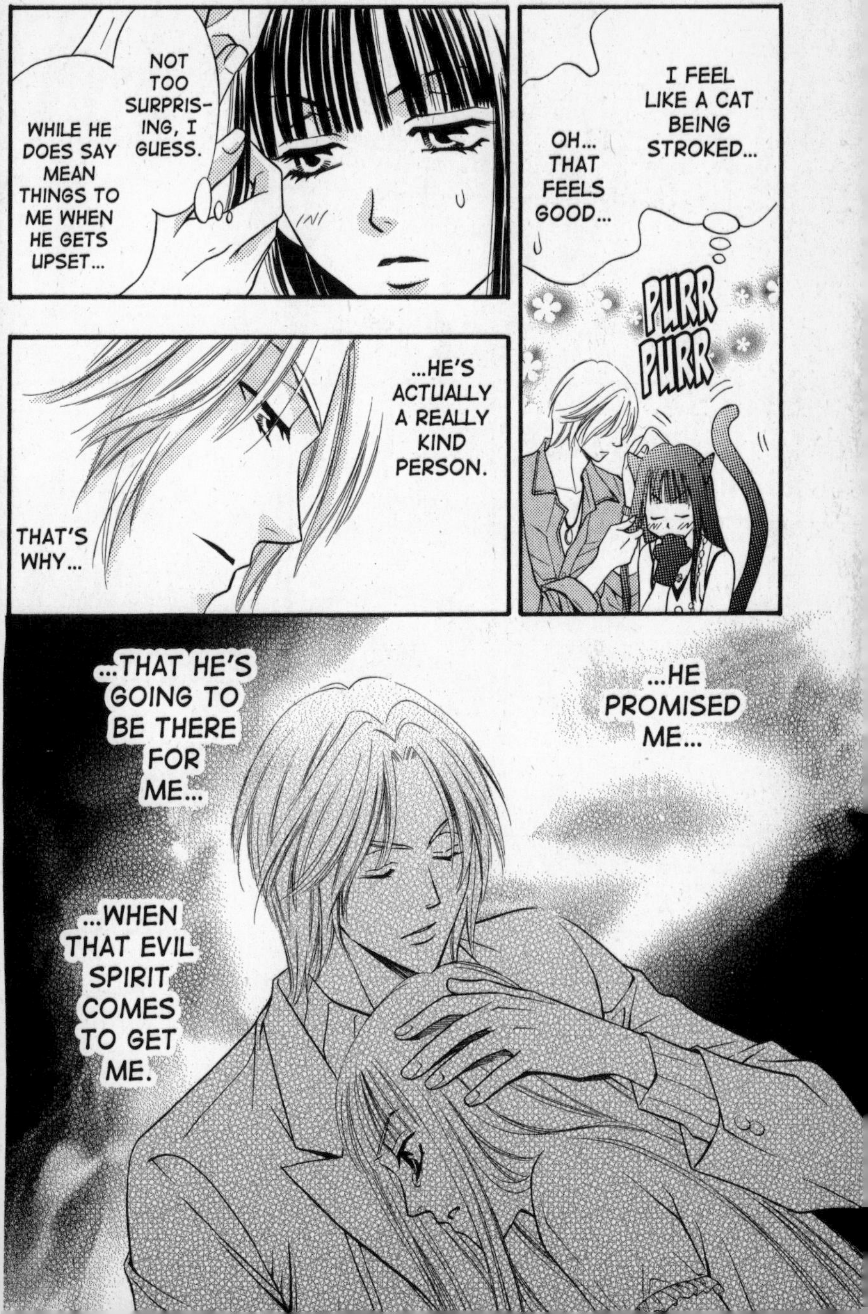
I FEEL LIKE A CAT BEING STROKED...
OH... THAT FEELS GOOD...
PURR PURR
NOT TOO SURPRIS- ING, I GUESS.
WHILE HE DOES SAY MEAN THINGS TO ME WHEN HE GETS UPSET...
...HE'S ACTUALLY A REALLY KIND PERSON.
THAT'S WHY...
...HE PROMISED ME...
...THAT HE'S GOING TO BE THERE FOR ME...
...WHEN THAT EVIL SPIRIT COMES TO GET ME.

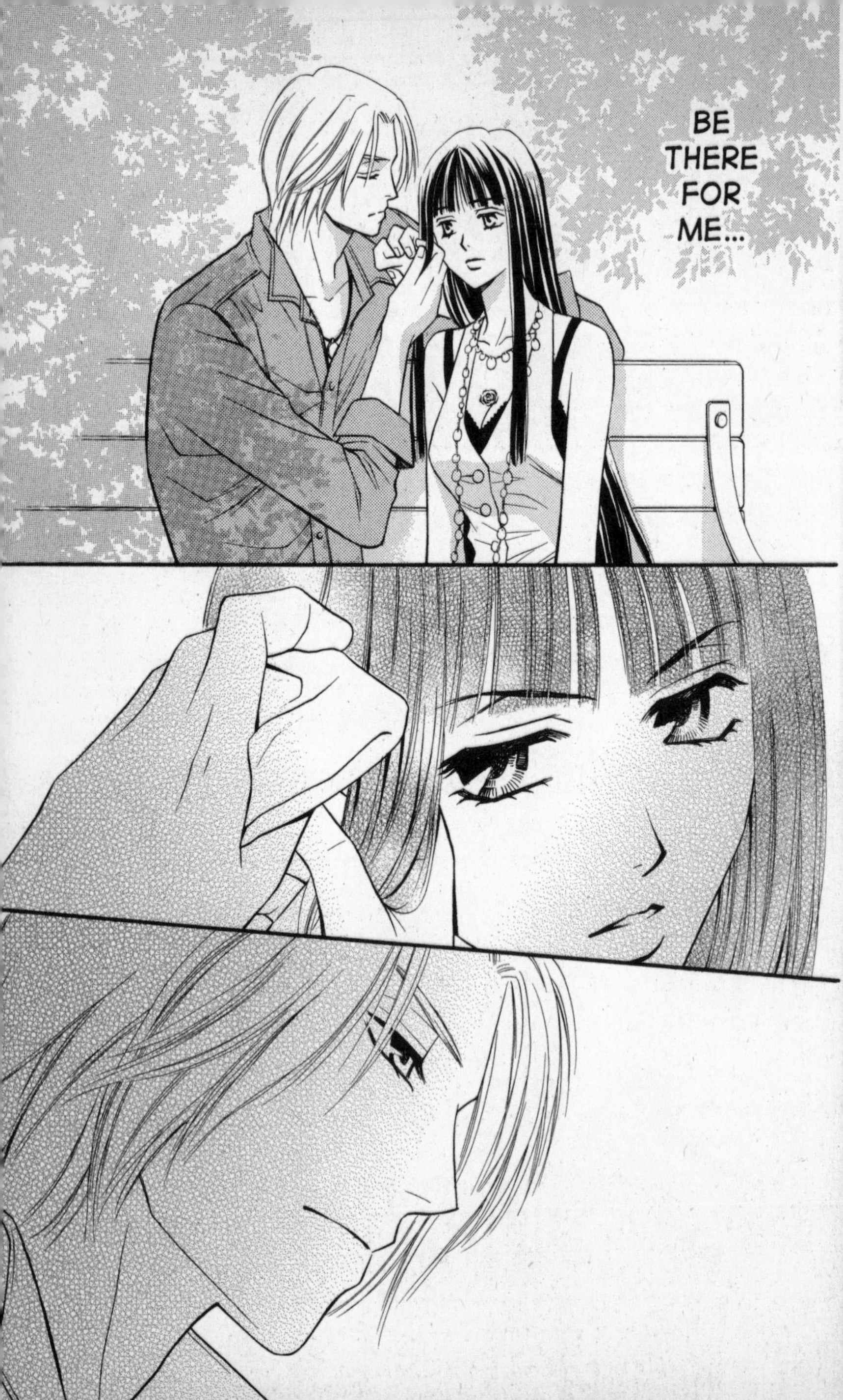
BE THERE FOR ME...

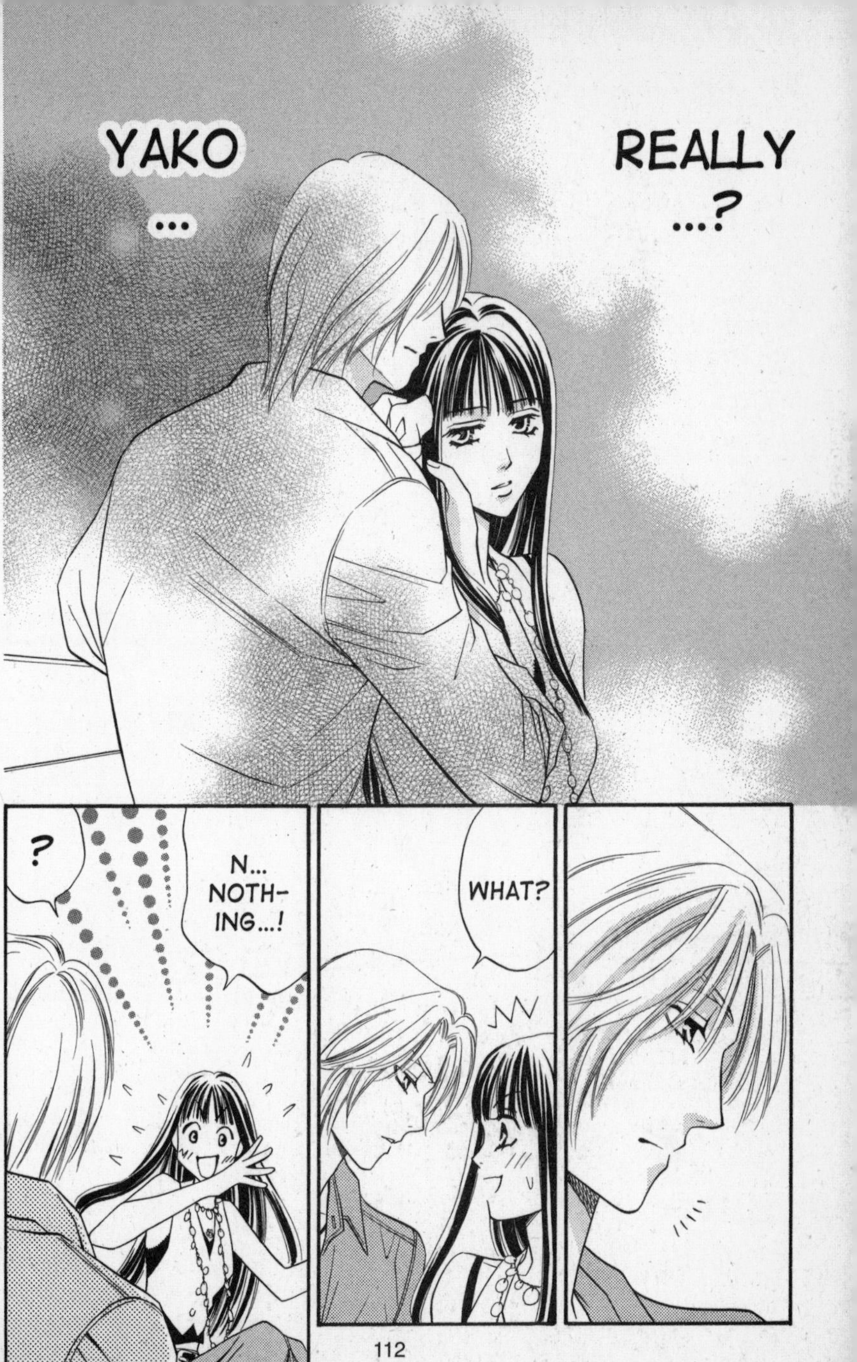
REALLY ...?
YAKO ...
WHAT?
N... NOTH-ING...!
?

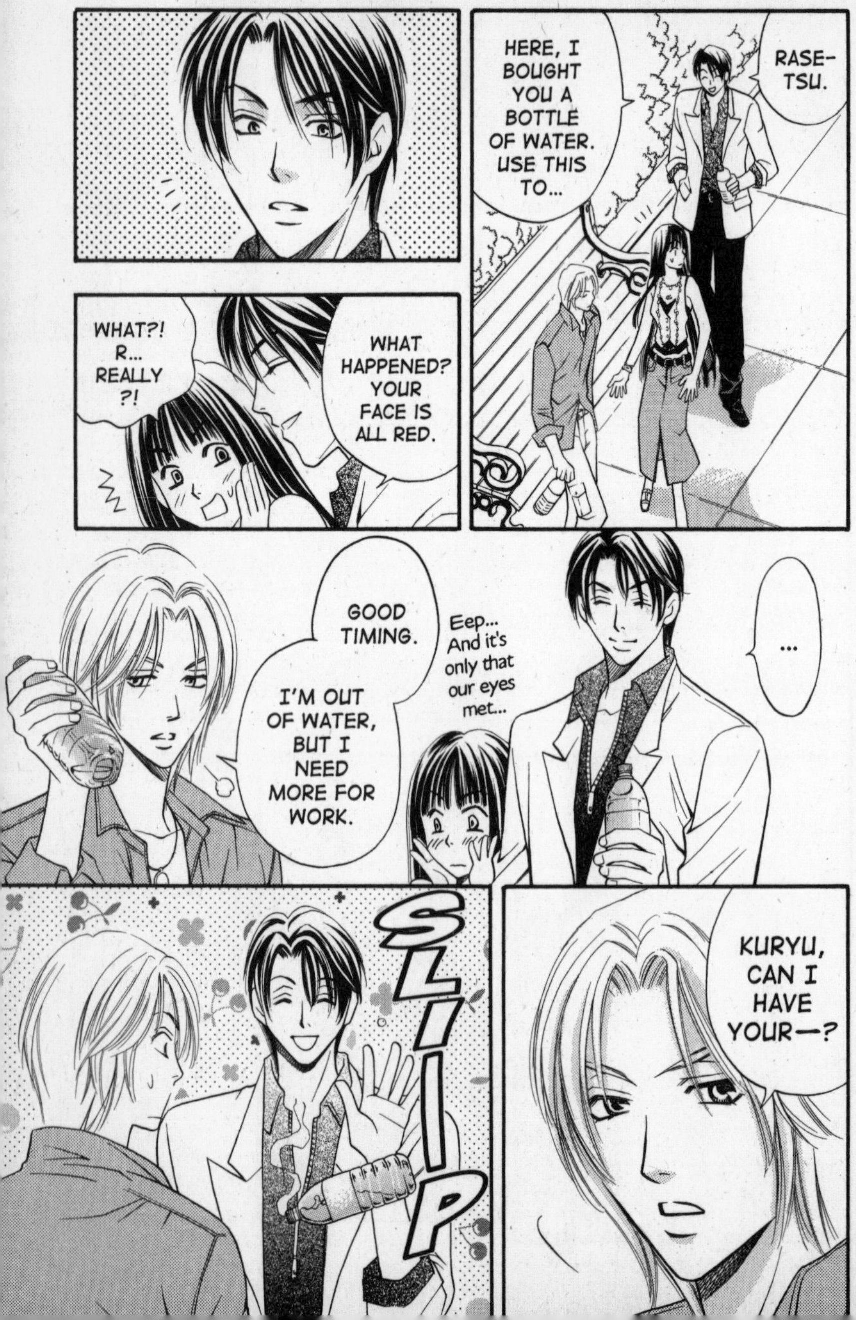
RASE-TSU.
HERE, I BOUGHT YOU A BOTTLE OF WATER. USE THIS TO...
WHAT HAPPENED? YOUR FACE IS ALL RED.
WHAT?! R... REALLY ?!
...
Eep... And it's only that our eyes met...
GOOD TIMING.
I'M OUT OF WATER, BUT I NEED MORE FOR WORK.
KURYU, CAN I HAVE YOUR—?
SLIIP

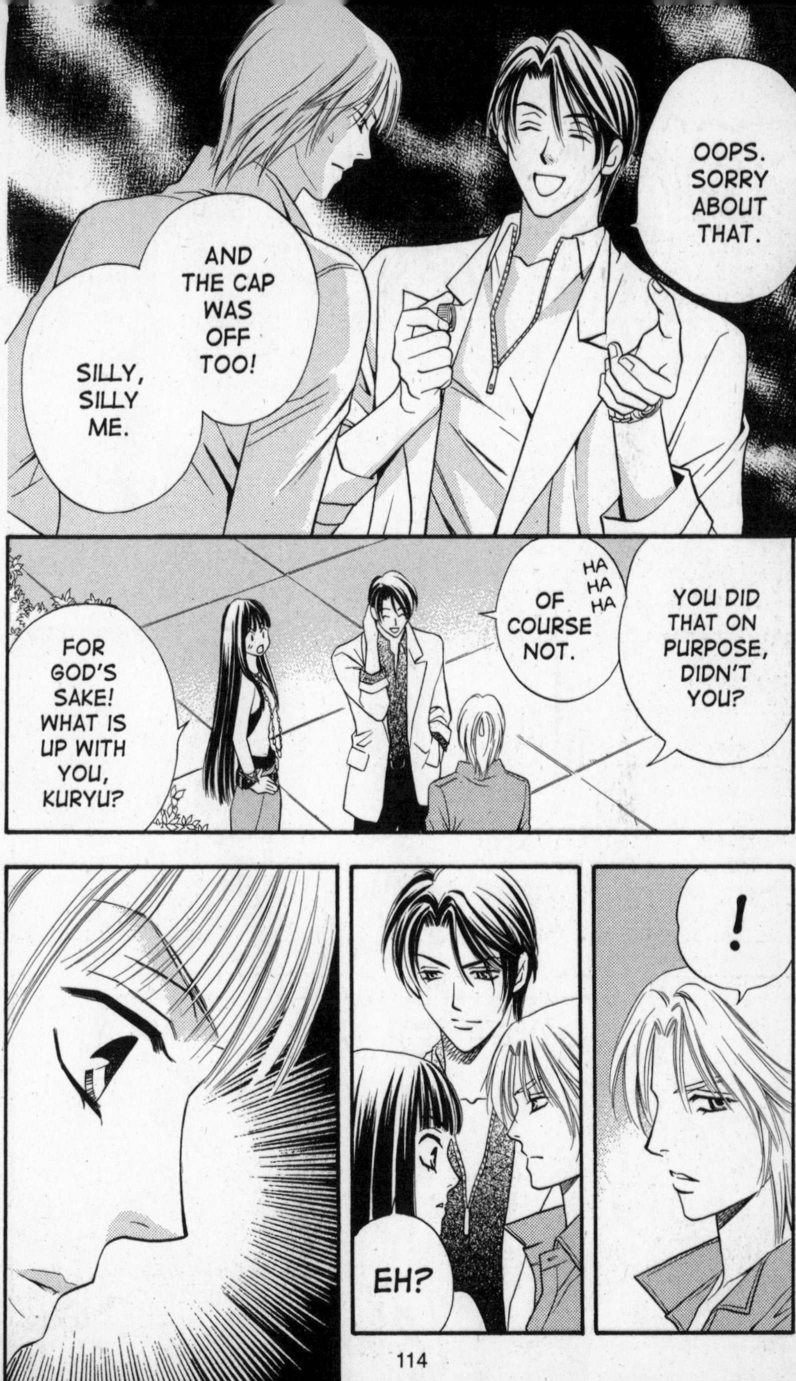
OOPS. SORRY ABOUT THAT.
AND THE CAP WAS OFF TOO!
SILLY, SILLY ME.
YOU DID THAT ON PURPOSE, DIDN'T YOU?
HA HA HA
OF COURSE NOT.
FOR GOD'S SAKE! WHAT IS UP WITH YOU, KURYU?
!
EH?

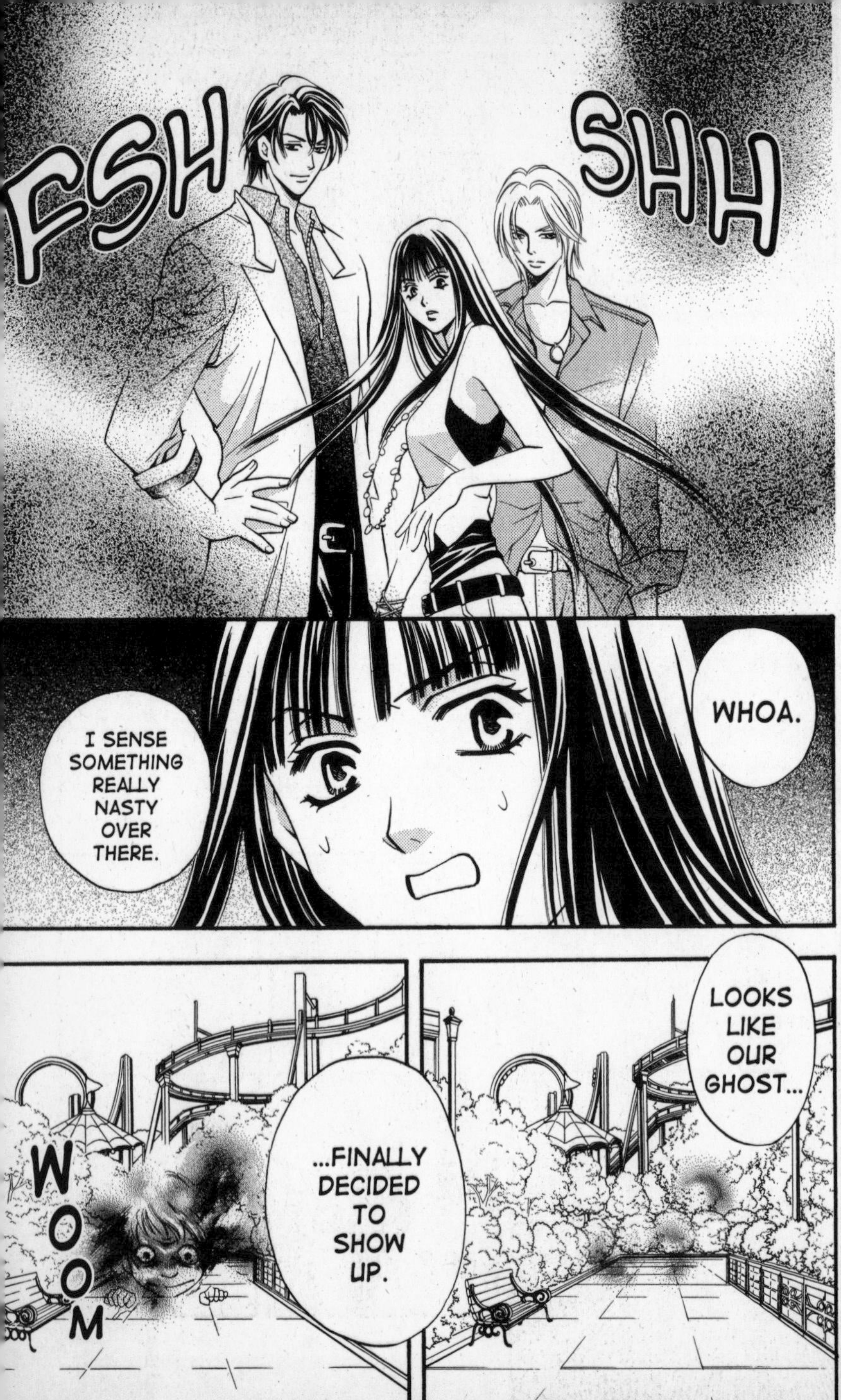
SHH
FSH
WHOA.
I SENSE SOMETHING REALLY NASTY OVER THERE.
LOOKS LIKE OUR GHOST...
...FINALLY DECIDED TO SHOW UP.
WOOM

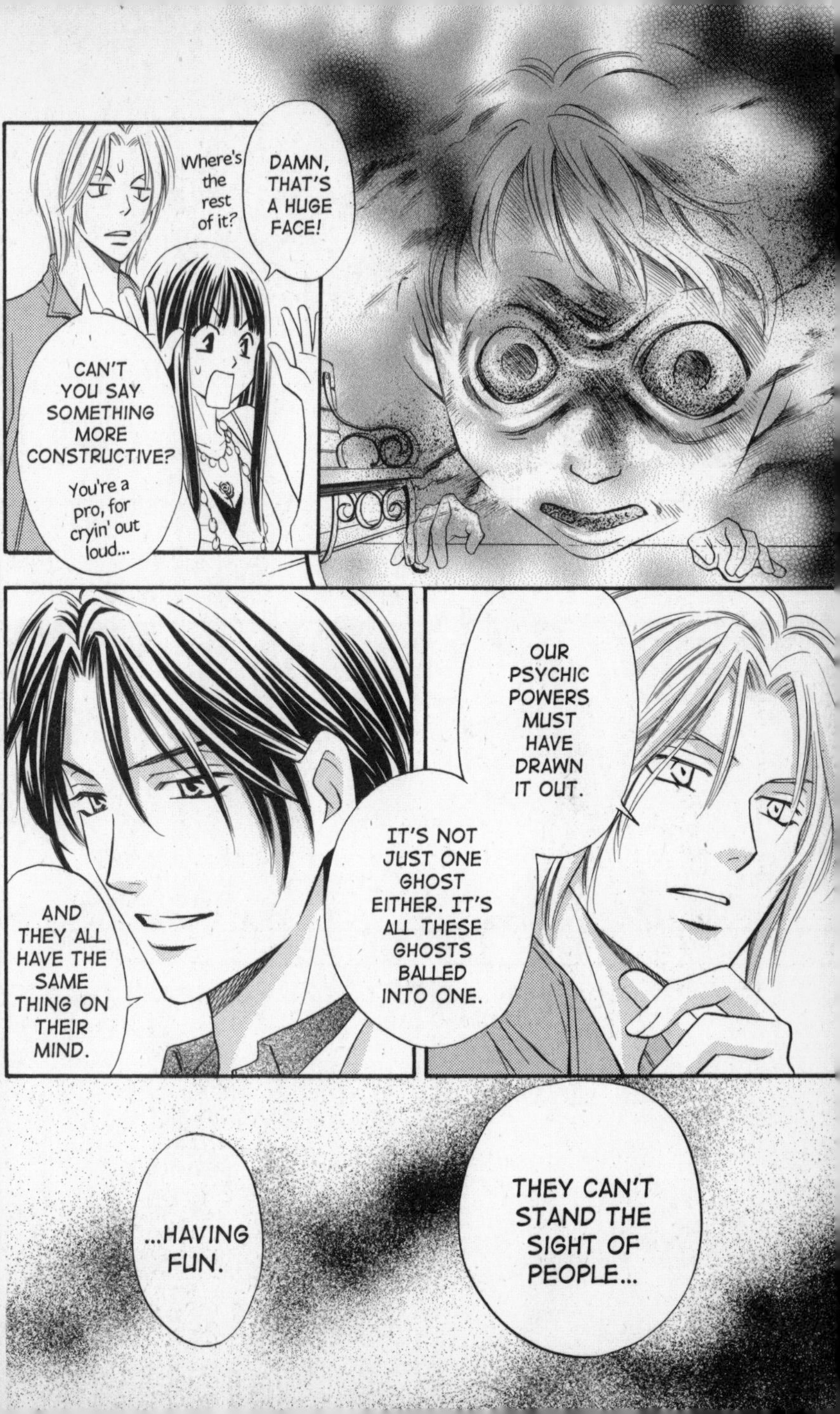
DAMN, THAT'S A HUGE FACE!
Where's the rest of it?
CAN'T YOU SAY SOMETHING MORE CONSTRUCTIVE?
You're a pro, for cryin' out loud...
OUR PSYCHIC POWERS MUST HAVE DRAWN IT OUT.
IT'S NOT JUST ONE GHOST EITHER. IT'S ALL THESE GHOSTS BALLED INTO ONE.
AND THEY ALL HAVE THE SAME THING ON THEIR MIND.
THEY CAN'T STAND THE SIGHT OF PEOPLE...
...HAVING FUN.

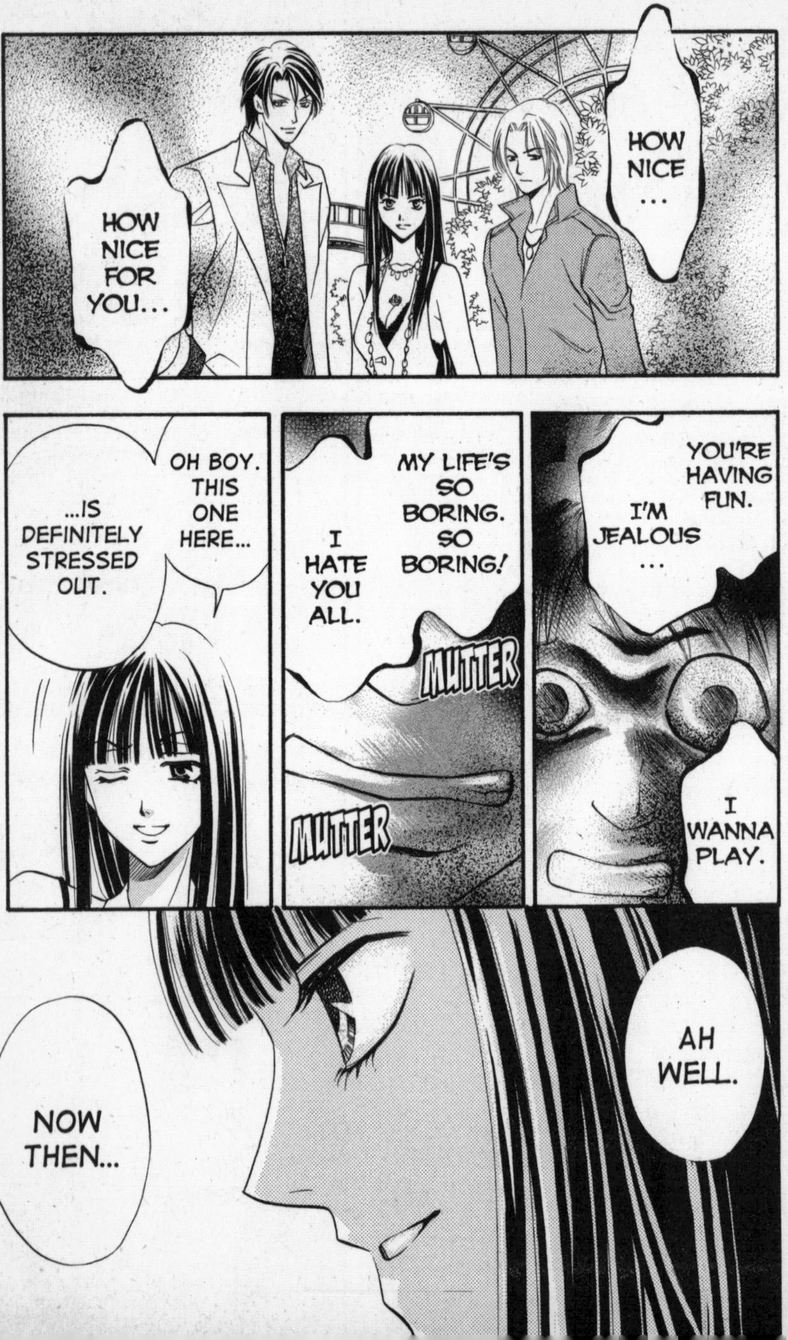
HOW NICE ...
HOW NICE FOR YOU...
YOU'RE HAVING FUN.
I'M JEALOUS ...
I WANNA PLAY.
MY LIFE'S SO BORING. SO BORING!
I HATE YOU ALL.
MUTTER
MUTTER
OH BOY. THIS ONE HERE...
...IS DEFINITELY STRESSED OUT.
AH WELL.
NOW THEN...

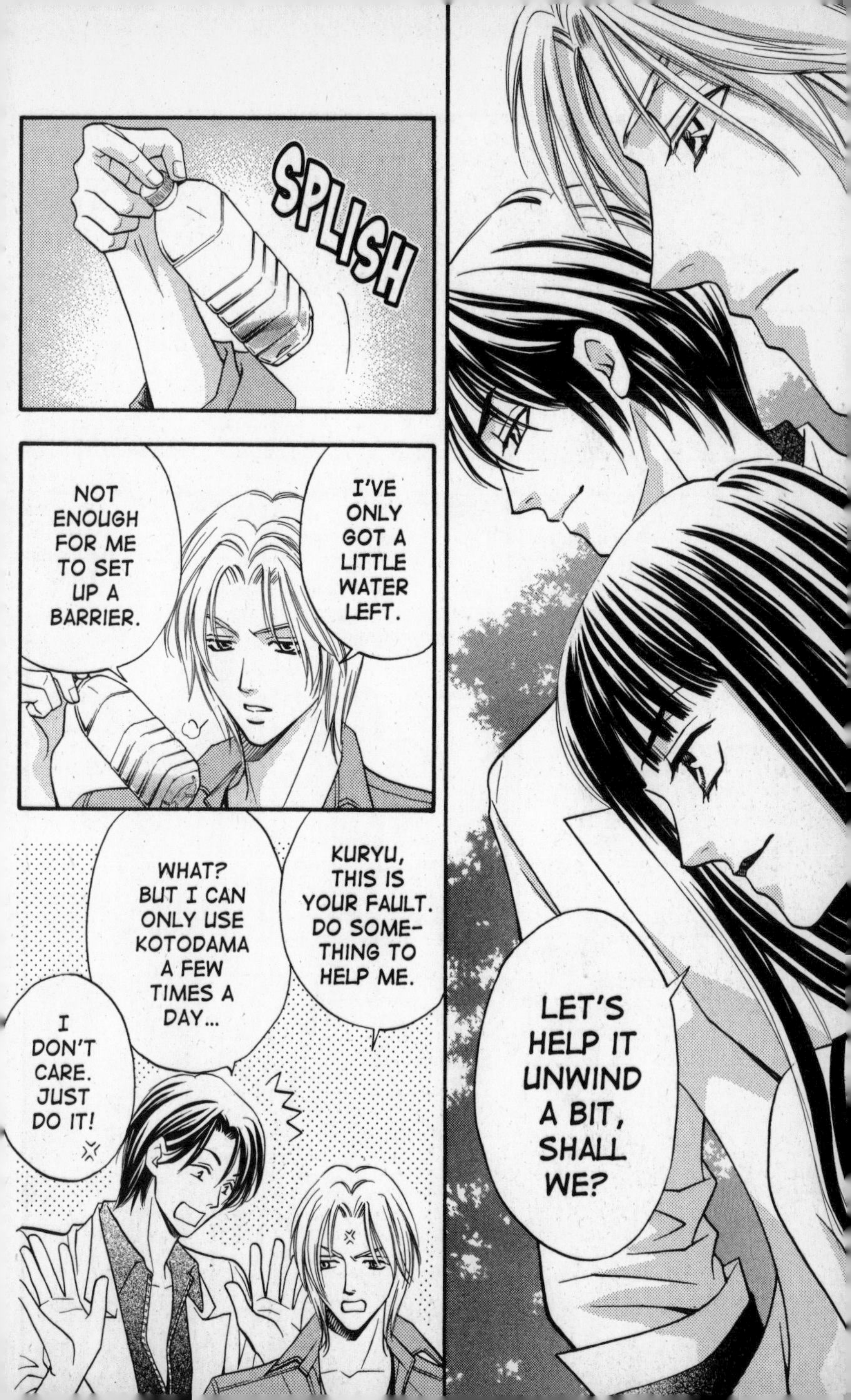
LET'S HELP IT UNWIND A BIT, SHALL WE?
SPLISH
I'VE ONLY GOT A LITTLE WATER LEFT.
NOT ENOUGH FOR ME TO SET UP A BARRIER.
KURYU, THIS IS YOUR FAULT. DO SOME-THING TO HELP ME.
WHAT? BUT I CAN ONLY USE KOTODAMA A FEW TIMES A DAY...
I DON'T CARE. JUST DO IT!

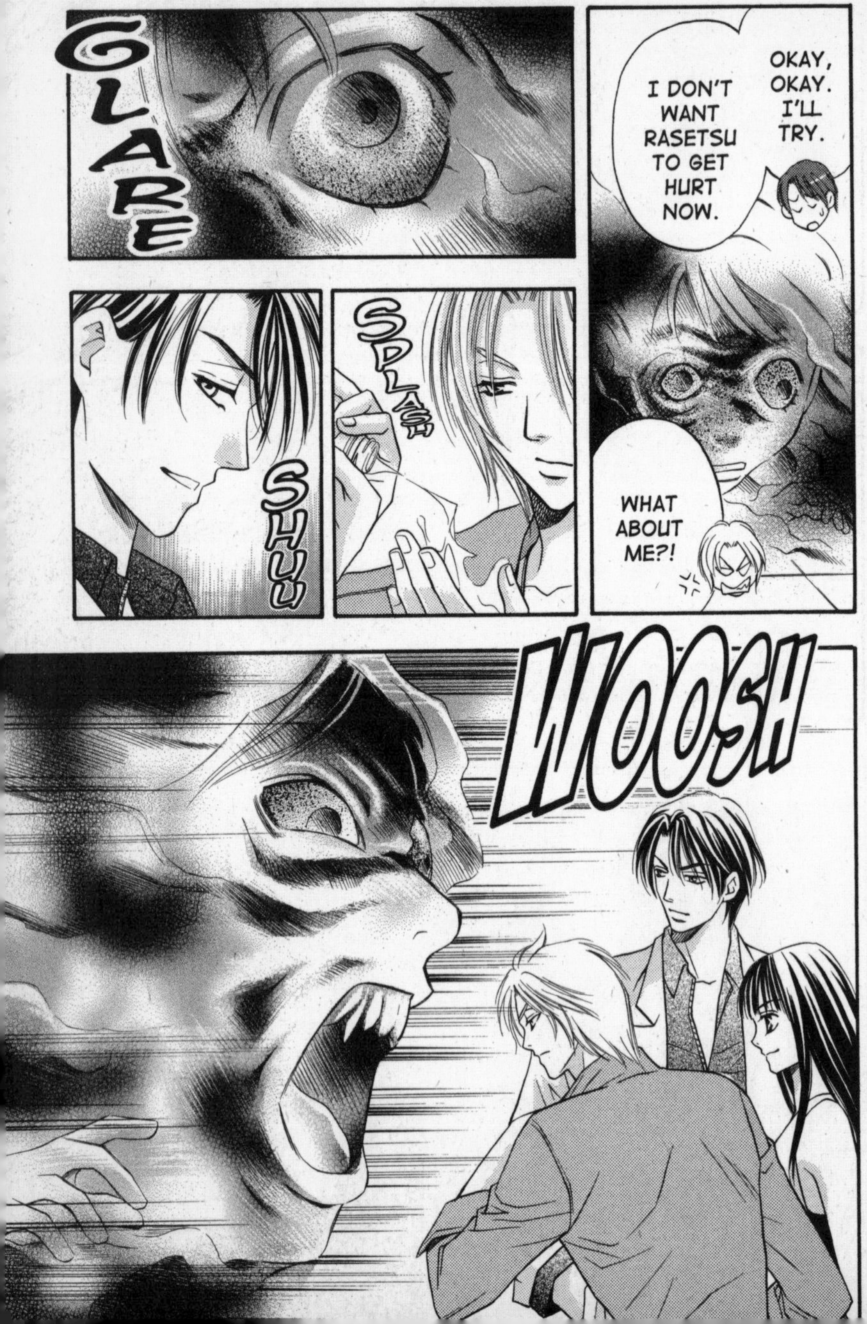
I DON'T WANT RASETSU TO GET HURT NOW.
OKAY, OKAY. I'LL TRY.
WHAT ABOUT ME?!
GLARE
SPLASH
SHUU
WOOSH

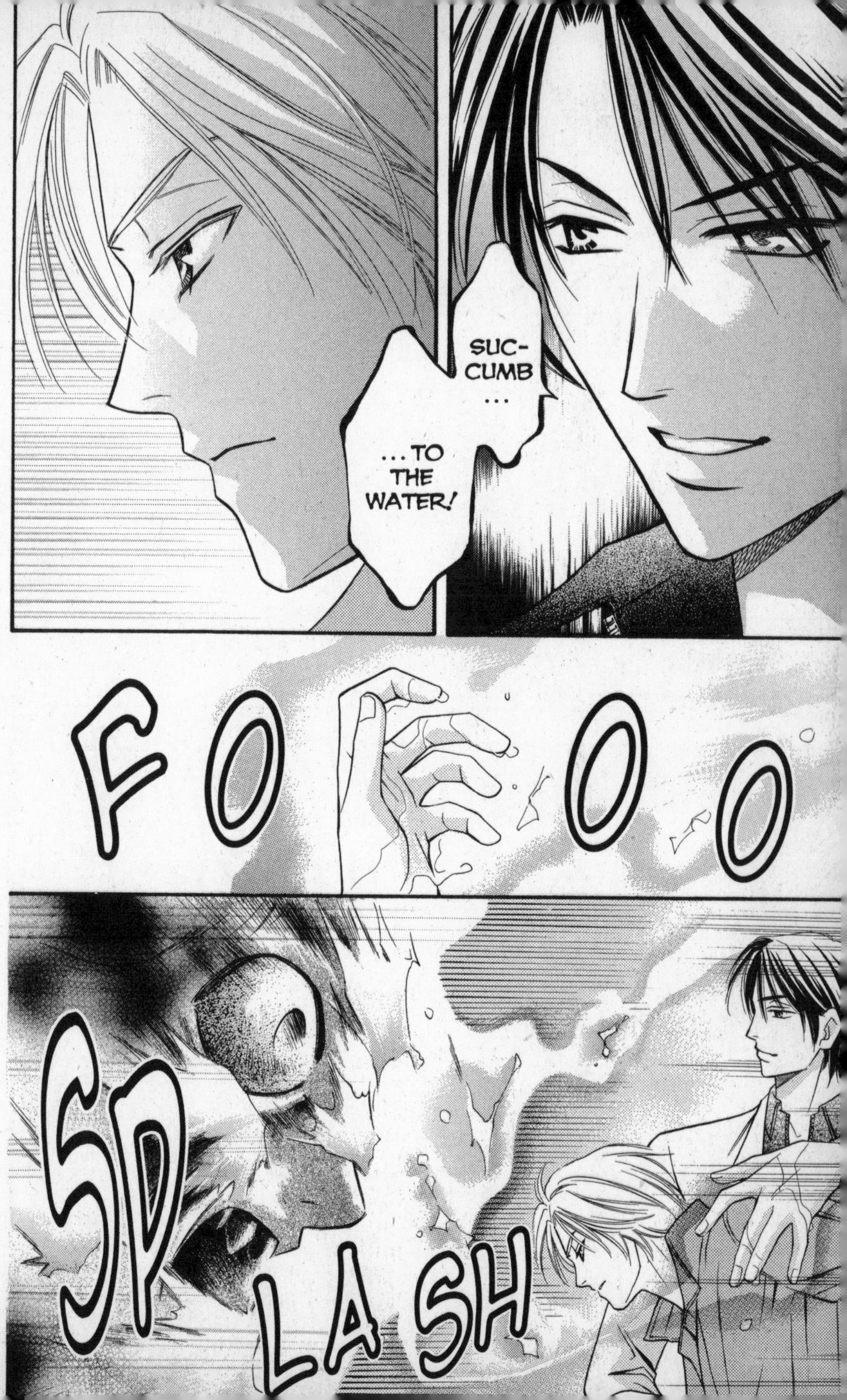
SUC- CUMB ...
... TO THE WATER!
FOOOO
SPLASH

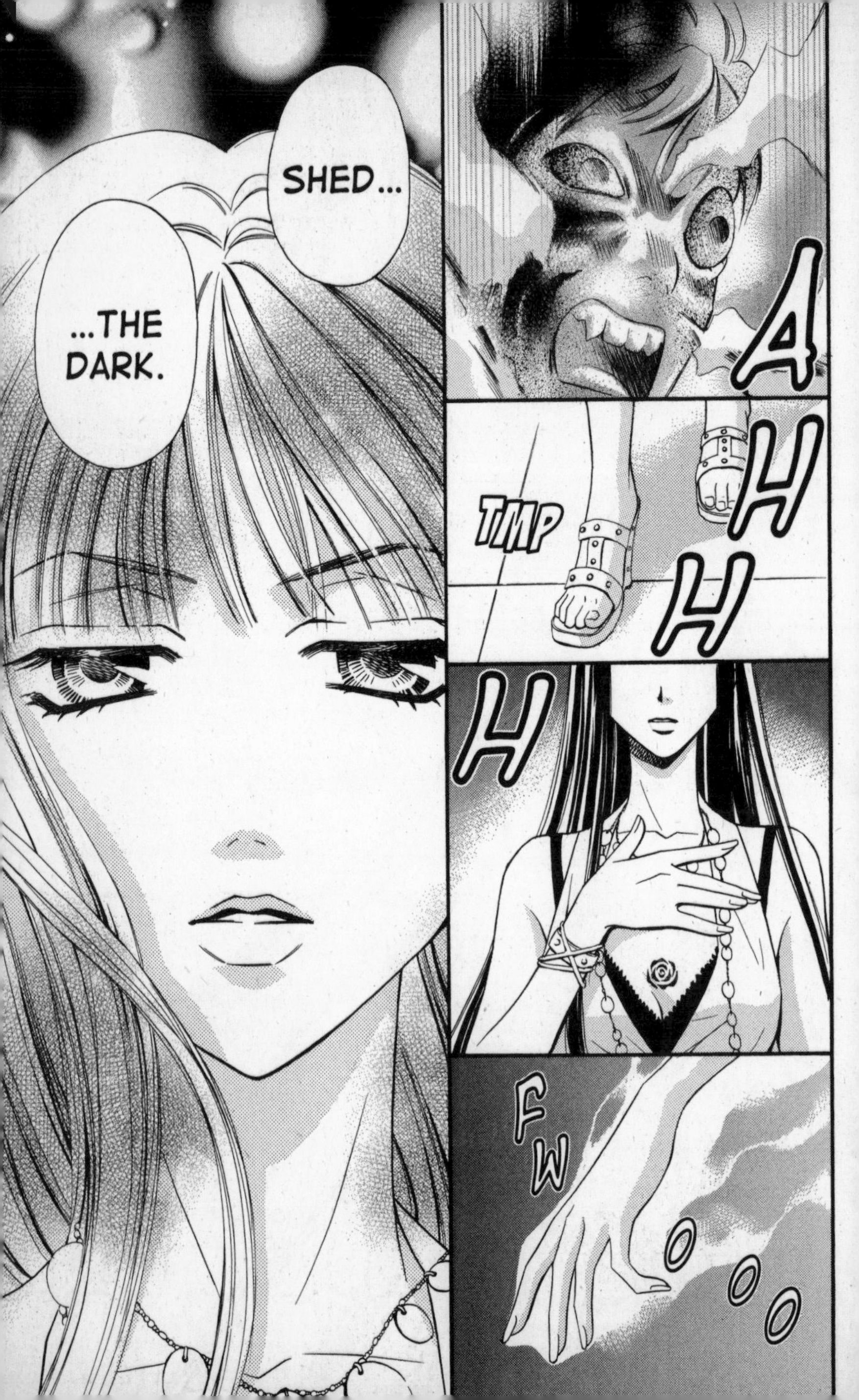
AHHH
TMP
FWOOO
SHED...
...THE DARK.

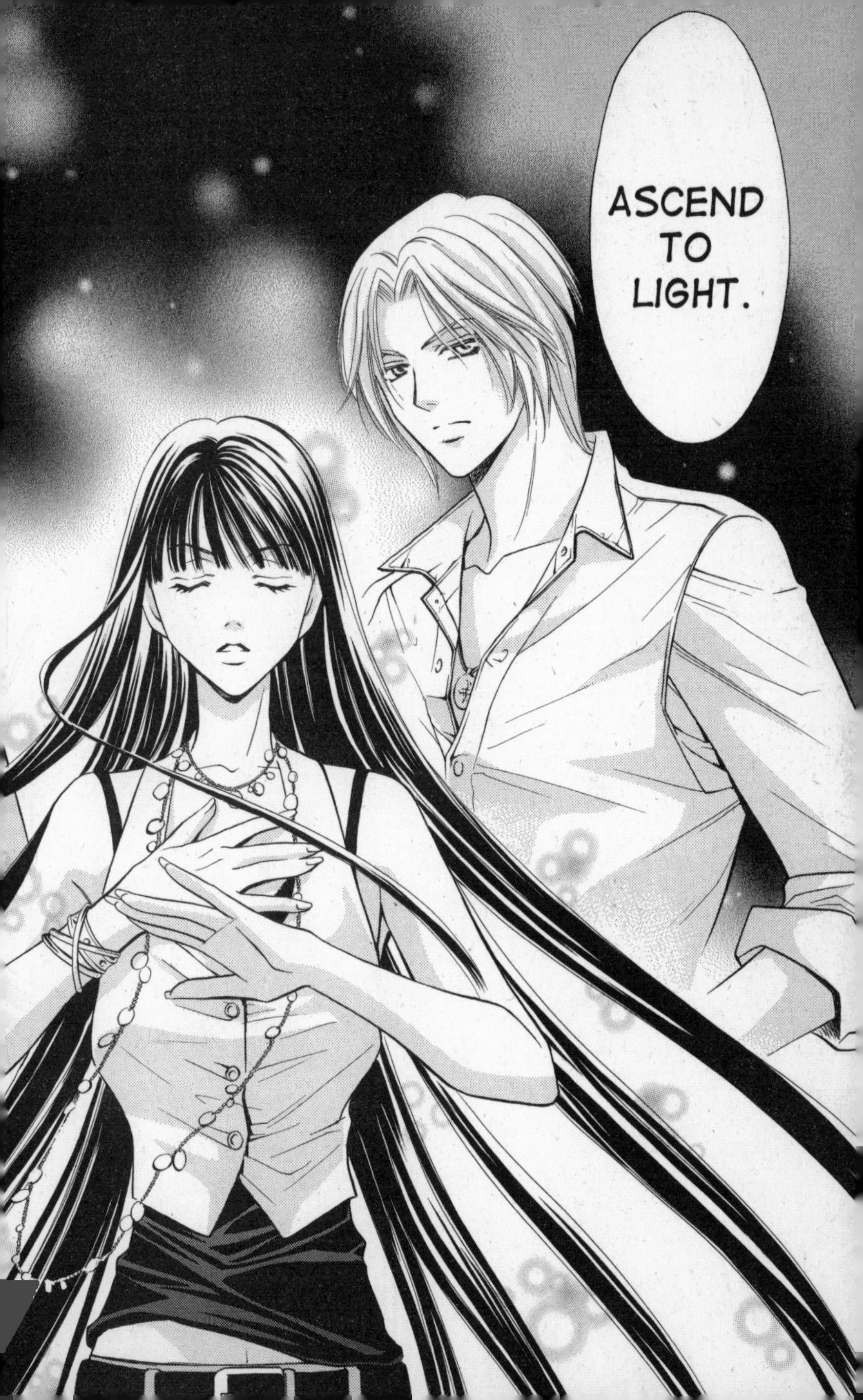
ASCEND TO LIGHT.

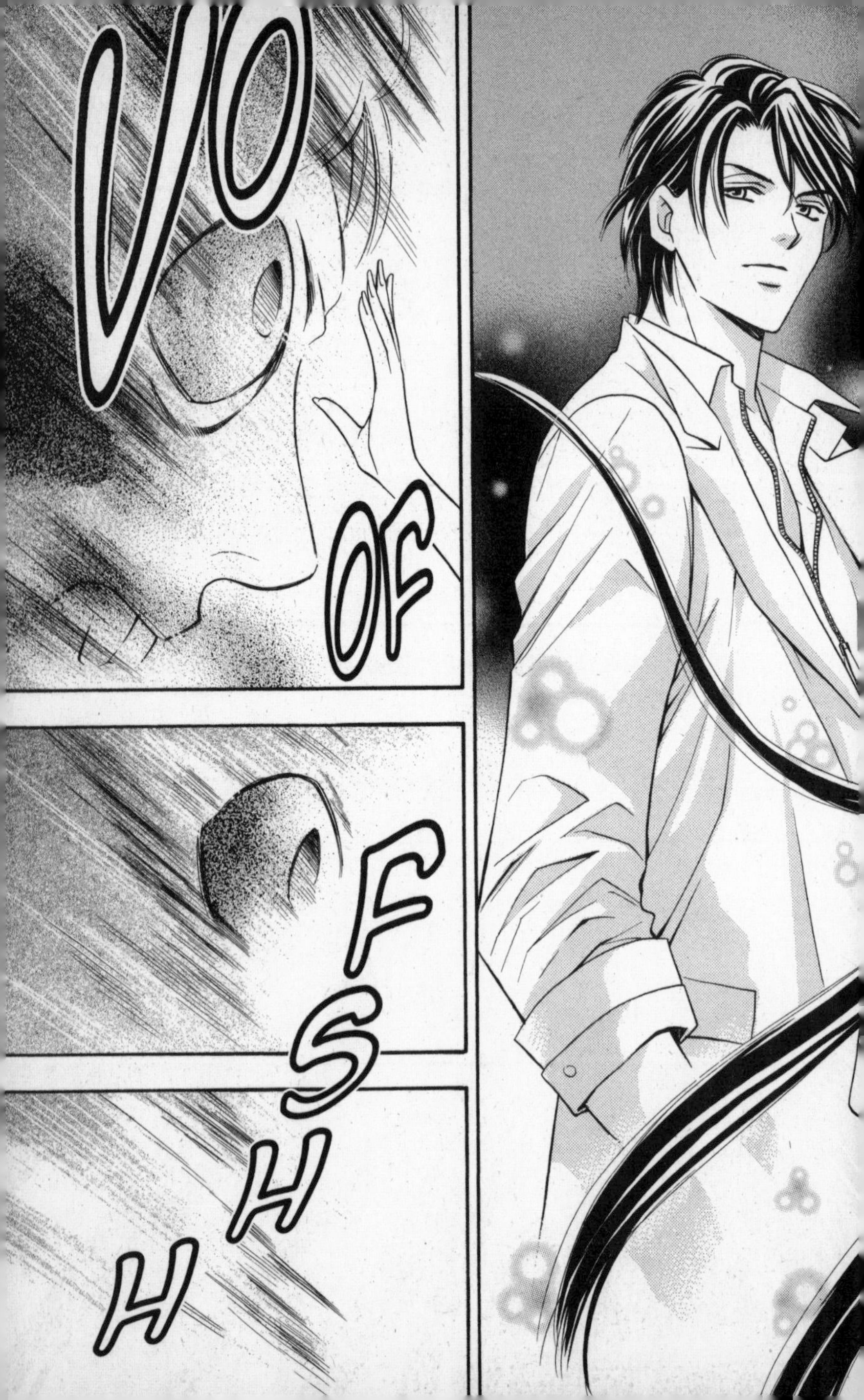
VO
OF
FSHH

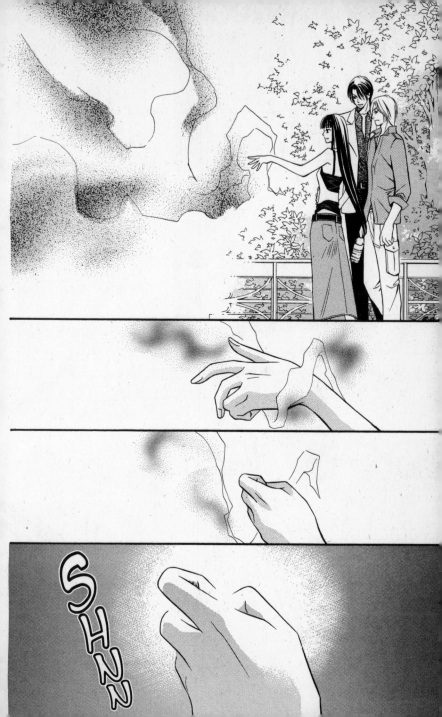

SHNN

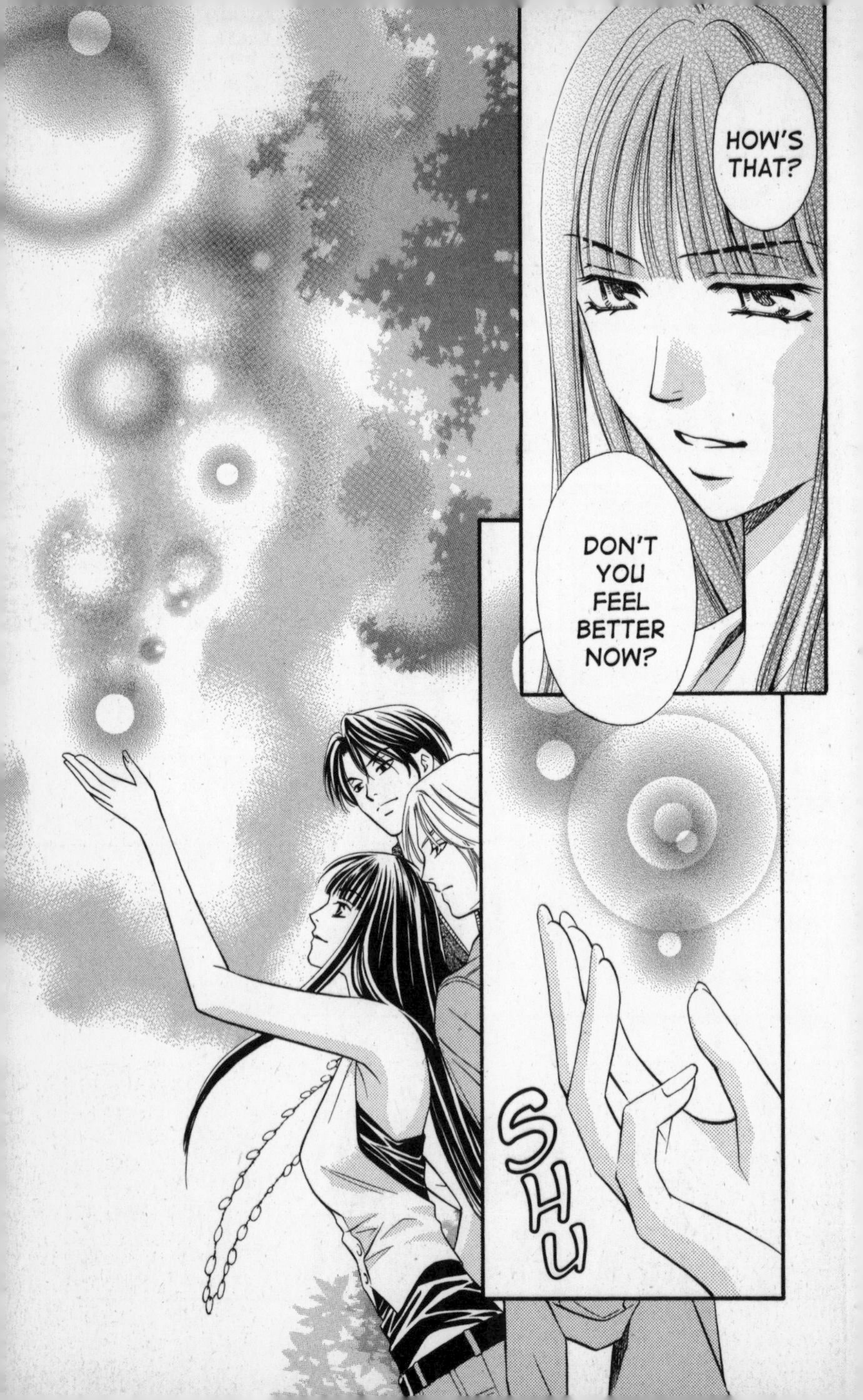
HOW'S THAT?
DON'T YOU FEEL BETTER NOW?
SHU

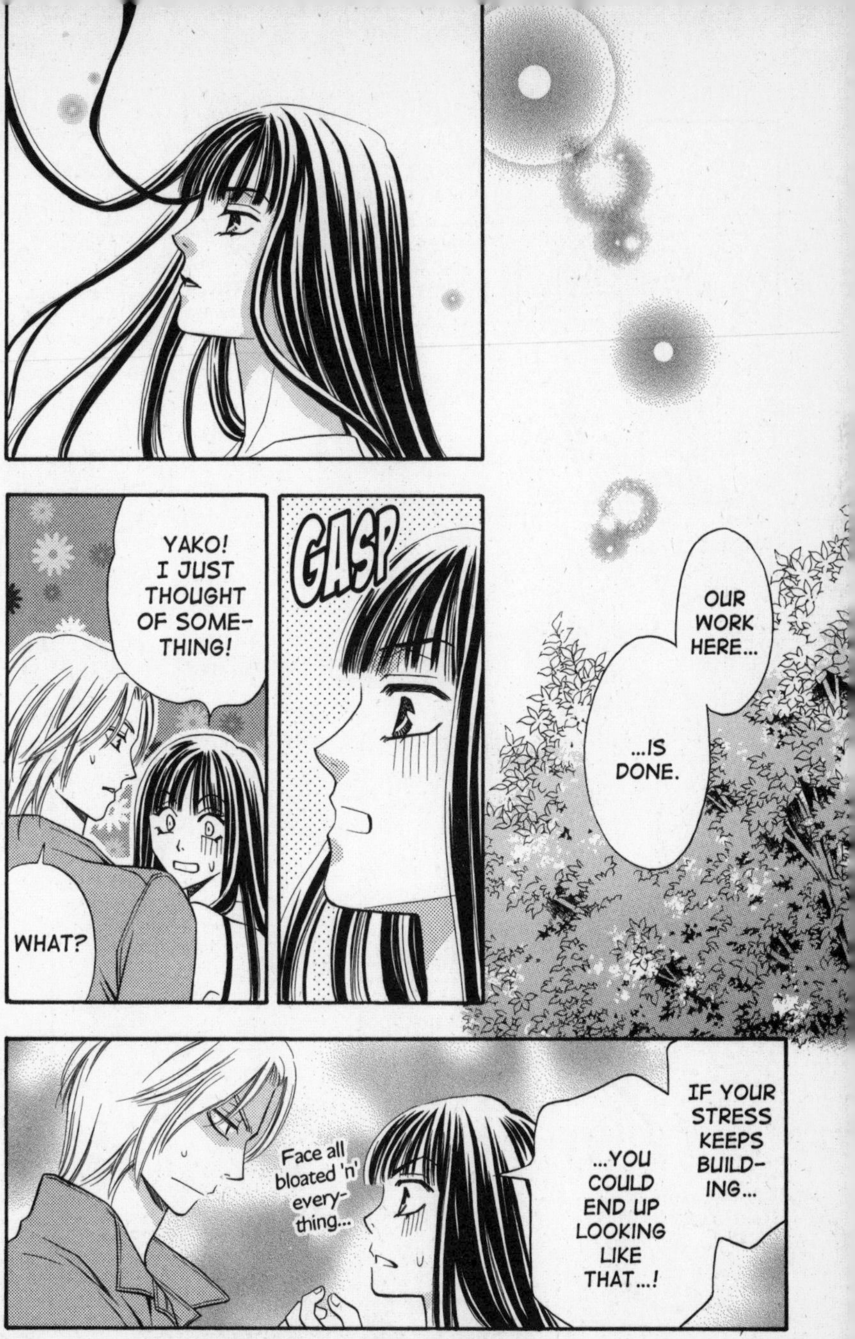
OUR WORK HERE...
...IS DONE.
GASP
YAKO! I JUST THOUGHT OF SOME-THING!
WHAT?
IF YOUR STRESS KEEPS BUILD-ING...
...YOU COULD END UP LOOKING LIKE THAT...!
Face all bloated 'n' every-thing...

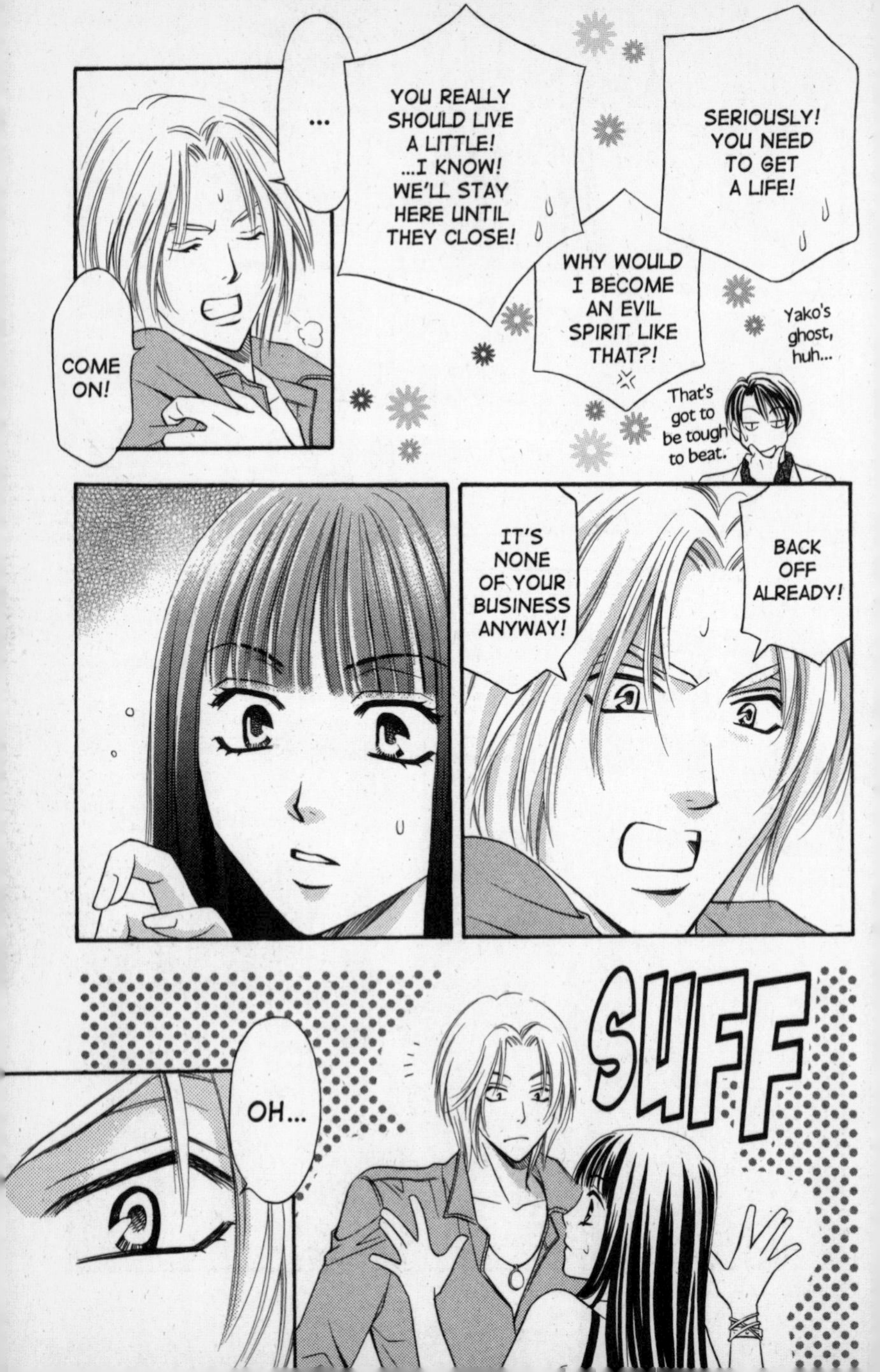
SERIOUSLY! YOU NEED TO GET A LIFE!
WHY WOULD I BECOME AN EVIL SPIRIT LIKE THAT?!
Yako's ghost, huh...
That's got to be tough to beat.
YOU REALLY SHOULD LIVE A LITTLE! ...I KNOW! WE'LL STAY HERE UNTIL THEY CLOSE!
...
COME ON!
BACK OFF ALREADY!
IT'S NONE OF YOUR BUSINESS ANYWAY!
SUFF
OH...

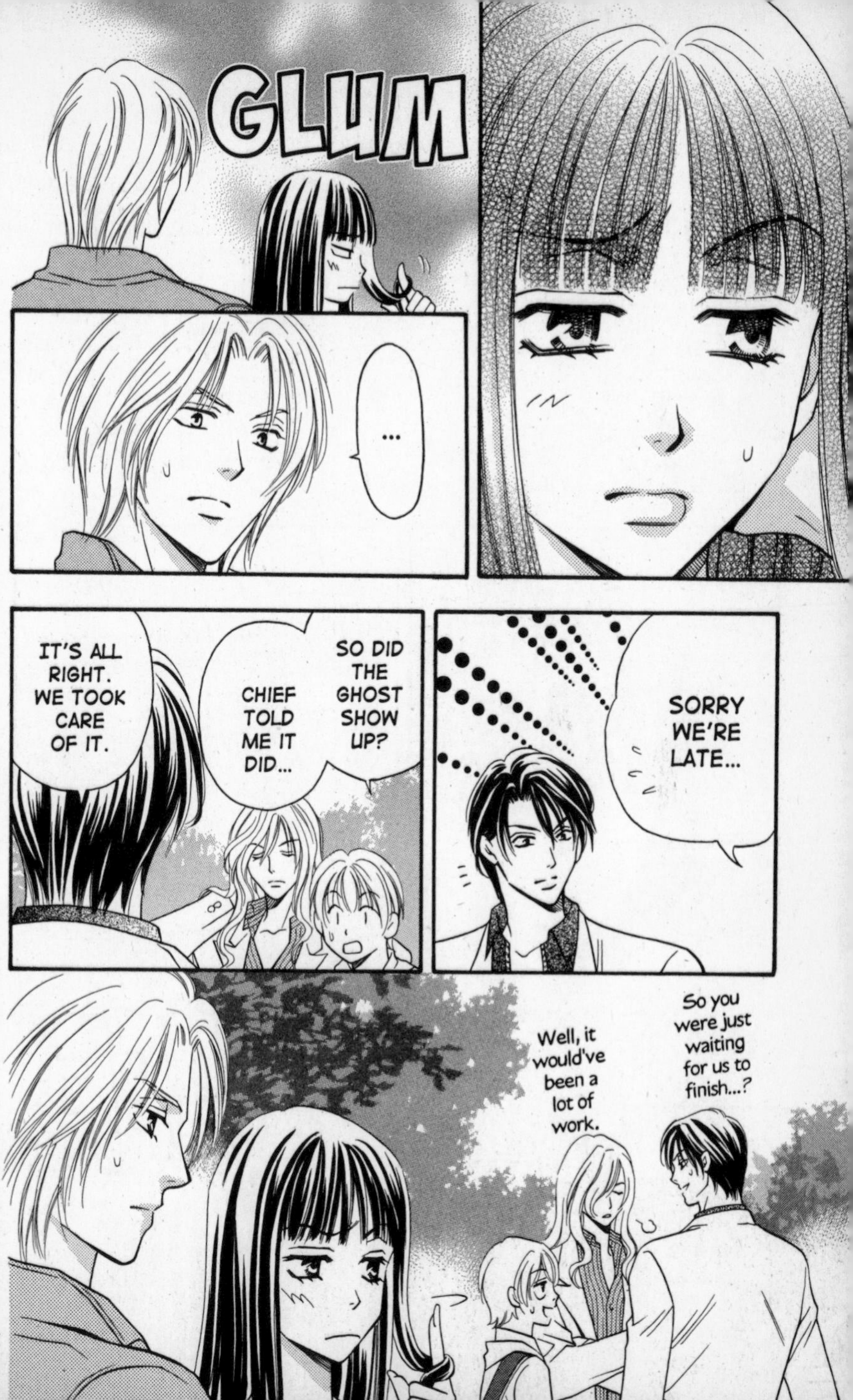
GLUM
...
SORRY WE'RE LATE...
SO DID THE GHOST SHOW UP?
CHIEF TOLD ME IT DID...
IT'S ALL RIGHT. WE TOOK CARE OF IT.
So you were just waiting for us to finish...?
Well, it would've been a lot of work.

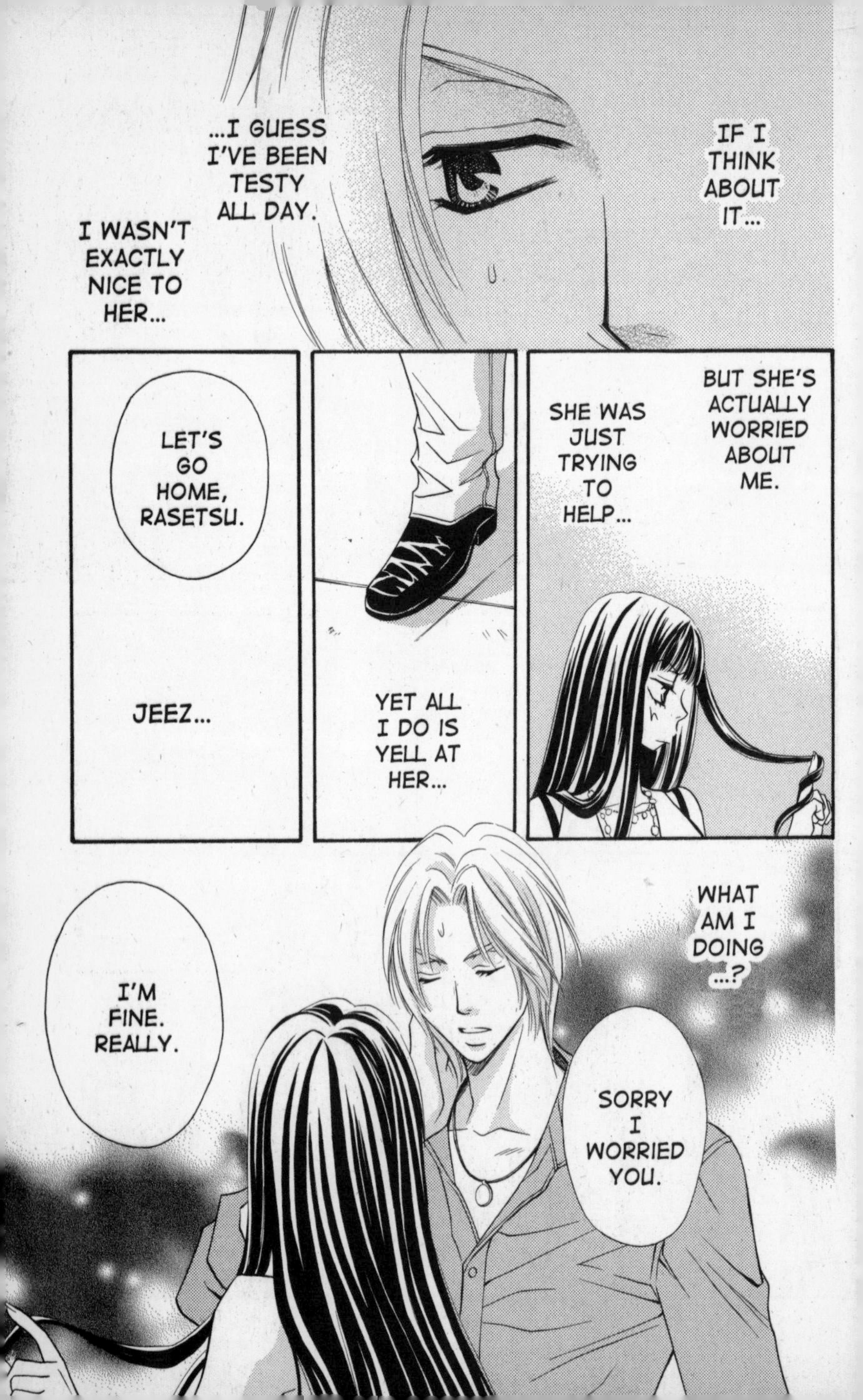
IF I THINK ABOUT IT...
...I GUESS I'VE BEEN TESTY ALL DAY.
I WASN'T EXACTLY NICE TO HER...
BUT SHE'S ACTUALLY WORRIED ABOUT ME.
SHE WAS JUST TRYING TO HELP...
YET ALL I DO IS YELL AT HER...
LET'S GO HOME, RASETSU.
JEEZ...
WHAT AM I DOING ...?
SORRY I WORRIED YOU.
I'M FINE. REALLY.

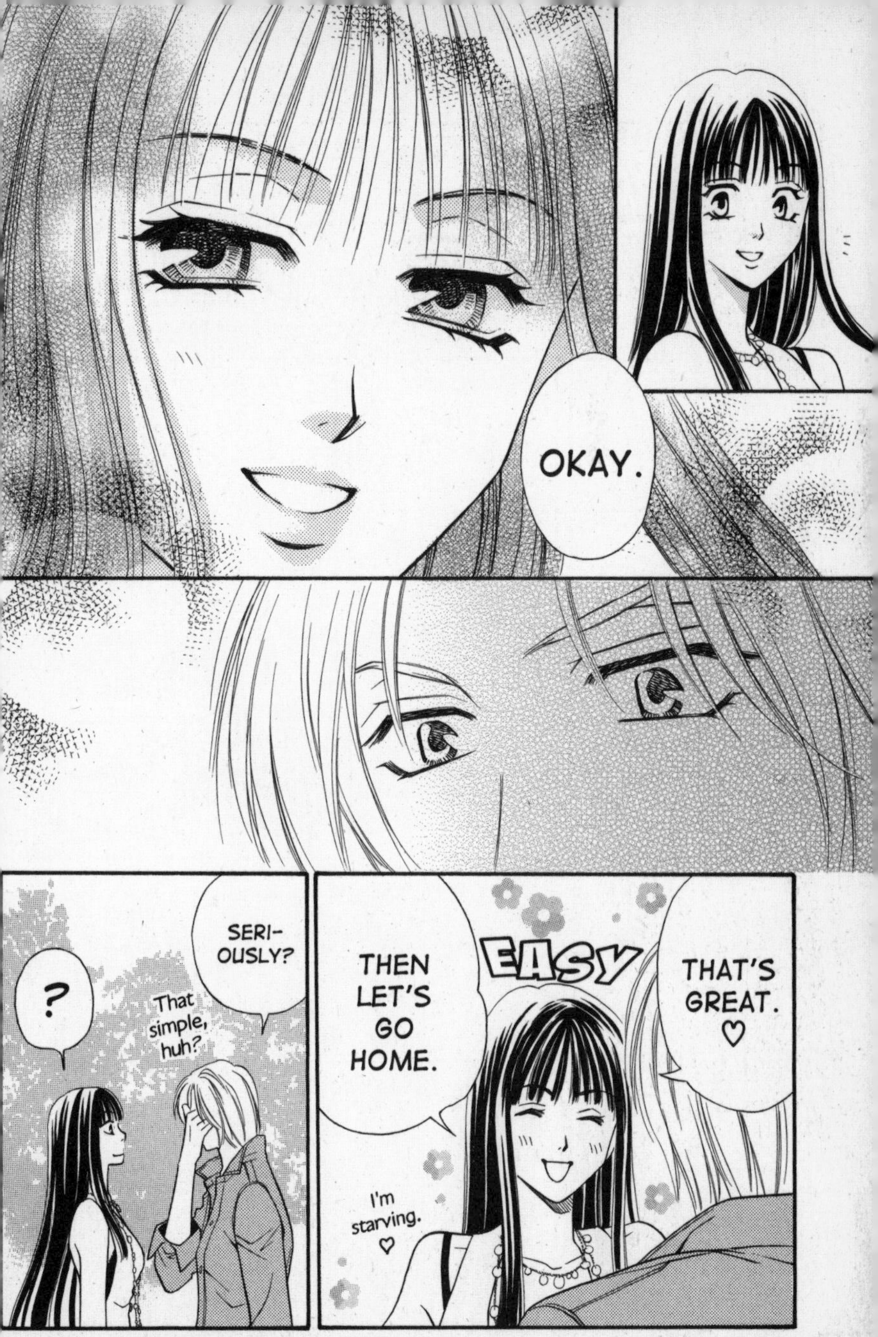
OKAY.
THAT'S GREAT. ♡
EASY
THEN LET'S GO HOME.
I'm starving. ♡
SERI-OUSLY?
That simple, huh?
?

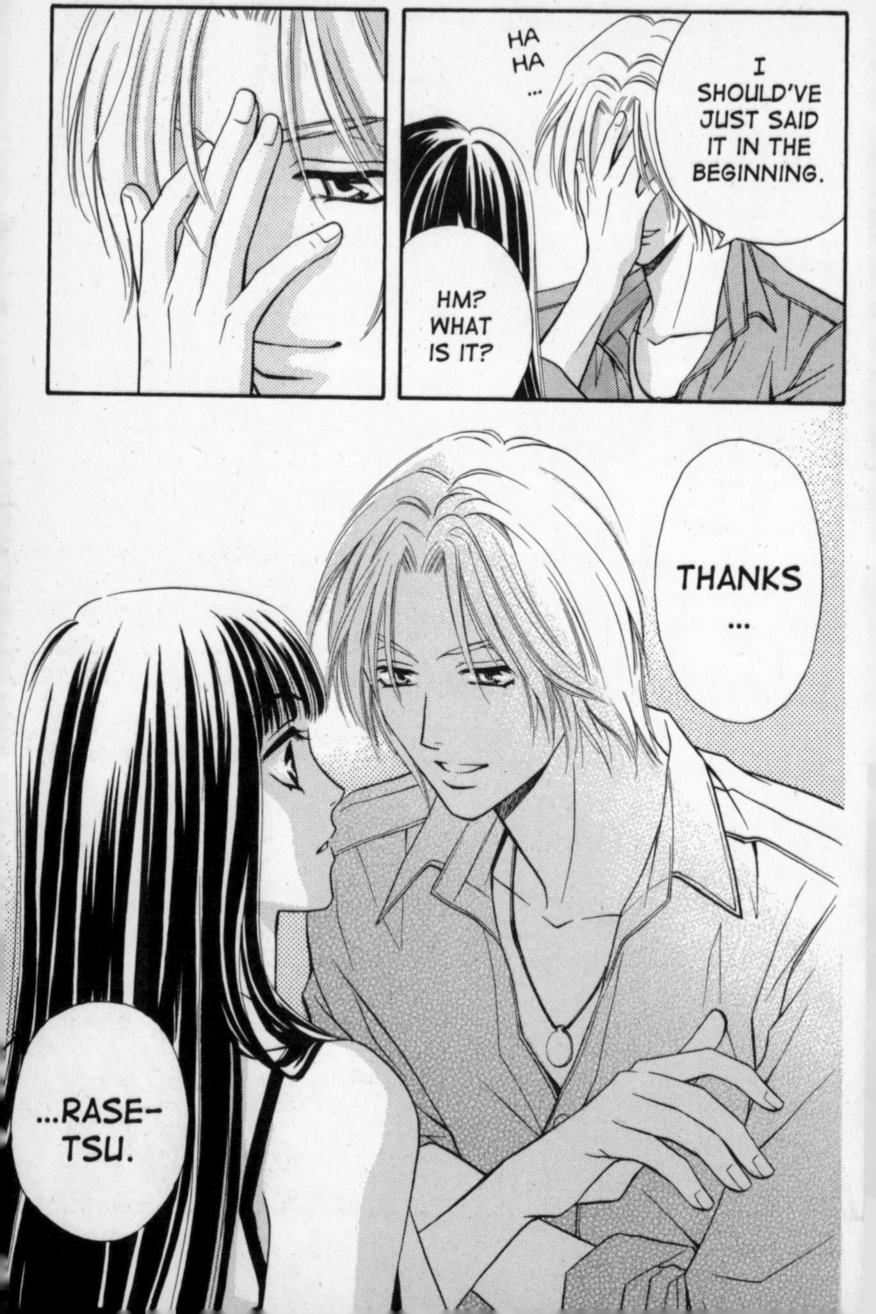
I SHOULD'VE JUST SAID IT IN THE BEGINNING.
HA HA ...
HM? WHAT IS IT?
THANKS ...
...RASE-TSU.

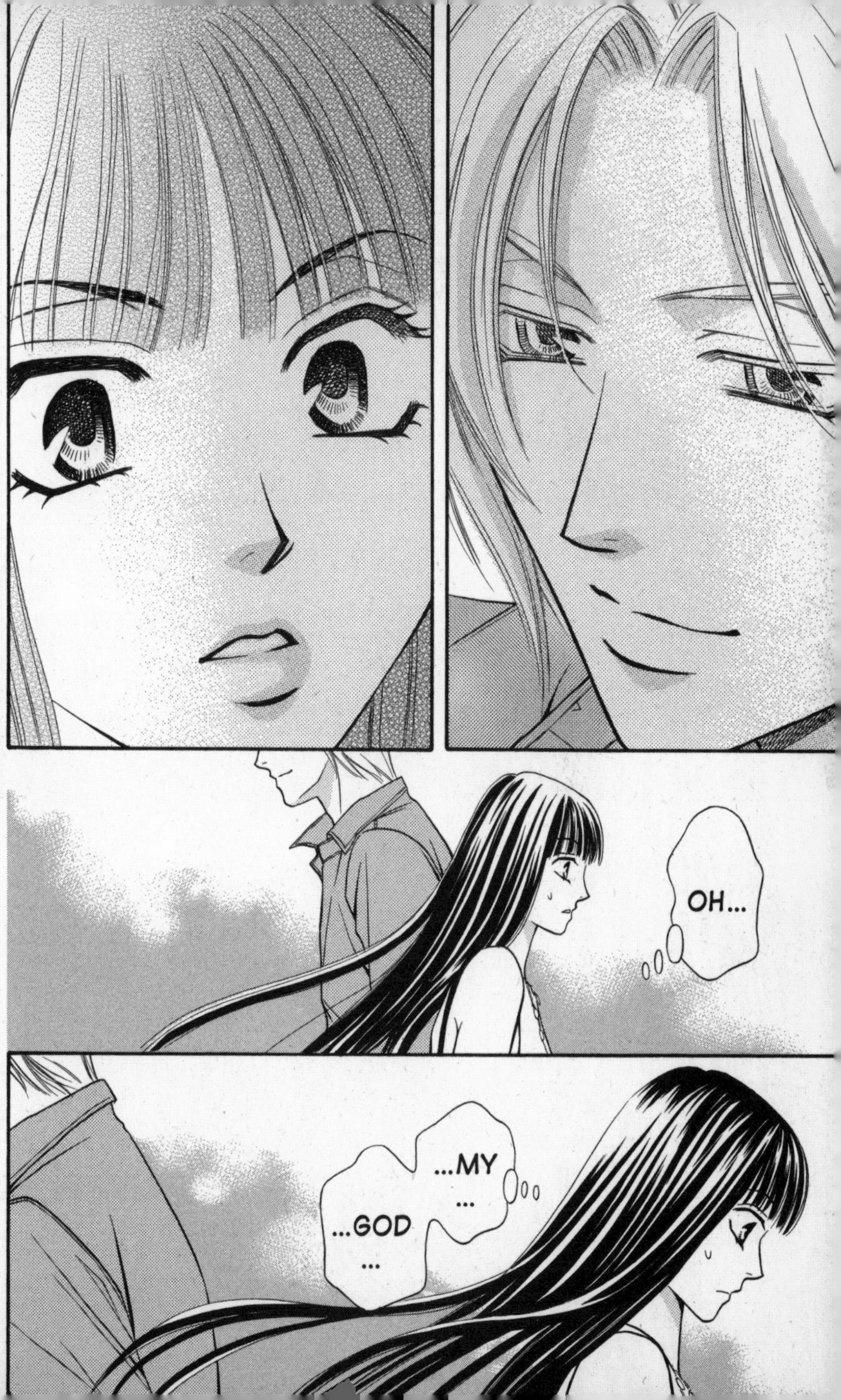
OH...
...MY ...
...GOD ...

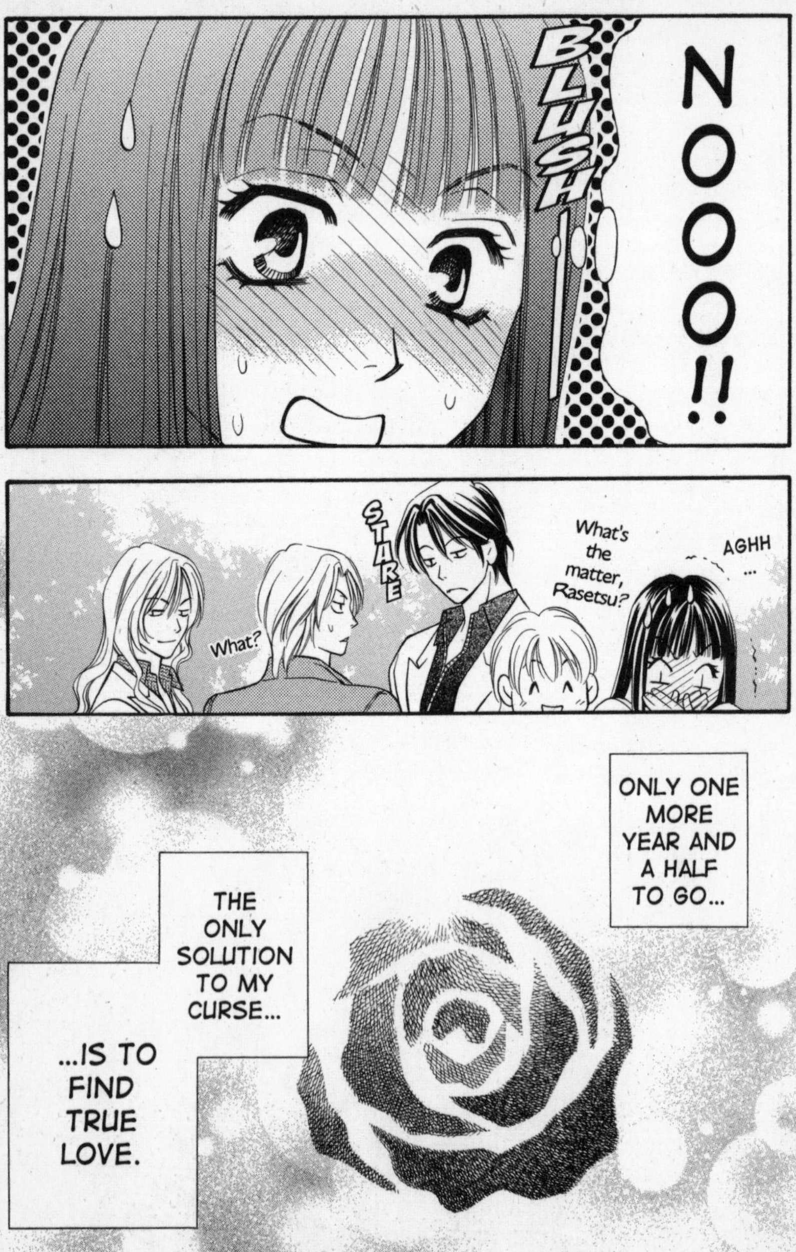
NOOOO!!
BLUSH
AGHH...
What's the matter, Rasetsu?
STARE
What?
ONLY ONE MORE YEAR AND A HALF TO GO...
THE ONLY SOLUTION TO MY CURSE...
...IS TO FIND TRUE LOVE.

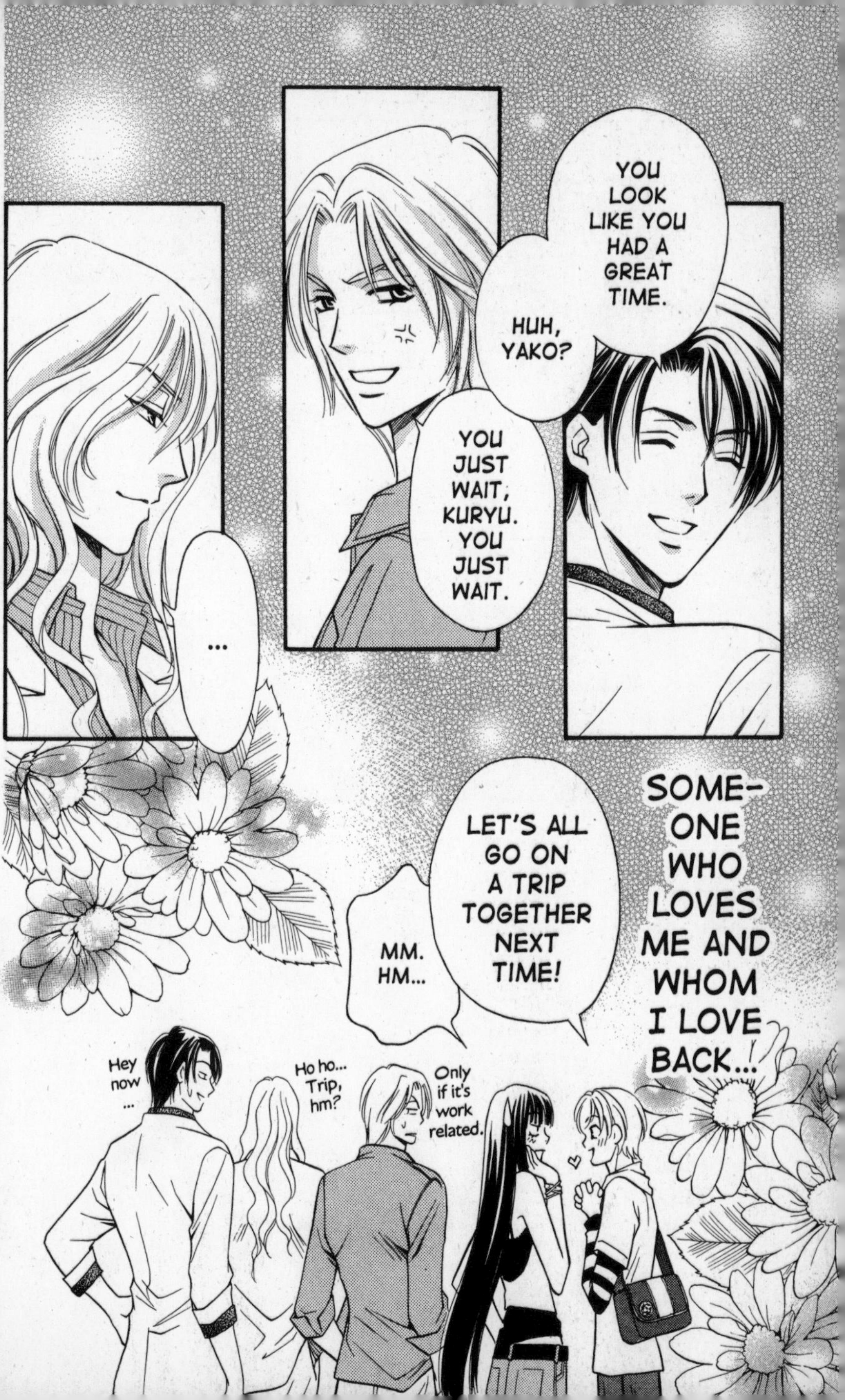
YOU LOOK LIKE YOU HAD A GREAT TIME.
HUH, YAKO?
YOU JUST WAIT, KURYU. YOU JUST WAIT.
...
SOME-ONE WHO LOVES ME AND WHOM I LOVE BACK...!
LET'S ALL GO ON A TRIP TOGETHER NEXT TIME!
MM. HM...
Only if it's work related.
Ho ho... Trip, hm?
Hey now ...

Chapter 7

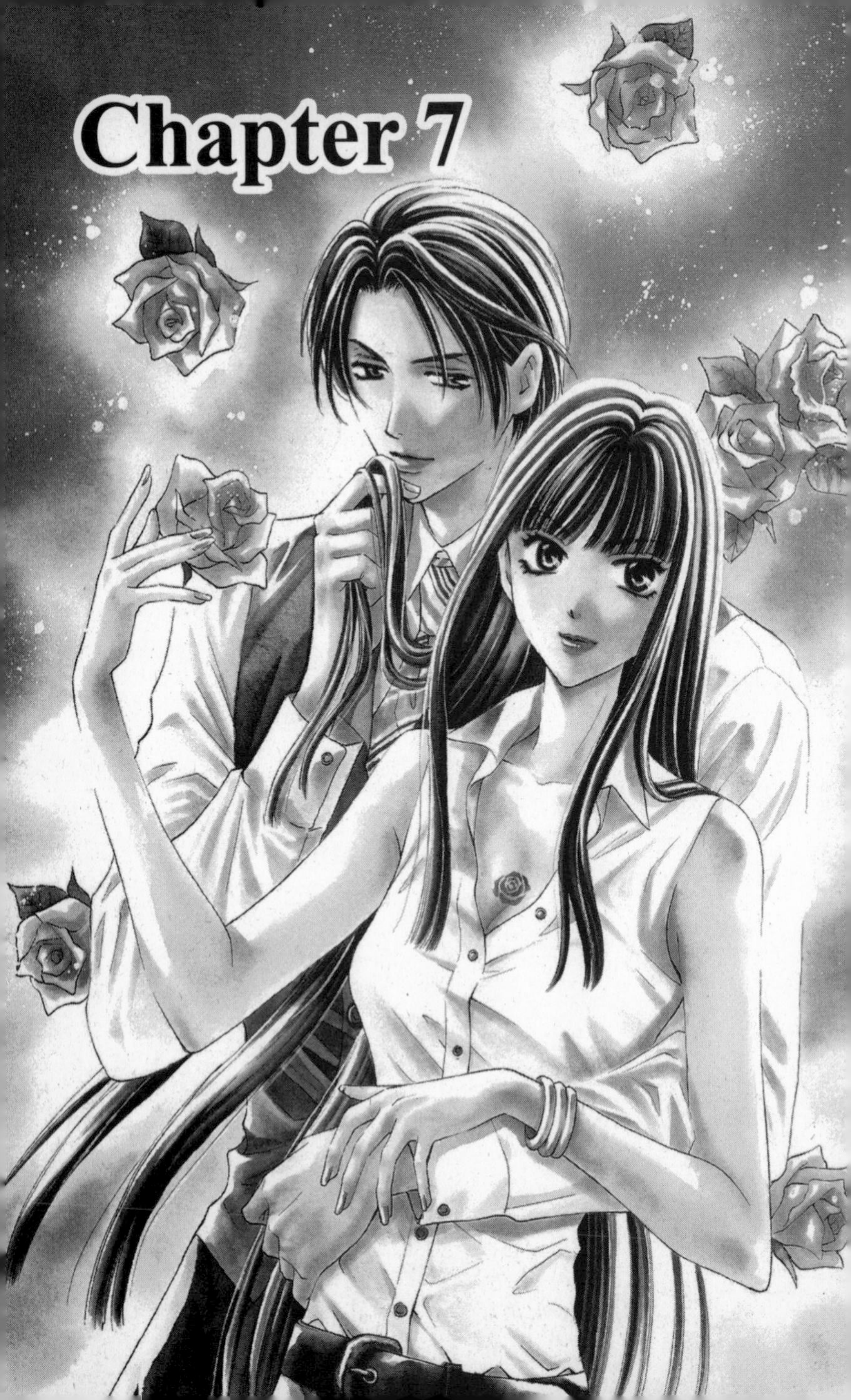

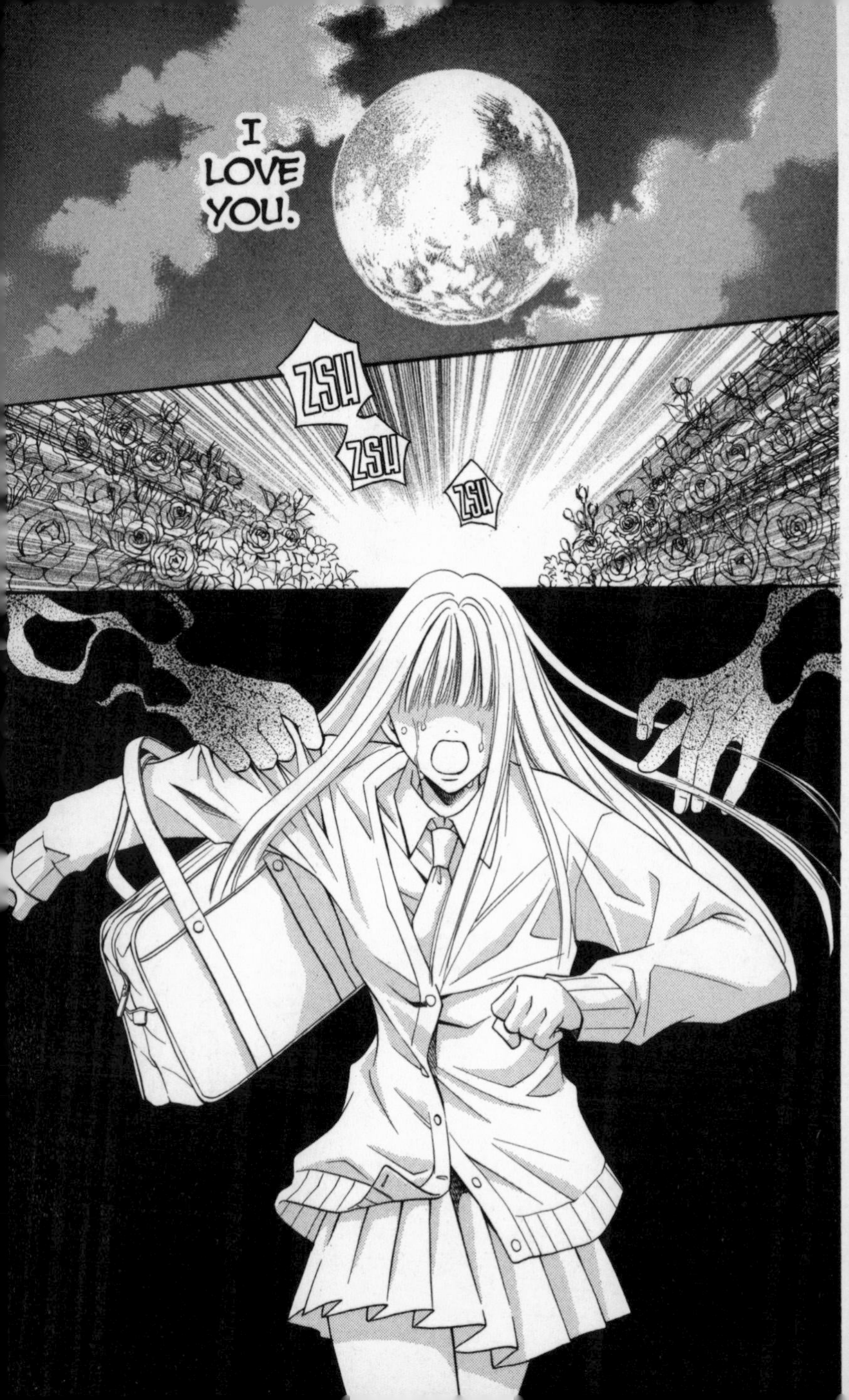
I LOVE YOU.
ZSH
ZSH
ZSH

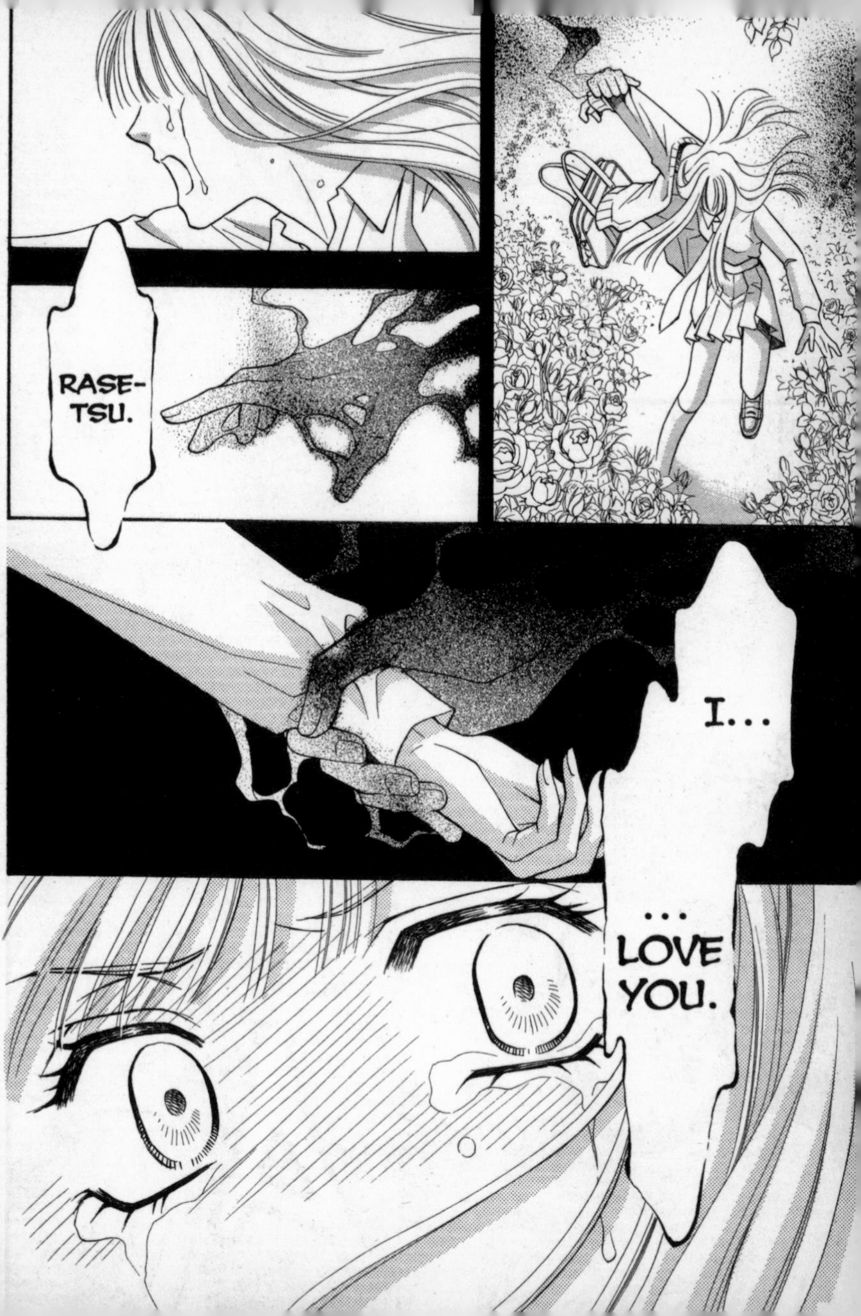
RASE-
TSU.
I...
...LOVE YOU.

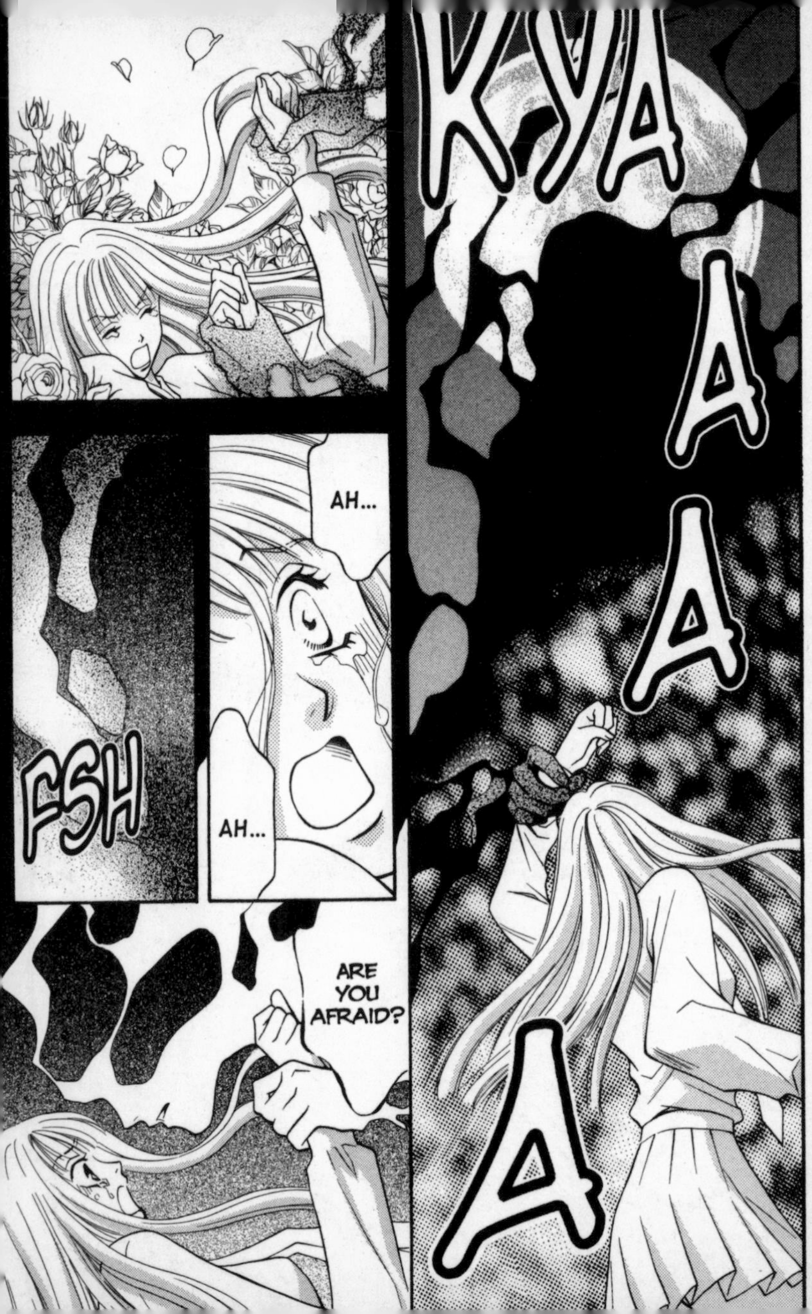
KYAAAA
AH...
AH...
FSH
ARE YOU AFRAID?

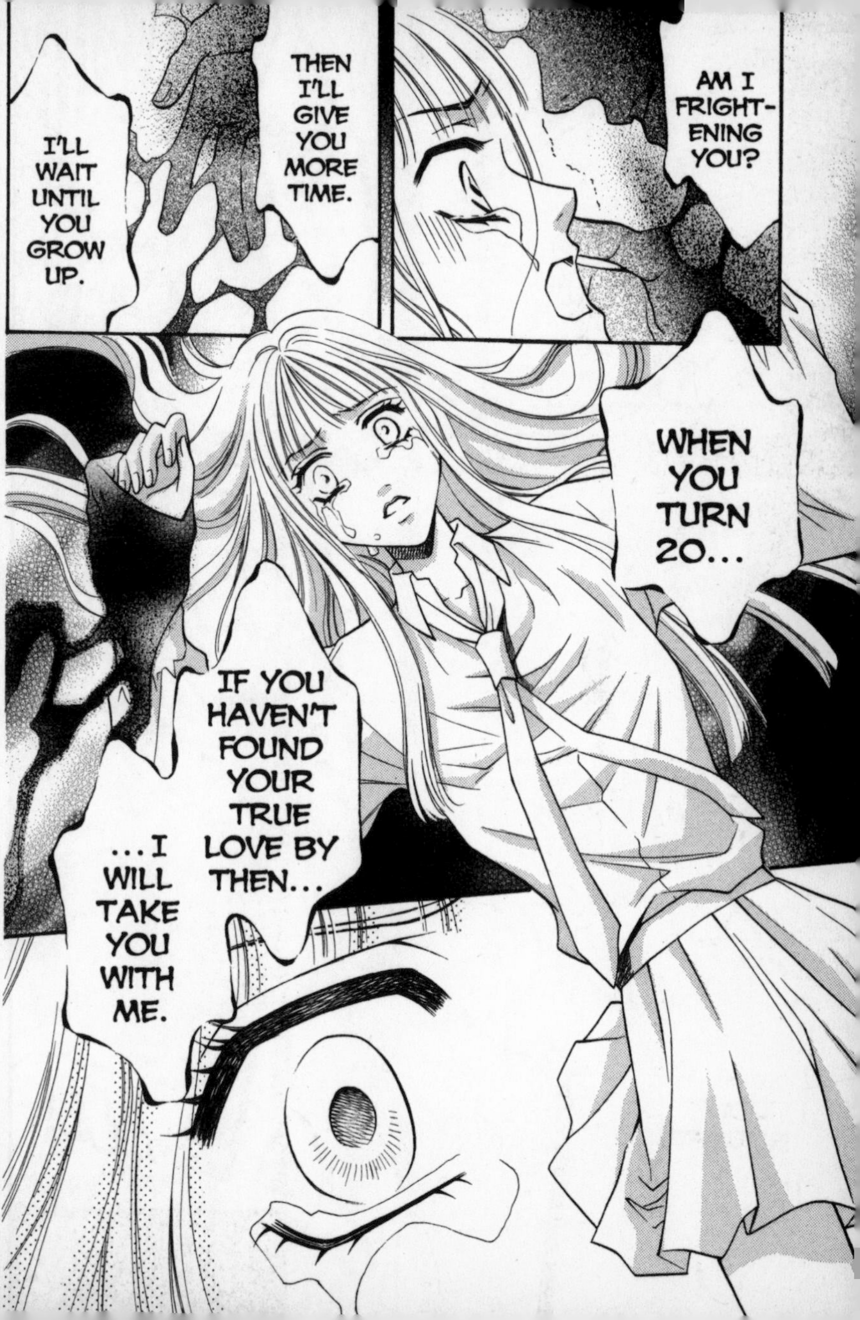
AM I FRIGHT-ENING YOU?
THEN I'LL GIVE YOU MORE TIME.
I'LL WAIT UNTIL YOU GROW UP.
WHEN YOU TURN 20...
IF YOU HAVEN'T FOUND YOUR TRUE LOVE BY THEN...
...I WILL TAKE YOU WITH ME.

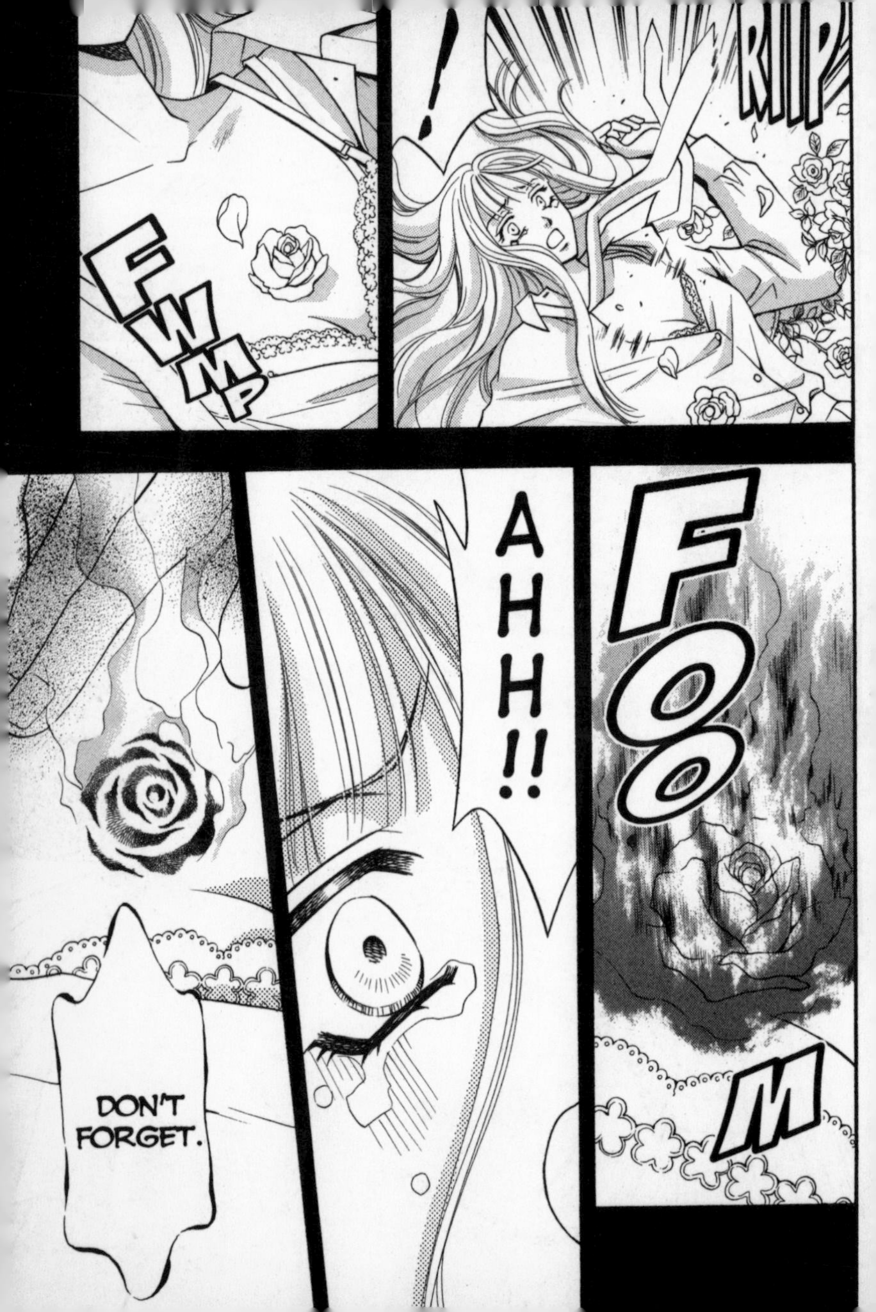
RIP
!
FWMP
FOOM
AHHH!!
DON'T FORGET.

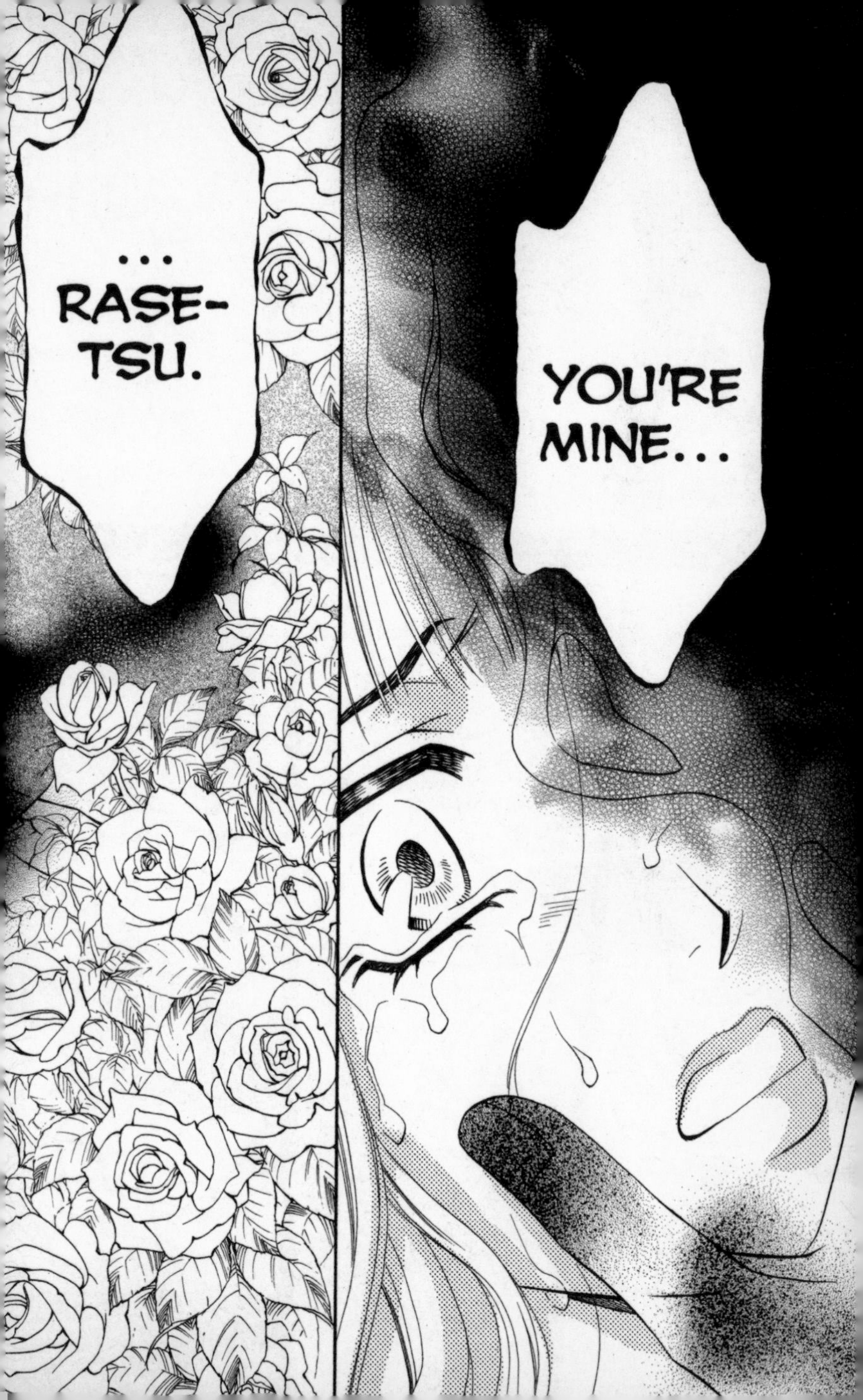
YOU'RE MINE...
... RASE-TSU.

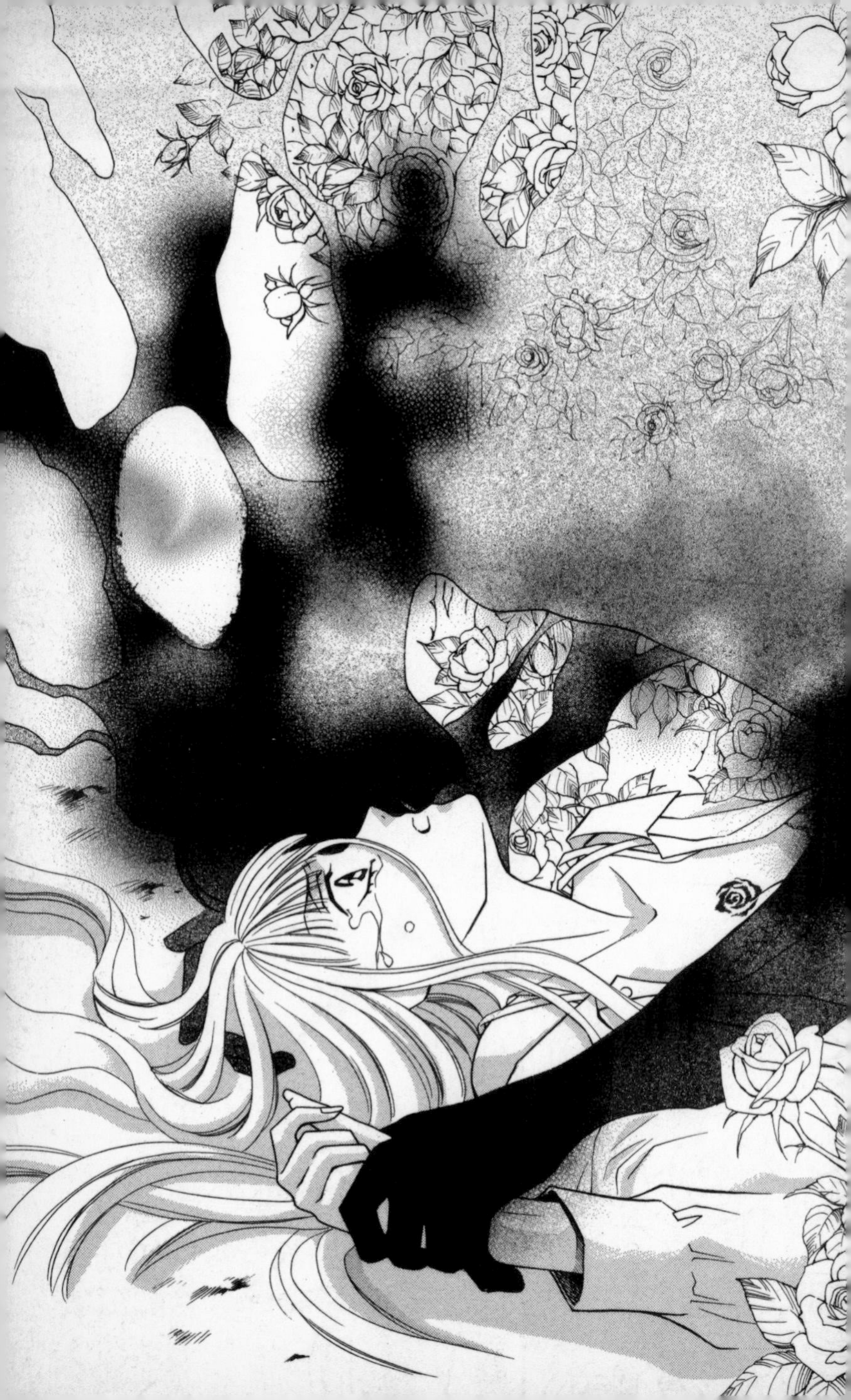

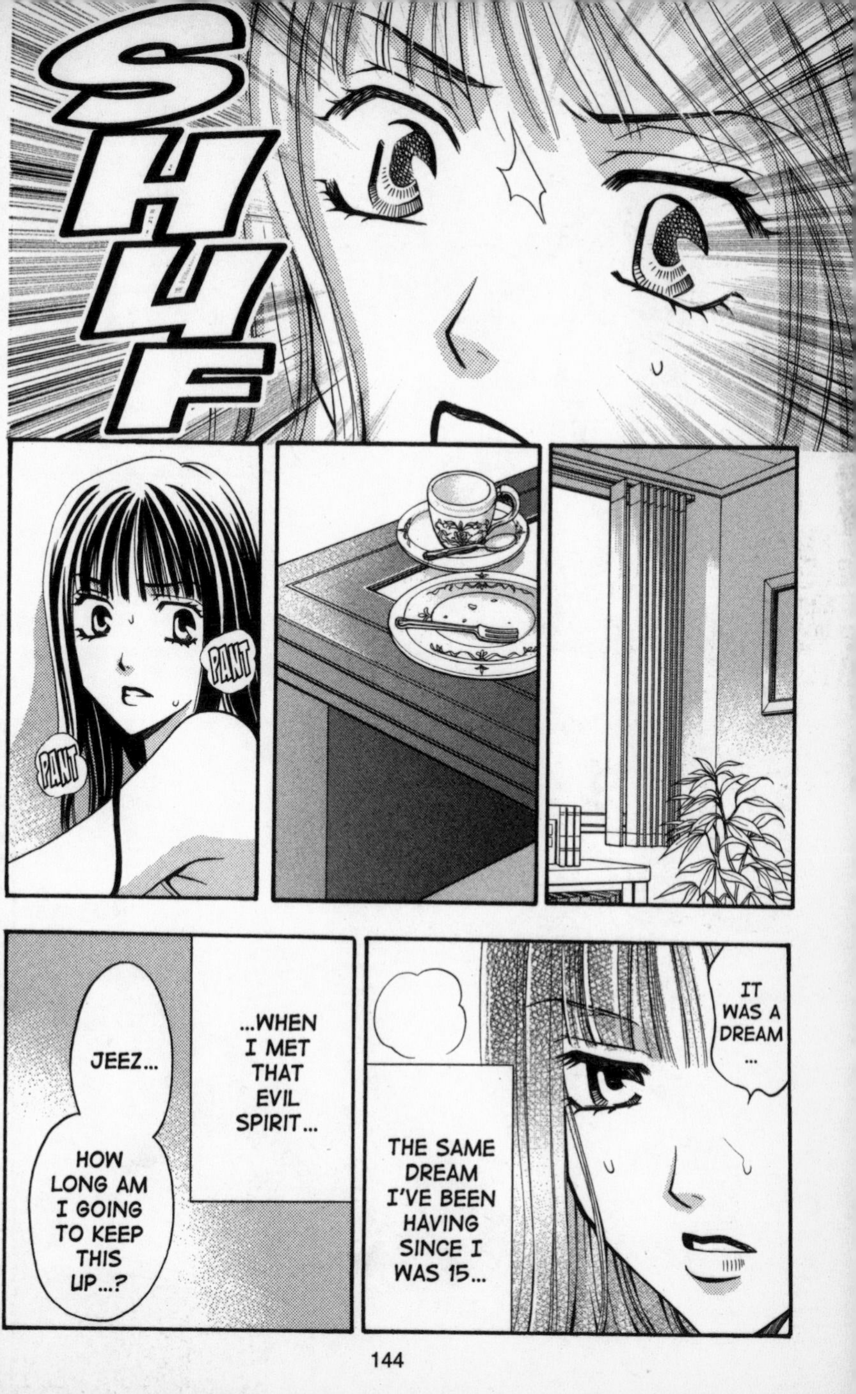
SHUFF
PANT
PANT
IT WAS A DREAM...
THE SAME DREAM I'VE BEEN HAVING SINCE I WAS 15...
...WHEN I MET THAT EVIL SPIRIT...
JEEZ...
HOW LONG AM I GOING TO KEEP THIS UP...?

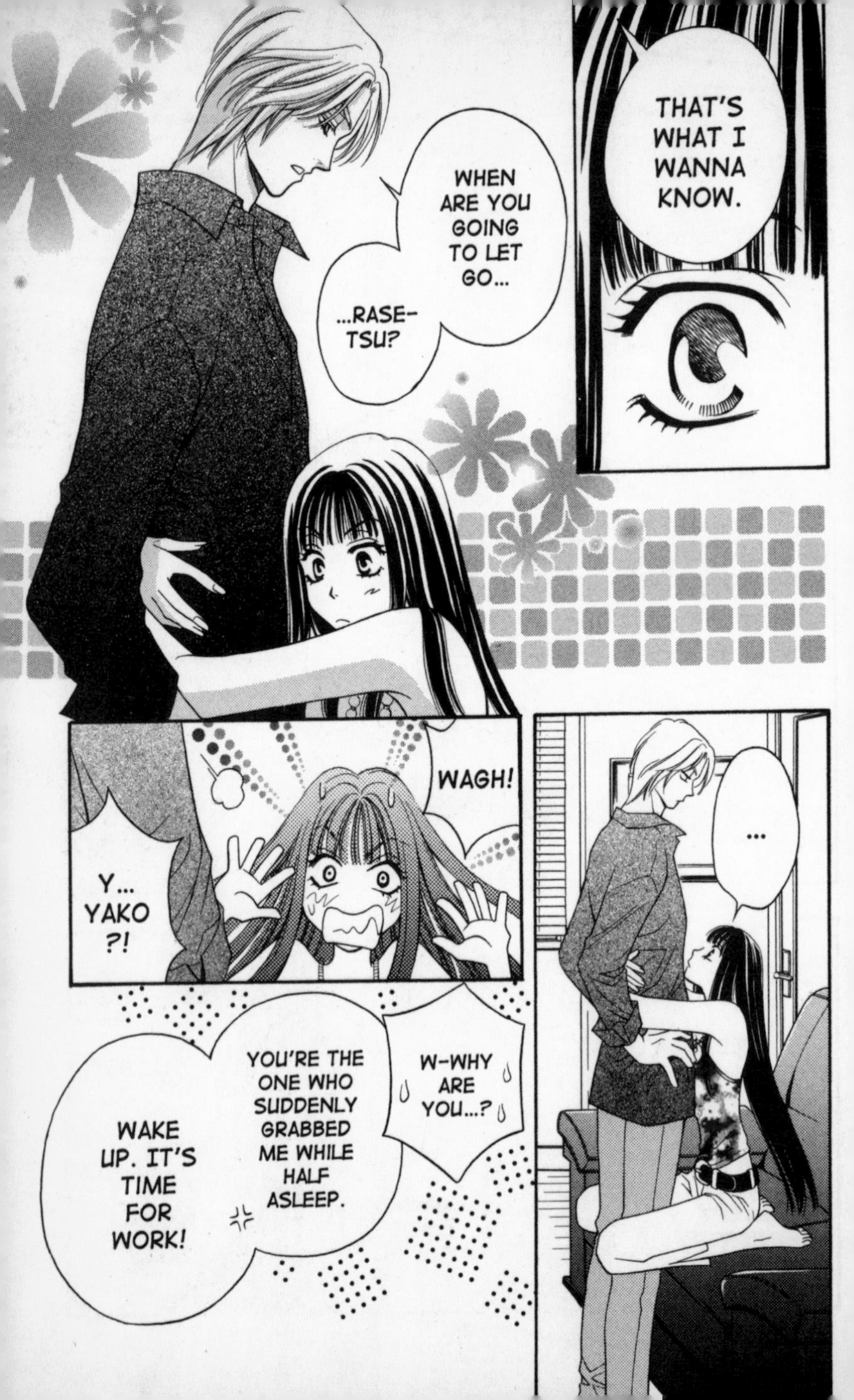
THAT'S WHAT I WANNA KNOW.
WHEN ARE YOU GOING TO LET GO...
...RASE-TSU?
...
WAGH!
Y... YAKO ?!
W-WHY ARE YOU...?
YOU'RE THE ONE WHO SUDDENLY GRABBED ME WHILE HALF ASLEEP.
WAKE UP. IT'S TIME FOR WORK!

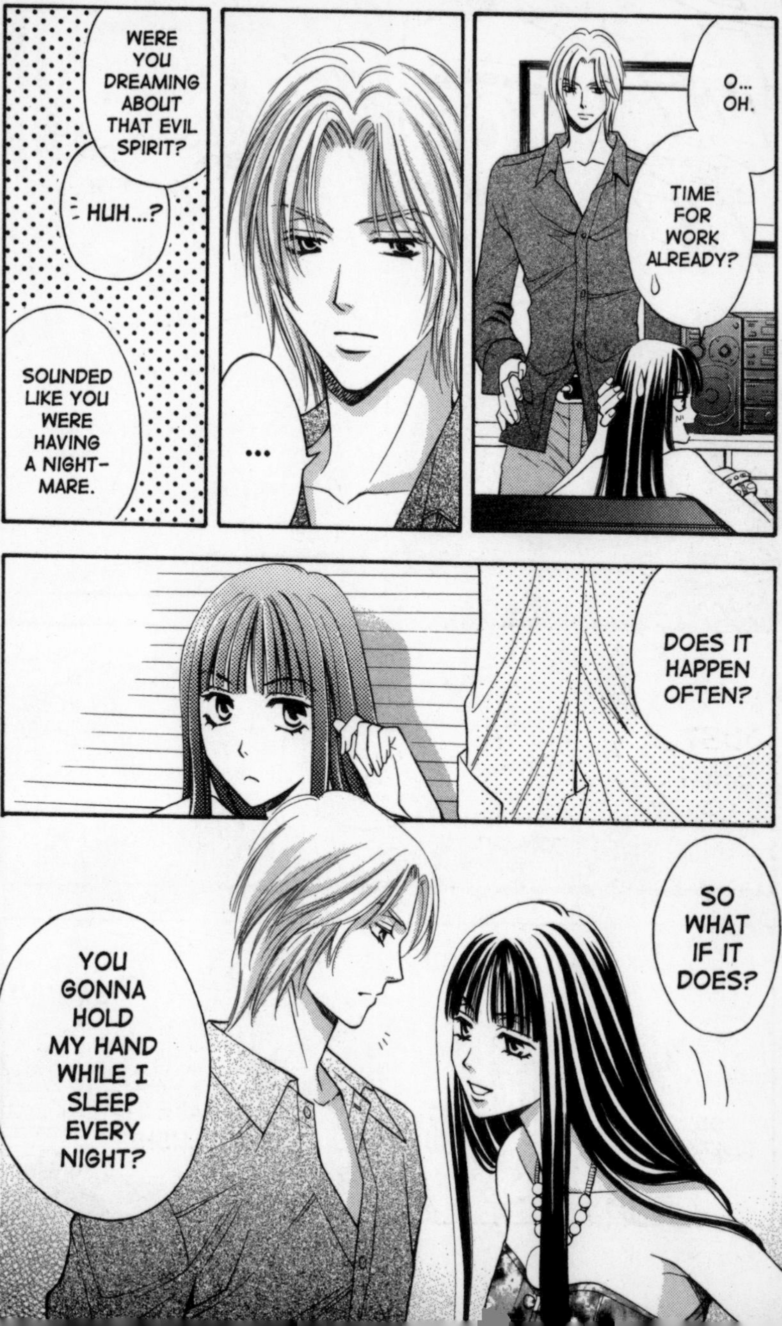
O... OH.
TIME FOR WORK ALREADY?
...
WERE YOU DREAMING ABOUT THAT EVIL SPIRIT?
HUH...?
SOUNDED LIKE YOU WERE HAVING A NIGHT-MARE.
DOES IT HAPPEN OFTEN?
SO WHAT IF IT DOES?
YOU GONNA HOLD MY HAND WHILE I SLEEP EVERY NIGHT?

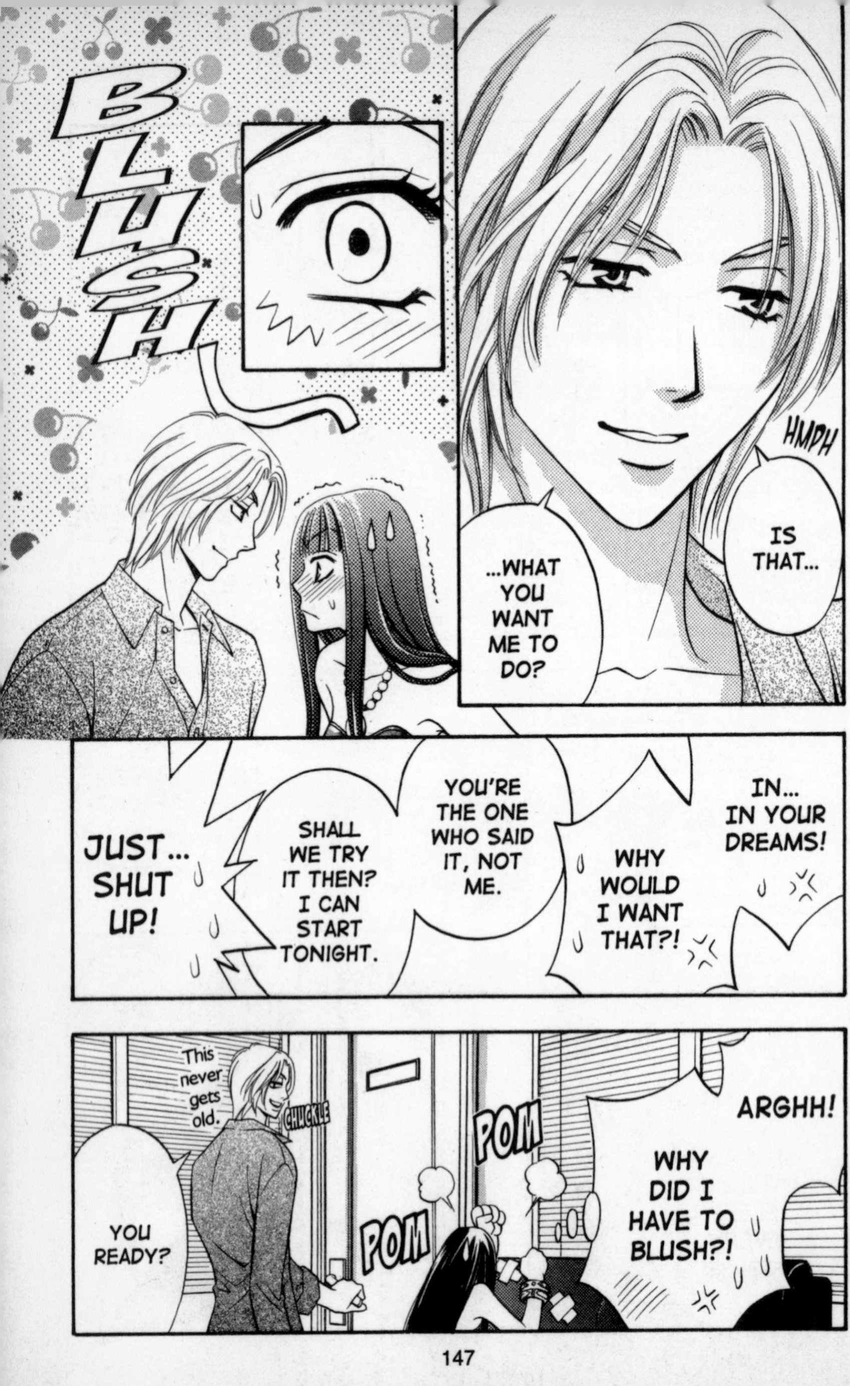
HMPH
IS THAT...
...WHAT YOU WANT ME TO DO?
BLUSH
IN... IN YOUR DREAMS!
WHY WOULD I WANT THAT?!
YOU'RE THE ONE WHO SAID IT, NOT ME.
SHALL WE TRY IT THEN? I CAN START TONIGHT.
JUST... SHUT UP!
ARGHH!
WHY DID I HAVE TO BLUSH?!
POM
POM
CHUCKLE
This never gets old.
YOU READY?

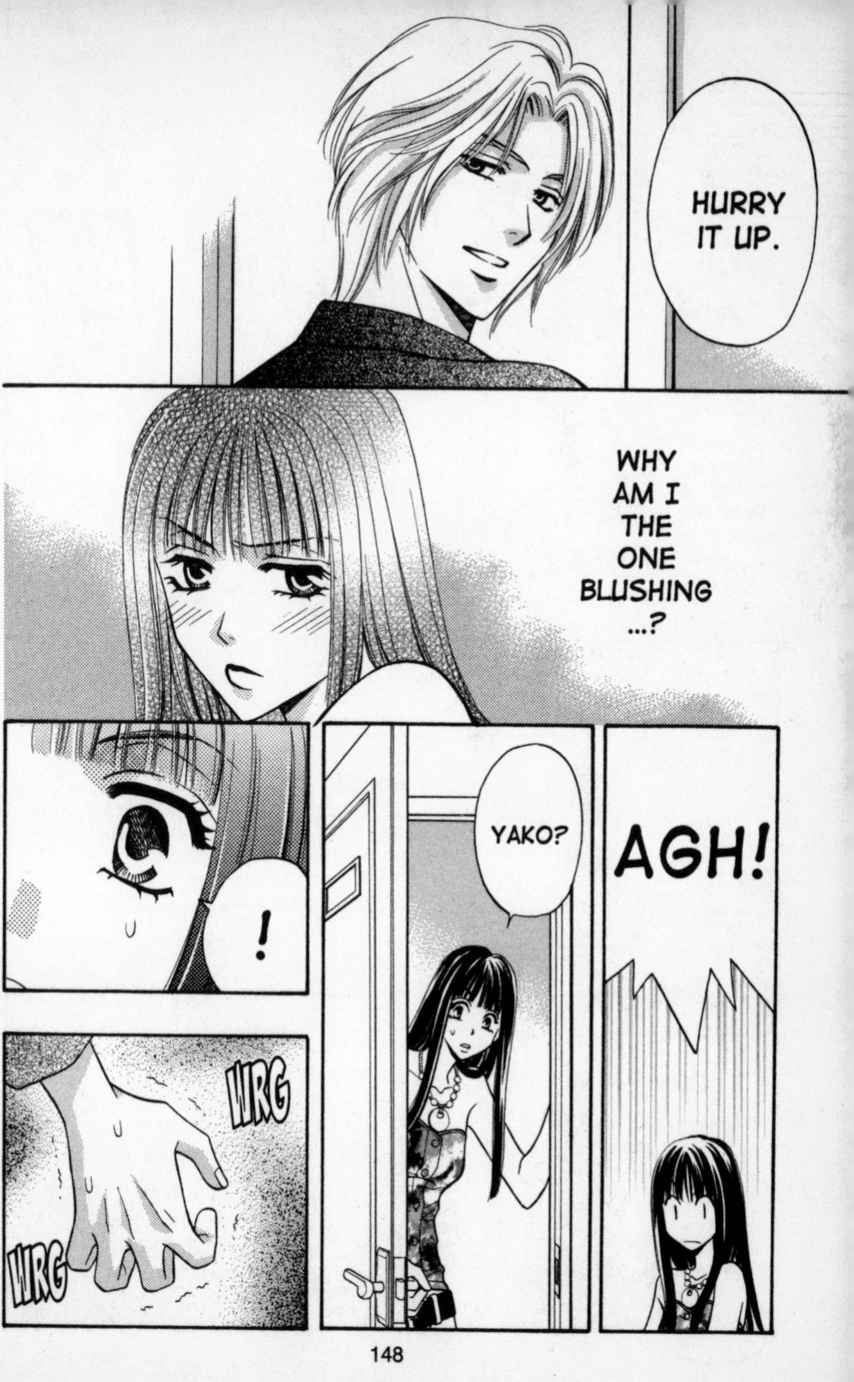
HURRY IT UP.
WHY AM I THE ONE BLUSHING ...?
AGH!
YAKO?
!
WRG
WRG

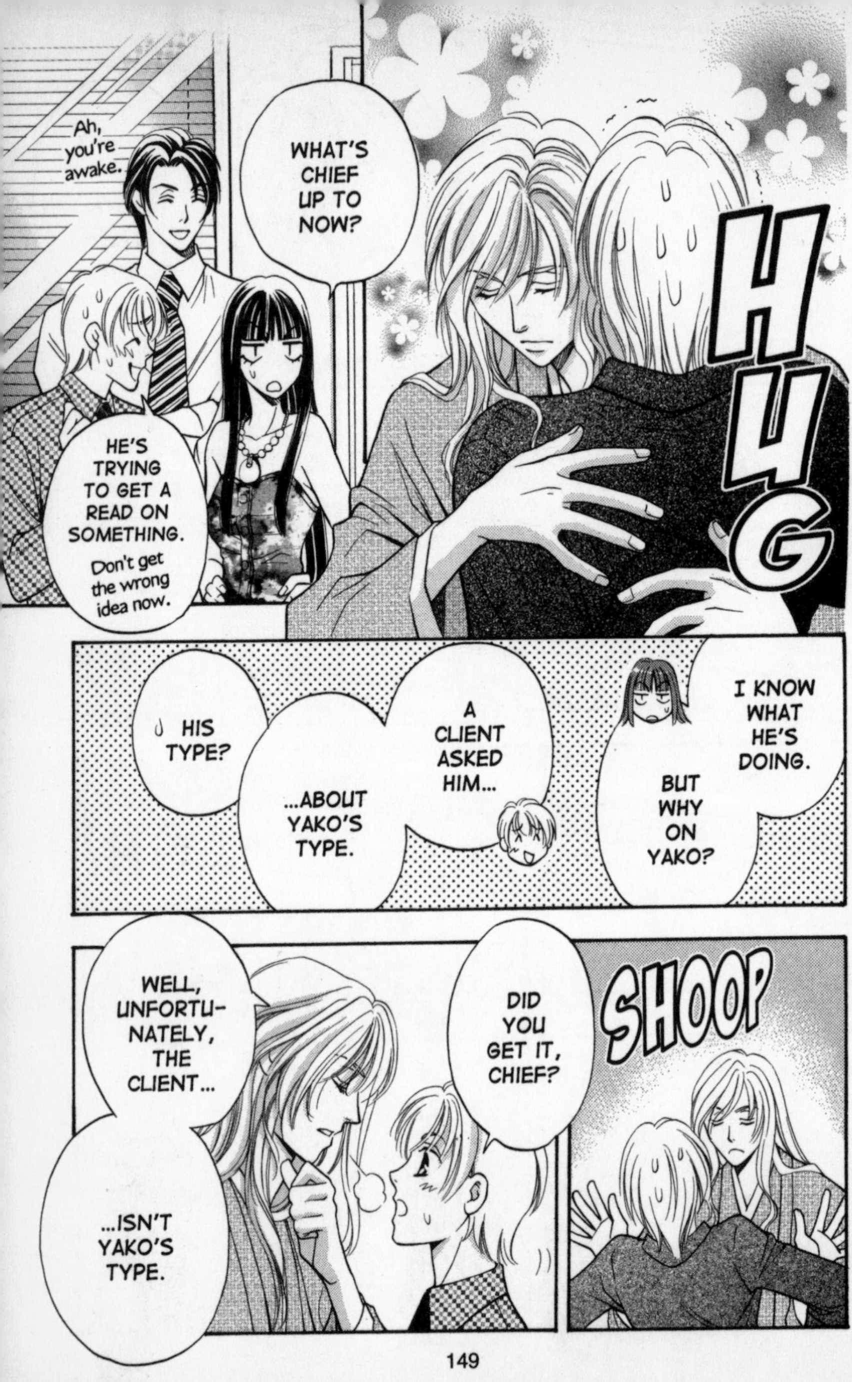
HUG
WHAT'S CHIEF UP TO NOW?
Ah, you're awake.
HE'S TRYING TO GET A READ ON SOMETHING.
Don't get the wrong idea now.
I KNOW WHAT HE'S DOING.
BUT WHY ON YAKO?
A CLIENT ASKED HIM...
...ABOUT YAKO'S TYPE.
HIS TYPE?
SHOOP
DID YOU GET IT, CHIEF?
WELL, UNFORTU-NATELY, THE CLIENT...
...ISN'T YAKO'S TYPE.

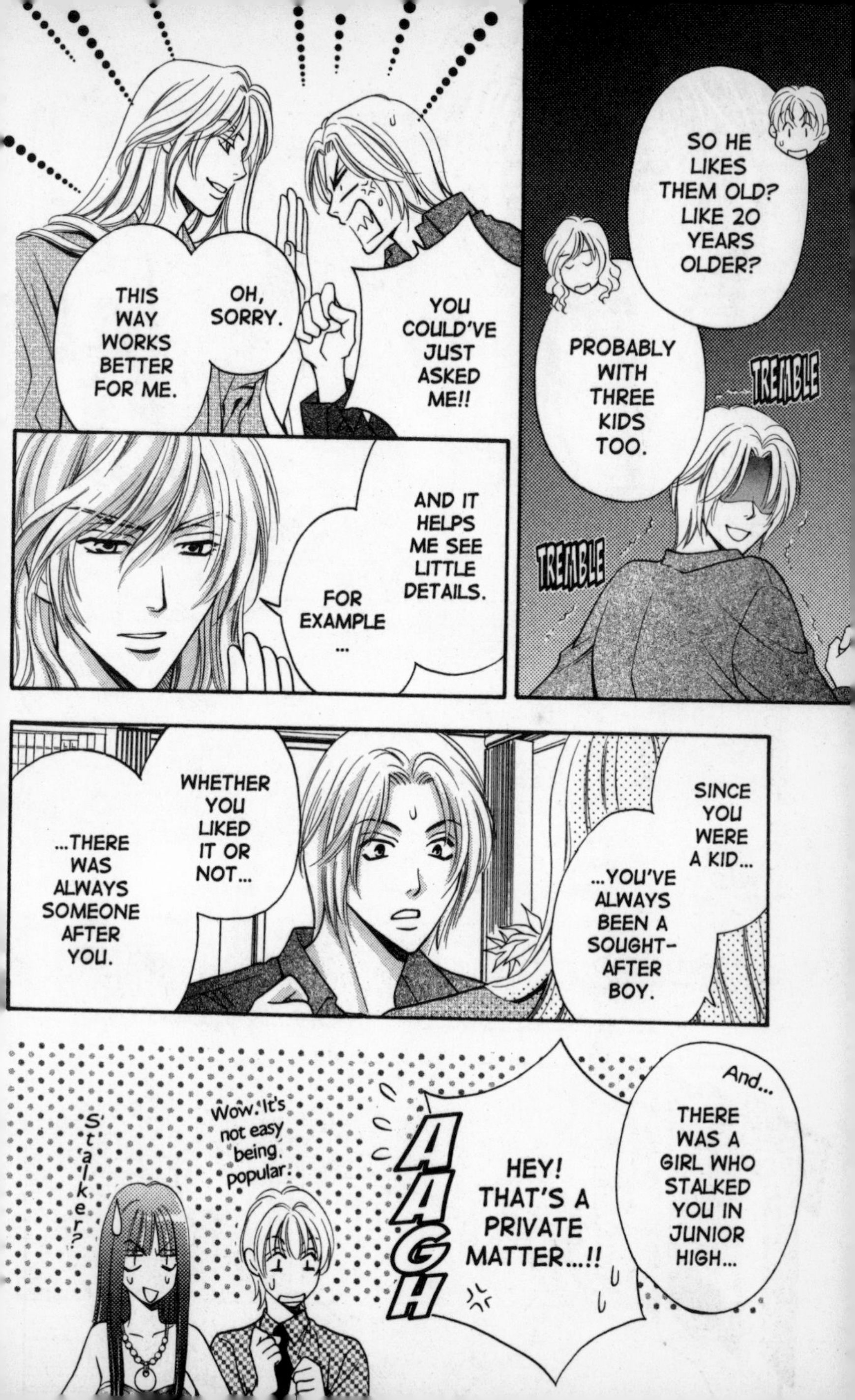
SO HE LIKES THEM OLD? LIKE 20 YEARS OLDER?
PROBABLY WITH THREE KIDS TOO.
TREMBLE
TREMBLE
YOU COULD'VE JUST ASKED ME!!
OH, SORRY.
THIS WAY WORKS BETTER FOR ME.
AND IT HELPS ME SEE LITTLE DETAILS.
FOR EXAMPLE ...
SINCE YOU WERE A KID...
...YOU'VE ALWAYS BEEN A SOUGHT-AFTER BOY.
WHETHER YOU LIKED IT OR NOT...
...THERE WAS ALWAYS SOMEONE AFTER YOU.
And...
THERE WAS A GIRL WHO STALKED YOU IN JUNIOR HIGH...
HEY! THAT'S A PRIVATE MATTER...!!
AAGH
Wow. It's not easy being popular.
Stalker?

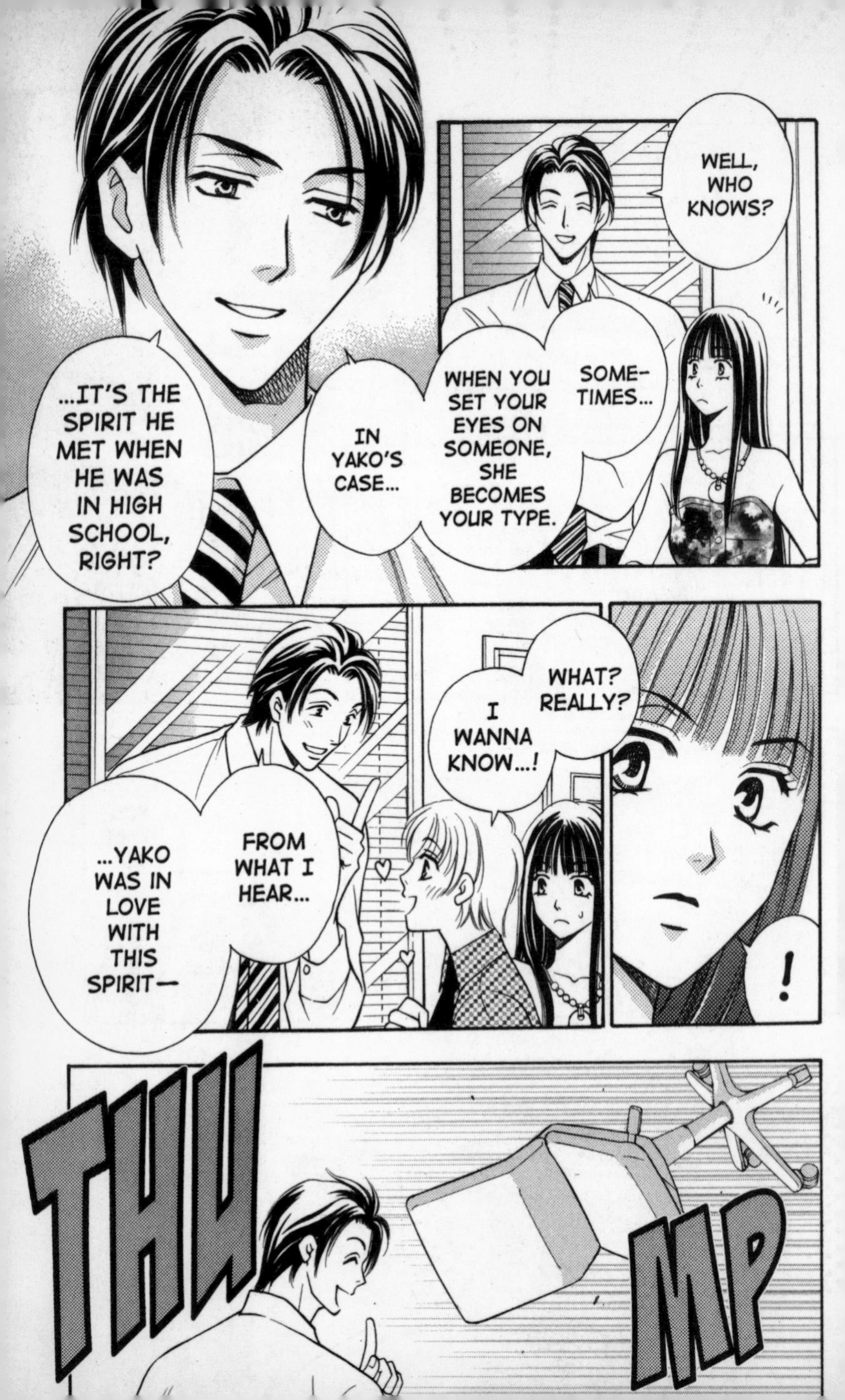
WELL, WHO KNOWS?
SOME-TIMES...
WHEN YOU SET YOUR EYES ON SOMEONE, SHE BECOMES YOUR TYPE.
IN YAKO'S CASE...
...IT'S THE SPIRIT HE MET WHEN HE WAS IN HIGH SCHOOL, RIGHT?
!
WHAT? REALLY?
I WANNA KNOW...!
FROM WHAT I HEAR...
...YAKO WAS IN LOVE WITH THIS SPIRIT—
THUMP

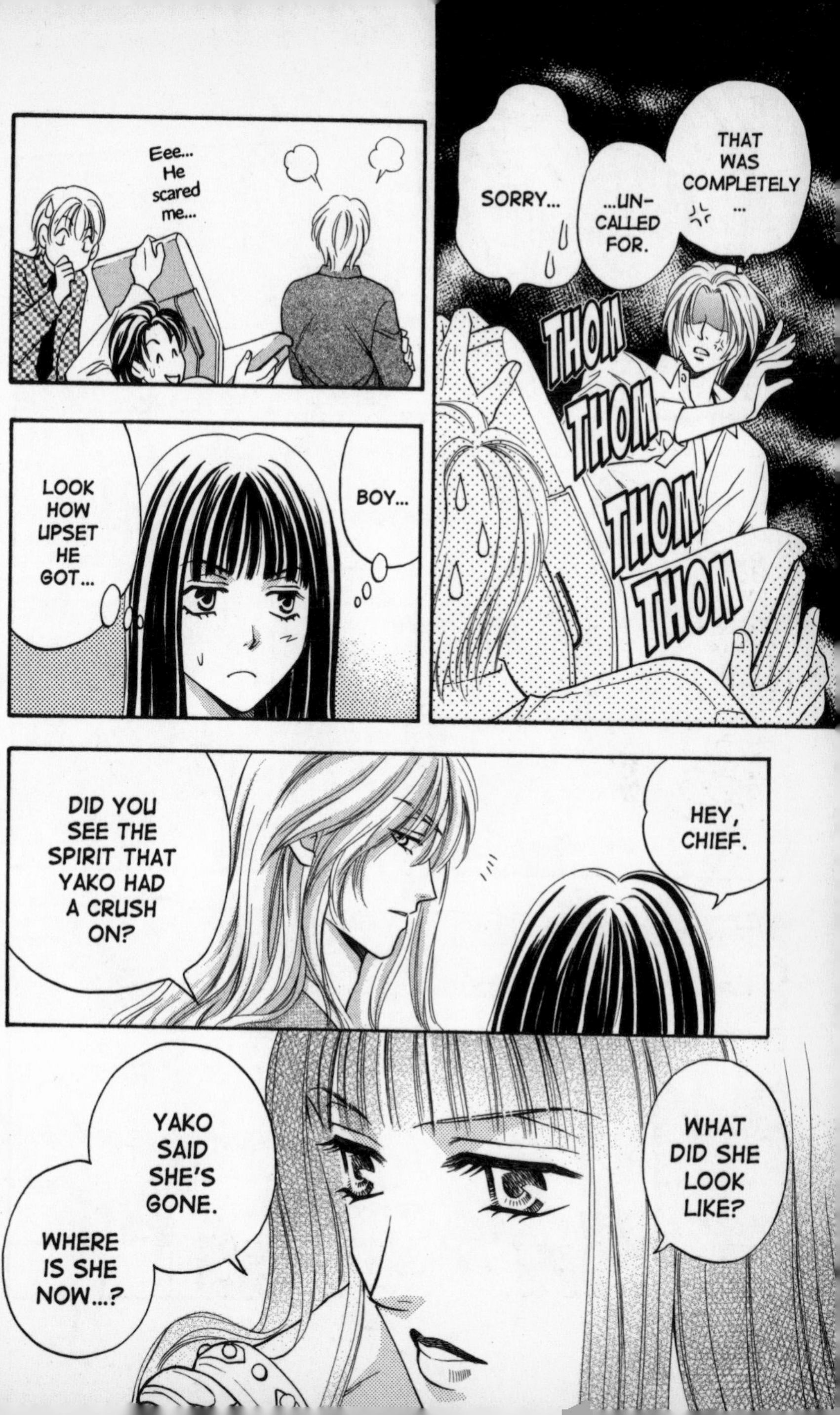
THAT WAS COMPLETELY ...
...UN-CALLED FOR.
SORRY...
THOM
THOM
THOM
THOM
Eee... He scared me...
BOY...
LOOK HOW UPSET HE GOT...
HEY, CHIEF.
DID YOU SEE THE SPIRIT THAT YAKO HAD A CRUSH ON?
WHAT DID SHE LOOK LIKE?
YAKO SAID SHE'S GONE.
WHERE IS SHE NOW...?

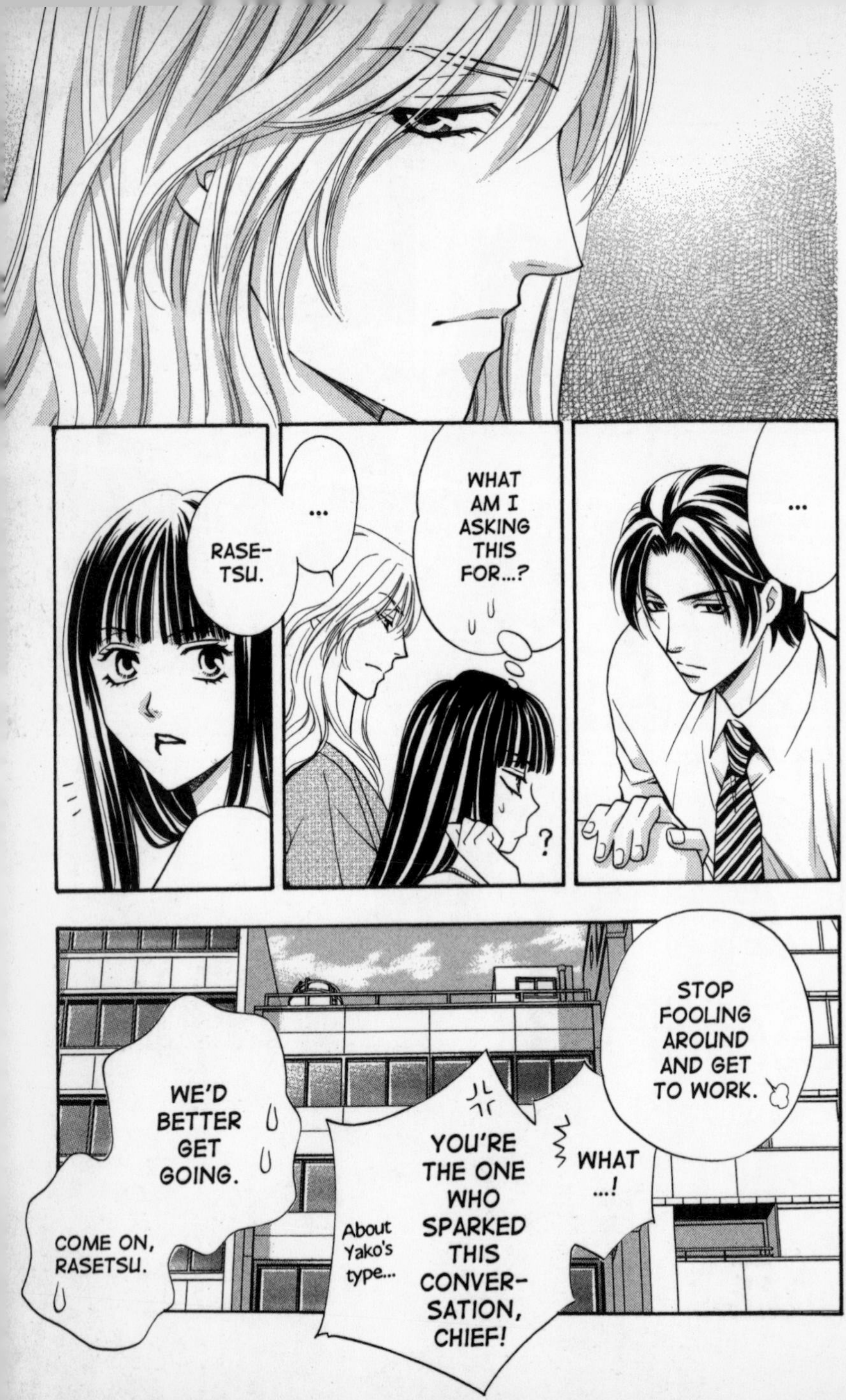
...
WHAT AM I ASKING THIS FOR...?
...
?
RASE-TSU.
STOP FOOLING AROUND AND GET TO WORK.
WHAT ...!
YOU'RE THE ONE WHO SPARKED THIS CONVER-SATION, CHIEF!
About Yako's type...
WE'D BETTER GET GOING.
COME ON, RASETSU.

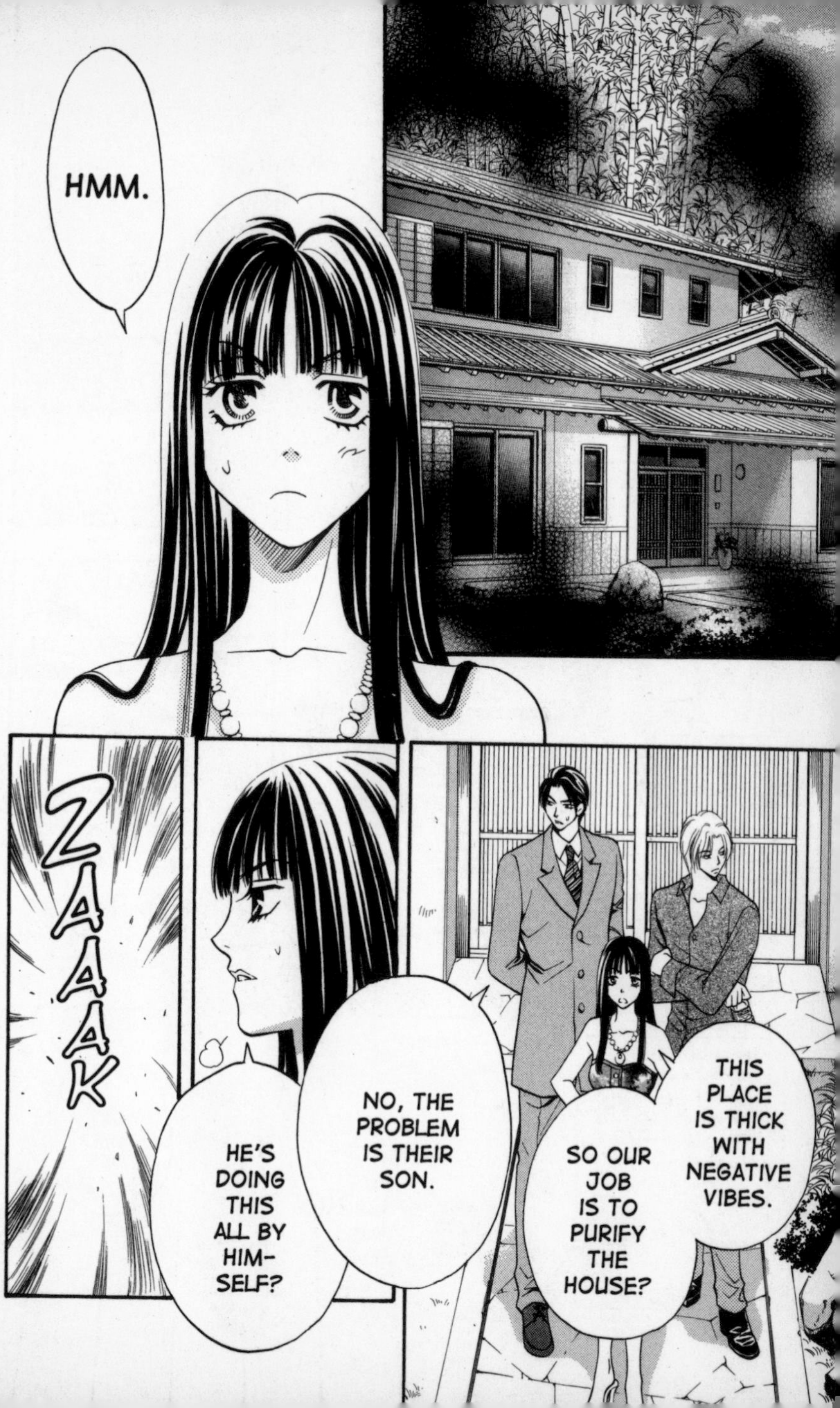
HMM.
THIS PLACE IS THICK WITH NEGATIVE VIBES.
SO OUR JOB IS TO PURIFY THE HOUSE?
NO, THE PROBLEM IS THEIR SON.
HE'S DOING THIS ALL BY HIM-SELF?
ZAAAK

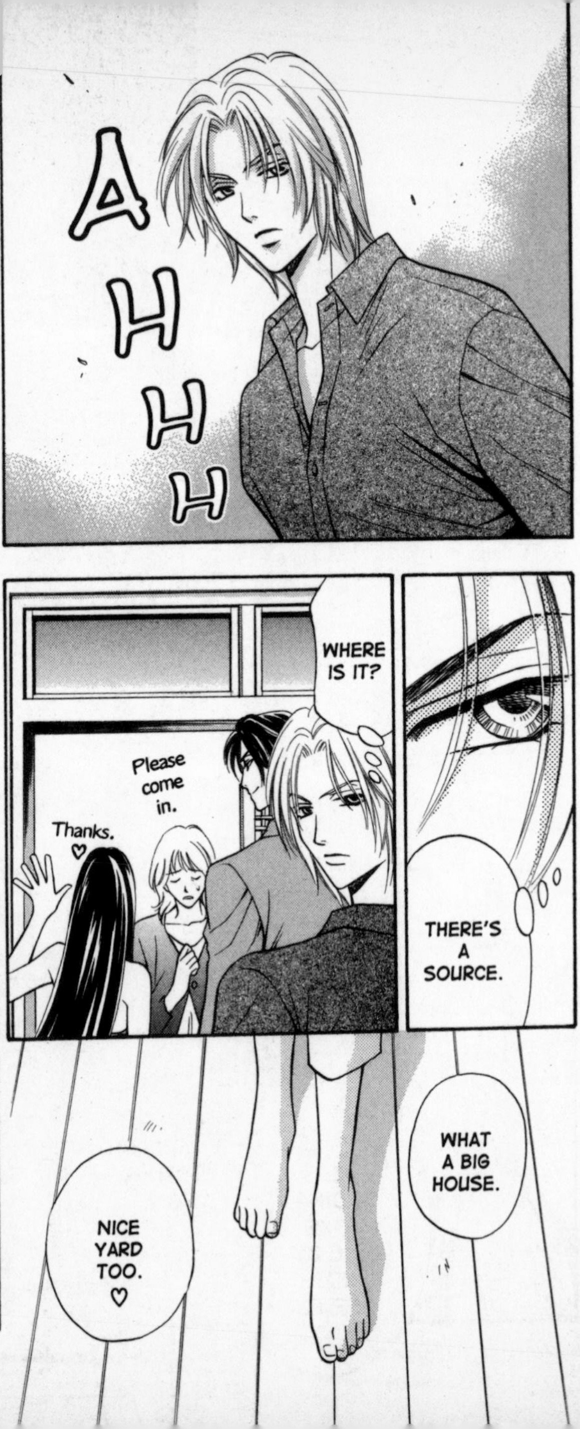
AHHH
THERE'S A SOURCE.
WHERE IS IT?
Please come in.
Thanks. ♡
WHAT A BIG HOUSE.
NICE YARD TOO. ♡

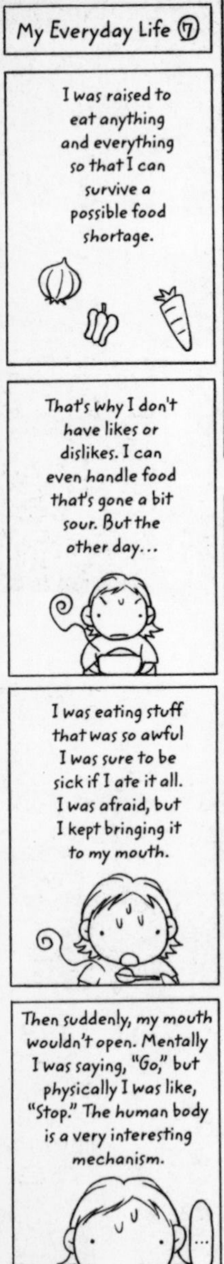
My Everyday Life ⑦
I was raised to eat anything and everything so that I can survive a possible food shortage.
That's why I don't have likes or dislikes. I can even handle food that's gone a bit sour. But the other day...
I was eating stuff that was so awful I was sure to be sick if I ate it all. I was afraid, but I kept bringing it to my mouth.
Then suddenly, my mouth wouldn't open. Mentally I was saying, "Go," but physically I was like, "Stop." The human body is a very interesting mechanism.
...

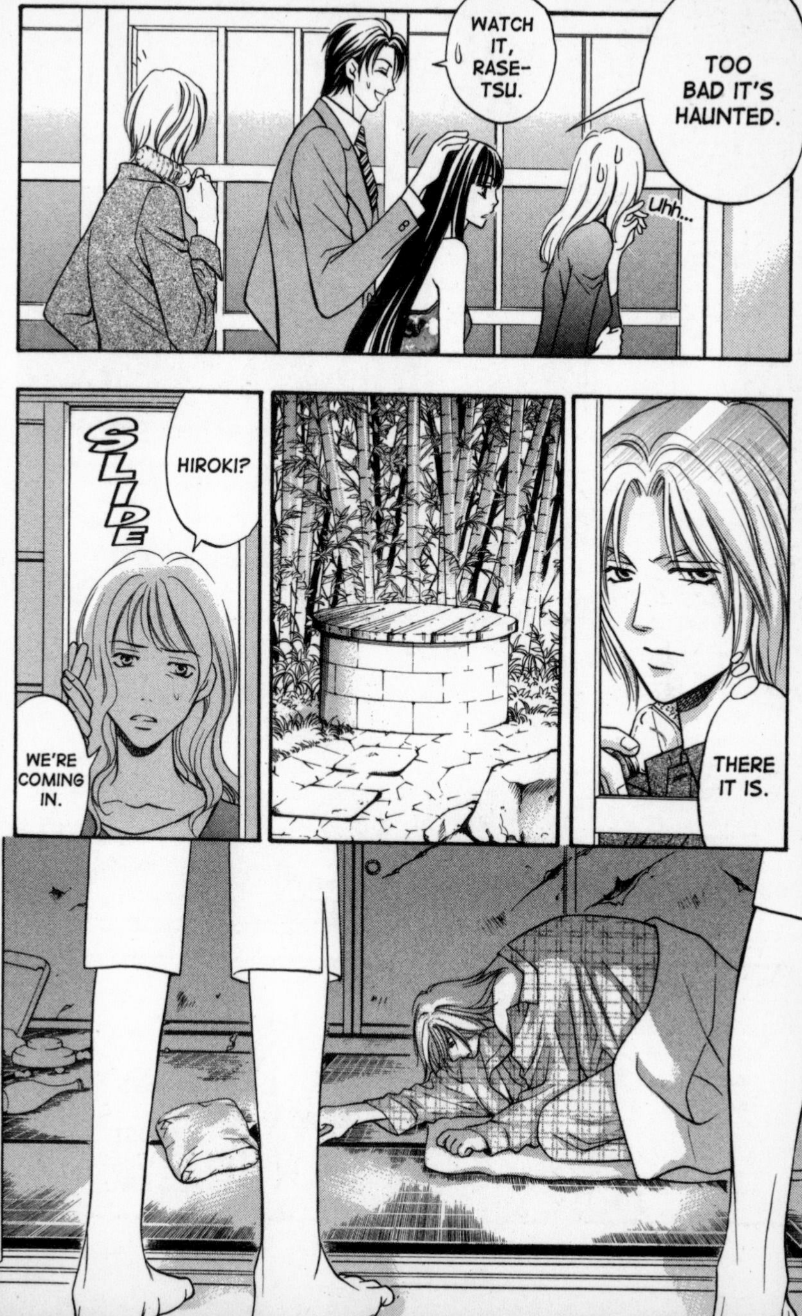
TOO BAD IT'S HAUNTED.
Uhh...
WATCH IT, RASE-TSU.
THERE IT IS.
HIROKI?
SLIDE
WE'RE COMING IN.

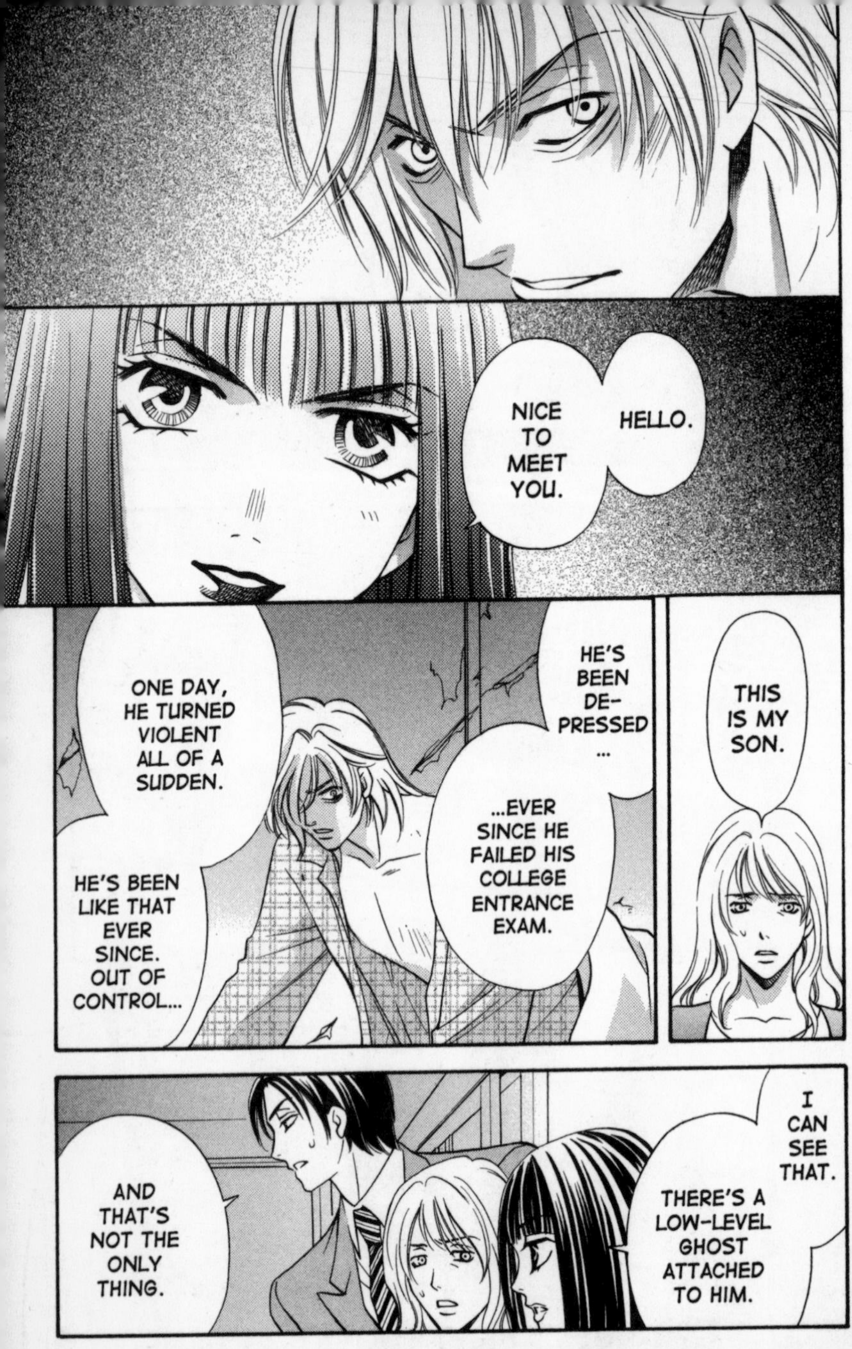
HELLO.
NICE TO MEET YOU.
THIS IS MY SON.
HE'S BEEN DE-PRESSED ...
...EVER SINCE HE FAILED HIS COLLEGE ENTRANCE EXAM.
ONE DAY, HE TURNED VIOLENT ALL OF A SUDDEN.
HE'S BEEN LIKE THAT EVER SINCE. OUT OF CONTROL...
I CAN SEE THAT.
THERE'S A LOW-LEVEL GHOST ATTACHED TO HIM.
AND THAT'S NOT THE ONLY THING.

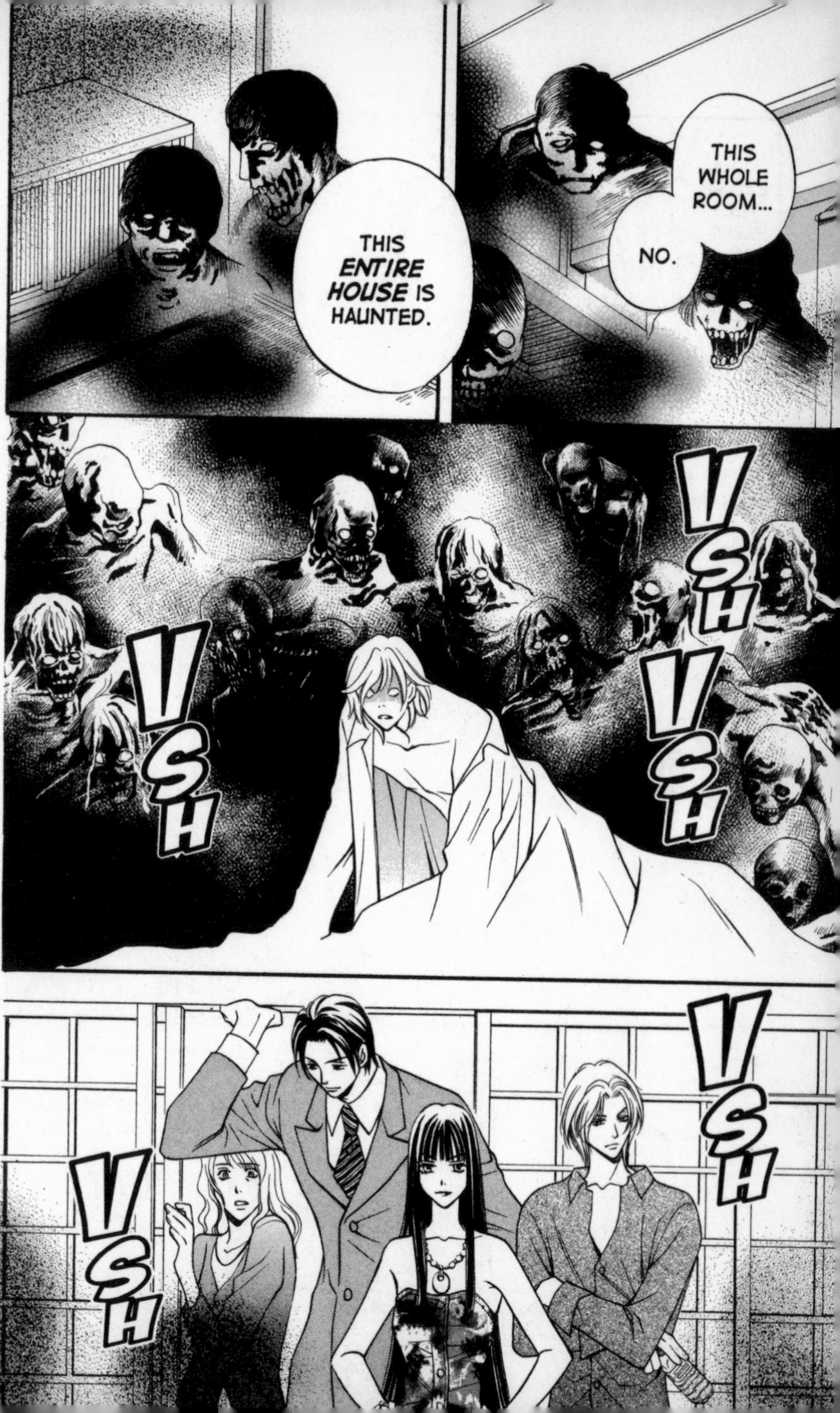
THIS WHOLE ROOM...
NO.
THIS *ENTIRE HOUSE* IS HAUNTED.
VISH
VISH
VISH
VISH
VISH

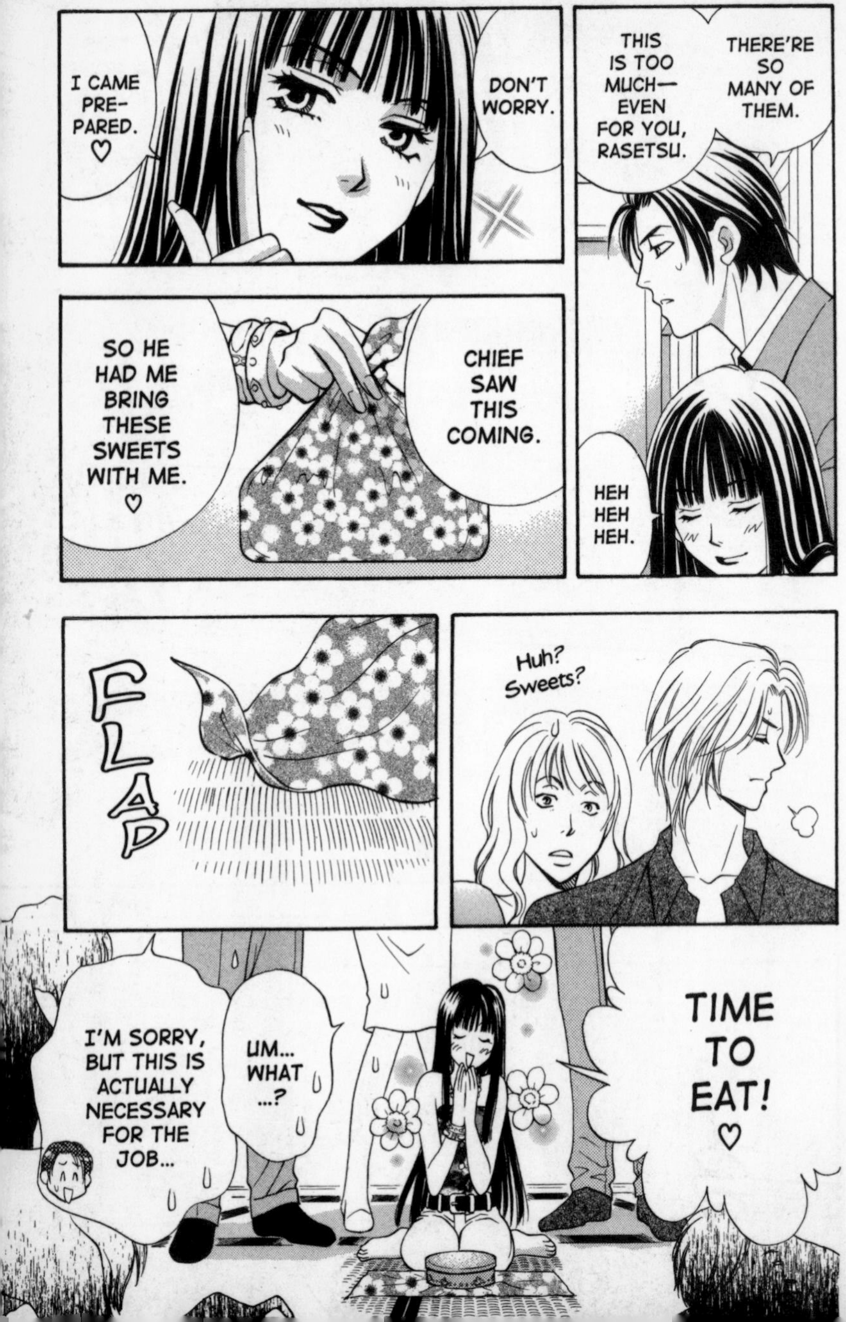
THERE'RE SO MANY OF THEM.
THIS IS TOO MUCH— EVEN FOR YOU, RASETSU.
HEH HEH HEH.
DON'T WORRY.
I CAME PRE-PARED. ♡
CHIEF SAW THIS COMING.
SO HE HAD ME BRING THESE SWEETS WITH ME. ♡
Huh? Sweets?
FLAP
TIME TO EAT! ♡
UM... WHAT ...?
I'M SORRY, BUT THIS IS ACTUALLY NECESSARY FOR THE JOB...

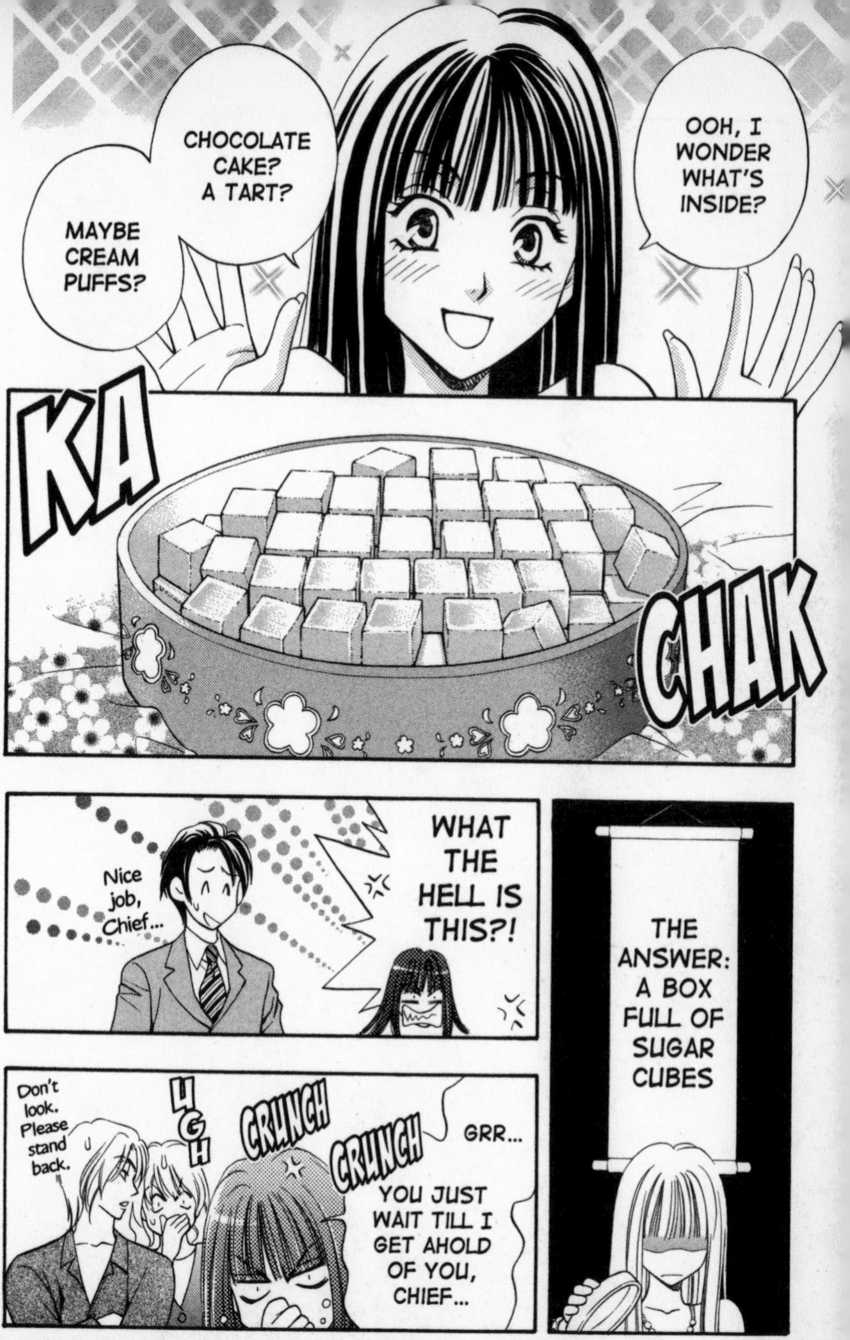
OOH, I WONDER WHAT'S INSIDE?
CHOCOLATE CAKE? A TART?
MAYBE CREAM PUFFS?
KA
CHAK
THE ANSWER: A BOX FULL OF SUGAR CUBES
WHAT THE HELL IS THIS?!
Nice job, Chief...
GRR...
YOU JUST WAIT TILL I GET AHOLD OF YOU, CHIEF...
CRUNCH
CRUNCH
UGH
Don't look. Please stand back.

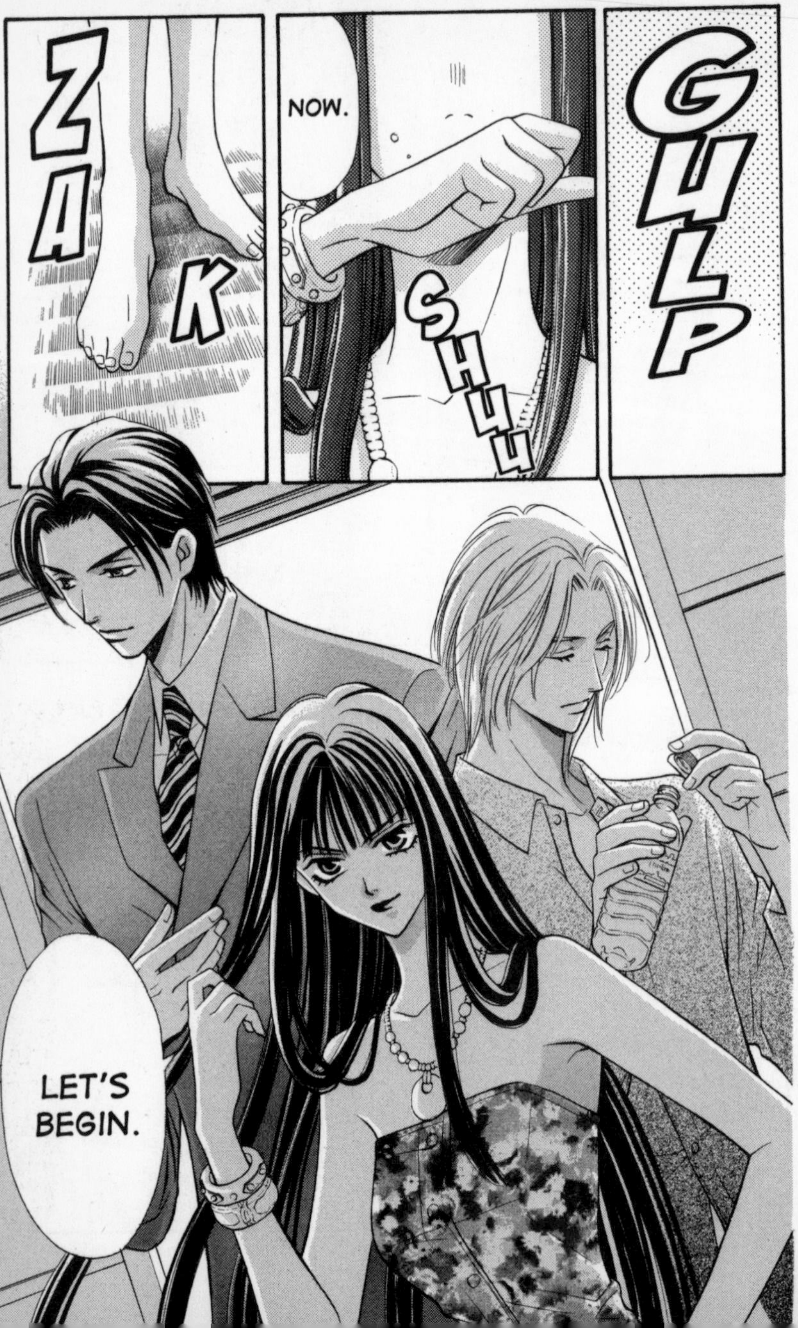
GULP
NOW.
SHUU
ZAK
LET'S BEGIN.

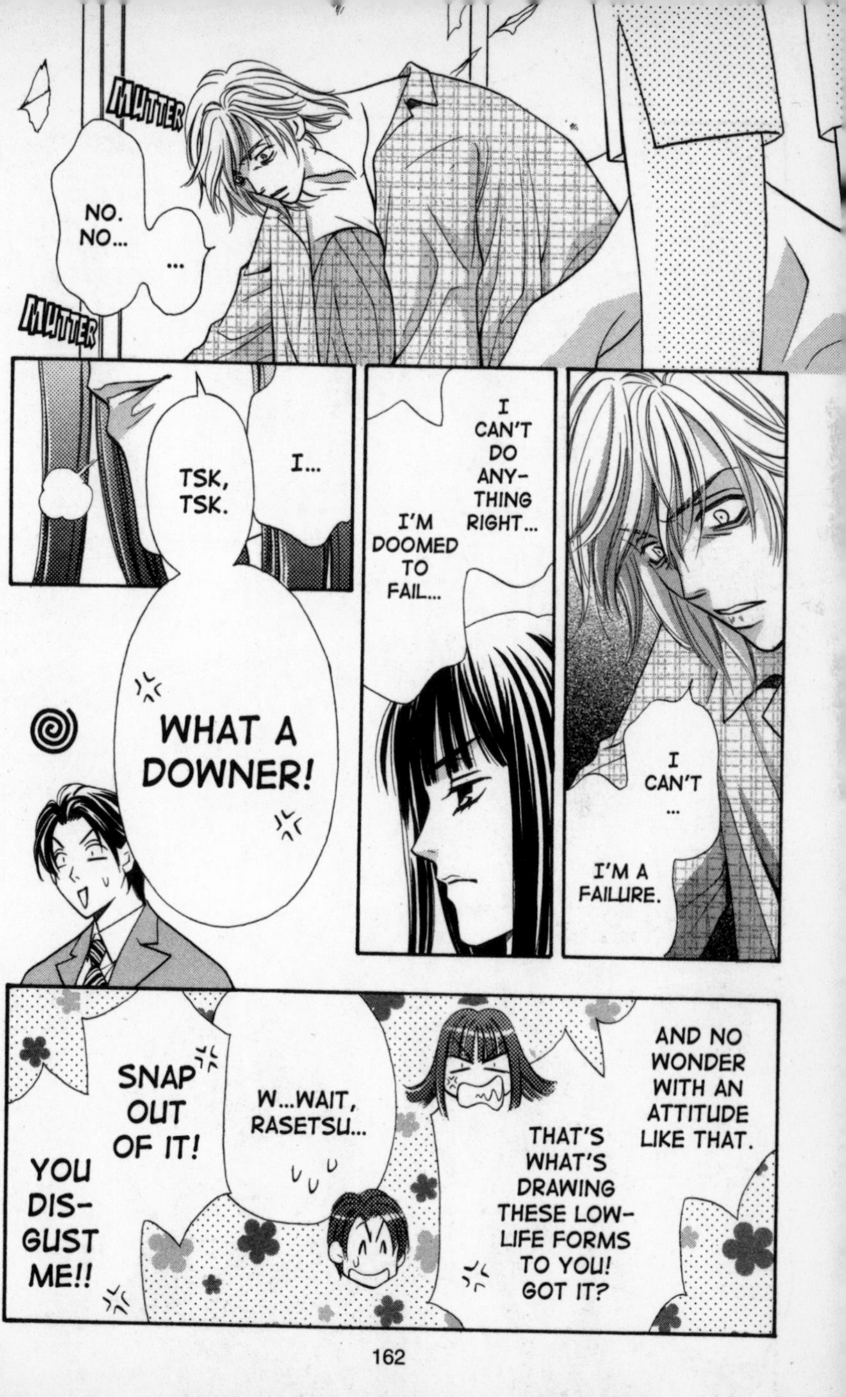
MUTTER
NO. NO... ...
MUTTER
I CAN'T ...
I'M A FAILURE.
I CAN'T DO ANYTHING RIGHT...
I'M DOOMED TO FAIL...
I...
TSK, TSK.
WHAT A DOWNER!
AND NO WONDER WITH AN ATTITUDE LIKE THAT.
THAT'S WHAT'S DRAWING THESE LOW-LIFE FORMS TO YOU! GOT IT?
W...WAIT, RASETSU...
SNAP OUT OF IT!
YOU DISGUST ME!!

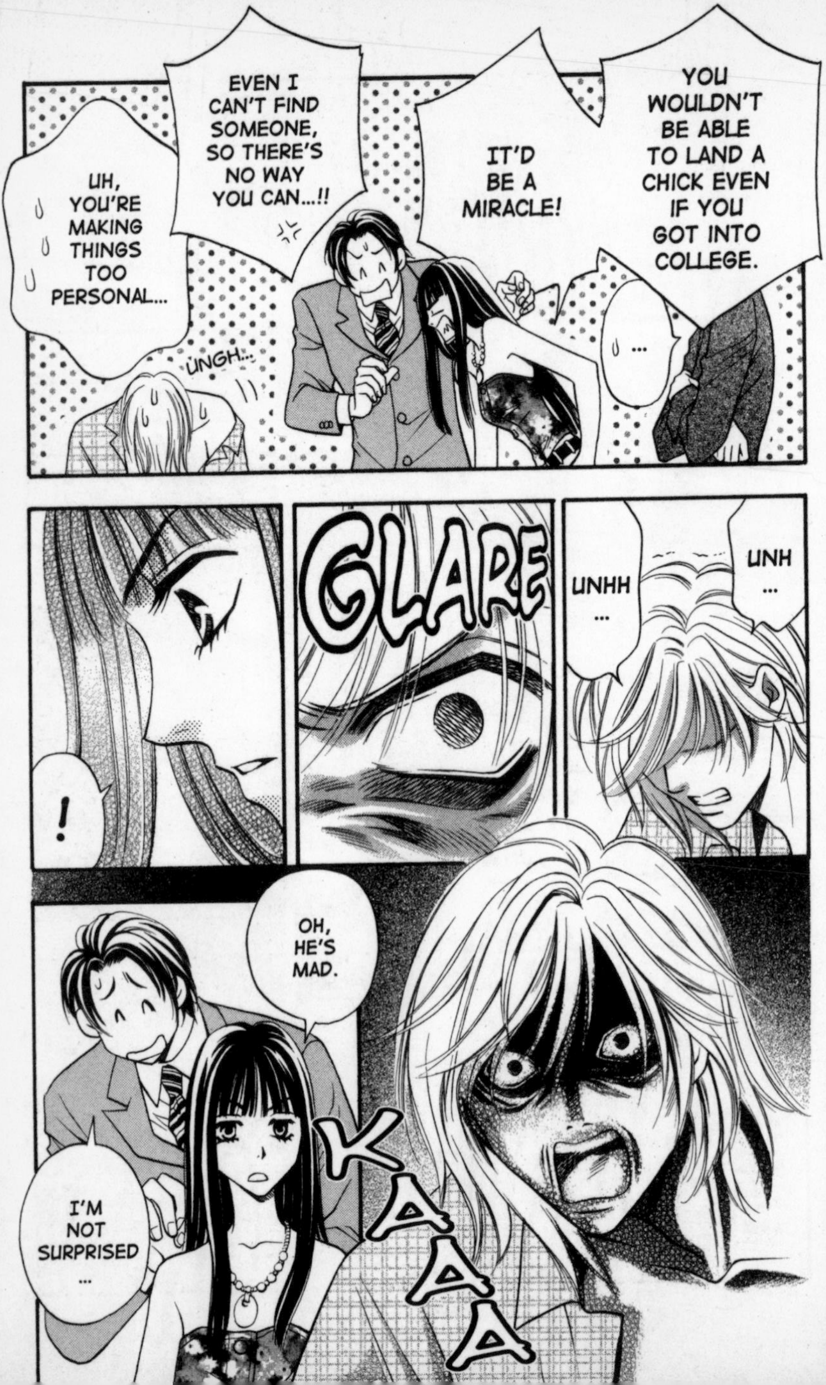
YOU WOULDN'T BE ABLE TO LAND A CHICK EVEN IF YOU GOT INTO COLLEGE.
IT'D BE A MIRACLE!
EVEN I CAN'T FIND SOMEONE, SO THERE'S NO WAY YOU CAN...!!
...
UH, YOU'RE MAKING THINGS TOO PERSONAL...
UNGH...
UNH ...
UNHH ...
GLARE
!
KAAAA
OH, HE'S MAD.
I'M NOT SURPRISED ...

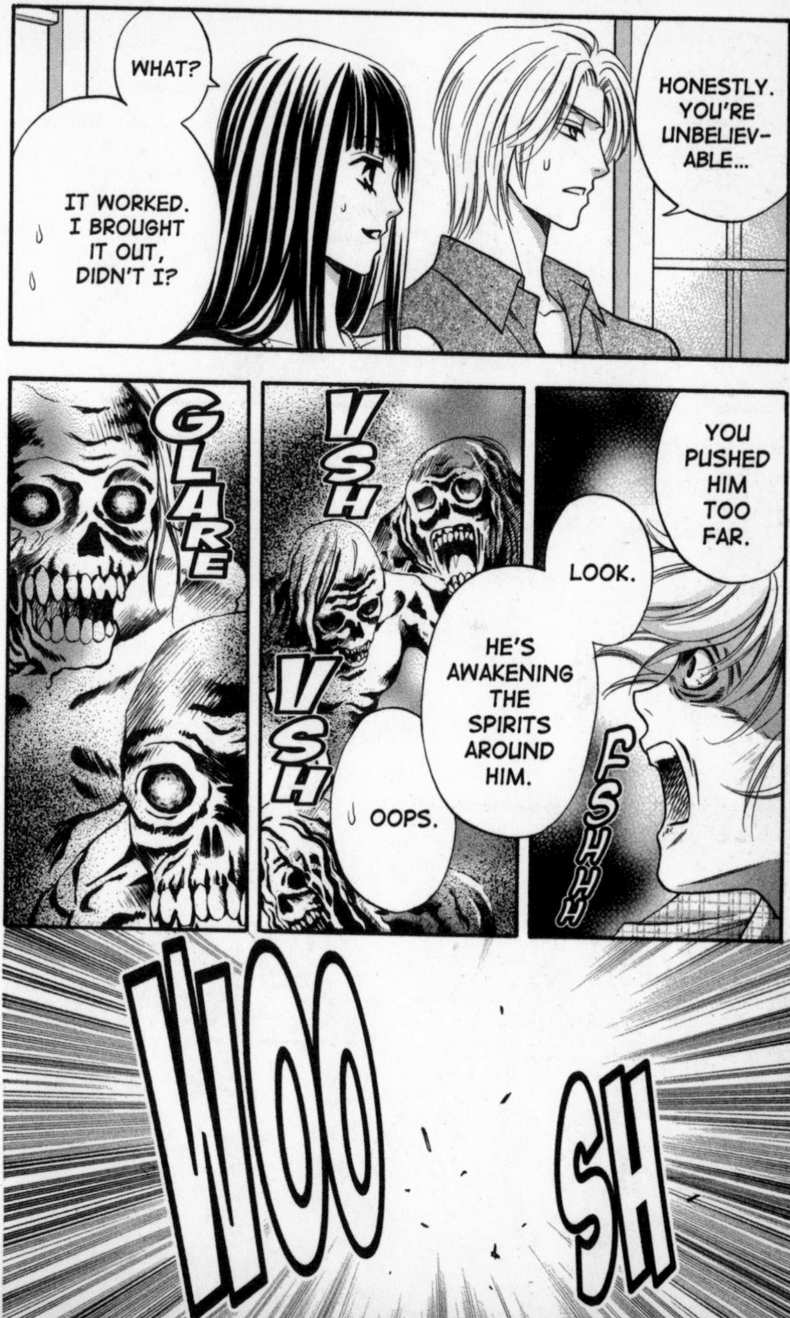
HONESTLY. YOU'RE UNBELIEV-ABLE...
WHAT?
IT WORKED. I BROUGHT IT OUT, DIDN'T I?
YOU PUSHED HIM TOO FAR.
LOOK.
HE'S AWAKENING THE SPIRITS AROUND HIM.
FSHHHH
VSH
VSH
OOPS.
GLARE
WHOO
SH

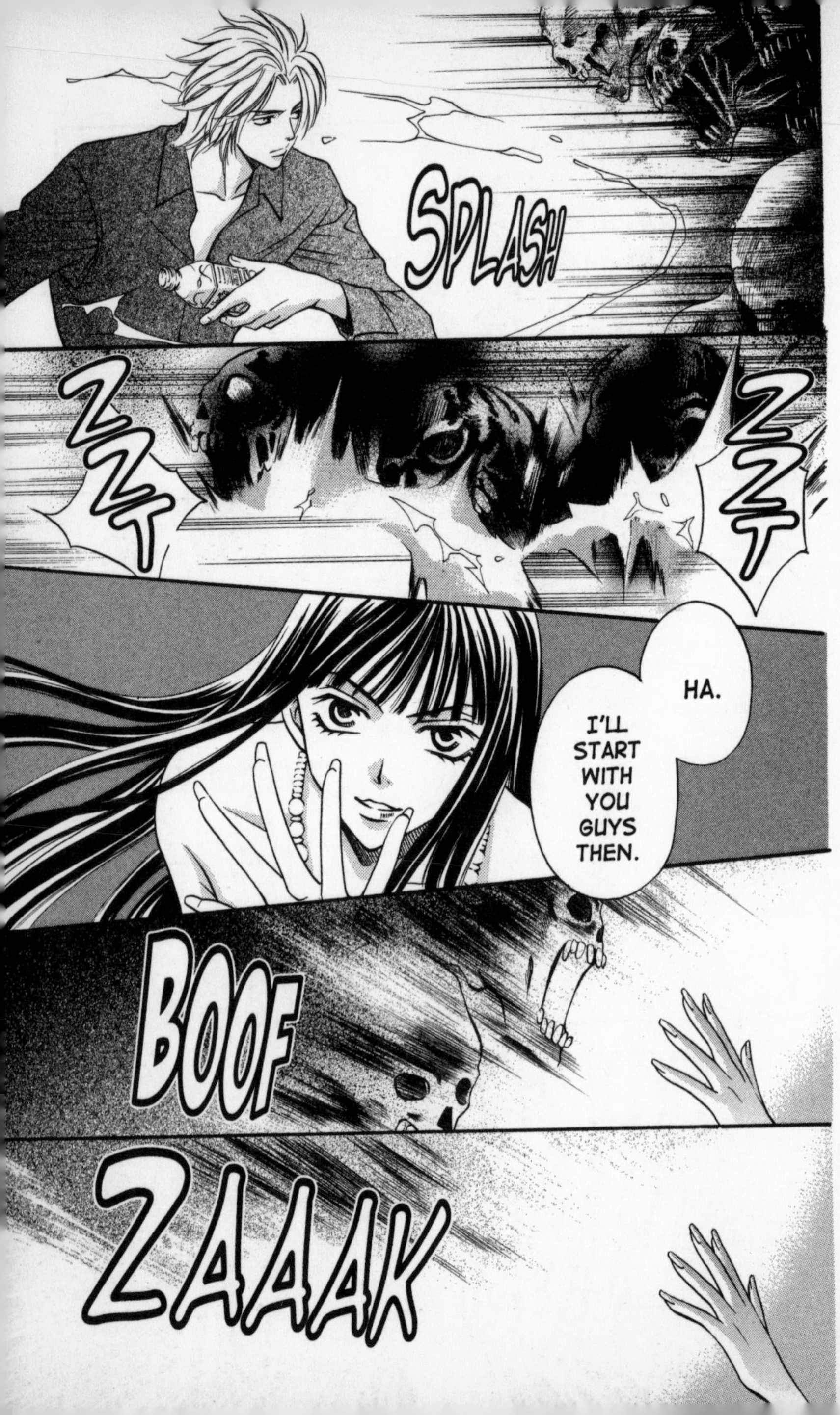
SPLASH
ZZZT
ZZZT
HA.
I'LL START WITH YOU GUYS THEN.
BOOF
ZAAAK

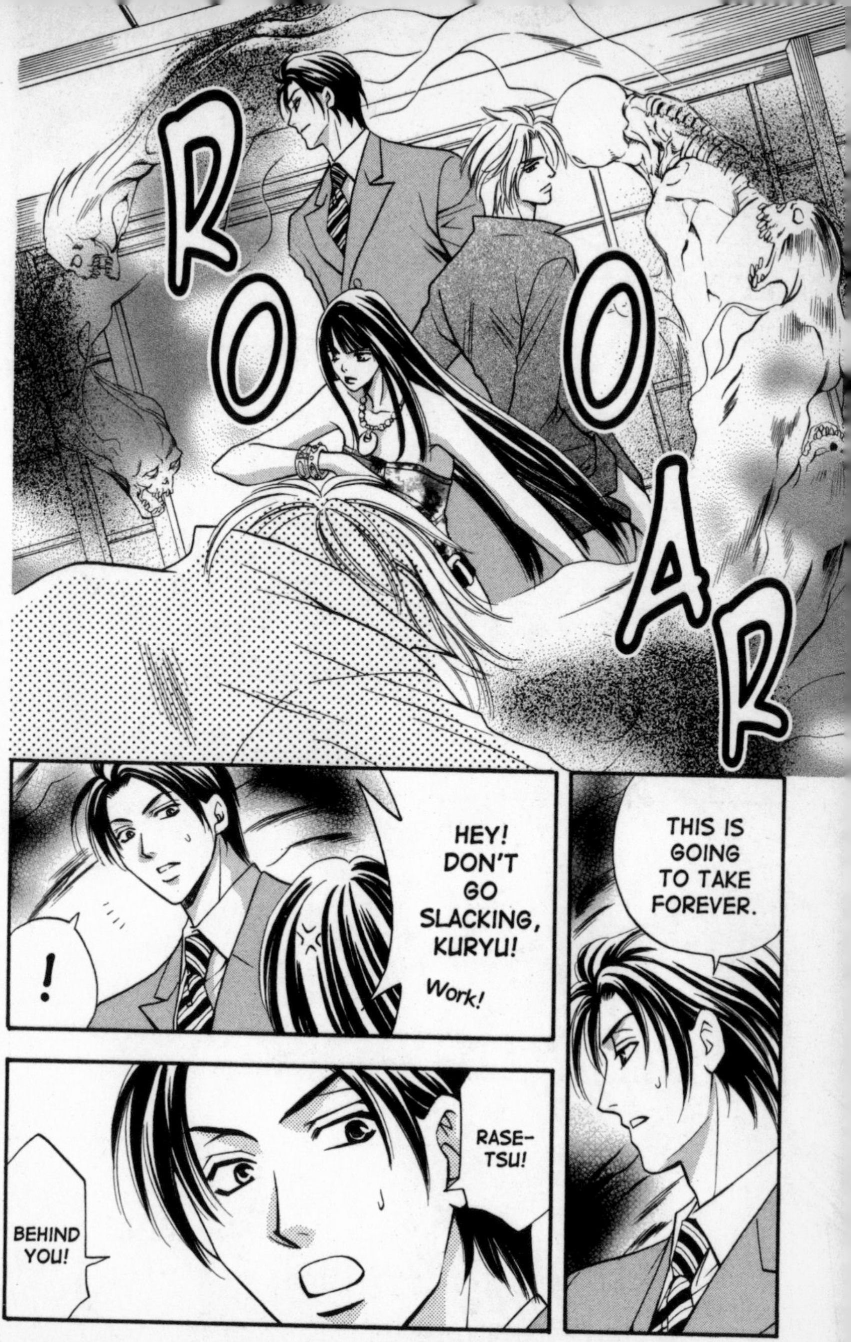
ROOOAR
THIS IS GOING TO TAKE FOREVER.
HEY! DON'T GO SLACKING, KURYU!
Work!
!
RASE-TSU!
BEHIND YOU!

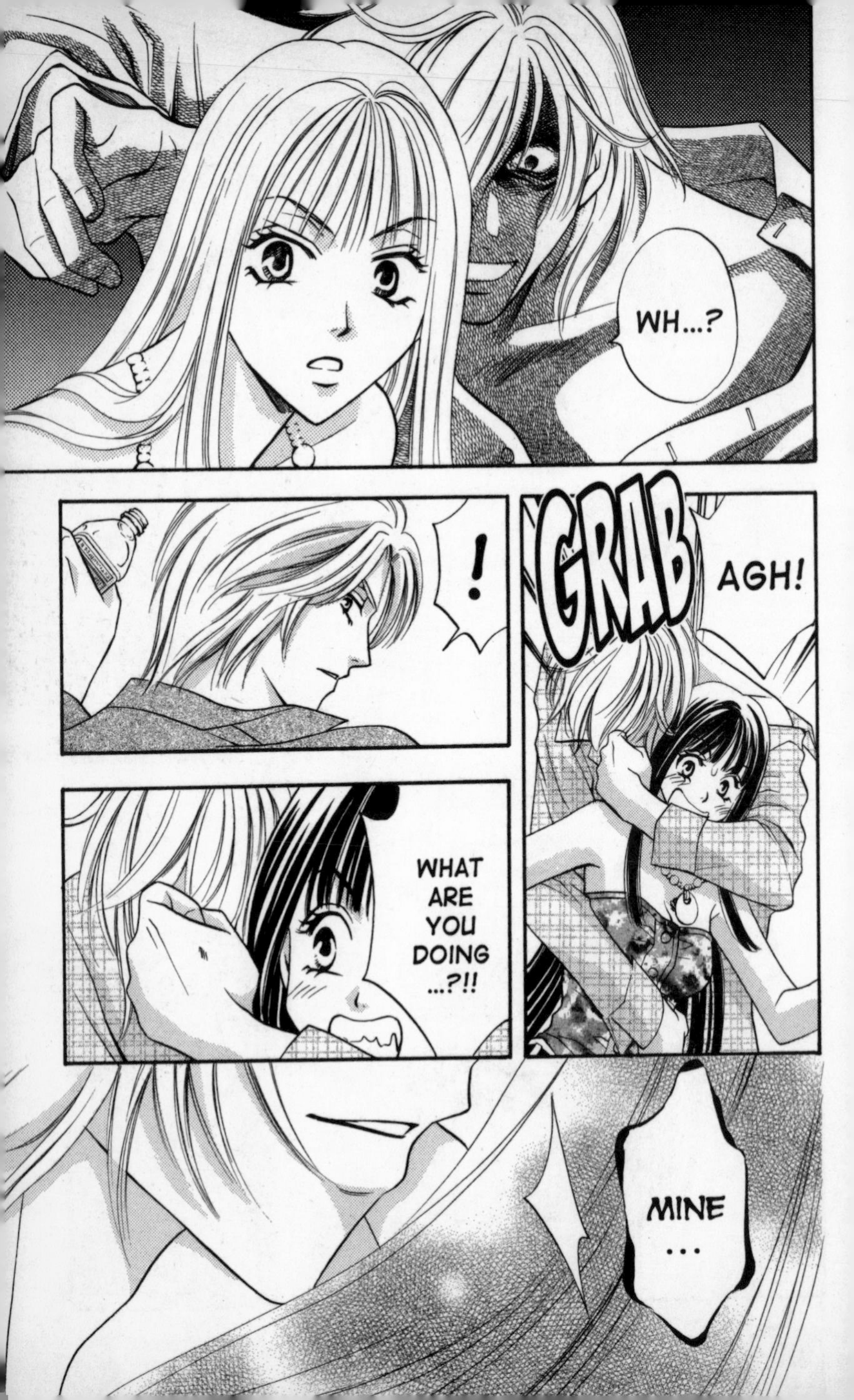

WH...?
GRAB
AGH!
!
WHAT ARE YOU DOING ...?!!
MINE ...

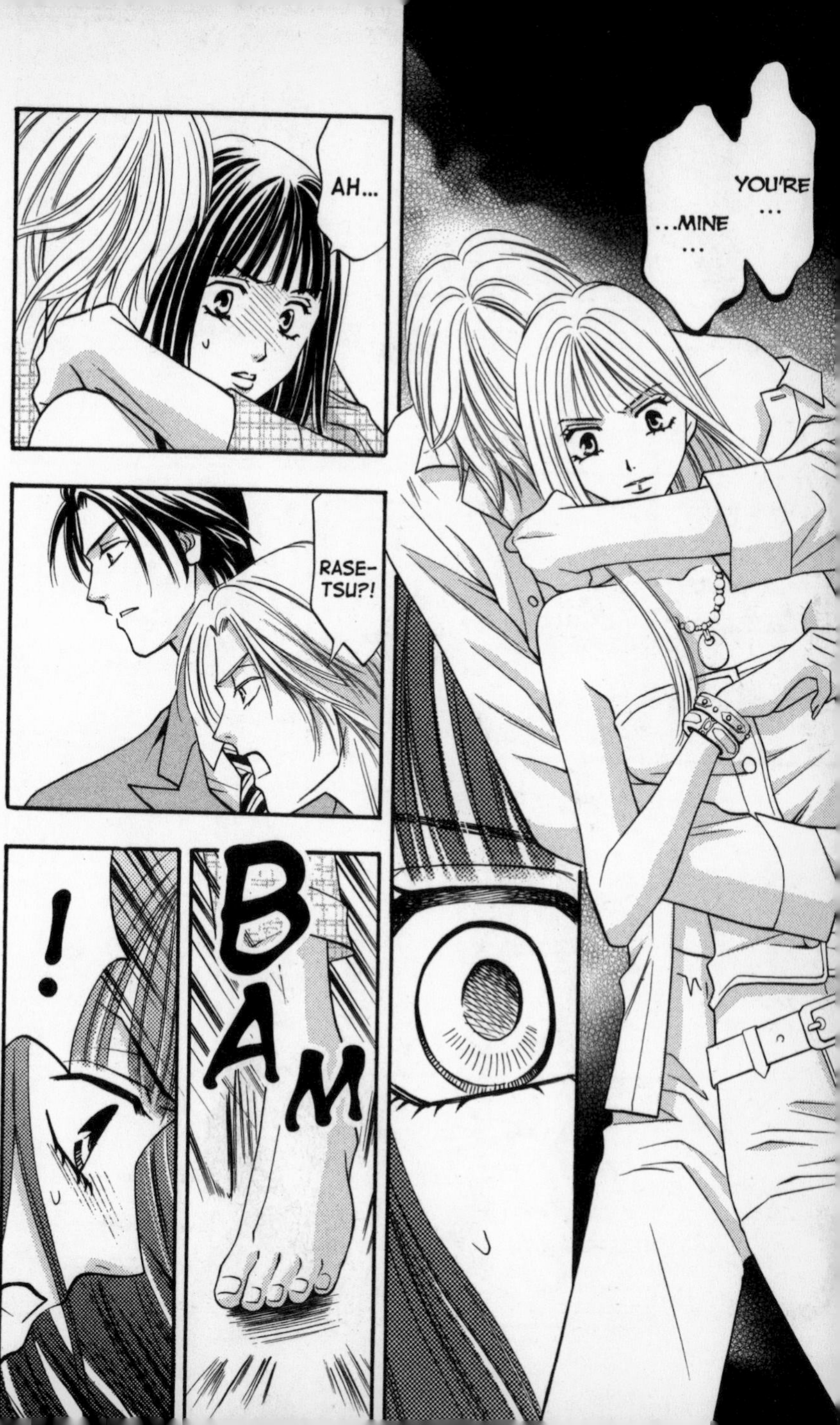
YOU'RE ...
...MINE ...
AH...
RASE-TSU?!
BAM
!

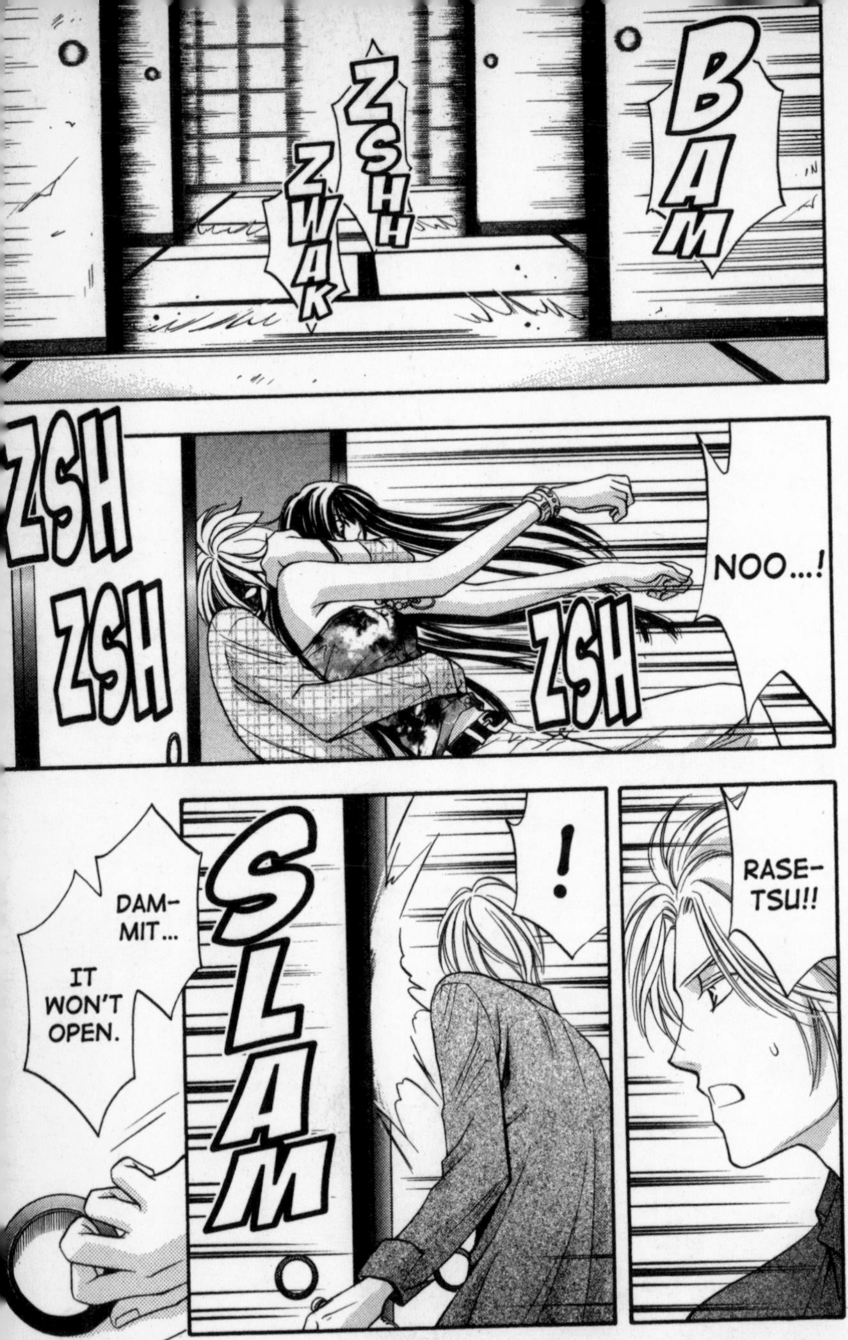
BAM
ZSHH
ZWAK
NOO...!
ZSH
ZSH
ZSH
RASE-TSU!!
!
SLAM
DAM-MIT...
IT WON'T OPEN.

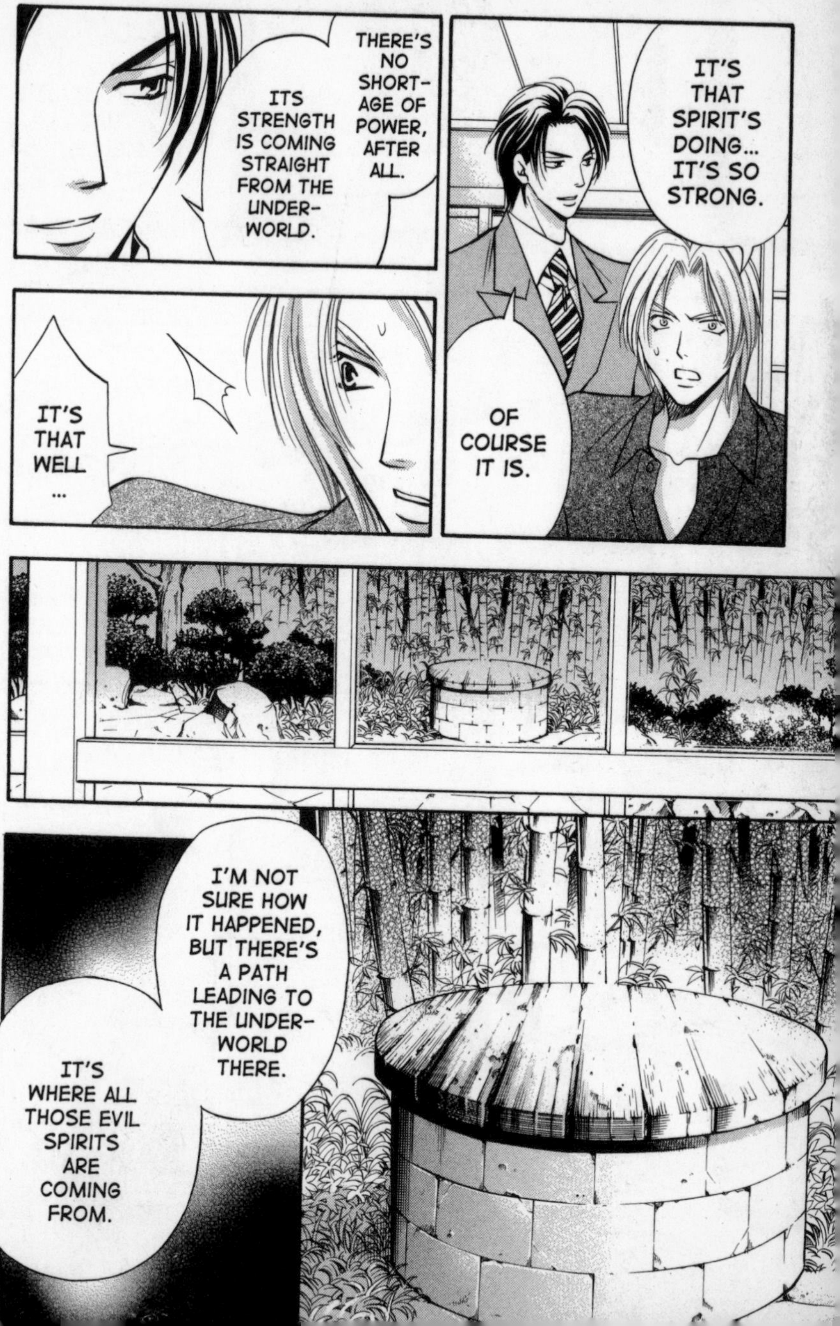
IT'S THAT SPIRIT'S DOING... IT'S SO STRONG.
OF COURSE IT IS.
THERE'S NO SHORTAGE OF POWER, AFTER ALL.
ITS STRENGTH IS COMING STRAIGHT FROM THE UNDERWORLD.
IT'S THAT WELL...
I'M NOT SURE HOW IT HAPPENED, BUT THERE'S A PATH LEADING TO THE UNDERWORLD THERE.
IT'S WHERE ALL THOSE EVIL SPIRITS ARE COMING FROM.

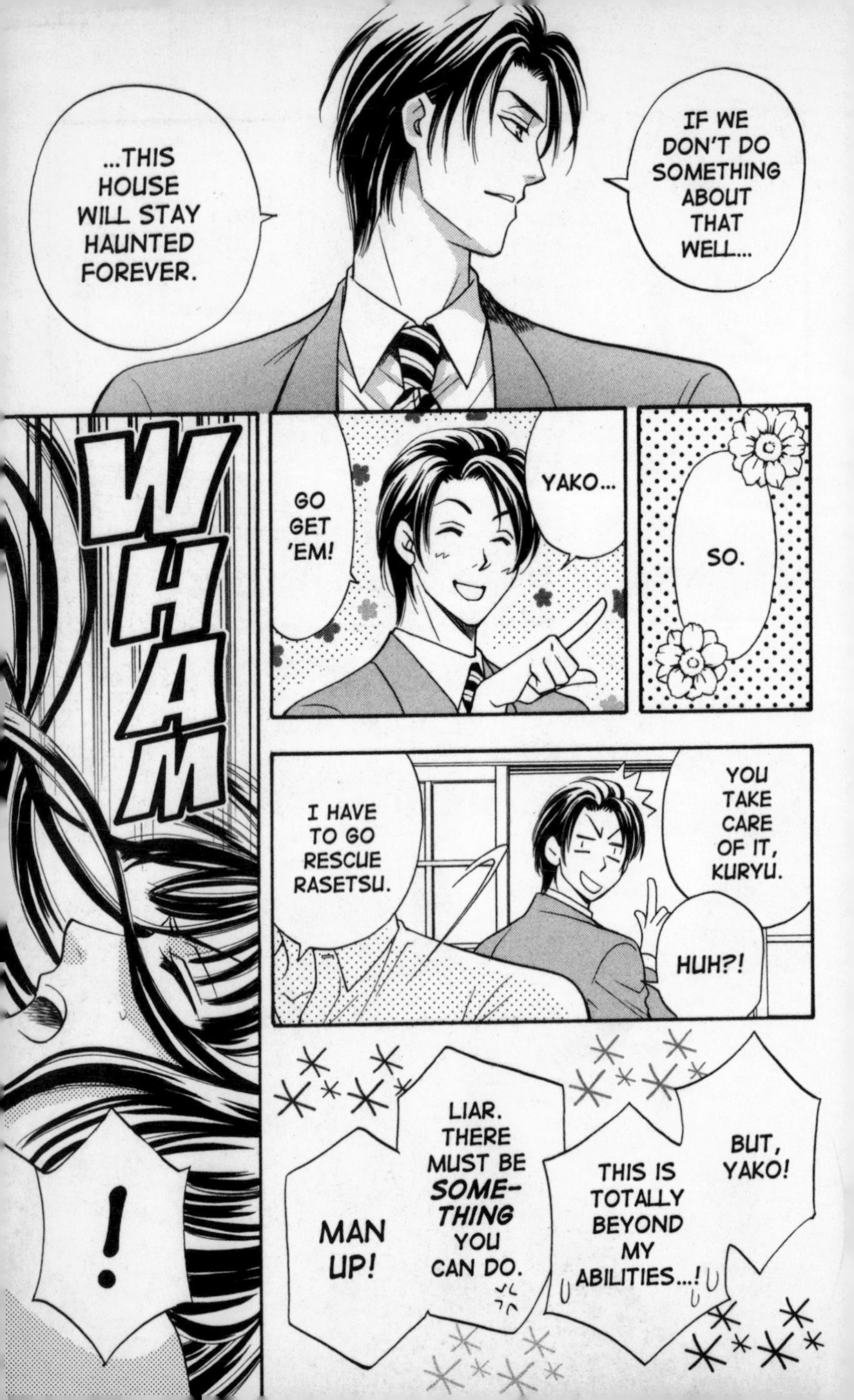
IF WE DON'T DO SOMETHING ABOUT THAT WELL...
...THIS HOUSE WILL STAY HAUNTED FOREVER.
SO.
YAKO...
GO GET 'EM!
YOU TAKE CARE OF IT, KURYU.
HUH?!
I HAVE TO GO RESCUE RASETSU.
BUT, YAKO!
THIS IS TOTALLY BEYOND MY ABILITIES...!
LIAR. THERE MUST BE *SOME-THING* YOU CAN DO.
MAN UP!
WHAM
!

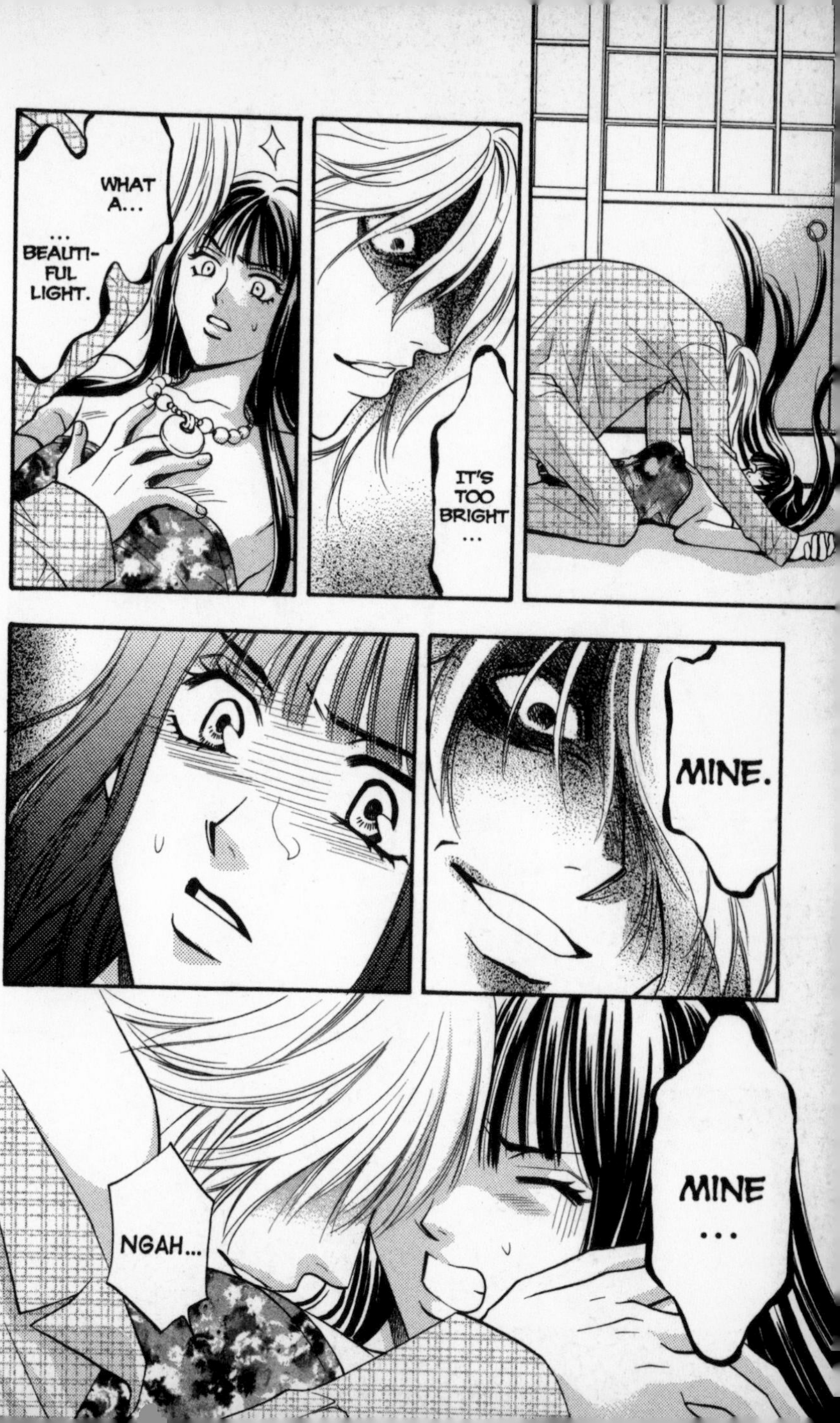
IT'S TOO BRIGHT...
WHAT A...
...BEAUTI-FUL LIGHT.
MINE.
MINE...
NGAH...

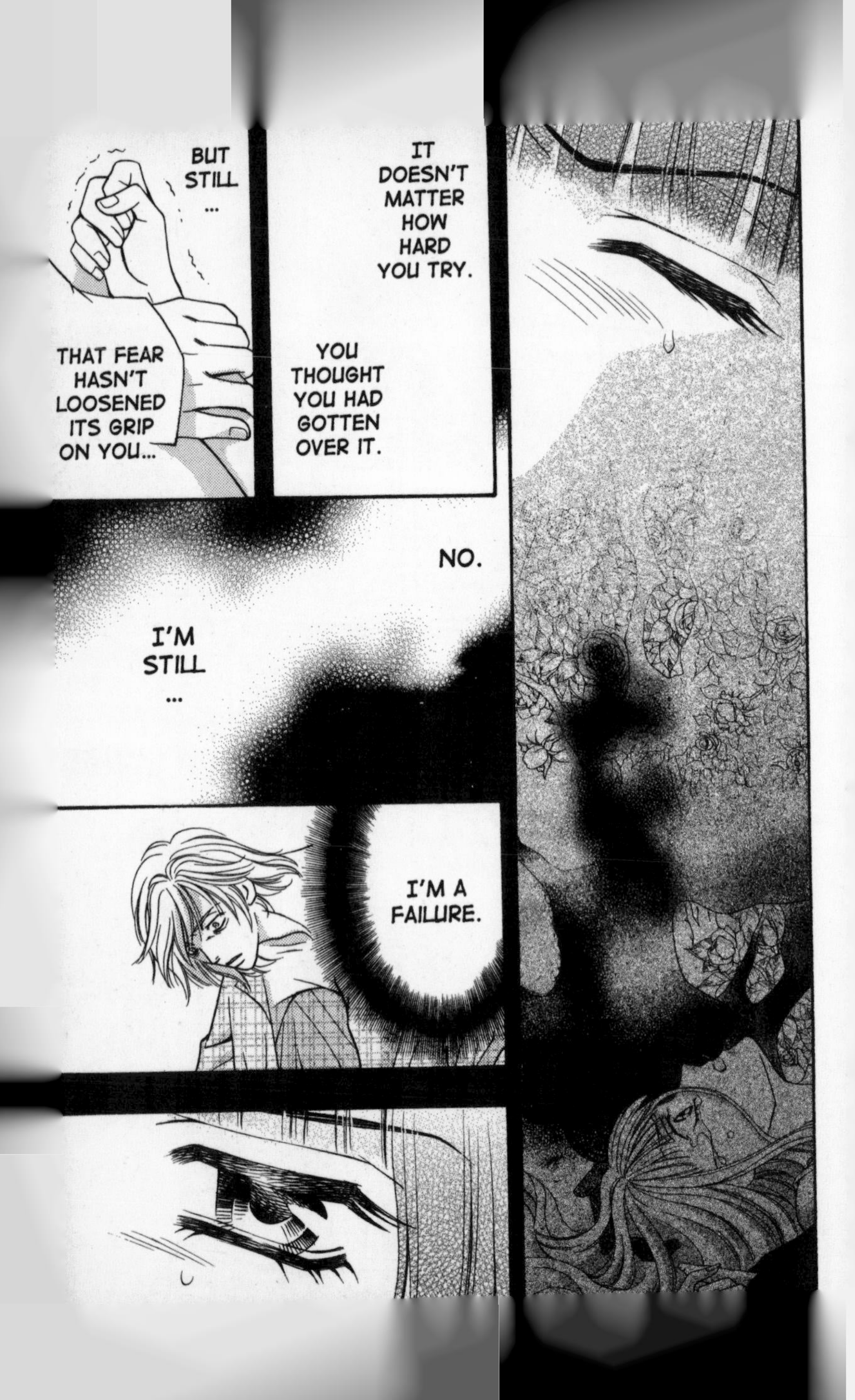
IT DOESN'T MATTER HOW HARD YOU TRY.
YOU THOUGHT YOU HAD GOTTEN OVER IT.
BUT STILL ...
THAT FEAR HASN'T LOOSENED ITS GRIP ON YOU...
NO.
I'M STILL ...
I'M A FAILURE.

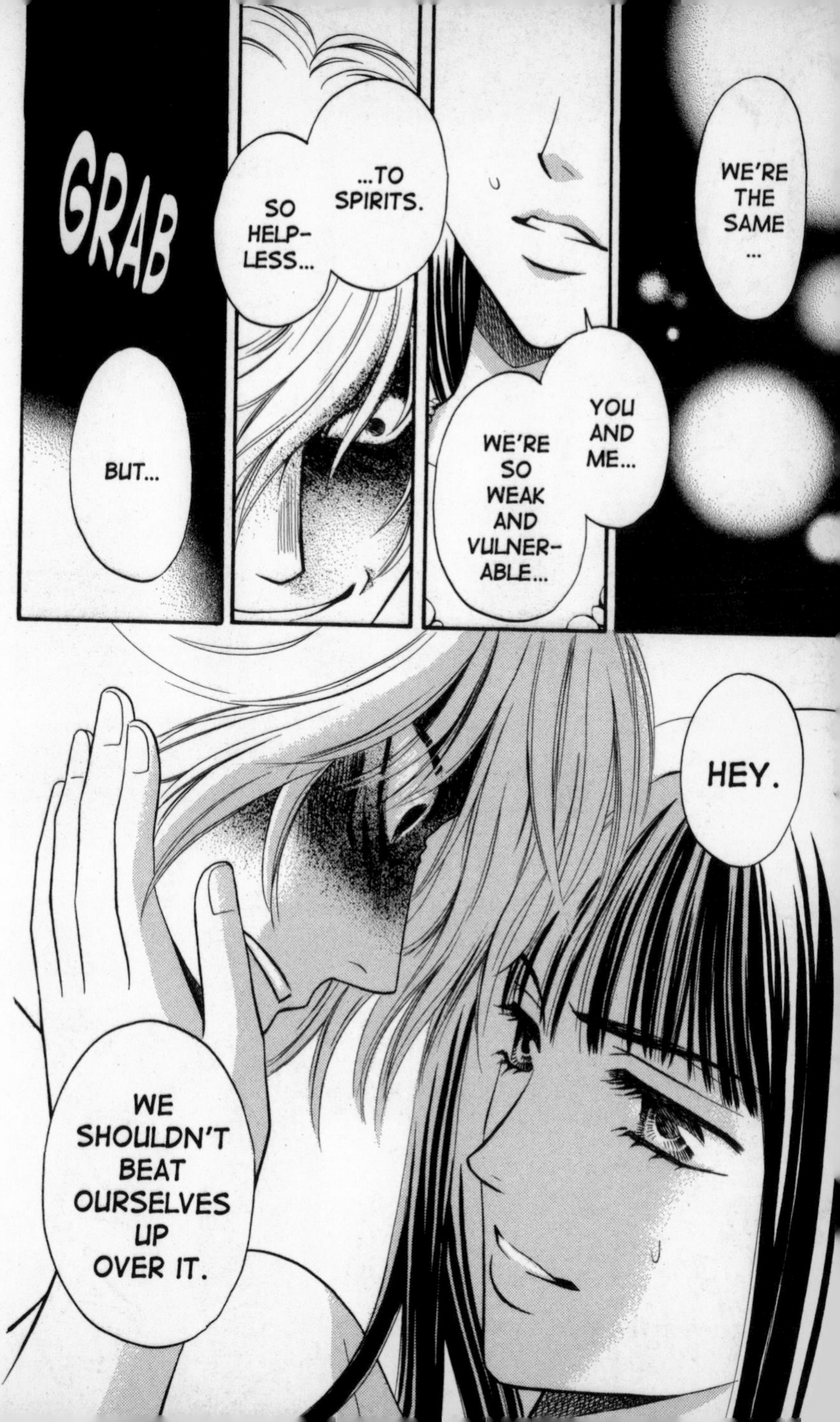
WE'RE THE SAME ...
YOU AND ME...
WE'RE SO WEAK AND VULNER-ABLE...
SO HELP-LESS...
...TO SPIRITS.
GRAB
BUT...
HEY.
WE SHOULDN'T BEAT OURSELVES UP OVER IT.

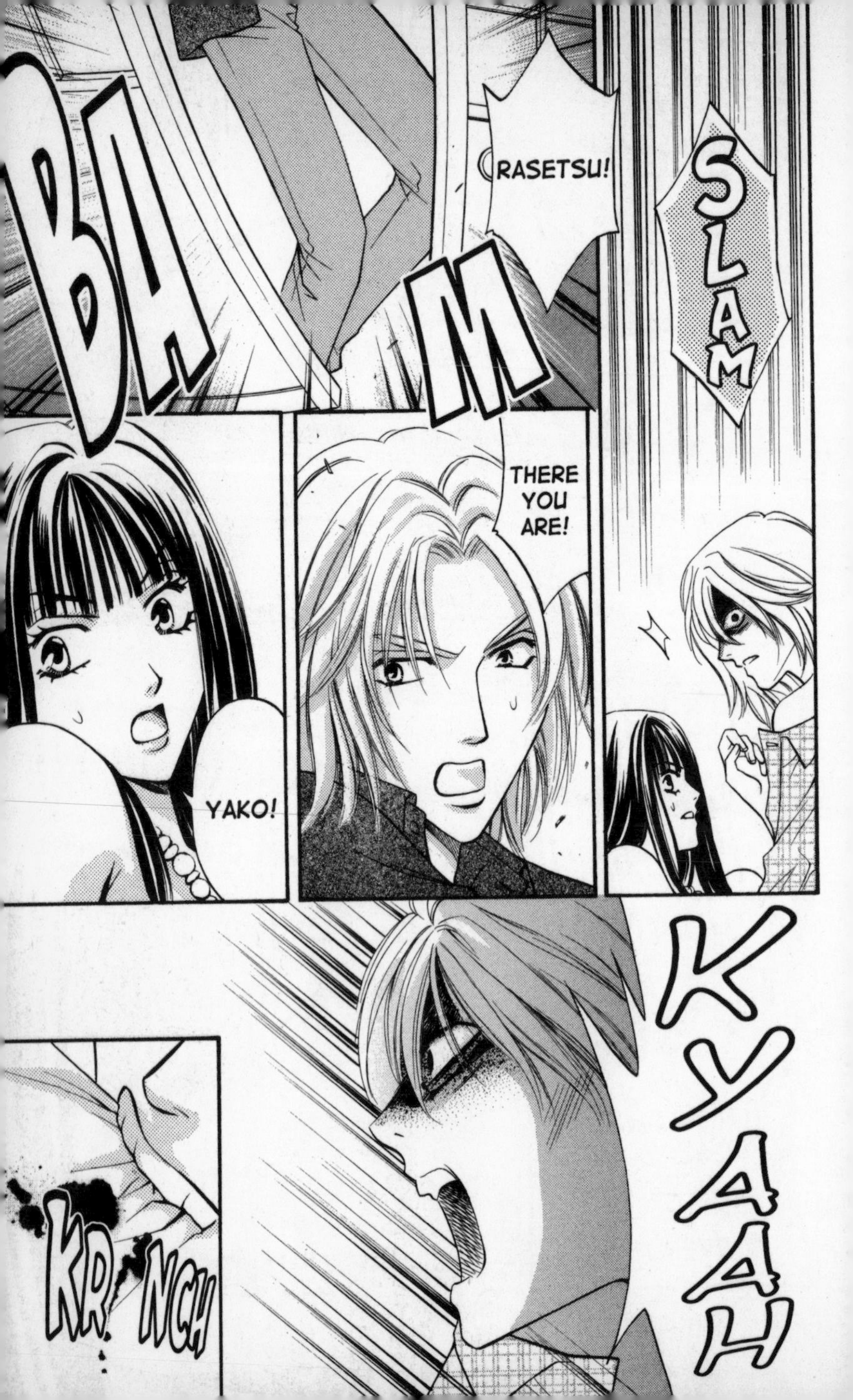
SLAM
RASETSU!
BAM
THERE YOU ARE!
YAKO!
KYAAH
KRNCH

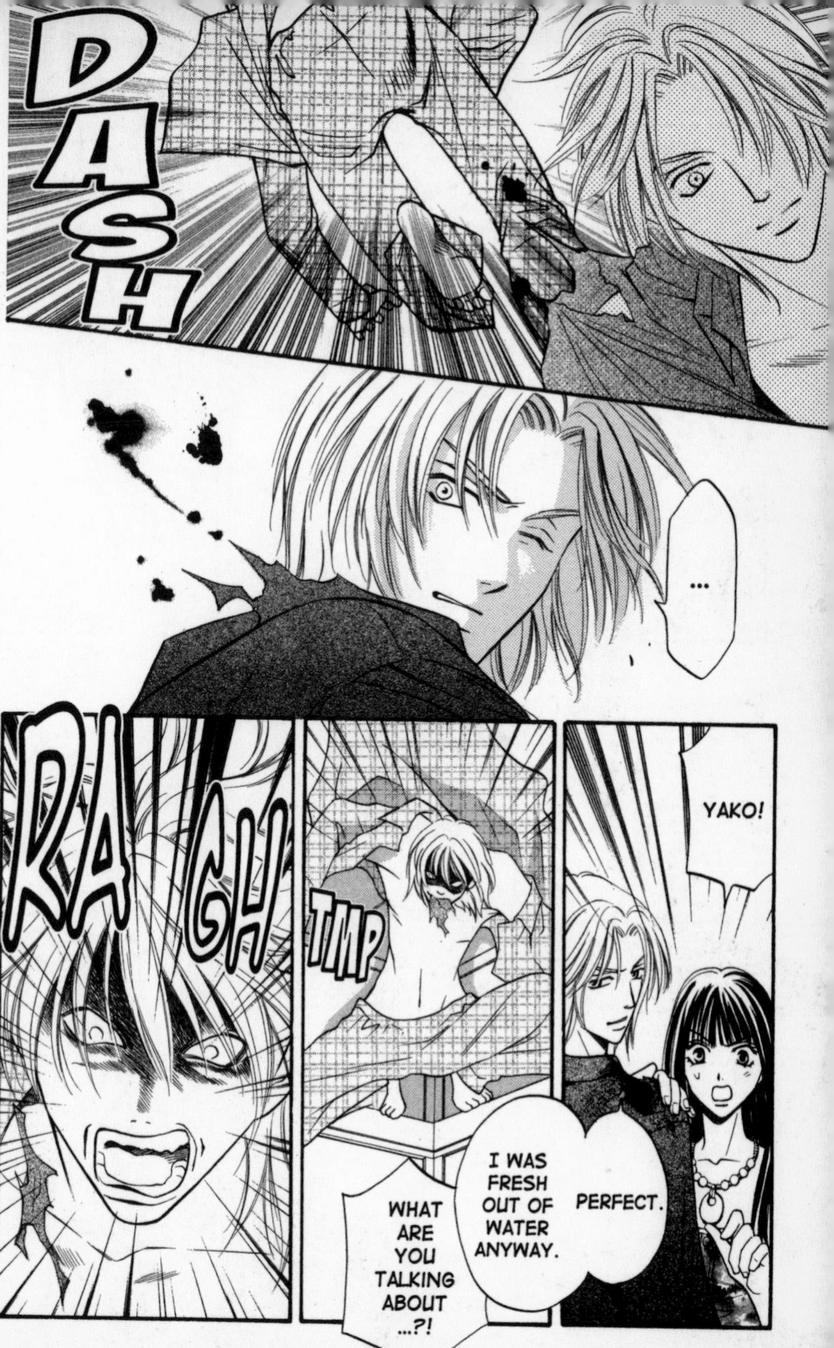
DASH
...
YAKO!
PERFECT.
TMP
I WAS FRESH OUT OF WATER ANYWAY.
WHAT ARE YOU TALKING ABOUT ...?!
RAGH

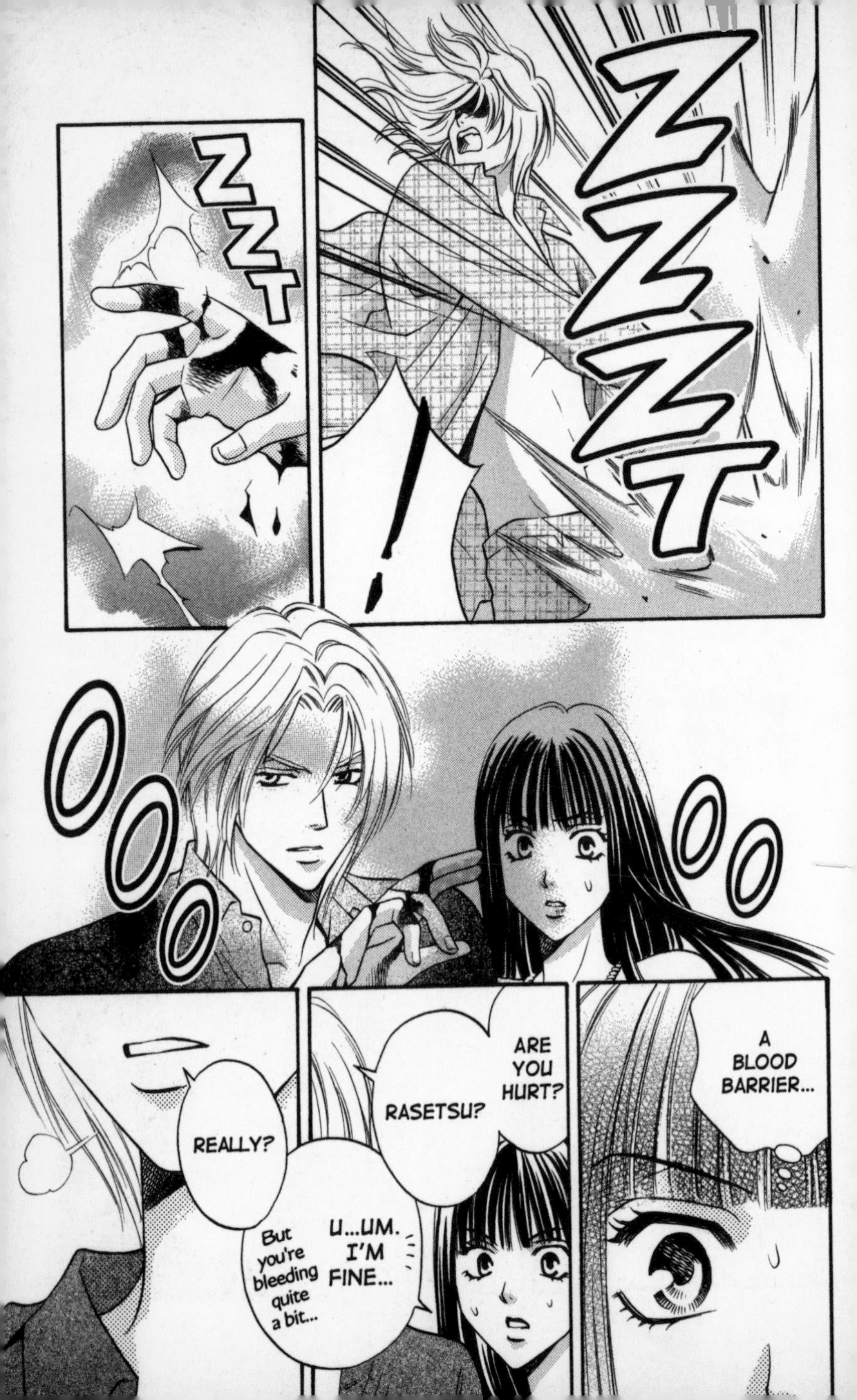
ZZZZT
ZZT
OOO
OOOOO
A BLOOD BARRIER...
ARE YOU HURT?
RASETSU?
U...UM. I'M FINE...
REALLY?
But you're bleeding quite a bit...

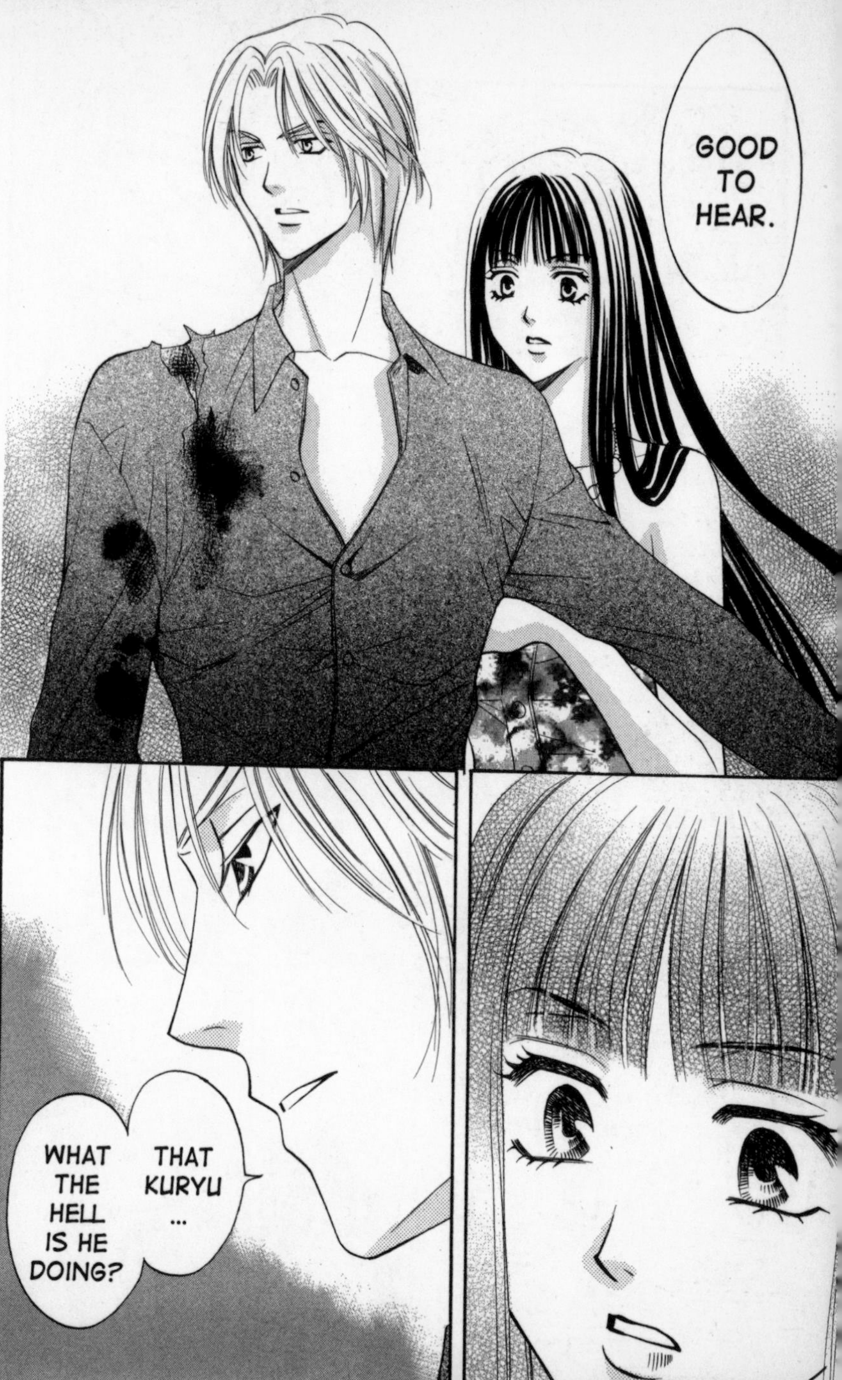
GOOD TO HEAR.
THAT KURYU ...
WHAT THE HELL IS HE DOING?

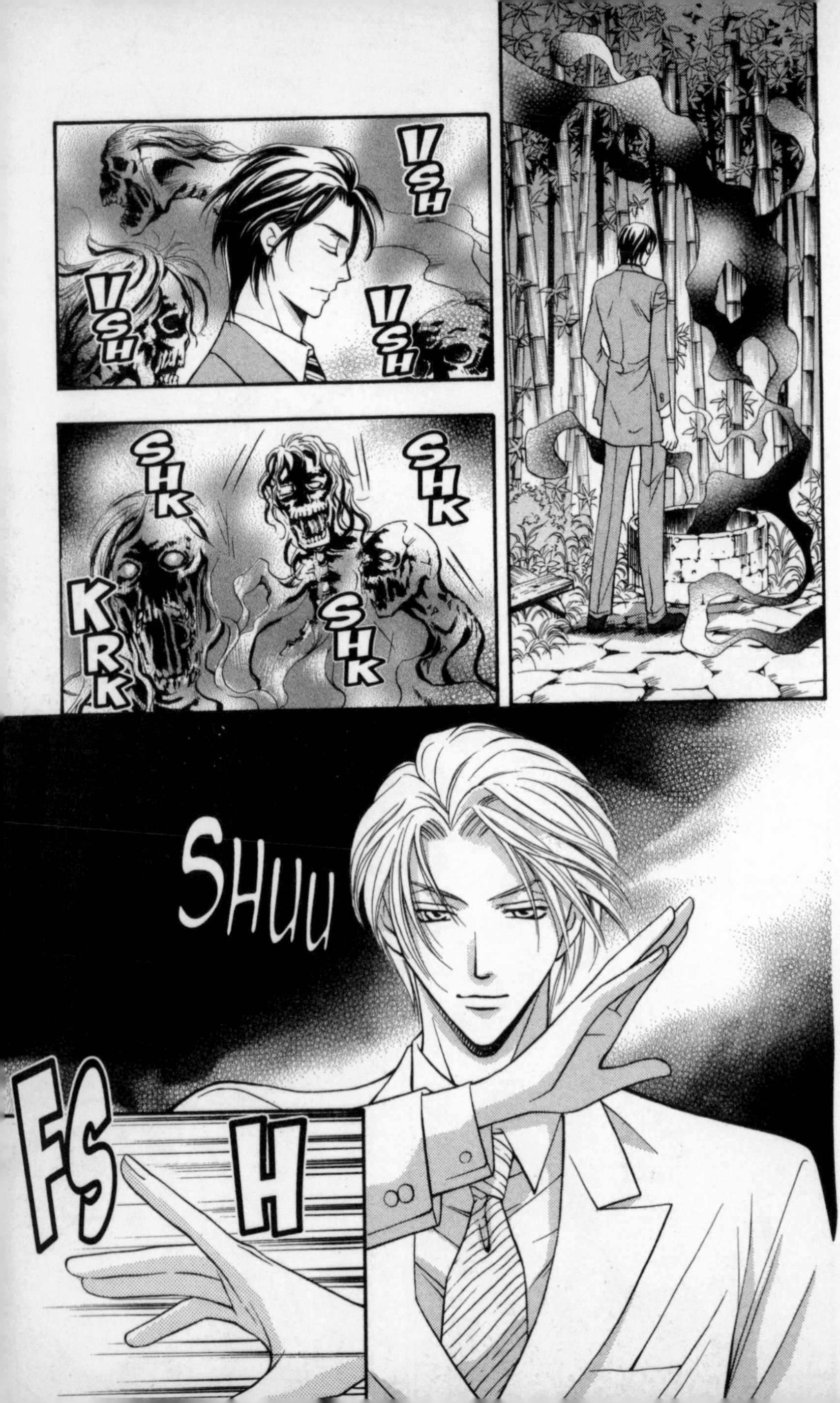
VSH
VSH
VSH
SHK
SHK
SHK
KRK
SHUU
FSH

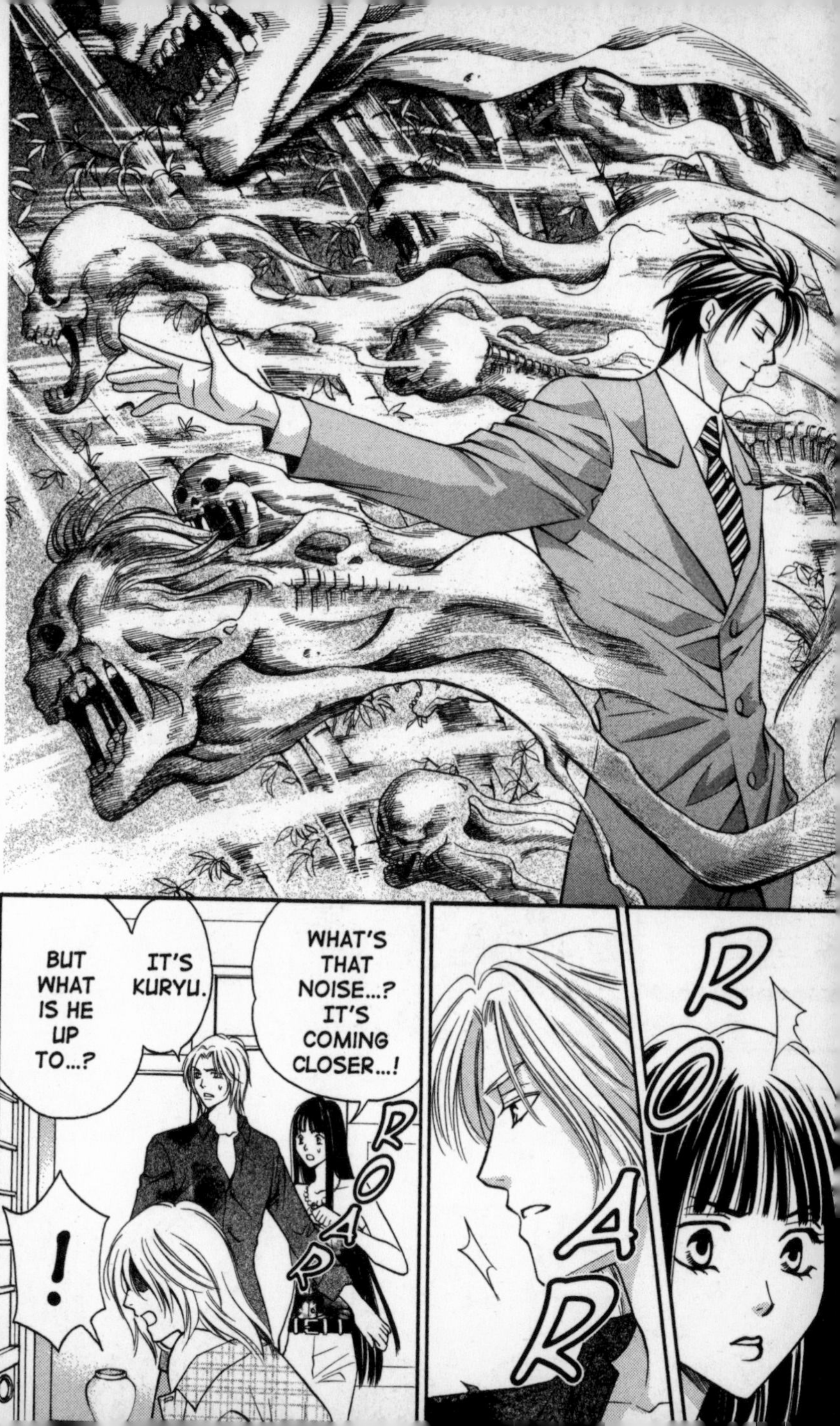
ROAR
WHAT'S THAT NOISE...? IT'S COMING CLOSER...!
IT'S KURYU.
BUT WHAT IS HE UP TO...?
ROAR
!

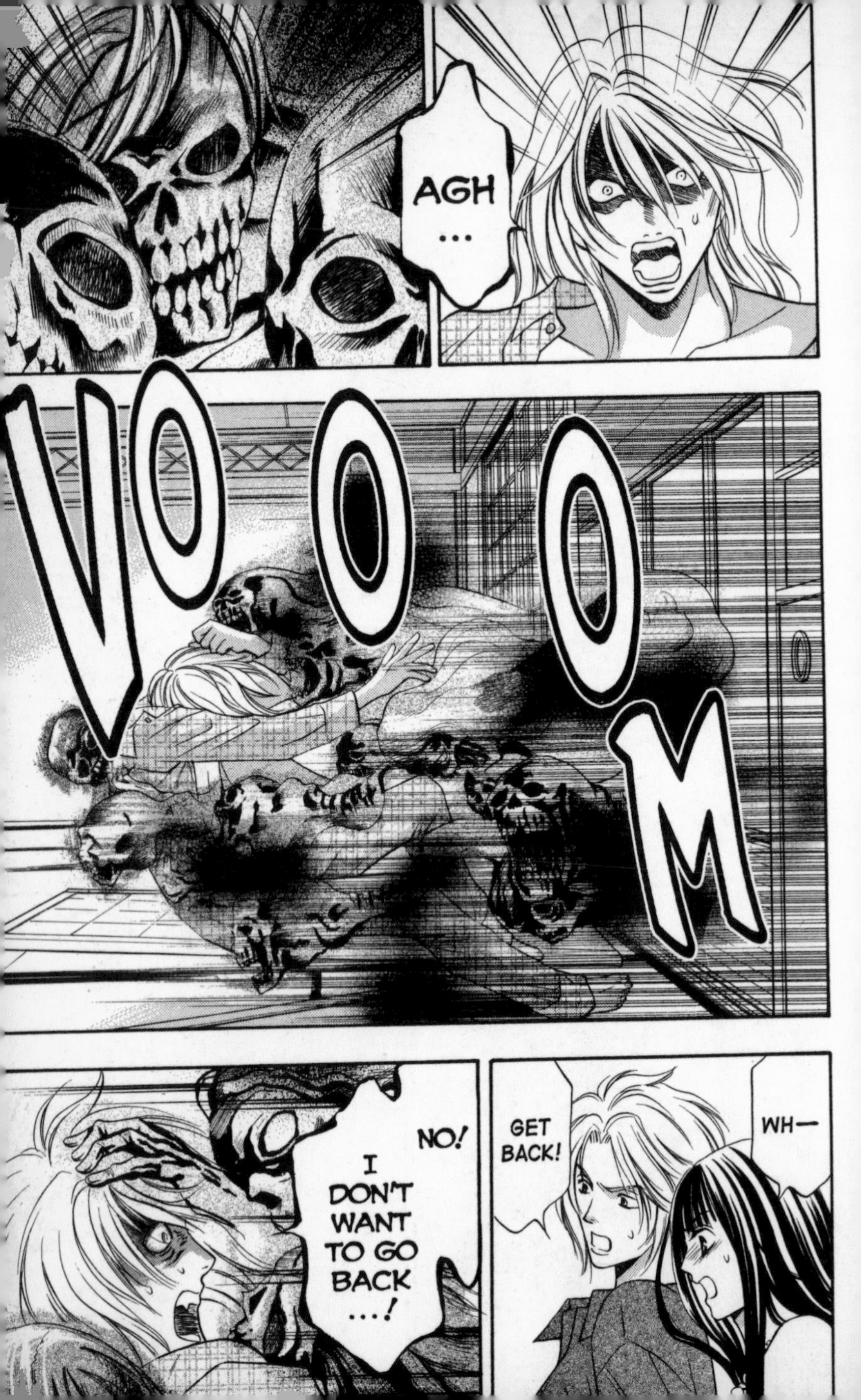
AGH
...
VOOOM
WH—
GET BACK!
NO!
I DON'T WANT TO GO BACK ...!

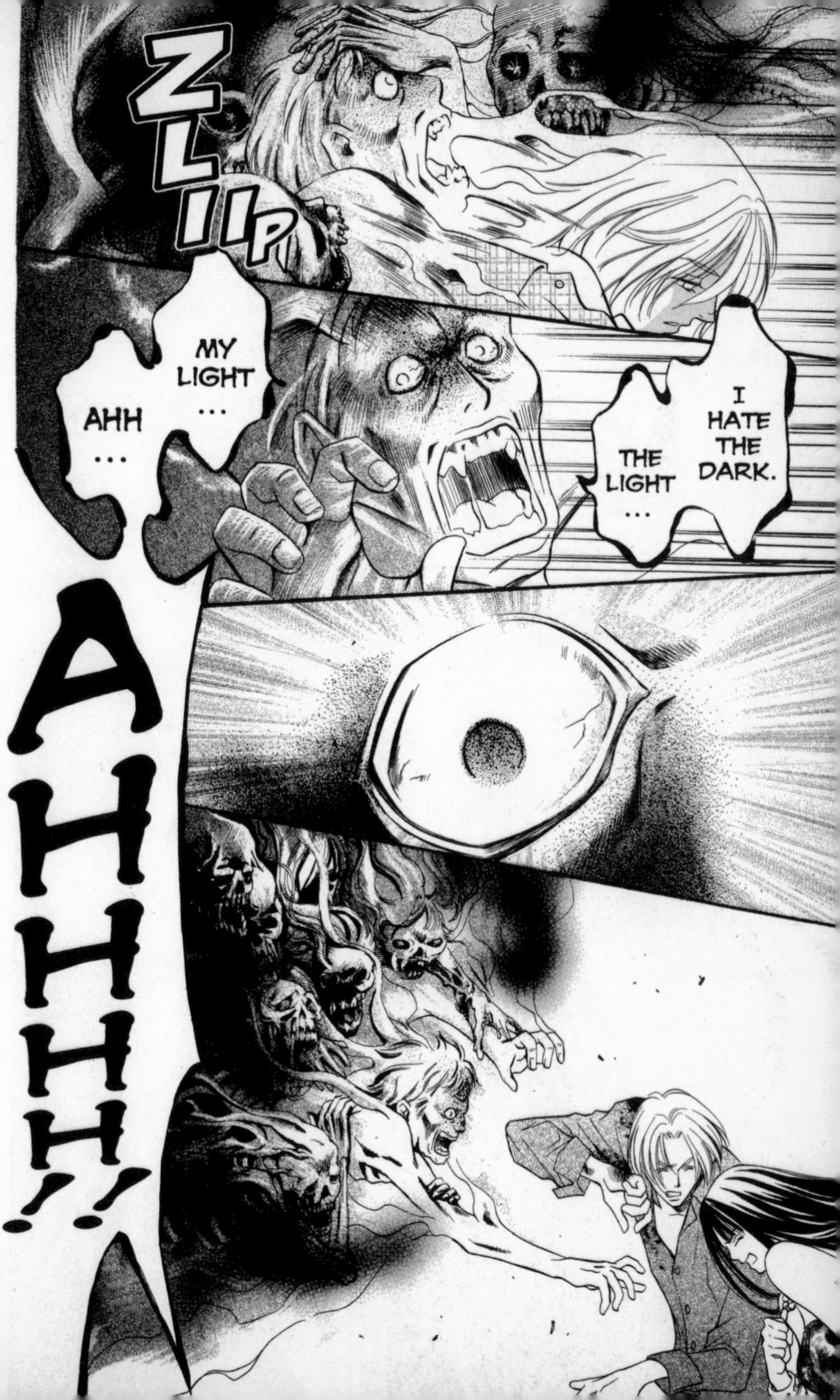
ZLIIP
I HATE THE DARK.
THE LIGHT ...
MY LIGHT ...
AHH ...
AHHHH!!

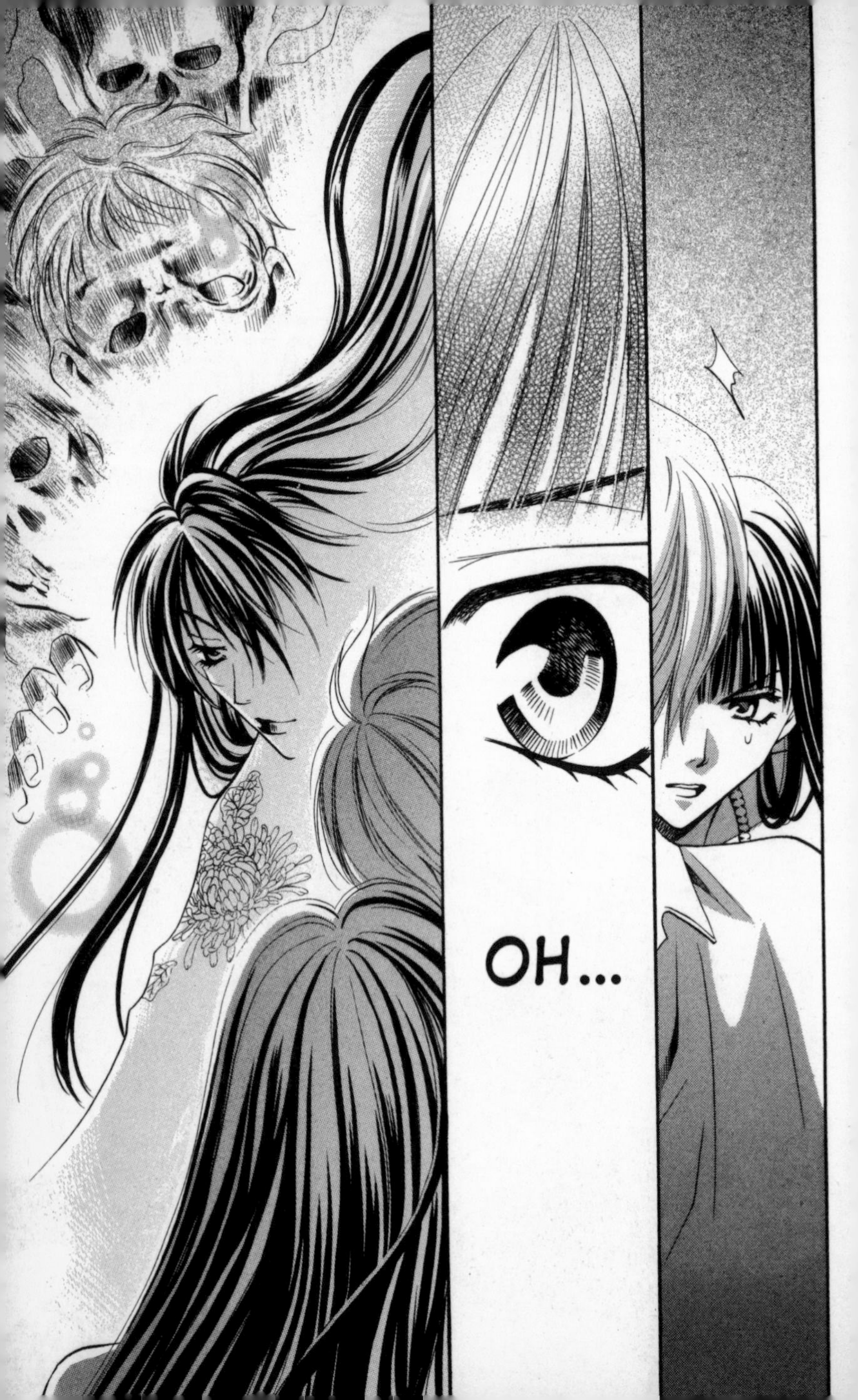
OH...

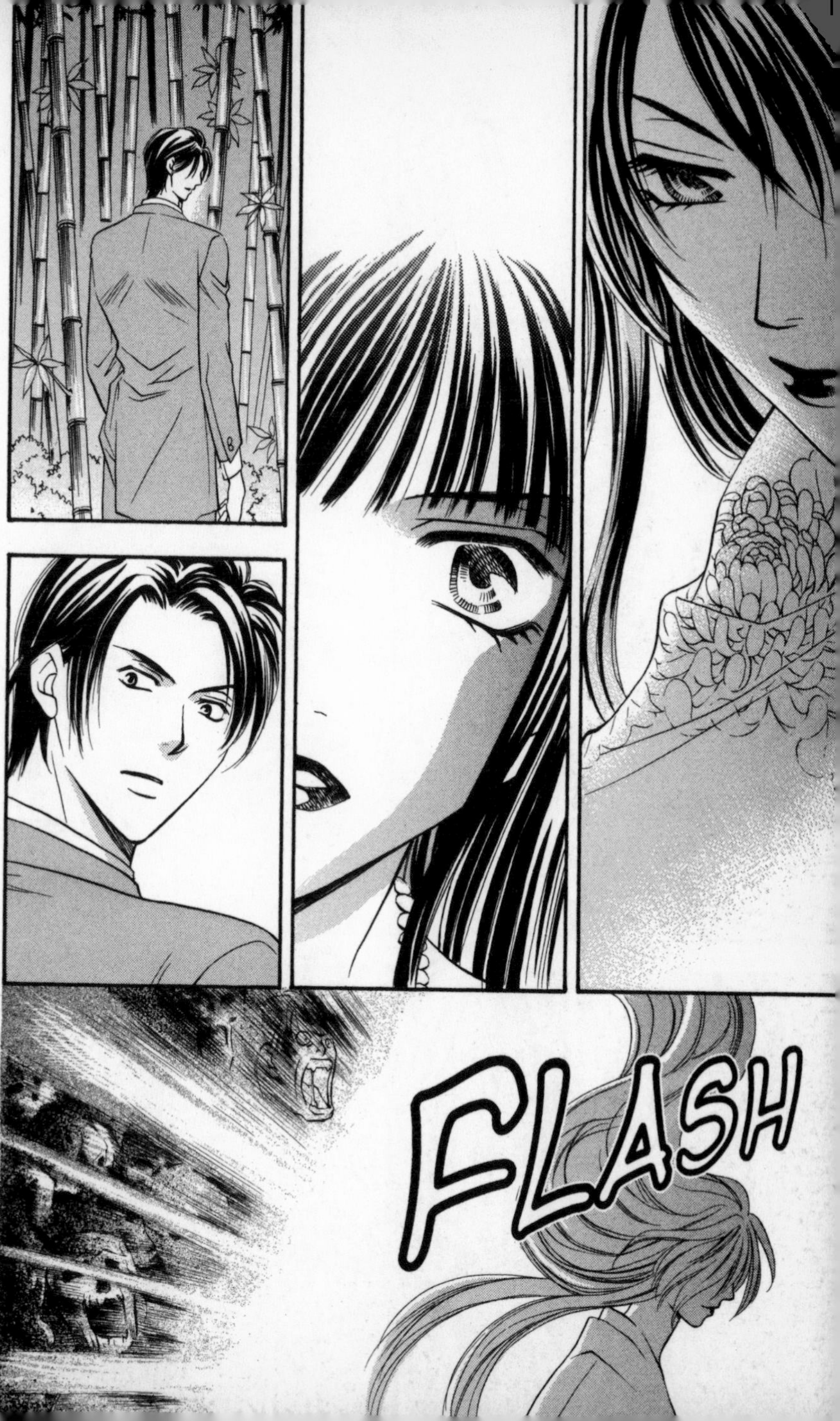
FLASH

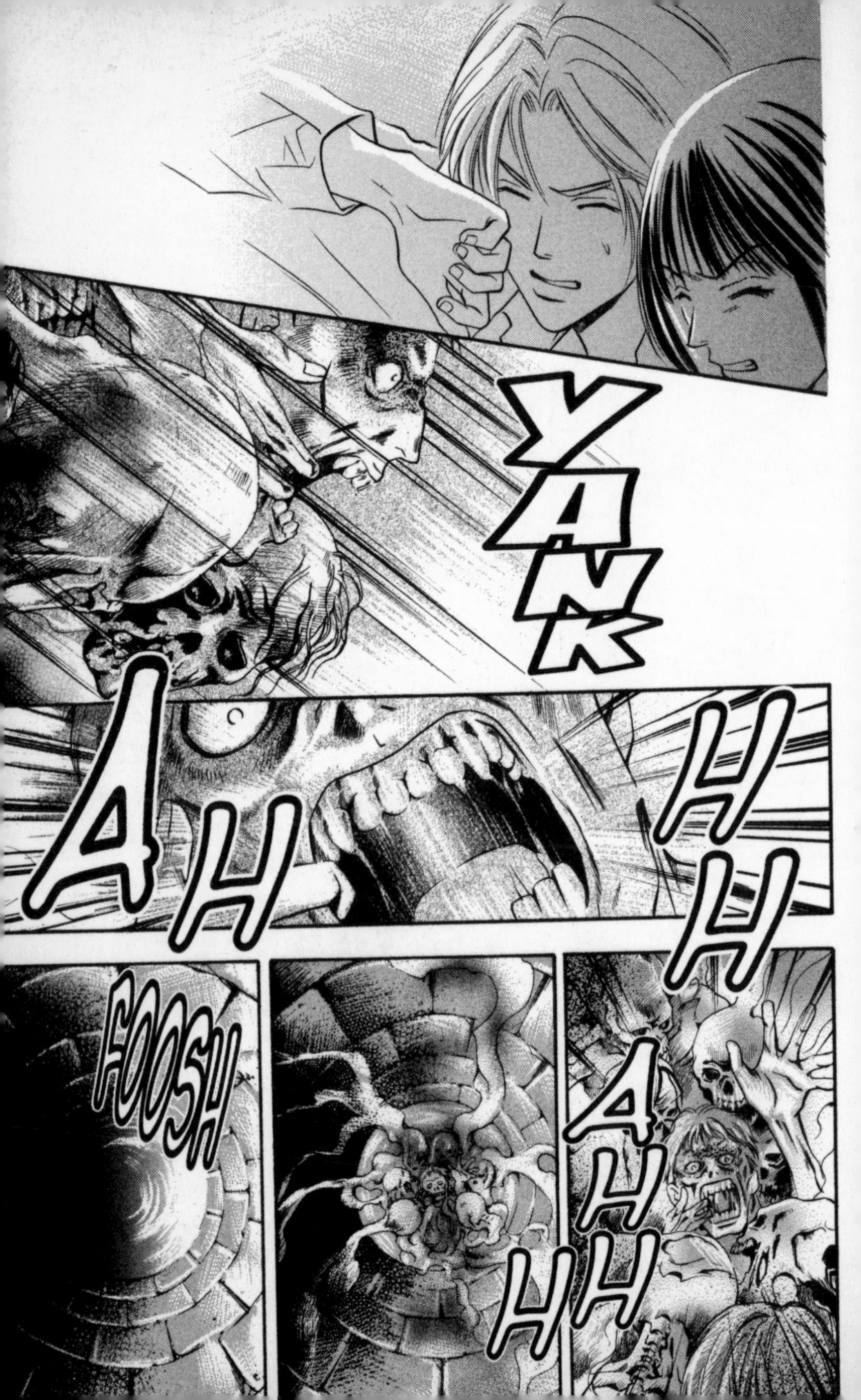
YANK
AHHHHAHHHH
FOOSH

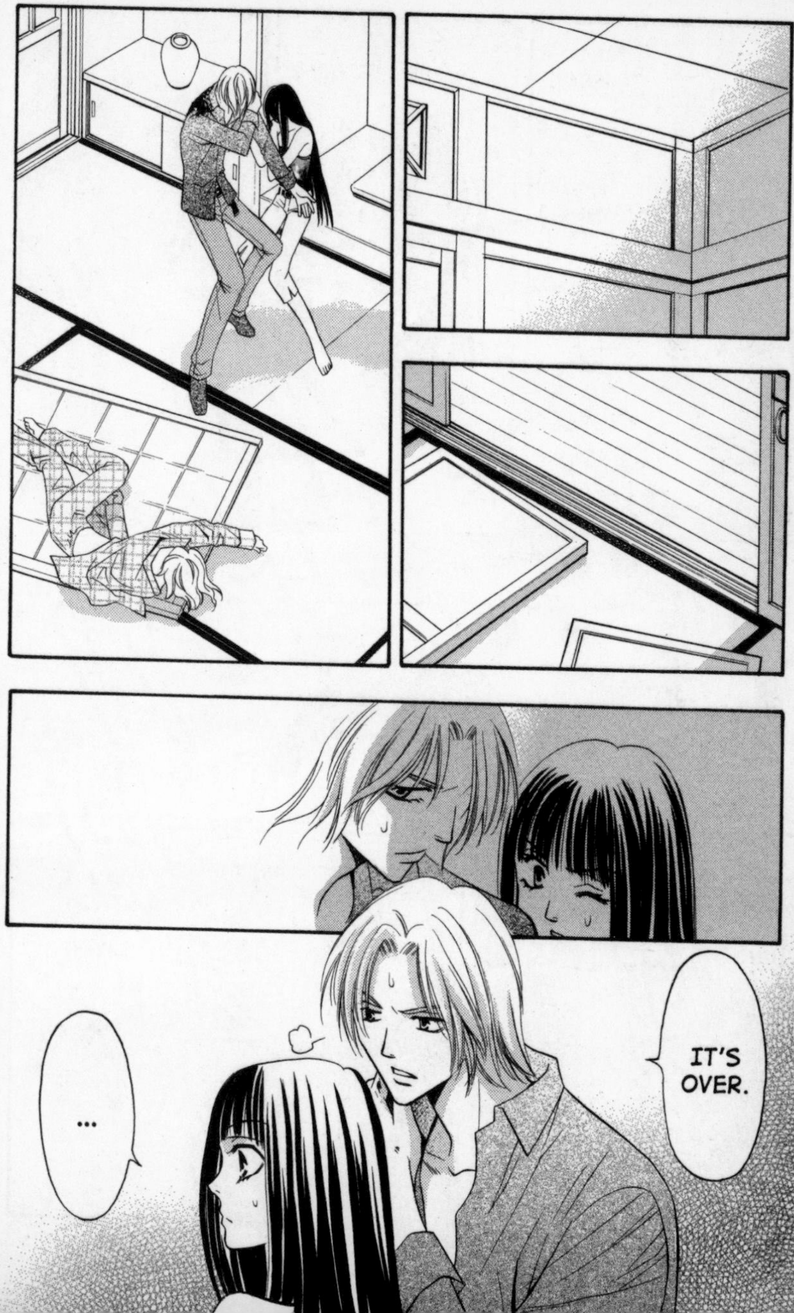
IT'S OVER.
...

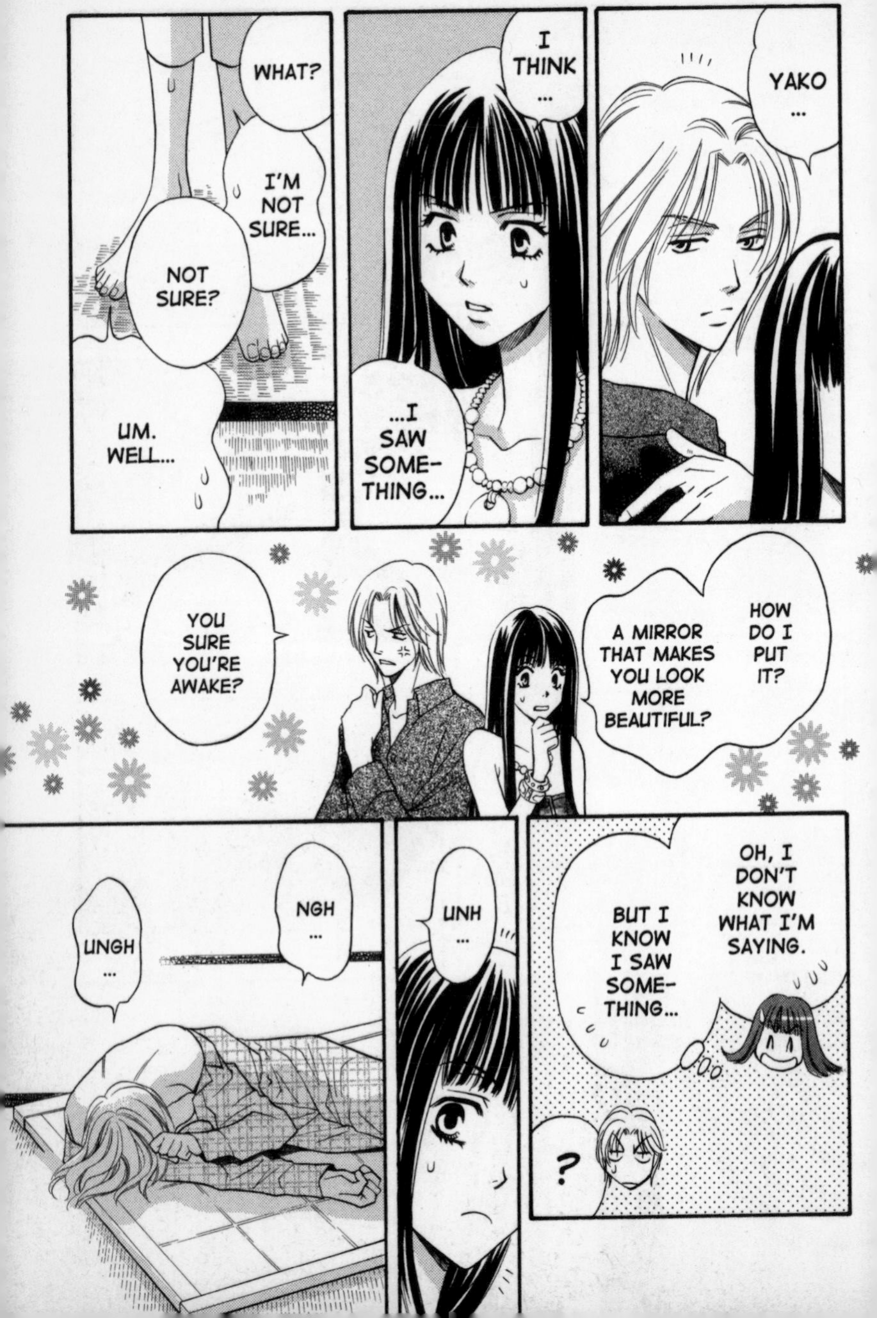
YAKO ...
I THINK ...
...I SAW SOME-THING...
WHAT?
I'M NOT SURE...
NOT SURE?
UM. WELL...
HOW DO I PUT IT?
A MIRROR THAT MAKES YOU LOOK MORE BEAUTIFUL?
YOU SURE YOU'RE AWAKE?
OH, I DON'T KNOW WHAT I'M SAYING.
BUT I KNOW I SAW SOME-THING...
?
UNH ...
NGH ...
UNGH ...

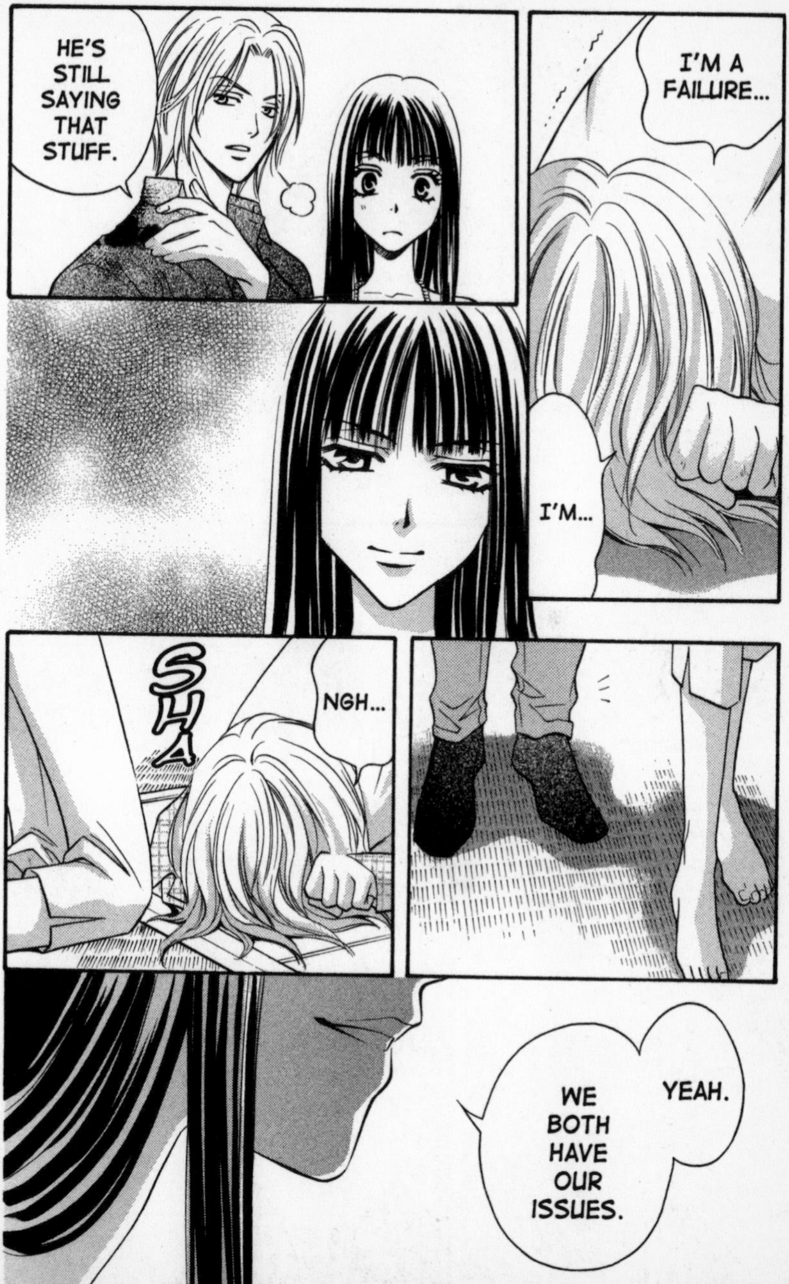
I'M A FAILURE...
I'M...
HE'S STILL SAYING THAT STUFF.
NGH...
SHA
YEAH.
WE BOTH HAVE OUR ISSUES.

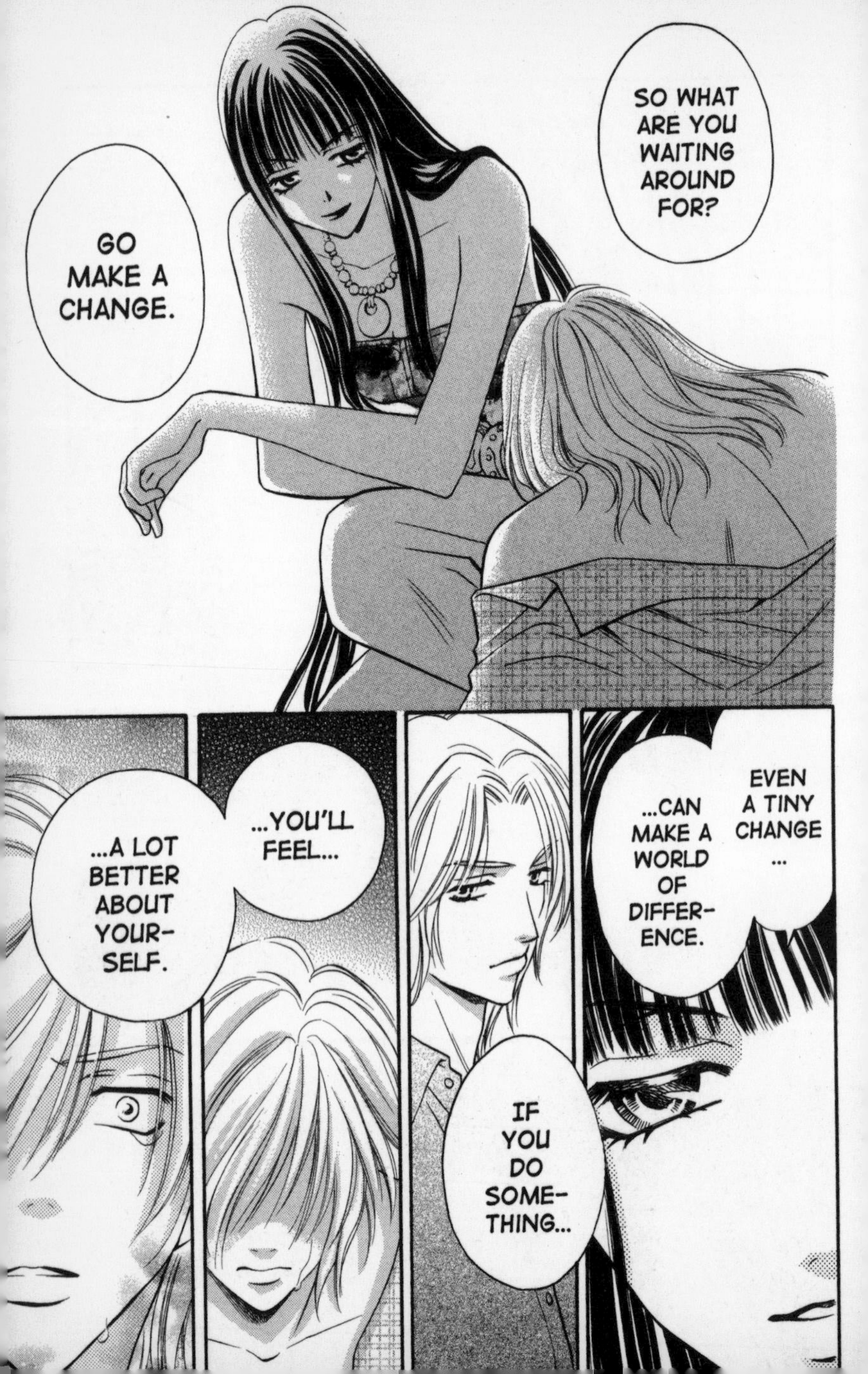
SO WHAT ARE YOU WAITING AROUND FOR?
GO MAKE A CHANGE.
EVEN A TINY CHANGE ...
...CAN MAKE A WORLD OF DIFFER-ENCE.
IF YOU DO SOME-THING...
...YOU'LL FEEL...
...A LOT BETTER ABOUT YOUR-SELF.

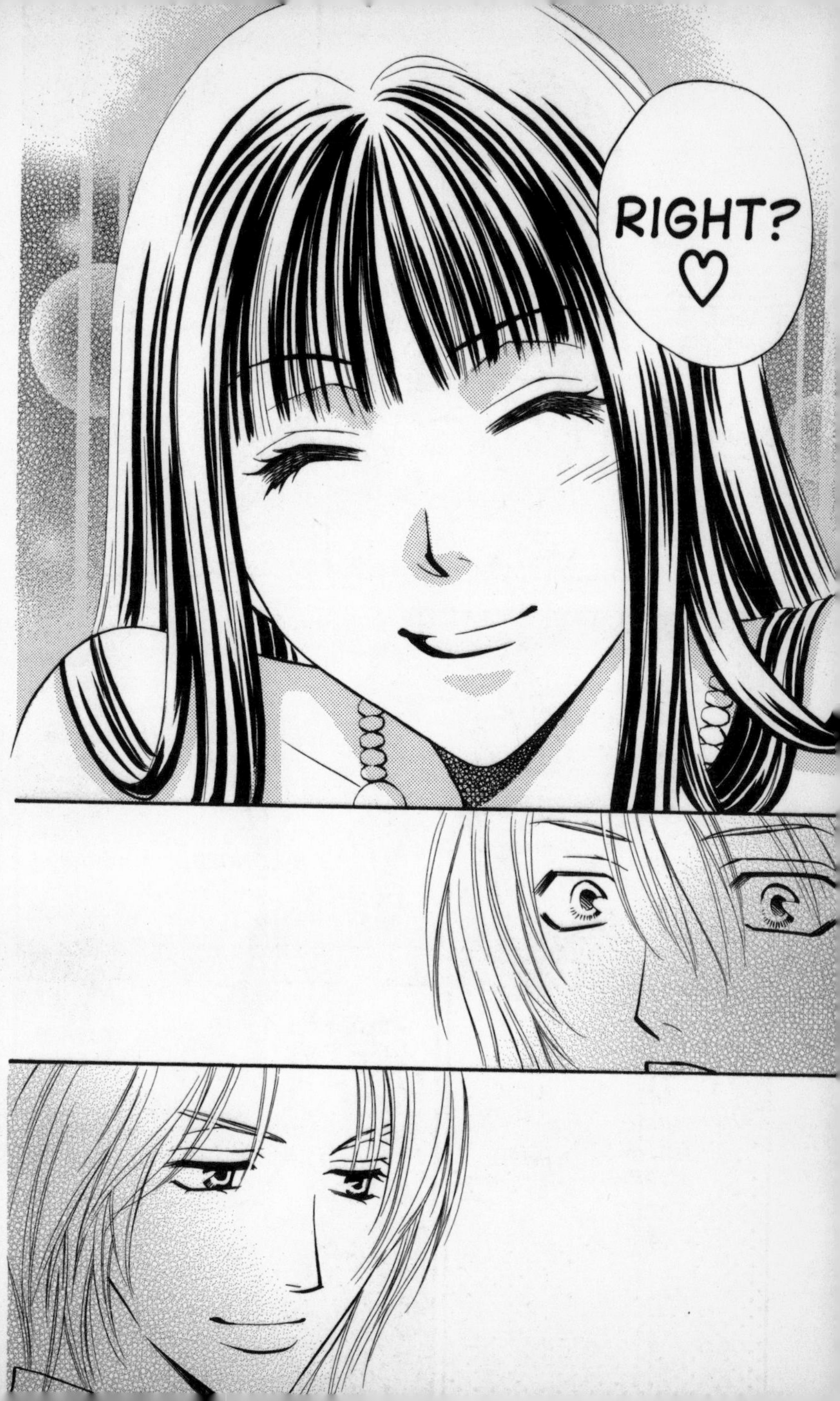
RIGHT? ♡

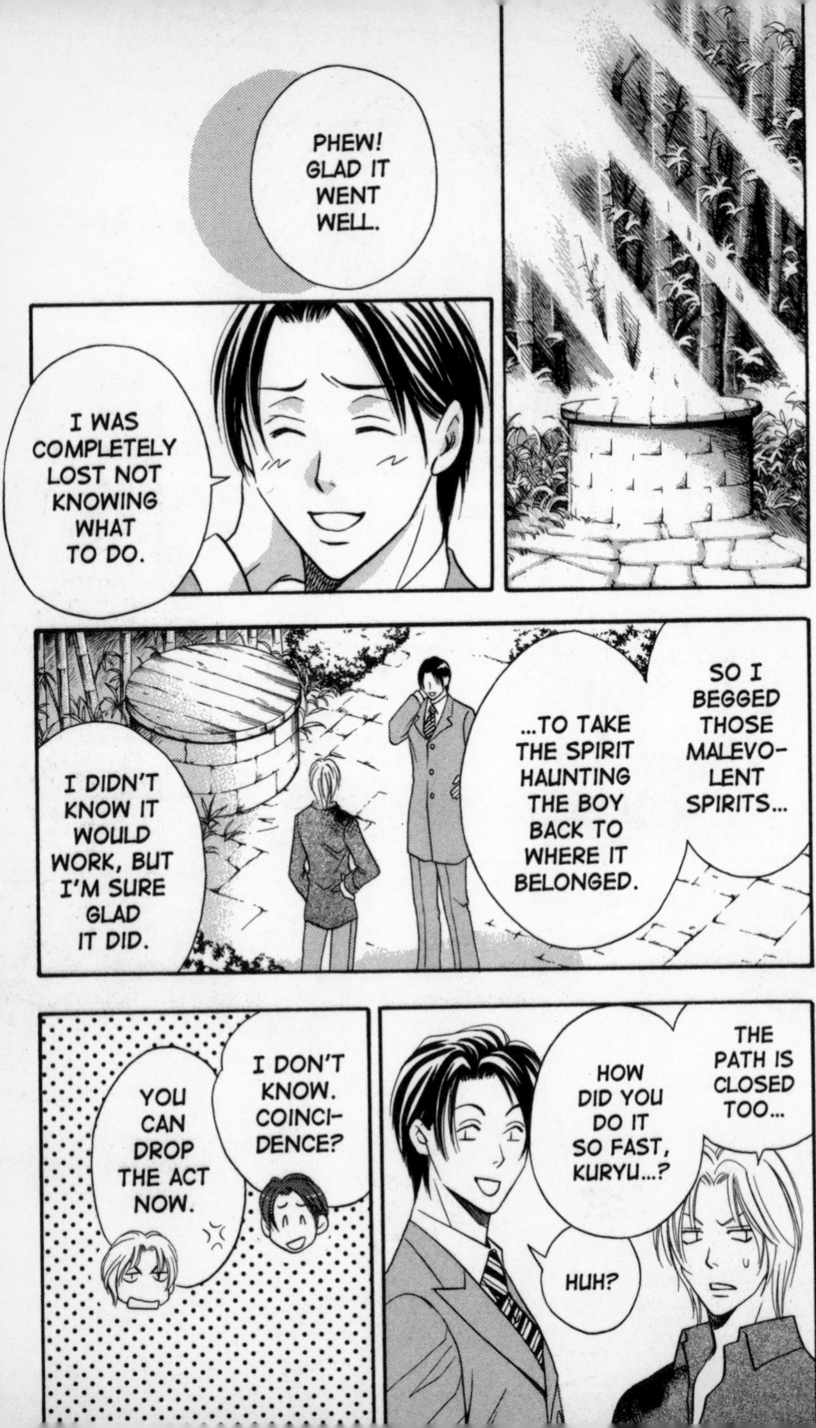
PHEW! GLAD IT WENT WELL.
I WAS COMPLETELY LOST NOT KNOWING WHAT TO DO.
SO I BEGGED THOSE MALEVO- LENT SPIRITS...
...TO TAKE THE SPIRIT HAUNTING THE BOY BACK TO WHERE IT BELONGED.
I DIDN'T KNOW IT WOULD WORK, BUT I'M SURE GLAD IT DID.
THE PATH IS CLOSED TOO...
HOW DID YOU DO IT SO FAST, KURYU...?
HUH?
I DON'T KNOW. COINCI- DENCE?
YOU CAN DROP THE ACT NOW.

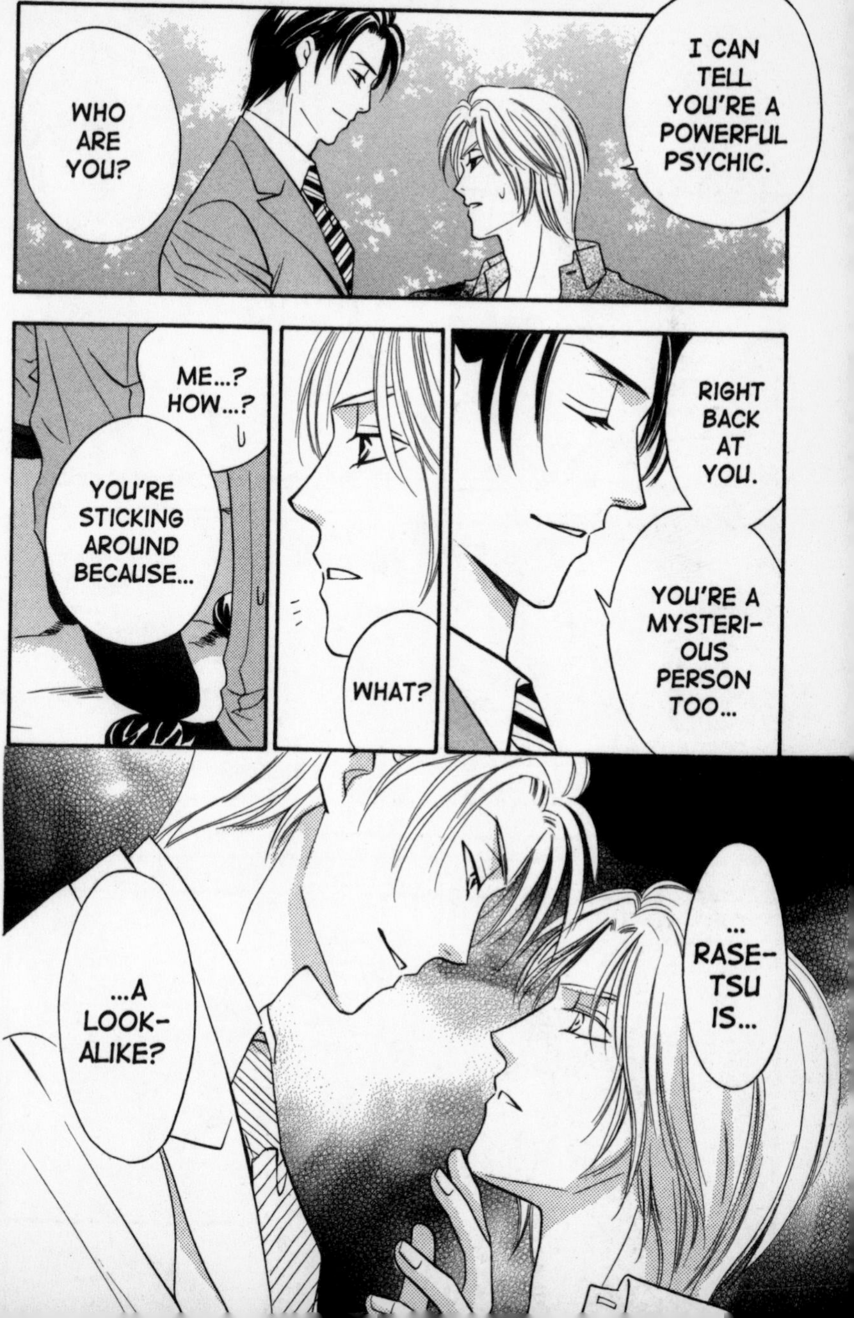
I CAN TELL YOU'RE A POWERFUL PSYCHIC.
WHO ARE YOU?
RIGHT BACK AT YOU.
YOU'RE A MYSTERI-OUS PERSON TOO...
WHAT?
ME...? HOW...?
YOU'RE STICKING AROUND BECAUSE...
...RASE-TSU IS...
...A LOOK-ALIKE?

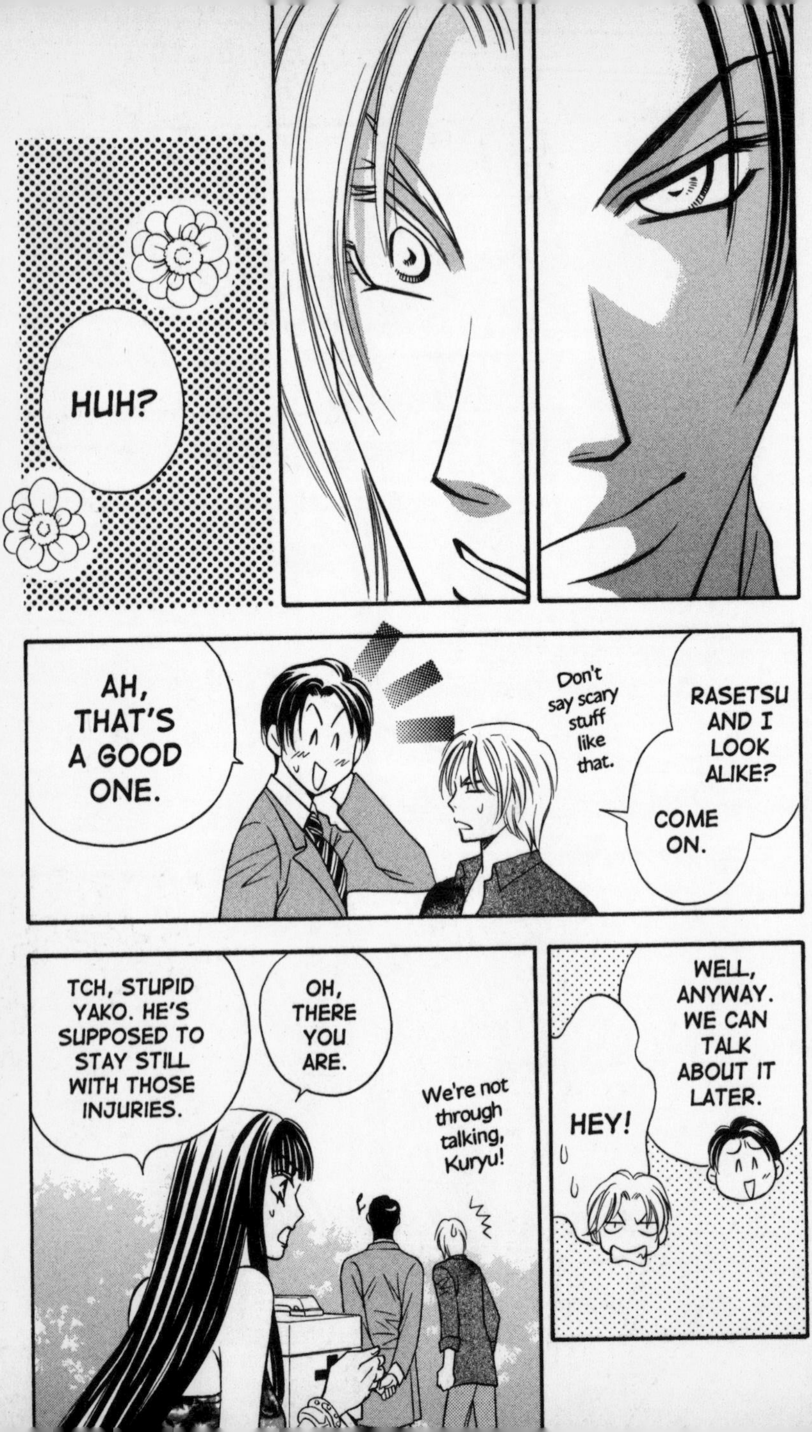
HUH?
RASETSU AND I LOOK ALIKE?
COME ON.
Don't say scary stuff like that.
AH, THAT'S A GOOD ONE.
WELL, ANYWAY. WE CAN TALK ABOUT IT LATER.
HEY!
We're not through talking, Kuryu!
OH, THERE YOU ARE.
TCH, STUPID YAKO. HE'S SUPPOSED TO STAY STILL WITH THOSE INJURIES.

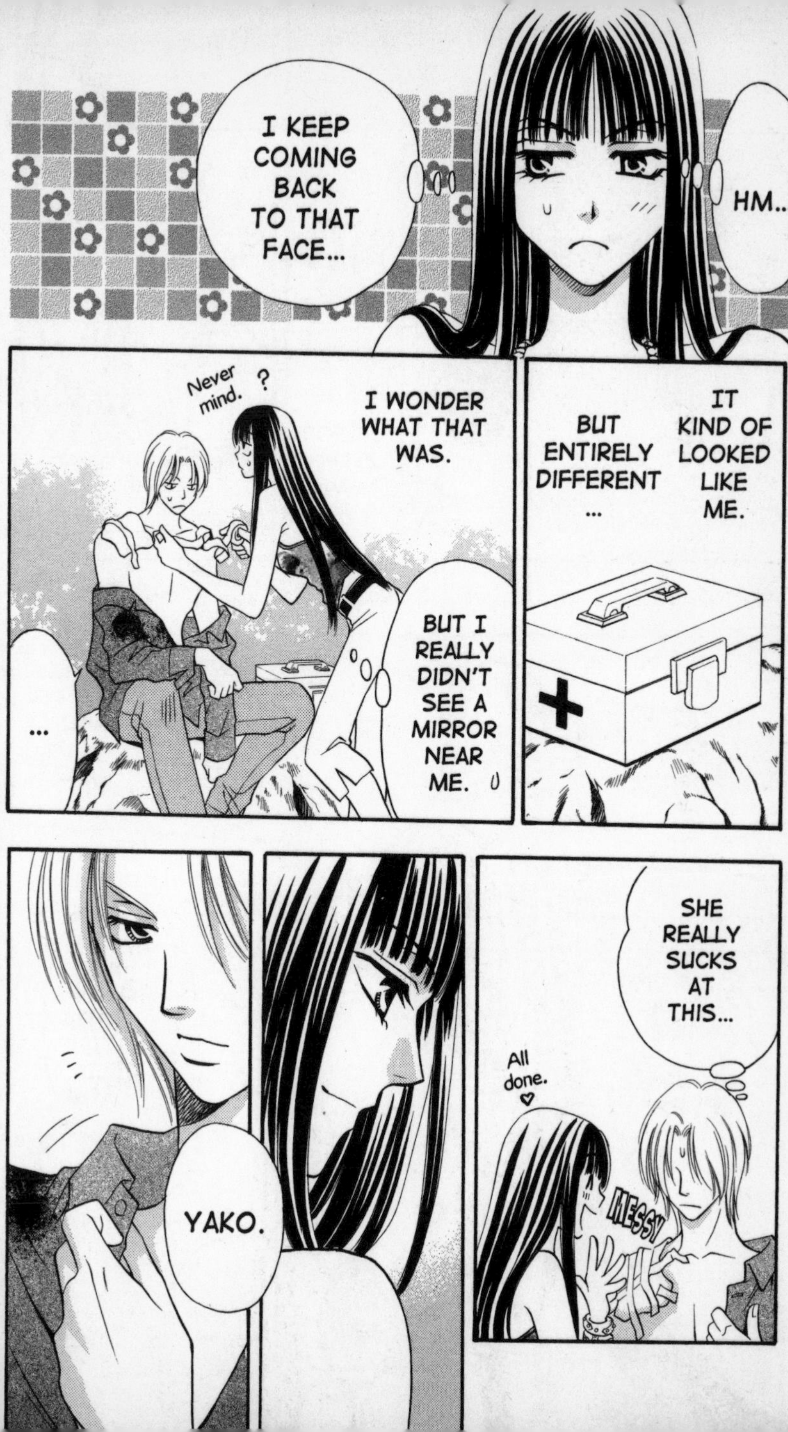
HM...
I KEEP COMING BACK TO THAT FACE...
IT KIND OF LOOKED LIKE ME.
BUT ENTIRELY DIFFERENT ...
I WONDER WHAT THAT WAS.
BUT I REALLY DIDN'T SEE A MIRROR NEAR ME.
?
Never mind.
...
SHE REALLY SUCKS AT THIS...
All done. ♥
MESSY
YAKO.

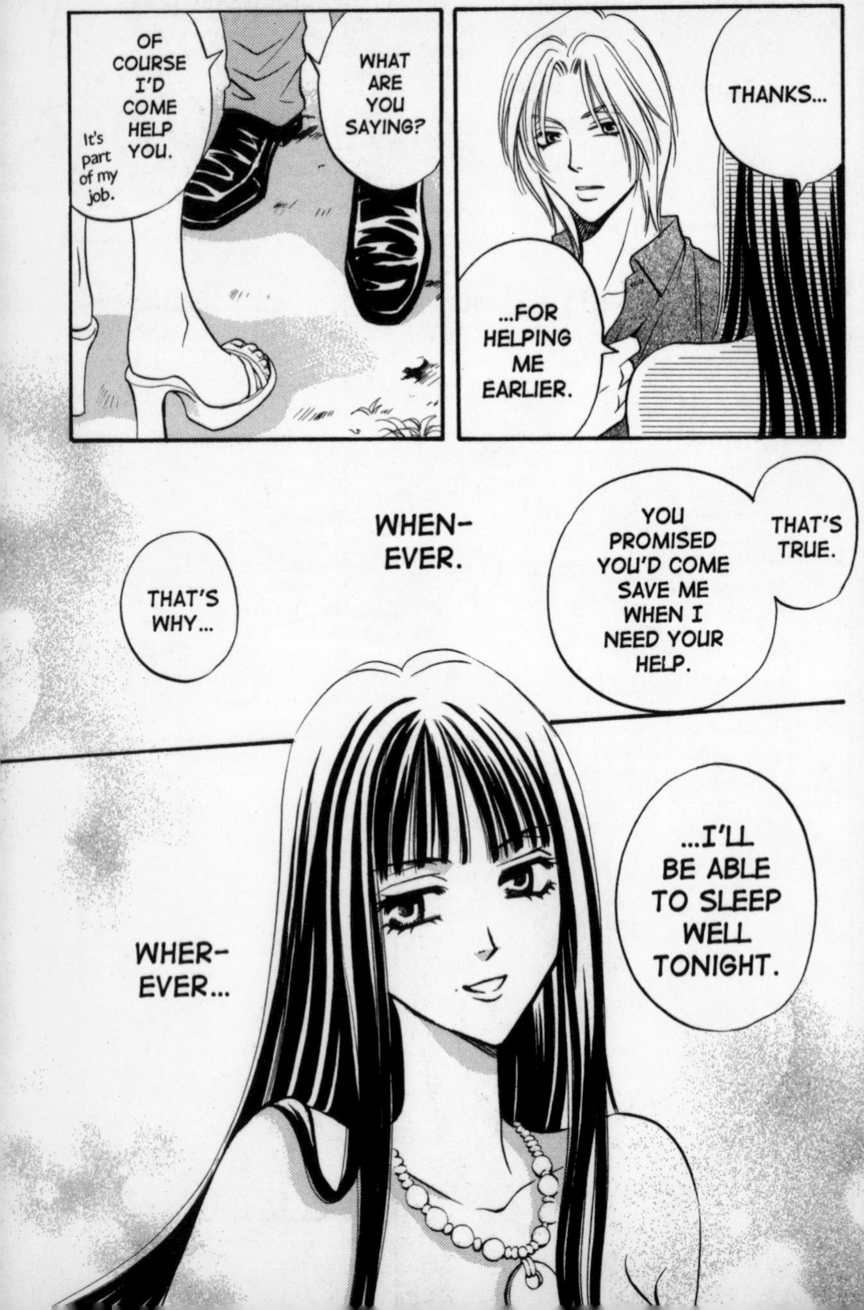
THANKS...
...FOR HELPING ME EARLIER.
WHAT ARE YOU SAYING?
OF COURSE I'D COME HELP YOU.
It's part of my job.
THAT'S TRUE.
YOU PROMISED YOU'D COME SAVE ME WHEN I NEED YOUR HELP.
WHEN-EVER.
THAT'S WHY...
...I'LL BE ABLE TO SLEEP WELL TONIGHT.
WHER-EVER...

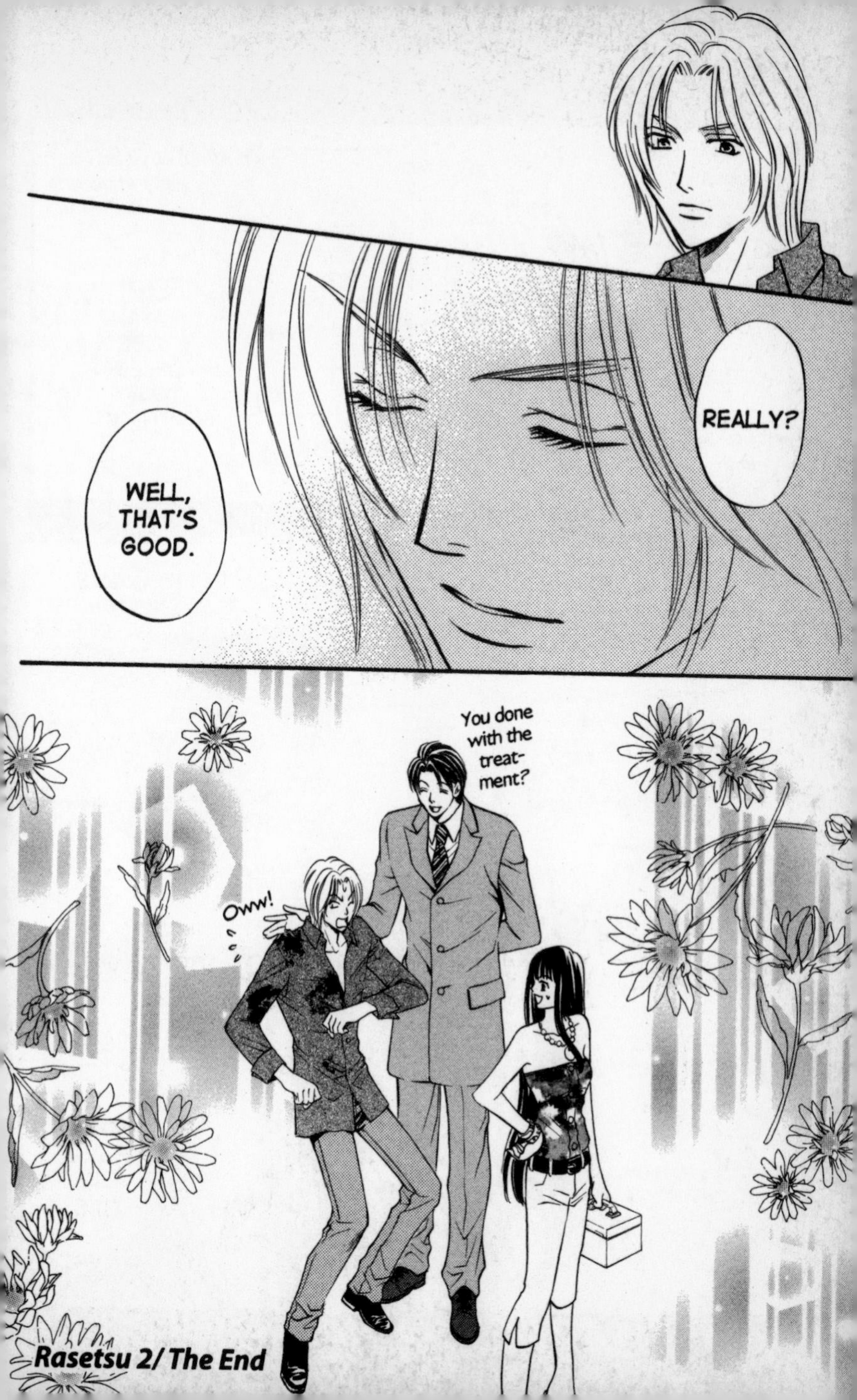
REALLY?
WELL, THAT'S GOOD.
You done with the treat-ment?
Oww!
Rasetsu 2/ The End

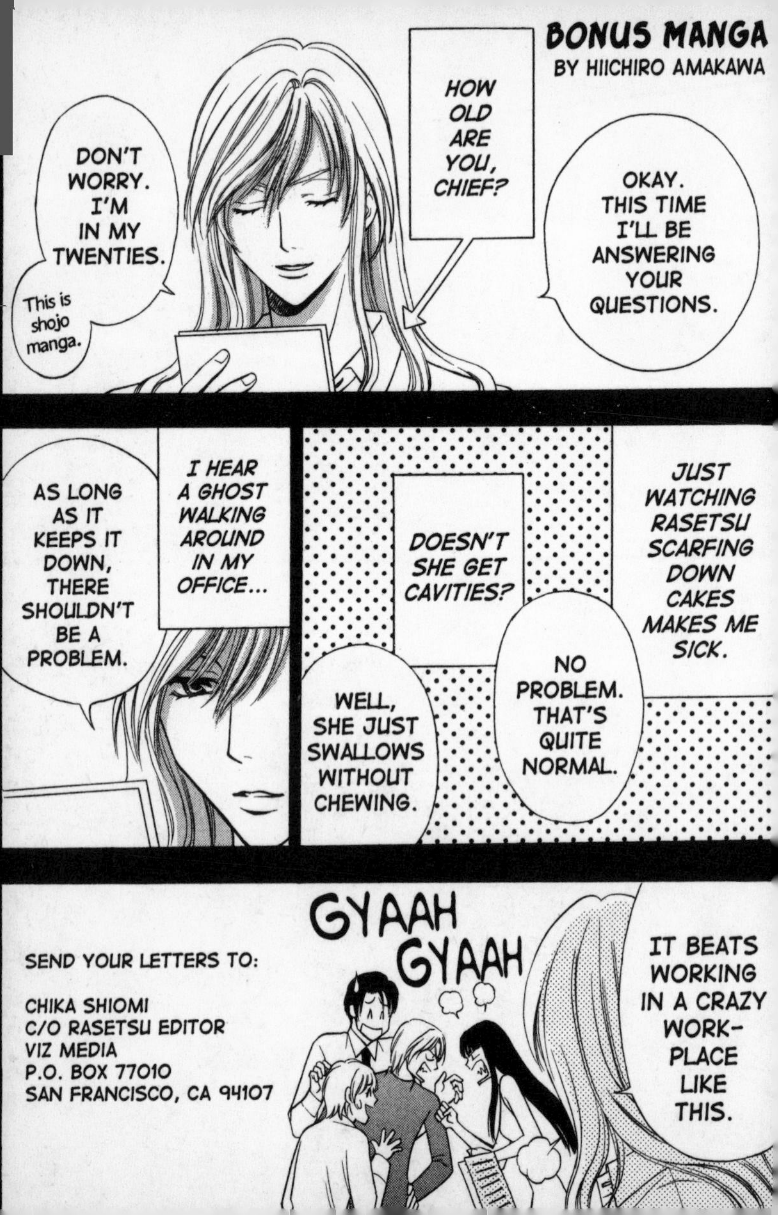
BONUS MANGA
BY HIICHIRO AMAKAWA
OKAY. THIS TIME I'LL BE ANSWERING YOUR QUESTIONS.
HOW OLD ARE YOU, CHIEF?
DON'T WORRY. I'M IN MY TWENTIES.
This is shojo manga.
JUST WATCHING RASETSU SCARFING DOWN CAKES MAKES ME SICK.
DOESN'T SHE GET CAVITIES?
NO PROBLEM. THAT'S QUITE NORMAL.
WELL, SHE JUST SWALLOWS WITHOUT CHEWING.
I HEAR A GHOST WALKING AROUND IN MY OFFICE...
AS LONG AS IT KEEPS IT DOWN, THERE SHOULDN'T BE A PROBLEM.
IT BEATS WORKING IN A CRAZY WORK-PLACE LIKE THIS.
GYAAH GYAAH
SEND YOUR LETTERS TO:
CHIKA SHIOMI
C/O RASETSU EDITOR
VIZ MEDIA
P.O. BOX 77010
SAN FRANCISCO, CA 94107

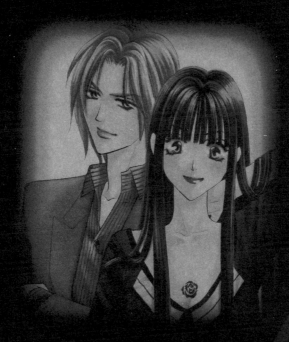

Chika Shiomi lives in Aichi Prefecture, Japan. She debuted with the manga *Todokeru Toki o Sugitemo* (Even if the Time for Deliverance Passes), and her previous works include the supernatural series *Yurara*. She loves reading manga, traveling, and listening to music. Her favorite artists include Michelangelo, Hokusai, Bernini, and Gustav Klimt.